I0821507

Records of the Moravians Among the Cherokees

March to Removal, Part 4

'They Shall Not Be Forsaken'

*Georgia historical marker at the site of the Moravians' Oochgeelogy mission on old Belwood School Road, Georgia. The Oochgeelogy mission house, built in 1821 by Joseph Crutchfield, sold to the Moravian Church in 1822 (*Records: Cherokees, *6:2828-30), stood until it was destroyed by fire in 1980.*

Records of the Moravians Among the Cherokees

March to Removal, Part 4

'They Shall Not Be Forsaken'

Volume 9

1830 – 1833

Richard W. Starbuck

Editor

Cherokee Heritage Press
Tahlequah
Oklahoma

Published by:
Cherokee Heritage Press, Tahlequah, Oklahoma,
a division of Cherokee National Historical Society, Inc.

Distributed by:
University of Oklahoma Press, Norman, Oklahoma

Funding for this project provided by:
Cherokee Nation
Eastern Band of Cherokee Indians
Cherokee Moravian Historical Association
Wachovia Historical Society
Friends of Moravian Archives

Library of Congress Control Number:
2018959317

ISBN 978-0-9994521-1-0

May God grant that everything turns out in their — the Cherokees' — favor. It is amazing how bravely they have acted, and are still acting, under oppression, and they are determined to continue thus until their matter is decided.

Gottlieb Byhan
Springplace, Cherokee Nation
to
Theodor Schulz
Salem, North Carolina
November 27, 1830

. . .[T]here is a prevalent belief that all missionaries are trying to persuade them to emigrate. Although we really cannot discuss this with the Indians, it is still desirable for it to come to this soon, because if the Cherokees hold out here with their previous infatuation, it is obvious that they will be spiritually and physically ruined and all efforts against this will remain fruitless. And so we really hope that this Nation might accept the liberal offer of the Government and leave this unfortunate country, and the sooner the better.

Henry G. Clauder
Connesauga, Cherokee Nation
to
Theodor Schulz
Salem, North Carolina
July 22, 1833

In case they do decide to move, the earlier advice given to our missionaries there is to be followed by Br. Clauder, if the Cherokees give occasion for it: That they are to be given to understand that they shall not be forsaken by us, with the request that in the move they keep together as well as they can, and that upon arrival in the land of their future repose that they also build as close as can be beside one another around their teachers.

Provinzial Helfer Conferenz
Salem, North Carolina
December 27, 1833

. . . [L]ast Sunday our Brn. and Srs. declared positively that, "We wait untill our Chiefs fail."

Henry G. Clauder
Connesauga, Cherokee Nation
to
Theodor Schulz
Salem, North Carolina
December 31, 1833

Contents

Documents, Names, Quotes, etc.

1830, part 3

1831, part 1

1831, part 2

1831, part 3

1831, part 11

1832, part 1

1832, part 2

1832, part 3

1832, part 4

Introduction

On July 13, 1801, the Moravian Church opened the first mission in the Cherokee Nation, called Springplace (*Records of the Moravians among the Cherokees*, 1:277-78). Barely nine months later, the State of Georgia and the federal government agreed to the Compact of 1802. Georgia ceded its western territory to the United States to become the states of Alabama and Mississippi. But by the fall of 1830 the federal government had not "extinguished" Indian land titles in the State of Georgia. The Cherokee Nation remained steadfast, unmovable.

All that was about to change.

Fresh on the heels of Congress giving Andrew Jackson, the frontier president, "power to remove" all Native Americans east of the Mississippi River in volume 8 of *Records: Cherokees* (4261), volume 9, covering August 1830 through 1833, continues the subtitle series *March to Removal.*

As volume 9 opens, all seems peace and quiet for our two Moravian Church missionaries, Brn. Gottlieb Byhan at Springplace and Henry Gottlieb Clauder at Oochgeelogy, begun in 1821 (6:2711-13). They tend to their duties of preaching the good news of salvation for the Cherokees, making visitations among their mission members, and spending hour after tedious hour, quill pen in hand, recording in mission diaries and lengthy letters the events they witness, which comprise *Records of the Moravians among the Cherokees.* But that peace and quiet is shattered in early 1831 by a law adopted by the State of Georgia to expand its jurisdiction over the Cherokee Nation. As of March 1, 1831, all white men in the Cherokee Nation must take an oath of allegiance to the state's laws, or they must leave the country (9:4360-61). The new law ushers in a year of upheaval, terror, and imprisonment that eventually becomes a national cause célèbre before the United States Supreme Court.

When Br. Byhan learns of the new law he writes: "We see clearly that this law is aimed especially at the missionaries among the Cherokees, because it is believed that the missionaries are to blame, or are the cause, that the Cherokees will not move to the West" (4359). The law has its dire effect in the Cherokee Nation. The Georgia Guards sweep the land of white laborers, artisans, and especially, as Br. Byhan reports, the "Yankee Missionaries" (4376) of the American Board in Boston.

One such missionary is Samuel Worcester, friend of the Moravians, who was instrumental in publishing the Moravian Church Litany as only the third booklet printed in the Cherokee syllabary at New Echota (see *Records: Cherokees*, v. 8). With the Georgia Guards on the prowl for him, Worcester reportedly declares: "If they wish to see me or take me, I shall be in my house" (4410). The jailing (4411) of Samuel Worcester eventually rises to the United States Supreme Court, which makes its ruling in Worcester's favor but with no power to enforce it (4614).

In 1831 alone, our two Moravian missionaries, Byhan and Clauder, fire off 57 frantic letters to Br. Theodor Schulz of their supervising church board, the Provinzial Helfer Conferenz (Helf. Conf.) in Salem, North Carolina, begging for advice when there is none, pouring out their anxiety as they live from moment to moment not knowing whether they would be summarily evicted from hearth and home or even dragged off in chains to the penitentiary.

To Brn. Byhan and Clauder, Georgia's oath of allegiance law is especially repugnant. Both well know the Moravian Church's longstanding tenet abstaining from swearing or taking oaths, since both were born and raised in Moravian Church communities. As for swearing allegiance to the "unjust" laws of Georgia, they agree they "could not, because this is completely against our conscience" (4364, 4369). Moreover, what would the Cherokees say if they took the oath? "Would they not say: Now we see how far your friendship toward us goes. All love, all trust in us would be gone" (4369).

Appeals to Georgia's governor (4432-33, 4444-45), unwanted friendliness of the Georgia Guard (4505-6, 4507), protection as "agent" of the federal government as postmaster at Springplace (4370) are to no avail. The Moravians must abandon their missions and find refuge across the state line in Tennessee (4402-3).

The first to go is Oochgeelogy (4506) with a final Sunday of "melancholy" services on July 17, 1831. Then on New Year's Day 1833 "at 3 o'clock in the afternoon 5 wagons and some carts and 15 to 20 people" arrive at Springplace and demand "possession of all of our houses" (4683). The Moravians' beloved Springplace is lost to the Georgia's lottery of land in the Cherokee Nation.

With the Moravians as the last missionaries to leave Cherokee country in Georgia (4373), the Cherokees must face their future on their own. A new treaty with the federal government is proposed in 1832, and Br. Clauder lists the terms (4632) and finds them "very advantageous, and if everything promised to them is carried out properly, the Cherokees will hardly find reason to regret their move" (4630). "Without a doubt," Br. Clauder predicts, "there will soon be a split among the Cherokees. They are already divided. One party is for selling the land, but by far the largest part of the nation, led by John Ross, is against it" (4638). For the first time the term "treaty party" appears in Moravian mission records (4646), and they are shouted down in Council as "traitors" (4640) to their Nation.

As volume 9 of *Records: Cherokees* comes to an end, Br. Clauder continues his mission work on the Conasauga River in Tennessee, safe from Georgia's reach. Rather than move to Arkansas, his congregation declares "positively that, 'We wait untill our Chiefs fail'" (4774-75). And from Salem, North Carolina, the Moravian Church's supervisory Helf. Conf. offers the assurance, the subtitle to *Records: Cherokees* v. 9: *They shall not be forsaken* (4773).

Records of the Moravians among the Cherokees concludes its *March to Removal* subtitle series with volume 10, covering 1834 to the autumn of 1838, with the subtitle *'This is not my home any more.'* Then volume 11 of *Records: Cherokees* opens a new subtitle series, *In New Land*, with the Moravian missionaries setting out on their journey west on what has come to be known in American history as the Trail of Tears.

Moravian Archives, Southern Province, wishes to express its gratitude to the Cherokee Nation for major funding of the *Records: Cherokees* project, the publishing of all the Moravian Church's Cherokee mission documents held at Moravian Archives in Winston-Salem, North Carolina. Wachovia Historical Society also supports the project through grants to the Moravian Archives book fund. Thanks also go to the many who have offered their input and encouragement, as well as you, the readers, who are taking this journey through *Records of the Moravians among the Cherokees*. This is the Cherokees' — and all America's — history of a people exiled from their ancestral homeland building anew their history and heritage.

Richard W. Starbuck
Moravian Archives
Winston-Salem, North Carolina
August 2019

Records of the Moravians Among the Cherokees

March to Removal, Part 4

'They Shall Not Be Forsaken'

1830, part 1

[M 414-5-28: Translated by Julie Tomberlin Weber. Addressed to: Revd. Theod. Schulz, Salem, Stokes County, North Carolina. Postmark: Springplace, Aug. 1. Free. Gottl. Byhan, P.M. Received Aug. 16.]

Springplace, July 31, 1830

Dearly beloved Br. Schulz,

Your kind letter of June 29, as well as the one from July 6 and a part of the Salem Diary Memorabilia of the congregation in Salem from the year 1829, reached my hands on the 25th of this month. We give you our best thanks for everything. I will send your letter of July 6th to dear Br. Clauder with the first opportunity. From this I see that you were concerned whether the $125 which you sent me in a letter with Mr. John Ridge reached my hands. I safely received the letter with the money on June 13th last year.[1] Since the last account I sent only went back to July 1st of last year, this money or the receipt of this amount was not included, but it can be found in the previous account, that is, in the sum of $1,829 which I received from Br. Theod. Shulz from Oct. 18, 1827, to June 30, 1829. So you can relax about <u>this</u>, because the money is unfortunately already used up and spent here.

Last Sunday, the 25th, was the baptism of the Indian woman Tucka. She received the name Sophia Carolina. We could sense the Savior in our midst. She was supposed to be baptized 14 days earlier on the 11th of this month with our Br. Boas's wife,[2] but she was prevented from coming on that day because of illness

---

1 See *Records: Cherokees*, 8:4030, 4032.

2 See *Records: Cherokees*, 8:4251.

in the family. I think I informed you that on the 11th of this month the Indian Br. Boas's wife was baptized with the name Lydia Elisabeth.[1] So once in a while a soul becomes the Savior's reward for His suffering. May He also maintain her in grace and keep her with Him!

Since my last letter to you on the 17th of this month,[2] there has not been the least thing I can report about or concerning the Indians. I must say we have heard nothing at all since then. All

is quiet and peaceful. Some time ago I reported to you certain circumstances concerning our Br. Wm. Abr. Hicks in Och_____y, and today I received a letter from Br. G. Clauder in which he writes the following about this unpleasant matter:

"Now with our Br. Hicks things have really not gone well. When I was with him last week he told me freely and openly, and I believe certainly with remorse and humility, about his sinful deeds in Washington. He assured me he was in despair over the treatment he experienced from his comrades when he sought worldly pleasures. Sorrowful! Who would have expected anything like this? What should be done now? He himself considers himself excluded from our company, and I told him that this would follow directly, despite his remorse, to avoid any offense, because his case will without a doubt be widely known and to some degree already is."

However, there is one cause for gratitude toward our dear Lord in this sad matter. This lost sheep now realizes and regrets his mistake, and when one considers how inexperienced he was in the fine temptations of a city, and how great the temptation, and that he turned away from paganism to become a believer, one cannot help but have compassion in his pitiful case. What do you dear Brn. think we should do now? Our idea is this, that he remain excluded until he has sufficiently proved the truth of his remorse through his actions, and then accept him again only at his request. In the meantime we will take special care of him.

---

1 See *Records: Cherokees*, 8:4258.

2 See *Records: Cherokees*, 8:4255.

Sun., Aug. 1. I had written this far yesterday and did not conclude the letter, so I could wait and see if perhaps something would arrive from you dear ones today, and indeed I just received your kind letter of July 19th in answer to mine to you of June 27. I will answer this letter this week. But I would like to say this much in advance, that there is no question that it is necessary for our Rachel to be brought back this fall. In the worst case, I will have to bring her and bear the travel costs myself. I will write more in my next letter, primarily about our recall. Sr. Byhan is currently very sickly. Everyone sends best greetings, and especially your friend and Br.,

G. Byhan

[Springplace (M 407-2) and Oochgeelogy (M 409-1) Diaries. Translated by Julie Tomberlin Weber. Handwritings are Henry G. Clauder's (Ooch.) and Gottlieb Byhan's (Spg.).]

Sun., Aug. 1. [Spg.] Today only a few Brn. and Srs. came for the services. This is usually the case if there was a baptism or Holy Communion the previous Sunday, because most of our Brn. and Srs. live far from here.

Sun., Aug 1. [Ooch.] Among the visitors was our Sr. Ridge along with her daughter Sarah. The latter was educated in the school in Salem. In a conversation with her, we found clear signs of the Holy Spirit's work of grace in her heart. With tears, she lamented her wretchedness as a sinner and her complete lack of faith in Jesus, the Friend of sinners. We tried to comfort her and give her hope, and we sincerely wished that the One who began the good work in her heart would soon continue it without resistance and might complete it for the benefit of her soul and to the glory of the One who shed His precious blood for sinners.

Aug. 3. [Ooch.] Sarah Bethiah Hicks visited us. She gave her daughter, who is in the school here and will be baptized soon now, a sincere and emotional admonition to use her current time of grace well. Mother and daughter were moved to tears during this.

Aug. 5. [Ooch.] I visited George Augustus, who had returned from the gold mines a few days ago. He and the rest of the Indians who work there were driven away by a regiment of soldiers, although that land is the Cherokees' property. In the evening I went to Wm. Abr. Hicks's and spent the night there. When asked, I led an evening devotion there; his entire large family was present and attentive.

Aug. 7. [Ooch.] I was asked to bury the body of a young white boy who died in New Echota, since the missionary who lives there, Worcester, was gone. The burial was at 5 o'clock in the evening. Most of the listeners were young, and the Daily Text for the 8th (Isa. 40:6,8) provided an opportunity to emphasize to them the uncertainty of life and the great danger of neglecting their eternal salvation in the enjoyment of youthful and sinful pleasures. Then in a very orderly manner we all went a quarter of a mile into the bush to where the grave had been prepared. While the sun was going down, we prayed part of our burial litany and we lowered the body to its rest. I returned home that same evening.

Sun., Aug. 8. [Spg.] Since only a few of our Brn. and Srs. had come for the services again, in the first service a sermon was read about the words [Rom. 1:16]: I am not ashamed of the gospel of Christ: for it is the power of God unto salvation to every one that believeth. In the second service was the Bible reading. Currently we are having extraordinarily dry weather. Everything in the field and garden is beginning to die. This year we will get hardly half as much corn as last year. All the garden growth like cabbage, cucumbers, etc., is dying, so that in fact it looks very gloomy. Today various Indians were in our fields collecting peaches in sacks, but there is an overabundance of these this year, so we are happy if they are used, because we are not in a position to dry all of them and use them.

[M 414-5-29: Translated by Julie Tomberlin Weber. Addressed to: Revd. Theod. Schulz, Salem, Stokes County, North Carolina. Postmark: Springplace, C.N., Aug. 15. Free. Gottl. Byhan, P.M. Received Aug. 31.]

Springplace, Aug. 14, 1830

My dear Br. Shulz,

Your kind letter of July 19th, in response to my letter of June 27th, and *Missy. Intelligencer* arrived here on Aug. 1st. We thank you sincerely for everything included in this. I wanted to answer your dear letter eight days ago, but time and circumstances did not allow it. However, nothing has been lost, because not the least noteworthy event has happened since my last letter to you.

All in the Nation is quiet; at least I have heard nothing about moving west. Last Aug. 2nd was the election for Members for the Council and Committee, and Joseph Vann and John Ridge were elected, among others. We do not hear much about the gold mines either. In brief, praise God, we are living in peace and quiet.

However, there is certainly much to reply to your dear letter if I could do so in person. And so I will answer just a few questions in it. I paid Jos. Vann $50 for the field in March 1829.[1] I already mentioned in one of my previous letters that I received the $125 which you sent with John Ridge.

Otherwise, it seems in your letter as if the Cherokees would not be able to tolerate one more year here, because they cannot live under the Georgia Law. It is true they are considered the same as Negroes in this, since they cannot bear witness against a white man. This point is difficult for them, but even so it does not move them to the west. I believe, and I am pretty certain, that

---

[1] See *Records: Cherokees*, 8:3982, 3983.

according to the current sentiment of the Indians, they would be more likely to let themselves be killed here than move west, and the Georgians are not allowed to do this to them. Generally it seems to me now, and I am only speaking of the current situation of the Nation, as if the Georgians have pulled in their wings a little, and it is my belief that the Government and Georgia will still be required to carry out the letter of the Treaties with the Cherokees. Because the Treaties and all the promises which the Government and the Georgians made to them still exist and are in black and white. This is my view of the matter, because when one is here personally on the ground, so to speak, as we are, where all these events and situations are taking place, then one can for the most part reach a conclusion about how things might go.

It is always true that the further one discusses these matters concerning the Cherokees, the more dangerous it becomes, and this is also the reason why I believe that you from 400 miles away believe that the Cherokees are in the most miserable circumstances in the world, which is not actually the case yet. God is sitting on the throne! He knows how to arrange everything for the best. The Cherokees are also His creatures. He also redeemed them with His precious blood. He will not completely abandon them, because if they moved to the west, they would be delivered.

He sometimes lets something difficult happen to a country or people, so that we seek Him in distress, and I must say that I and everyone who has paid attention to this will have to say that many of the Cherokees have turned to God in heaven in their difficult situation and have called to Him for help. They claim that if humans will not and cannot help them out of their situation, God in heaven will certainly do so. It can at least be concluded that this claim says a lot.

And can God fail to answer these cries of the poor, and to answer this trust in Him? I say — no! He will save them in an instant! This is my firm belief. Therefore, we want to lay the poor residents of this land diligently before His faithful heart in our prayers, and He will hear our prayer.

Now concerning the idea that the Indians must move west in the end, it seems to me from your dear letter that this mission will soon have reached its end, and we will therefore be called to tolerate things here longer until the Indians have moved west despite the poor health of my dear wife and my inability to take care of this post, which I often painfully feel. In response to this, it seems that another Br. and Sr. cannot be found to take our place here, and it is already late in the year. So in this case we will stay here. The Savior alone will help us.

However, it is essential that a change be made in our family. This means that a change must take place regarding our Nathanael, and it is a shame that it did not happen last fall. I also declare here once again that our Rachel must be taken back to Salem this fall, since circumstances require it and she really wants to go back. And so I have decided, if there is no other opportunity, to take her back myself this fall, which would be preferable to me and us, since I could then tell you in person about the mission here, which I also really want to do. I beg you to answer this as soon as possible. If there is concern that travel costs would keep me from bringing Rachel, this concern can be overcome, because we are willing to take this on ourselves.

Our Br. Samuel recently had an unpleasant experience as well, when his son Flea, who was here in the school, tried to spread lies in the country concerning our family, although he himself did not directly make them up. When his father, Br. Samuel, defended his son, we found it necessary to explain his son's behavior to him and speak lovingly with him in the presence of many Indian Brn. But he became somewhat heated, as happens easily with him, and he left saying he would think about it and give me an answer. However, I have not seen him again since then. All the Indian Brn. said that Br. Samuel believes everything his son Flea tells him and that they know that he is a bad boy.

Otherwise, Br. Samuel seems much too sure of himself lately, and he had paid too much attention to other Brn. and Srs. and in the process unfortunately forgot himself. He is also very attached to the Methodist side lately. His son Flea was recently baptized by them, although when I asked him what baptism was and what it meant he did not know. We also hear that Br. Samuel lives very disharmoniously with one of his wives — it is known that he has two — so that he has offended our Brn. and Srs. Time will tell what will happen with him.

Now I must close. It is very hot. The thermometer reads 102°. We currently are having an extraordinary drought. Everything is starting to die; even the peach trees, the fruit and leaves, are starting to dry up.

We send our best greetings to all, and you, dear Br., accept another special greeting from your sincerely loving, humble Br.,

Gottl. Byhan

[Springplace (M 407-2) and Oochgeelogy (M 409-1) Diaries.]

Sun., Aug. 15. [Spg.] A pretty large number of our Indian Brn. and Srs. came for the services. The Bible reading was repeated by Br. Solomon in the Cherokee language. Since some of our Brn. are planning to go to the gold mines this week, we took the opportunity to tell them lovingly and confidentially that we of course could not prevent them from going there to gain something, but wanted to ask them as our Brn. and advise them to let God's Spirit protect them from all diversions and from things which were not suitable for believers and to stay together as much as possible and generally to behave as children of God, so that the world might see what children of the Spirit of God they are. They seemed to take this admonition very lovingly and promised to follow this.

This afternoon we once again had a refreshing rain after several weeks of long drought and heat, and also on

Aug. 16. [Spg.] we received a refreshing rain shower. Our field and garden crops, however, have suffered so much through the long-lasting drought and heat that this rain shower was of little use. In the evening at 8 o'clock it suddenly became as light in our yard as if a fire had suddenly broken out. When we looked around, however, we saw a large fiery ball in the northeastern sky, which caused this light. This ball was visible about 8-10 seconds.

Mr. David St. Tazizi was also here overnight. He is on his way to the gold mines. His two brothers who are going with him camped at our Spring Branch. Many Indians are now going to the gold mines, since their fieldwork is mostly finished, to earn something, as they say, to pay their debts.

Sun., Aug. 15. [Ooch.] This was a day the Lord made for us, and we joyfully baptized into Jesus' death the often mentioned baptismal candidate from among our scholars, with the name Margaret Mary. There was a powerful feeling of the presence of our dear Savior, who is also the Savior of all heathen. Even those who have served sin with hard hearts for a long time showed signs of inner emotion. Immediately after this proceeding our Br. and Sr. George Augustus's baby boy was brought to the Savior in holy baptism, with the name David. In the evening our house congregation brought the Lord our humble gratitude for all the blessings we received on this day.

Aug. 17. [Spg.] Since last night we had another small shower of rain, today we could finally get our turnip field in order and sow it. We were not able to do this earlier because of the drought.

Aug. 18. [Spg.] In the morning our Br. Josua came to our place and told us that he is also planning to go to the gold mines in a couple of days, and he told us that most all of our Brn. would go and stay there for a couple of weeks. He was cordially advised not to get involved in arguments with other Indians about gold digging, much less with white people about the right to land, which he promised to do. At his request we lent him a spade which he wants to dig for gold.

Wed., Aug. 18. [Ooch.] Br. Clauder visited Wm. A. Hicks and other neighbors. Entire families are sick with fever, which is probably due to the use of bad drinking water, the continuous heat and drought, etc. With grateful hearts we rejoice we are enjoying good health, as are all our children.

[M 414-5-30: Translated by Julie Tomberlin Weber. Addressed to: Revd. Theodor Schulz, Salem, Stokes County, North Carolina. Postmark: Springplace, C.N., Aug. 22. Paid 18¾. Received Sept. 6.]

Ooyugillogy, Cherokee Nation, Aug. 16, 1830

Dear Br. Schulz,

On June 10th I sent you a thick letter containing the Diary from Ooyugill____y through the end of May. I recently received a letter from my parents in answer to a letter to them included in the packet for you, and from this I assume that you received it although I have not yet received your reply to it. My last thorough letter to you left Spring Place on July 11th, and I have not received any answer to that one either. This leads me to presume that your letters were taken at some point and kept, since I know for certain that one of my parents' letters never arrived here. In the hope that this letter has better luck, I will try to inform you of our current situation, internally as well as externally.

General consideration of the inner life of this mission gives us many reasons to offer our Lord our humble gratitude for the proofs of grace He has shown us thus far, most especially considering the current extremely difficult and oppressive circumstances under which this country is suffering. Most especially encouraging was the baptism yesterday of our Peggy Hicks, during which she received the name Margaret Mary, as well as the request for baptism made some time ago by our white neighbor Austin Copeland. This delighted us and caused us to lift our deepest thanks to the Lord God for the grace which He has shown our weak efforts to extend his kingdom.

Our George Augustus Hicks, who has been working at the gold mines since April with pretty good luck, also returned home a number of weeks ago. It is known that an indescribable godlessness prevails there, through which some of the recently converted Cherokees were swept up again in the current of ruin. Praise God, however, the protective hand of God not only kept our George from all spiritual harm but also from all external attacks from the Georgian authorities. Many Cherokees were taken prisoner there, but he always remained free. Otherwise, the few godfearing people gathered each evening in his tent where they strengthened their souls together despite the mockery and scorn they had to endure.

Our Srs. Hannah and Sussannah Fields are still with their husbands at a recently discovered gold mine in the interior of our Nation. All the rest are at home, and as far as we know in a pleasant spiritual condition except for our dear old Wm. Abr. Hicks.

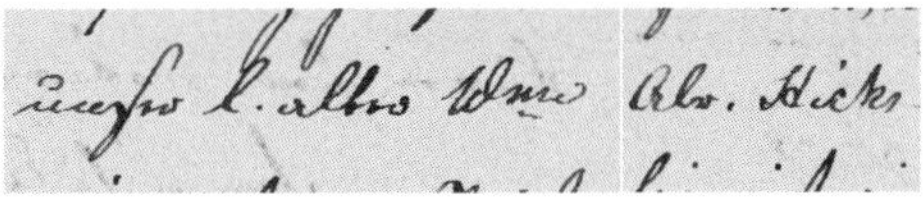

Now I come to sad matter in which we face a difficult test. Here is a pitiful example of the weakness of humans and the basic depravity of the human heart. One who otherwise is so firmly grounded in everything good is now swept away by passions which could have a sad end, although we hope God prevents this. Some days after his return from Washington he informed me with an apparently heavy heart, with tears and sighs, that in desperation due to the mean and base treatment he received from two of his fellow delegates, he had pursued the appealing temptations of the city and had enjoyed all worldly pleasures and desires. He expressed his remorse and his willingness to do whatever we required of him, etc. There was still hope here he would begin anew on the narrow path of life he had left, through thorough repentance, especially since I made it my business to pursue him and win him again in love.

Unfortunately, his son George came here this morning and told me with a heavy heart that since his father had not been present at all at the recently held Council, he would now be put on trial, because there was doubt about his loyalty to the affairs of his Nation. He, an influential man, one of the head chiefs, is being accused of treason. This is an unfounded accusation made by his enemies, the same ones who treated him badly in Washington, and now he is planning revenge.

He is threatening not to rest until one or the other of them is in the earth. He will do what will put his name on the black register of murderers! Now his son is asking me to try to quiet him down and guide him to do what is right, in order to prevent the shedding of blood.

His behavior at the baptism yesterday was strange and called attention, but we did not yet know anything about this matter. In this service, during which George was the interpreter, he was moved to tears, especially during the address to all who had renounced sin in holy baptism, during which they were sincerely reminded of their covenant and their promise. Before the service ended he went out and then left without saying good-bye to us, as he usually does.

On the one hand there is joy and hope; on the other there is deep, searing pain. What should be done! I will not neglect words and admonitions with this poor confused man, but it requires a stronger voice than that of a human to save him from his confusion and to humble him enough in this. Pray for all of us and for the poor Cherokee believers.

Concerning external matters, we must confess with gratitude toward the One who has given all good things that we are enjoying more than we deserve. We are all healthy and active. Currently we have had so much to do that we took in another hired worker today. Our fruit trees are almost breaking under the weight of all the fruit. We are all, even some of the children, busy with cuttings and spend almost half the nights with this work. Otherwise, there is a general drought here, through which the corn fields are suffering a lot. Everything is wilting in the intense heat.

The school continues in its usual routine with 15 scholars. We are expecting two more, who are at home on a visit. We cannot complain that our scholars go home too often. We introduced a rule quite successfully that no child is allowed to leave the school except in the case of illness. If their parents ask to take them home anyway without good reason, they are not accepted back again. However, during vacation days, which are in September, they can go home for a visit. We are now planning to hold a public examination of our scholars on Sept. 10. May the Lord grant success in this. Unfortunately, the Sunday school, which was so enjoyable for the children and has been beneficial and blessed, had to be discontinued here as well, as had been done earlier in Spring Place, because I could not get a reliable assistant. After a trial, I found it too difficult to lead the school and services alone, and so found it necessary to let this beautiful and blessed work go, at least for now.

We have not heard anything about the Indians moving. Since I have been in this country, there has never been a time when there was so little discussion of this matter as now. I really do not know what to make of this remarkable quiet. Perhaps it is the predecessor of great unrest, because the Cherokees continue to act according to their own laws. They hold elections, Courts, and Councils to the public mockery of the Georgia law.

The 19th. Yesterday I was at William Hicks's almost the entire day, and I had an opportunity to give him a serious reminder of his baptismal covenant, etc. He is still very friendly toward us and gratefully accepts everything we tell him. I told him it was his duty to forgive those who had offended him and to humble himself before God. I reminded him of his misdeeds toward God and that if he did not forgive his enemies he could not experience forgiveness himself. I then emphasized that if he did not renounce his unchristian, vengeful thoughts and behave as a Christian believer, he could not remain in our covenant. I was happy to see that he is not yet too hardened to shed tears and to promise the best. May God grant that he keeps his promise. I am planning to set out for Spring Place [page torn] day to talk with Br. Byhan about this sad situation. May the Lord reveal Himself to us mercifully and grant us wisdom, with love and seriousness.

Some weeks ago I was called to New Echota to bury a young person who [page torn] had died from a high fever. He was from Alabama, was [page torn] Wheeler, a brother of the printer of the *Phönix*. As far as I could learn, he died without giving the least indication of a change of heart. The printer, Wheeler, whose wife is the daughter of our Christian David, often comes here to the services, and from the frequent conversations I have had with him, during which he has been trusting and open-hearted, we have the best reason to conclude that he is thoroughly awakened. Some weeks ago a Presbyterian congregation was organized in

Echota under Mr. Worcester's leadership. Wheeler will probably join there. His wife is a member there.

In closing, we here (Copeland and Sr. Gambold) greet you all and commend ourselves to your prayer and loving remembrance. Your faithfully obliged Brother,

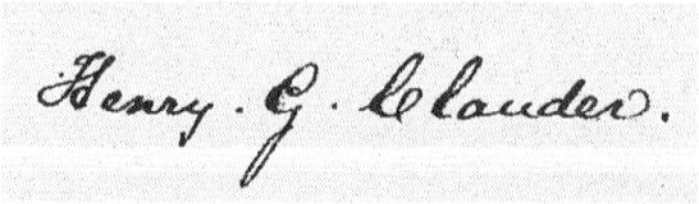

Henry G. Clauder

[Br. Clauder concludes his letter to Br. Schulz in English:]

P.S. Spring-Place, Aug. 20

Dear Brother, on my arrival here I received your favour of the 19th July to my great joy. I perceive you had received my two letters alluded to in the beginning of this. Remember my best love to Henry Aug. Shulz. I have received his favour of July 4th. In coming up today I heard from good authority of the arrest of Alexander McCoy at Echota and several other Cherokees by one of the Georgia sheriffs for the crime of — debt. This is becoming the order of the day. Oppression and sufferings have commenced. Your,

H. G. Clauder

[Springplace (M 407-2) and Oochgeelogy (M 409-1) Diaries.]

Fri., Aug. 20. [Ooch.] At dawn Br. Clauder began his journey to Spring Place, and he returned from there the following day.

Aug. 19. [Spg.] We received a nice, soaking rainstorm, for which the dry ground has been longing for a long time. We were grateful to our heavenly Father for this. Already a couple of months ago the mills in our neighborhood were almost still due to a lack of water, so that we could not get our corn milled for bread. And so on

Aug. 20 [Spg.] we had to send our workers to Mr. Harlen's mill 11 miles from here, as we did a number of weeks ago.

Aug. 21. [Spg.] They returned and could get milled only half the corn they had taken along. Br. Clauder was here visiting at Spring Place yesterday and today.

[M 414-5-31: Translated by Julie Tomberlin Weber. Addressed to: Revd. Theodore Shulz, Salem, Stokes County, North Carolina. Postmark: Springplace, C.N., Aug. 22. Gottl. Byhan, P.M. Free. Received Sept. 6.]

Springplace, Aug. 21, 1830

My dear Br. Shulz,

Your dear letter on behalf of the Prov. Helf. Conf. in Salem to the Mission Conf. here, dated Aug. 3, arrived here safely on the 15th of this month. Since we had a pleasant visit here this week from Br. Clauder, we were able to share this with him right away, and he took it with him this morning to Ooyugilogy to share it with the rest of the Brn. and Srs. there. I would be very happy if my letter to you dated the 14th of this month reached your hands very quickly, so that you could answer it just as quickly, and I hope you will be good enough do so as soon possible.

Since my last letter, nothing particularly new has taken place in the Nation except that the Georgia sheriffs, according to Georgia Law, are working among some halfbreeds, because the latter are in debt. Today we hear that the Georgia and Tennessee [page torn] have had fights at the gold mines, and that the Georgians had to flee. Dear God, what else will happen! This week most of our Indian Brn. also went to the gold mines to earn some money. When they told me this last Sunday, I admonished them to behave there as children of God and to show what spiritual children they are. They accepted the admonition with much love and promised to stay together there as much as possible.

Today we also heard that the Georgians will not allow the Cherokees to hold their Council in October. Time will tell if this turns out to be true.

You will receive a letter from Br. Clauder with this mail. We here in Spring Place are all pretty well, praise God, except for Nathanael, who has suffered a lot for some time now from toothaches and headaches.

Currently we are very busy drying peaches; we have unheard-of quantities of them. Everyone sends greetings. Please greet our children for us as well and tell them that I am waiting for a letter from them. I remain your faithfully obliged Br.,

Gottl. Byhan

I am enclosing the Diary from Jan. and Feb. of this year. It will be continued.

[Springplace (M 407-2) and Oochgeelogy (M 409-1) Diaries.]

Sun., Aug. 22. [Spg.] Since most of our Brn. and Srs. are at the gold mines, only 2 communicants and 3 of our closest neighbors came to our services today, which was also the case the following *Sun., Aug. 29.* Throughout this whole month we had unusually dry weather, although sometimes storms came up but always went past us. Otherwise, everything was still and quiet in the Nation, because most Indians, at least from our neighborhood, are at the gold mines so that we currently see few Indians.

Sun., Aug. 22. [Ooch.] We had only our Br. and Sr. Hicks at our service. We nourished ourselves by reading the Holy Scriptures and gave a brief admonition to place our faith only in God the Lord during the current time of trial. In conclusion we bowed and knelt in the dirt before Him, the only Comforter and Helper in all distress, and we brought Him praise and thanksgiving for all the proofs of His love and merciful protection we have enjoyed thus far in such an unearned manner, and we pleaded for further assistance and further childlike trust in all of His ways through darkness, which lead to the kingdom of light, which is promised to all faithful believers.

Sun., Aug. 29. [Ooch.] After the usual services, we considered it our obligation to try to correct an old misunderstanding which has been going on between two of our Brn. and Srs. However, we were sorry to find that with one of them, despite all requests and admonitions, nothing could be improved. She remained implacable and left us with obvious signs of anger. Such cases are always extremely unpleasant and discouraging. May the good, faithful Shepherd also bring the lost sheep back in love to the flock with God's staff, and keep us in communion with all those He has redeemed from sin in the spirit of peace, which is higher than reason, until the final day.

Heinrich Gottlieb & Elisabeth Clauder

[M 414-5-33: Translated by Julie Tomberlin Weber. Addressed to: Revd. Theodor Shulz, Salem, Stokes County, North Carolina. Postmark: Springplace, C.N., Aug. 29. Free. Gottl. Byhan, P.M.]

Springplace, Aug. 28, 1830

My dear Br. Shulz,

I received your kind letter of the 10th of this month on the 22nd, and we thank you sincerely for this. The view you expressed about the Cherokees therein is absolutely correct and agrees completely with our idea that the Supreme Court of the U. St. will decide whether the Cherokees can remain here or not. And I think some people who have even the least familiarity with the relationship between the U. St. and the Cherokees and with the Treaties which exist can only believe that it will be decided in favor of the Cherokees, because, as I confidently believe, no partisan spirit will rule there. It does not seem right to me that some people believe that the U. St. Court will decide against the Cherokees, because they have established their own Government among themselves, which they indeed are permitted to do according to their Treaties, unless it were the Georgians. The Cherokees are an independent Nation, and they are allowed to make their own laws which do not concern the white people. The Treaties are still in force as long as they have not been declared null and void. According to the Act, until they are set aside, they remain an independent Nation and can make as many laws as they want to, and they will surely do this. And I think this will be the main question in the Supreme Court.

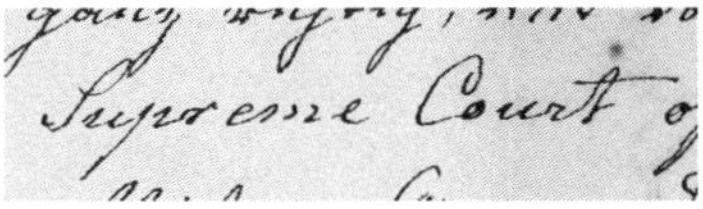

Otherwise, everything here is quiet. Many Indians are at the gold mines now. We have not heard of any problems there, except what the Regulars and the white people have done to each other. Gold is being found closer and closer to us now. People say that some has been found in Coosawatee, about 20 miles from us.

Currently we are all pretty healthy, praise God! except that Nathanael is bothered a lot by toothaches and headaches. Many of our children have a cough. We are currently very busy drying peaches, which are very plentiful. We have already dried about 30 bushels! And the trees are still thick with more. We are having extremely dry weather. Everything is wilting and the heat is very intense. Even as I am writing this, the thermometer shows 98° Fahr. in my little room.

You will have seen from my previous letters that I am planning to bring our Rachel to Salem this fall because circumstances and parental duty require this. We really need an answer concerning this situation, in reply to my previous letters. Everyone sends best greetings, especially your familiar friend and humble Br.,

Gottlieb Byhan

Enclosed is our Diary from the beginning of March to May 10.

N.B. On Br. Clauder's last visit with us, he told us that he will hold a public examination with his children in Ochgelogy on Sept. 9th or 10th. <u>We</u> will <u>not</u> have one because of circumstances.

[Springplace (M 407-2) and Oochgeelogy (M 409-1) Diaries.]

Sun., Sept. 5. [Spg.] Since some of our Brn. and Srs. have returned from the gold mines, they came back to our Sunday services today. Today we heard that a white man from Tennessee who had spent the night at Mr. Vann's brought the news that the President, Andr. Jackson, will visit in the Cherokee Nation in a number of weeks. Time will tell if this news turns out to be true. Our Indian Br. Israel also brought us the news today that about 4 days ago two travelers from our area in North Carolina had been at the gold mines and were planning to visit in Oochgelogy. And so we concluded that it must be a couple of Brn. from Salem who were in South Carolina or Georgia on business and are now planning to visit the mission among the Cherokees. If it really is a couple of Brn. from Salem, we will surely soon hear more from them.

Sun., Sept 5. [Ooch.] In the sermon we considered the Gospel lesson for today about the good Samaritan, during which we discussed love for our neighbor, since out of love for us like a good Samaritan, Christ gave the most precious oil, His life, to heal our wounds caused by wretched sin, and on the arms of His mercy He guides us to our complete salvation in the eternal heavenly home. After the sermon we had the grace of strengthening our needy souls in Holy Communion, with a small number of our communicants.

Sept. 6. [Spg.] Heavy storms blew in from the southwest. Accordingly we were already looking forward to rain, which we would get with this. But it moved past us without any rain. Our gardens look as they do in winter. Most everything is wilted or dried out. We must be patient. The heavenly Father knows best what is good for His children!

Mon., Sept 6. [Ooch.] We had a brief visit from the printer Wheeler and his wife, who is an Indian. We had a brief uplifting conversation with him and were delighted to see that the Holy Spirit has begun a good work in his heart.

Sept. 7. [Spg.] Br. Byhan, Sr., and Rachel Byhan visited in Oochgelogy today. In the evening we had some rain. This somewhat softened the soil, which in many places was torn up from the drought.

Sept. 7. [Ooch.] Br. Byhan visited us from Spring Place, accompanied by his daughter Rahel. This was a delight and encouragement for us.

Sept. 9. [Ooch.] They returned to their post.

[M 414-5-34: Translated by Julie Tomberlin Weber. Addressed to: Revd. T. Schulz, Salem, North Carolina. Postmark: per Br. Byhan. Received Oct. 7.]

Ooyugillogy, Sept. 6, 1830

Dear Brother Schulz,

I received your kind letter of Aug. 9th on the 30th to my great joy and encouragement, for which I sincerely thank you. I can easily imagine that while the entire world has its eyes directed on this unfortunate country, the eyes of our dear Brn. and Srs. in the Gemeine, particularly the Gemeine in Salem, look longingly and probably also sometimes with tears to God the eternal ruler, while offering urgent prayers, and they are commending us and our brown flock to Him.

Reflecting on this reassures and encourages us. We are not alone. God is with us and even if the enemy powerfully attacks us so that our weak flesh and blood would have to succumb, he still cannot steal from us the pearl which the soul possesses in Christ. Now, praise God, we do not lack comfort and courage, although the feeling of nothingness and so many shortcomings and misdeeds sometimes cause tears to flow. But there is also joy in this, because the tears are seeds which have already brought forth such glorious harvests and will certainly continue to do so.

We really know nothing yet, and we can hardly guess what the Cherokee Nation will do. We do not hear a word about it here; everyone is still and quiet about moving except when a Georgia officer occasionally makes an official visit in the nation. However, people expect that by the next Council significant encroachments of the Georgia law will have taken place, as has already happened in the Creek Nation where the negotiations of the Council were interrupted by the military.

My own opinion about moving with the Cherokees in the case of a general emigration is the same as it was a year ago. I will surrender myself completely to divine guidance and let myself be led by His spirit if the hour and day finally arrive. I could promise a lot now and raise your expectations, but then disappoint you in the end and not keep my word when the time actually came.

The human heart is a weak-spirited thing. I do not trust it at all. My own heart has already deceived me too often. And so I turn away from humans and turn to the One who is eternal, who is faithful, and whose word stands immovable. If the dear Indians moved today, I would joyfully go with them. If the Lord wants me to go along, then He will also open a way and maintain this attitude in me.

On this occasion you will receive our Diary for the last 3 months. With this I commend myself to your patience and that of all who read it.

A number of days have passed since I began this letter, and in that time we were delighted by the birth of a healthy baby boy on Sept. 7. Today (the 9th) my dear wife is quite peaceful again, and we are even more grateful for this, since she suffered a great deal yesterday and last night. The past days have been days of trial. Young Copeland is also suffering from an abscess on the left side of his face, which had to be opened yesterday. Our scholars are all still here. Tomorrow we will try to hold an examination, and I will add more about this since this will not be sent until the day after tomorrow.

We were delighted that Br. Byhan visited us in recent days. Because of this, you will be able to learn more thoroughly about the inner and outer circumstances of this mission from him than I now have time and opportunity to describe to you. I gave Br. Byhan a memorandum for the things I really need that we would like to request, and for which we will be grateful. Another special item which I did not add to this but which Br. Byhan will persuade you is necessary: a small farm wagon and a horse and harness. The wagon here came here with Proske and is now falling apart. The same is true with the old horse which Br. Gambold brought here in 1823. This faithful old servant is really unfit for work now and would not serve us for another summer.

Our old Br. Hicks is doing somewhat better now. I always find that one does not get along with Indians through a direct manner of speaking. What one wants to say must be done through reflection. In this way, I hope that this sheep who has gone astray will be won back through God's grace. Last Sunday we celebrated Holy Communion in the most blessed manner. Wm. Ab. H., however, is excluded from this for the time being. Many of our promising Indians (those we hoped to win) have returned to their old sinful ways because of their stay at the gold mines. It is true what Wm. Hicks said, these gold mines are in all respects the ruin of this Nation.

The 10th. Today were the examinations, and many of our friends and neighbors attended. All went quite well, and the children's singing was especially pleasant. They were more satisfactory than expected in reading, spelling, and arithmetic, and our Margaret Mary Hicks answered the questions about History and Geography of the U.S. quite beautifully. Most went home for a visit or to see their relatives. We are planning to begin this beautiful work anew in 4 weeks with renewed courage.

Greet your dear family and dear fellow Brn. of the P.H.C. from your Brother, bound in love,

H. G. Clauder

N.B. Srs. Gambold, Copeland, and my wife, who is very weak, send sincere greetings.

[Springplace (M 407-2) and Oochgeelogy (M 409-1) Diaries.]

Sept. 9. [Spg.] Three Methodist preachers stopped in at our place on their way to Capt. Dav. McNair's area, since a camp meeting will be held there in the next days.

Sept. 10. [Ooch.] Our scholars had an exam, which was the first public one at this post. Many of our friends and neighbors enjoyed attending it. One of the older children had made significant progress in geography, as well as in American History, and answered all the questions correctly and without the shyness which is typical of the Indian children. In reading, spelling, and singing they exceeded all our expectations. Since there will be no school for about 5 weeks now, most of them went home for a visit.

Sept. 10. [Spg.] Mr. Dav. Steiner Tazizi came past here today from the gold mines with his brother. He told us that a new order has been given, that the white people as well as the Cherokees are supposed to stop digging for gold, and that to this end the regular troops from Augusta are supposed to be strengthened. They have orders to burn all huts, tents, and equipment belonging to the gold diggers and to take away their cattle. In brief it is said they will now chase them away in all seriousness. Mr. Tazizi said that the Cherokees do not want to act disobediently but to go home, and then when everything is quiet and the white people are all gone, to go back and dig for gold. God alone knows what the end of this matter will be!

Sept. 11. [Spg.] In the evening Mr. Wheeler came to our place with his wife and her sister and spent the night here.

Sun., Sept. 12. [Spg.] The Sunday services were as usual. The Litany was prayed by our Indian Br. Solomon as well in the Cherokee language. Afterward the Brn. and Srs. were informed that we would have Holy Communion next Sunday. We also spoke with Br. Solomon about his spiritual walk. In the evening we had a Singstunde during which Mr. Wheeler and company, who had returned this evening from the camp meeting, were present. Most of our Brn. and Srs. have now returned from the gold mines. Everyone said they had found only a little gold.

Sun., Sept. 12. [Ooch.] In our Sunday service we sang and prayed and then read an uplifting sermon on the parable of the sower and the various kinds of soil. In all the trials we have endured during the present time and shared with our dear Cherokees, it is a special cause for gratitude toward our dear Lord that we occasionally experience the love and gratitude of some of our Brn. and Srs. in an encouraging manner. One Sister said, among other things, "We are happy and grateful that you all are here. We could not live without teachers anymore, because they encourage us to put our trust only in our Savior. What would we do if we did not know where to find comfort and strength for the oppressed and weak?"

Wed., Sept. 15. [Ooch.] Toward evening many of our Brn. from Spring Place came here and spent the night. They are planning to attend the Methodist camp meeting which will be held in this neighborhood in the coming days. We spent the evening happily together. Samuel led the evening devotions in

Cherokee, which was very enjoyable even though we couldn't understand it.

Thurs., Sept. 16. [Ooch.] Last night we were disturbed by our dogs barking and guessed it was a nocturnal thief visiting. This morning, though, we saw two wolves had been slinking around close to here to steal during the night.

Fri., Sept. 17. [Ooch.] Br. Clauder visited the above-mentioned camp meeting, where he made the pleasant acquaintance of a Mr. Owen, the superintendent of the Methodist mission in this country. He assured us of his interest in the work of the Brethren in this country and generally showed more gentleness and Christian love toward other confessions than has been the case with some other preachers of that confession. Br. Clauder spent the day in a beneficial manner there in the company of many preachers and teachers, and in the evening he said an emotional farewell ~~in love and unity~~ with the feeling of love. Because of the unusual and long-lasting drought, the Indian corn harvest did not turn out not very well, and so it is reasonable to expect there will be a great shortage of bread in this country. Some days ago an Indian with his wife and child came here and asked for food, and he assured us they had not eaten anything in 3 days. We could not turn away such hungry people, although their lack of food is also partly attributable to their inborn indolence. We have also found clear signs a number of times already of robbery from our cornfields by people who do not want to beg.

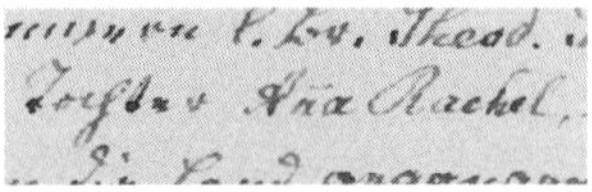

Sun., Sept. 19. [Spg.] Our Brn. and Srs. came to the services in large numbers. In the last service we had a blessed enjoyment of the body and blood of Jesus in Holy Communion. After this Br. Byhan, Sr., informed the Brn. and Srs. that he had received a letter with the mail today from our dear Br. Theod. Shulz in Salem in which he is given permission from the Pr. H. Conf. in Salem to take his daughter Anna Rachel back to Salem at her request. She has now served the mission for 3 years in external matters and helped her parents faithfully with the household. They are planning to begin their journey there next Tuesday the 21st, God willing. The Brn. and Srs. wished them a safe journey with tears in their eyes, asked them to greet all the Brn. and Srs. in Salem sincerely from them, and tell them even though they do not know each other personally, yet they sincerely love them. The Brn. and Srs. were lovingly advised to act worthily of the Gospel in Br. Byhan's absence and to allow themselves to be protected from the things of this world and to diligently attend the Sunday services as usual, as they would be led by Br. N. Byhan. They answered all this with a clear Yes, and one could clearly see their love for us all. They were also informed that we were planning to take along the single Br. Benj. Alexander to help on the journey, and for a visit in Salem, about which they were very happy. Afterward we spoke with our baptismal candidate, the Indian woman Waky, Br. Emanuel's wife, and informed her that soon after Br. Byhan's return from Salem she would have the grace of being baptized into Jesus' death. She was very happy about this.

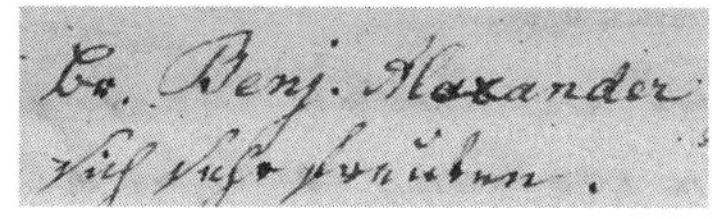

Sept. 20. [Spg.] Toward evening our Sr. Hanna came to Springplace with her husband Conondoah to see the traveling company depart from here tomorrow, as they said. They spent the night here.

Sept. 21. [Spg.] The above-mentioned company departed from here for Salem.

[M 414-5-35: Translated by Julie Tomberlin Weber. Addressed to: Revd. Theodore Schulz, Salem, Stokes County, North Carolina. Post stamp: New Echota, Cher. Na., Sept. 25, 18¾. Received Oct. 11.]

Ooyugillogy, C.N., Sept. 23, 1830

Dearly beloved Br. Shulz,

On the 17th of this month I received your kind letter of Aug. 31 and the enclosure of $100, and I thank you sincerely for this. I am now in a position to satisfy all creditors and will also keep a nice sum in my cash box. Henry is the only one who has demands against us, and last week we sold him 2 oxen for $25 against our debt.

The real reason I am writing you again so soon is this: Br. Copeland, who has already worked here faithfully and diligently for a year and has taken care of our agricultural work, recently said he has decided to move with his family to Indiana to be with the Brethren who have settled there. This statement was not completely unexpected, since I had previously noticed that he was really mulling over what to do about the future, and from time to time he had said he was unfit to serve as an assistant at this mission or anywhere else. I then asked him to consider this matter again before I wrote to you about this, and I told him at the same time that if he would prefer to continue here for a salary like other hired workers, we would rather have him than anyone else, and since he was well skilled at all kinds of work we could probably pay him a higher wage than the others. Experience has also already taught us that single workers whom we did not know could cause many problems with our female scholars, some of whom are almost adults.

After thorough consideration we agreed on the following terms, but I must first have your approval before it could be binding. Copeland is willing to remain here and work faithfully and diligently for $12 per month, board included. Sr. Copeland will assist in the housework and primarily with the school as previously, as her strength allows, for food and clothing for herself and her young son.

I just remembered a letter which I received from you a long time ago, in which you wrote to us that if Copeland would rather work for wages we should pay him cheaply. And so I hardly doubt that significant objections will be made by P.H.C. to the above-stated agreement. I am glad to be able to assure you that no misunderstandings have led Br. Copeland to this step.

Would it be inappropriate for Br. and Sr. Copeland to receive the articles noted for them on the memorandum sent through Br. Byhan? They are really quite short on clothing. It would perhaps also be better to have those things be sent to them to prevent any bad feelings in the future; he will pay for these things himself. I would like to ask for your prompt response to this matter.

Last week was a camp meeting 4 miles from here. Our poor baptismal candidate John Fields joined the Methodists there. He had not been here for a very long time already. When I visited there, I experienced much friendship from the preachers, and I was asked to preach but turned the honor down.

George Augustus is at the gold mines again and was arrested for a brief time by the U.S. troops, but he is free again now. People are very much in debt and are afraid of the Georgia Laws. On his last visit he took his note here through cash payment. May the Lord protect him now from all harm. Things are going better again with his father, old Wm. Abr. The good faithful Shepherd will find this lost sheep again. He is remorseful and humble and friendly toward us. His daughter Margaret Mary, who was baptized here on Aug. 15th, brought us great joy with her simple, childlike statements.

My dear wife is recovering very slowly. She is still very weak. However, the baby is healthy and well.

Praise and thanks to the Lord for all the good things we have received undeservingly from His blessed hands. May He give us and all of His servants and maids the power and grace to carry out a powerful work for Him, gathering the reward for His pain.

Br. and Sr. Copeland, Sr. Gambold, and my wife greet you and your dear colleagues, but most especially accept the greetings of your faithfully obliged, unworthy fellow Brother in Christ,

Henry G. Clauder

The 24th. Luckily something else occurred to me before I sent this letter, and I would just like to add this as a reminder for you: a gravestone for our blessed Br. Gambold's grave. Br. Byhan could certainly bring one along. We forgot this when we had an opportunity last year.

1830, part 2

[M 414-5-36: Transcribed by Grace S. Robinson. Addressed to: Revd. Theodore Shulz, Salem, Stokes County, North Carolina. Postmark: Springplace, C.N., Sept. 26, 18¾, via Knoxville. Received Oct. 11.]

Springplace, Cher. N., Sept. 25, 1830

Worthy Br. Shulz,

It falls to to my lot to write to you, since my Father left here on Thuesday last the 21st inst. on his journey to Salem. He reqested me to make mention to you, that he is now on the way, intending to go thro' Jonesborough, & Wilkesboro, to acquaint himself better with the road. At such a late time, this letter may not arrive sooner than he arrives, to give you notice. In case he was detained on the road by some accident, or some other occurance, you would have been notified beforehand; they will probably travell slow, 20 to 25 miles a day, having considerable baggage.

We expect Br. Clauder from Ochge. here to-day, but it is uncertain. We could hear from them at the other station again, as not having heard from there in more than a week. My Mother is in tolerable good health, as also the rest of the family. During council we intend to have school vacation, & to let the schollars visit their parents & friends. This we have done for a few years past. But whether there will be a Cher. Council this year is uncertain, as rumours are abroad, that the Gov. will not permit the session, & to send an armed force into the Nation to prohibit the same. This, in my opinion, is nothing else but to frighten them.

26th. We have been looking for Br. Clauder yesterday in vain. He will certainly be here to-morrow, as Mother will probably go with him to Oche.

Nothing particular has occurred since the departure of my father. I therefore beg to accept this little from me. We all join in love toward you, remaining
your ever faithfull,
Nathaniel Byhan
Revd. Theo. Shulz, Salem

[Springplace (M 407-2) and Oochgeelogy (M 409-1) Diaries. Translated by Julie Tomberlin Weber. Handwritings are Henry G. Clauder's (Ooch.) and Gottlieb Byhan's (Spg.). The Springplace Diary continues in Br. Byhan's hand even during his visit to Salem September 21 to November 6.]

Sun., Sept. 26. [Spg.] Few Brn. and Srs. had come to the services. A sermon was read on Matt. 7:21.

Sun., Sept. 26. [Ooch.] The sermon was on Eph. 6:11, and only a few of our friends and neighbors were present. The following day Br. Clauder went to Spring Place, and he returned from there with Sr. Byhan on *the 29th*. She stayed and visited until Oct. 4.

Sept. 27. [Spg.] Today Br. Clauder came from Ochgeloogy to take Sr. Byhan to Ochgeloogy for a visit. Mr. Tazizi also arrived here with his young brother on their way to Talony. They spent the night here and went further on the morning of *the 28th.*

Sept. 29. [Spg.] Br. Clauder and Sr. Byhan left from here for Ochgeloogy.

Sun., Oct. 3. [Spg.] Many of our Brn. and Srs. were here for the services. A sermon on Luke 18:13 was read.

Sun., Oct. 3. [Ooch.] There were more visitors than usual present for our services. In one of them was the baptism of the baby born on the 7th to Br. and Sr. Clauder; he received the name Charles Ignatius.

Oct. 4. [Spg.] In the evening Sr. Byhan returned from Ochgeloogy and with her came Br. and Sr. Copeland for a visit here.

Oct. 4. [Ooch.] In the evening an Indian came here with his wife, and they spent the night. They have been here often, but we had never had an opportunity to tell them anything about the One Thing Needful [Luke 10:42], or to speak with them about spiritual matters. When asked if he had ever attended a Christian service and heard anything about Jesus, he answered no. Then I told him something about the story of the suffering and death of Jesus, to save us His lost people from sin and the power of the devil. Both of them listened attentively during this, but did not say anything which would indicate a desire for such things as salvation from the power of sin and to have eternal life. Still this is typical for the Indian character, even if their hearts are full of unrest and fear. Since this man could read the language of this country well, I gave him a copy of the Gospel of Matthew, and he read this until late in the evening.

Oct. 5. [Ooch.] I visited some of our neighbors at the mill 1½ miles from here where 4 white families live consisting of 20 persons. Almost everyone is ill with the fever.

[*Records: N.C.*, 8:3926: Salem Diary. Translated by Douglas L. Rights.]

Oct. 6. In the evening Br. Byhan, Senior, arrived with his daughter Rahel, whom he brought here to stay. With him also was the young man Benj. Alexander, a communicant member of the Cherokee Mission in Springplace.* The latter contributed

Oct. 7. to the pleasure of the annual meeting of the Wachovia Brethren's Society for the Spread of the Gospel among the Heathen, at which Br. Byhan spoke of conditions in our mission among the Cherokee, which on account of its restricted condition is a special object of the interest and prayer of this society. At the lovefeast the Cherokee young man was induced, to the pleasure

* The Cherokee Mission had been begun in 1801.

of those present, to read something out of the Church Litany translated into Cherokee.

Oct. 13. In the afternoon, principally for the pleasure of Br. Byhan, but also for others present, Haydn's musical composition *The Creation* was presented.

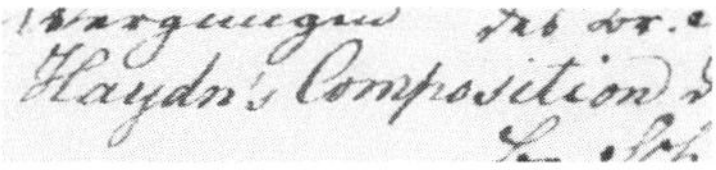

[B 61-3: Provinzial Helfer Conferenz, meeting in Salem. Translated by C. Daniel Crews.]

Thurs., Oct. 14. Our Br. Gottlieb Byhan arrived here for a visit on the 6th as agreed by the P.H.C. (With him came his daughter Rachel, who moved into the Girls Room in the Sisters House.) We had a face-to-face extensive discussion of the situation of our missionaries there including external circumstances as well as that of the Brethren and Sisters belonging to their Gemeinen. We also talked about the Brn. and Srs. serving in this Work of the Lord because we cannot now foresee what outcome the precarious situation of the Cherokee Nation will take. It was therefore very good for us to learn from Br. Byhan that he and his dear wife — in spite of her great weakness and illness —are willing and inclined to remain faithfully at their post at least another year or until the final decision of whether the Cherokee Nation will remain or migrate — which will be referred to the Supreme Court of the United States. We had this discussion with Br. Byhan so that however things may turn out, we might assure him of our sympathy, and also encourage our Gemeinen there with heartfelt greetings to our dear white and brown Brethren and Sisters there.

Because their own particular situation makes it necessary for them to do some farming, and they must hire a day laborer at a high price for this, it was opportune for Br. Byhan and for us that a young man belonging to Friedland, our faithful Br. Naeman Rominger, is willing to go with him to Springplace for the cheap salary of $8 a month. This will also give us the opportunity to fulfill Br. Clauder's request for a horse and a small wagon, which Br. Rominger can drive.

[*Records: N.C.*, 8:3927: Salem Diary.]

Oct. 21. Br. Byhan began the journey to return to Springplace with the Indian young man Benj. Alexander. Also went with him the single Br. Naeman Rominger to serve in secular affairs (outer economy).

[Springplace (M 407-2) and Oochgeelogy (M 409-1) Diaries.]

Oct. 6. [Spg.] We heard that Sister [blank: Anna Ayosta], Br. Josua's wife, is very ill. Sr. Byhan went there accordingly to visit her. She had the fever. But she found her somewhat better, because it was not right on the fever day. Br. and Sr. Copeland returned to Ochgeloogy.

Oct. 8. [Ooch.] I visited Wm. Abr. Hicks and had the opportunity to have a spiritual talk with him.

Sun., Oct. 10. [Spg.] In the first service we read on the text Rom. 10:1. Afterward the single Br. Solomon led a service in the Cherokee language. After a long drought we had a nice rainstorm toward evening, which refreshed the earth.

Sun., Oct. 10. [Ooch.] We had our usual visitors for the sermon, which was on Isaiah 53, of the meritorious sufferings and death of Jesus. During this we painted the heartrending scene at Gethsemane and Golgatha for the listeners with sincere warmth. Some of them are still unconverted and heathen, and we directed them to Jesus, who canceled our debt of sin. Some of them listened to us attentively; others, however, remained apathetic and practically denied the salvation offered them.

Oct. 12. [Spg.] Mr. McNair came here on his way to the Cherokee Council and spent the night here and traveled on Oct. 13th.

Mon., Oct. 11. [Ooch.] The Council of the Nation gathered in New Echota.

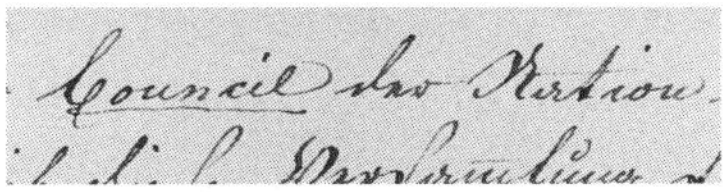

Oct. 13. [Ooch.] Br. Clauder visited there. Until then this gathering had remained free of the threatened attack by the court officials in Georgia, and the Indians began to feel hopeful that they would be able to end their business in peace. But on the 17th a small regiment of United States troops passed through our neighborhood going toward the above-mentioned place, and people presumed they did this to prevent the further meeting of the Council. However, this military visit had a completely different goal. The purpose was to capture all the white traders, gamblers, and hucksters who have come into this country without permission from the appropriate authorities, and now are carrying out their business in Echota, and to take them outside of the borders of the country. During the night all the houses and camps were attacked at once. All the said white people were arrested, and all the alcohol of those who traded in it was destroyed. Many Indians who know the harmful effects of this trade helped. Only a few white people succeeded in escaping. After a number of weeks, during which there was complete peace and order there, this Indian Council meeting finished its business.

Sun., Oct. 17. [Spg.] Few Brn. and Srs. were here for the services.

Oct. 18. [Spg.] We heard that the U. St. troops had arrived in New Echota to put in prison those white people who have no right to be there during the Council, following an order of the President of the United States.

Oct. 19. [Spg.] Br. Nathl. Byhan went today to New Echota and Ochgeloogy on a visit, and returned on the 20th with the news that the U.S. troops had already withdrawn from New Echota the day before and had taken some prisoners with them. Everything at the Council had been quiet and orderly.

[M 414-5-37: Transcribed by Grace S. Robinson. Addressed to: Revd. Theodor Shulz, Salem, Stokes County, North Carolina. Postmark: Spring Place, C.N., Oct. 24, 18¾, via Knoxville. Received Nov. 9. Lightly edited.]

Springplace, C.N., Oct. 23, 1830

Beloved Br. Shulz,

Wishing to inform you of our well doing here at Springpl., since my last letter to you of the 26th [25] Sept. — which I hope you have received — I again address myself to you with the information of our good health. Mother has not been seriously indisposed since my last. I have wrote 2 letters to my father since his departure, hoping their safe arrival.

The Chers. are — as far as I can understand — yet in Council, probably will adjourn to-day, but it is not certain. Few laws have passed, among which is one vis.: "That all those living in the Nation, Chers. or whites, who seek protection under the Georgia laws, are not considered hereafter as citizens." This I understood when there at the Council on Tuesday & Wednesday last, being anxious to see the U.S. Troops who had arrived at Echota & had taken several white men prisoners on the charge of having no business there & considered as intruders according to the "Intercourse law." The Cherokees were left unmolested to deliberate in Council. Here we may perceive that it was but a false report that the troops would arrest the members of Council. They only came to take such prisoners as had no licenses or permits from the Cher. authority.

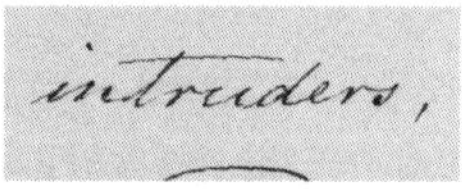

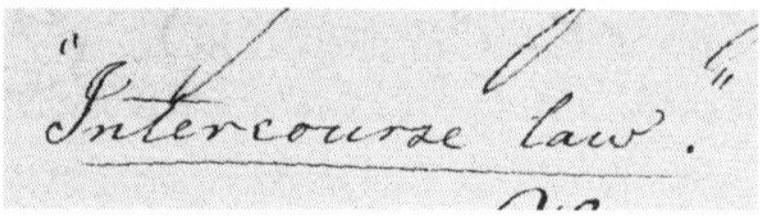

Col. Lowrey from East Tenn., formerly a Mem. of Cong., is a commissioner sent by Government to ascertain the disposition of the Cher. with regard to their removal. He has no full powers to treat with them; he only acts as an Agent. He proposed, among other matters, that the Chers. should send competent individuals to reconnoiter the country west of the Miss. & report at the next

Council or otherwise the situation of the country, quality, &c. This, however, the Cher. declined, thinking it might bring contention among their own tribe. As with regard to treaty, they believe that if Govmt. is not faithful to treaties here, they cannot be so there.

When at N. Town I also visited Ochgl. Br. Clauders were both well as also the rest of the Mission family. Br & Sr. Clauder were at N. Town on Wednesday last. They have at present an adult candidate for Baptism, you will undoubtedly have been informed hereof. Nothing particular has occured at this station since my last to you. Wishing you God's blessing. I remain your ever faithfull

Nathaniel Byhan

Revd. Theodor Shulz, Salem, N.C.

[Springplace (M 407-2) and Oochgeelogy (M 409-1) Diaries.]

Sun., Oct. 24. [Spg.] In the service a sermon was read. Very few of the Brn. and Sr. were here.

Sun., Oct. 24. [Ooch.] We had a nice number of listeners at our service, during which we considered the words of James 3:6, and this provided an opportunity to explain the sins of the tongue, through careless and damaging talk, which disrupt peace and love. All those present were very attentive, and we hope that they received the desired uplifting impression. After the sermon we had individual talks with some of the young people. A young man who was previously a scholar of the blessed Sr. Anna Ros. Gambold in Spring Place said, among other things: "I realize my confusion, and I am concerned about becoming converted and leading a life that will please God. Pray for me," he continued, "so that the day will soon come when I experience assurance of the forgiveness of my sins."

Oct. 28. [Ooch.] Br. and Sr. Clauder visited a white woman in this neighborhood who is ill and who belongs to the Methodists. We repeated this visit in the following days.

[M 414-5-38: Transcribed by Grace S. Robinson. Addressed to: Revd. Theodor Shulz, Salem, Stokes County, North Carolina. Postmark: Spring Place, C.N., Oct. 31, paid 18¾, via Knoxville. Received Nov. 16. Lightly edited.]

Springplace, C.N., Oct. 30, 1830

Dear Br. Shulz,

On the 24 inst, Mother & myself received a letter from you for which we were thankful to hear of Father's safe arrival at Salem amongst his Brethren and friends. Last Sunday the 24th I wrote a letter to you, hoping you may have received the same, in the which I mentioned our good health, & as yet — through the mercy of God — in good health. In my last to you was mentioned also something about the Cher. Council. Nothing has been done worth relating since that time. Indeed, I never knew when Council adjourned until to-day when I heard that they adjourned on Tuesday last. Many laws have not been made. With Col. Lowry they had a talk. The *Cher. Phoenix* gives a very good description of the performance. He done nothing with them, as the Chers. were determined to stay & not remove.

31st: We received a few lines from Revd. C. F. Shaaf, to our great joy, in which we perceive that Father is on his return to Springplace. Having not recd. a line from Father, we were thank-full for these few lines. Not having much time now to write more, wishing you the blessing of God, I subscribe myself your Fr. & Br.

Nathaniel Byhan

Revd. T. Chulz, Salem

[Springplace (M 407-2) and Oochgeelogy (M 409-1) Diaries.]

Sun., Oct. 31. [Ooch.] Once again we had the grace of baptizing a sinner justified in Christ into Jesus' death. This is our neighbor, the surviving husband of the blessed and now deceased Sr. Sarah Copeland, who died on June 10. Her blessed ending made a deep and healing impression of Jesus' love for sinners and the bliss of God's children. As usual on such occasions, our Saal was full of listeners who heard the comforting invitation of our Redeemer, Come unto me, all ye that labour and are heavy laden, etc. [Matt. 11:28], first in English and then through the help of the translator in their own language. At the conclusion of these blessed services, we joined our communicants in celebrating the memorial meal of our crucified Savior. One candidate observed for the first time, and three guests of other confessions participated emotionally.

Mon., Nov. 1. [Ooch.] School began again after a period of 6 weeks. Eleven of our previous scholars had returned.

Nov. 4. [Ooch.] We received a pleasant visit from Mr. Thompson and his wife, missionaries who live on the Hightower River about 25 miles from here. They left the next morning and continued on their way.

Nov. 6. [Spg.] Today we had the joy of seeing Br. Byhan, Sr., with his escort Benj. Alex. Sanders, arrive here healthy and well at our place again from their visit in Salem They had a competely safe trip there and back, for which we joined them in bringing our dear Lord emotional thanks.

Sun., Nov. 7. [Spg.] Many of our Brn. and Srs. came for the Sunday services. In the morning, after the praying of the Church Litany, was a sermon on Rom. 1:16: I am not ashamed of the gospel of Christ: for it is the power of God unto salvation to every one who believeth. In conclusion the Brn. and Srs. were invited to the Holy Communion next Sunday.

Nov. 8. [Spg.] Br. Clauder came from Ochgeloogy on a visit to our place. He came primarily to pick up his horse, wagon, and the things Br. Byhan had brought along from Salem for the mission post in Ochgeloogy. Since our neighbors' horses had begun breaking into our Indian corn fields every night, today we began harvesting the corn from them. A ten-acre field had already been harvested some time ago.

Mon., Nov. 8. [Ooch.] Br. Clauder went to Spring Place, despite the rainy weather, and he was happy to welcome Br. Byhan, who had returned on the 6th from his visit in Salem. The Female Missionary Society and individual friends in Salem sent items for this post along with many gifts for our poor Cherokee children. This moved us to sincere gratitude toward our dear Brethren and Sisters. May the Lord enable us to return and maintain their loving interest in these missions, through happy news about the progress of His kingdom among this people.

[M 414-5-39: Translated by Julie Tomberlin Weber. Addressed to: Revd. Theodore Schulz, Salem, Stokes County, North Carolina. Postmark: Spring Place, C.N., Nov. 14, paid 18¾. Received Nov. 29. Br. Schulz has written in the address: O______ee acct. from May to Nov. 1830 & to May 1831.]

Spring Place, Nov. 8, 1830

Dear Brother Schulz,

On the 3rd of this month I received your kind letter dated Oct. 12. It delighted all of us, since we had not had the pleasure of any communication from Salem in over a month. We sincerely thank you for the encouragement your dear notes always provide us, and it is certainly no less of a pleasure when we can send you and all the other friends of this work good news. Things are no different here than at other missions in this respect: Joy and suffering alternate with each other, a glorious arrangement of the only wise Ruler of all things.

We are all in good health except for Sr. Gambold, who has not been very well for a number of weeks now. Occasionally she has had to stay in bed. Still we join her in hoping that she might recover soon. Sr. Clauder has regained her strength and is busy with the household.

On Oct. 31 we had the pleasure of seeing our Gemeinlein increased by one through the baptism of our neighbor Austin Copeland. He received the name Isaac Austin. Many observers had gathered for this event. The Lord was gracious in all the services. He was especially close to us during the enjoyment of the holy sacrament in the late afternoon of the same day, when our Margaret Mary watched as a candidate and 3 members of other confessions (Widow James Fields, Mrs. Wheeler, & Mrs. Adair, the first 2 are Presbyterian, the latter Methodist) were fervent fellow participants. We expect that Mr. Wheeler, the printer of the *Phoenix* who often attends our services and seems to be thoroughly awakened, will soon join here. He is very openhearted toward me. Last Sunday evening I had a thorough 3-hour heart-to-heart conversation with him, as we did with Stand Watie (Boudinott's brother) the previous Sunday evening. In one conversation he also declared we could believe that God's Spirit is busy in his heart.

John Fields is now with the Methodists, where Crutchfield is now Class leader, and never attends here. He seems to be unhappy with me because I did not want to take back the $10 counterfeit he claimed to have received from Br. Schmidt, in exchange for a good one. Despite this, his wife Maria Rosina visits us regularly and does not let him influence her against us.

I arrived here this afternoon and had the pleasure of sincerely welcoming our dear Br. Byhan and receiving all the things sent with him, including the horse and wagon. I sincerely thank you for this. May the Lord reward you for your fatherly care, which we feel with deep humility. Tomorrow I am planning to drive back to Oochgeloogy, since our school, which began again on the 1st of this month, is already well attended, and Sr. Copeland cannot manage the school well alone during the continued troublesome weakness of our dear Mother Gambold. Sr. G's complaint is peculiar to the sex at that period of life.[1]

You will be able to learn about all the political news from the *Phönix*, so I will remain silent about this. I would like to ask you to submit my name to Br. Benzien as a subscriber to the *Illustrations of the Mission Places of the Brethren*. I also ask you to extend my most obliged thanks for his efforts to have Battier's sermons sent to me.

---

1 The sentence is in English in the original German manuscript.

Wm. Hicks was not well last week because of a bad cold, but yesterday he was here at our place again. I hope you will find the enclosed account satisfactory. Greet your dear family and especially Henry; I received his letter of Oct. 17th today. That's all, in haste. Your faithfully obliged friend and Brother,

Heinrich G. Clauder

Account Current of cash receipts and expenditures
From May 5 to Nov. 5, 1830

1830	Expenditures	
May 22	Expenses to cash for the Indian pans	$0.75
	Pd. Lavender for Sunday school books $2.75; swat oil $0.50; Bateman's drops $0.25; combs $0.25; cravats $1.50; cambric $1.50 tucking comb $0.62½; ½ yard muslin $0.37½	7.75
June	Pd. ferriage $0.50; postage $1.00; 7 milk pans $2.00	3.50
July	Pd. Jesse Copeland for work, 2 mos., 9 days	23.00
	Pd. ferriage $0.25; Elias Boudinot for Litany $7.00* *(the balance $13 settled in acct.)	7.25
July 15	Pd. for shoes $3.375; medicine $0625; 1 doz. Cherokee mats $2.00	6.00
	Pd. an Indian for a pot & 2 baskets	0.75
Aug.	Pd. Jesse Copeland for 1 day of work at the peach kiln	0.50
	Pd. 2 hands for work at fodder pulling	3.75
	Pd. ferriage of Blum's wagon returning last fall	1.00
	Pd. J. Wallace for ½ month work	4.50
Sept.	Pd. Saml. Henry on acct. for sundries	20.00
	Pd. for nutmeg $0.50; ferriage $0.25	0.75
Oct.	Pd. for postage $0.38; 13 lbs. coffee @ $0.25 $3.25	3.63
	Pd. for 1 quart wine for Sr. Gambold	0.75
	Advanced N. Byhan for Spr. Place treasury	20.00
Oct. 22	Pd. G. Lavender for sundry articles for Copelands: shoes, combs, osnaburg, etc., $9.875; 1 lb. cinnamon $0.75; spelling books, etc., for the mission $3.75	13.62½
	Pd. Elias Boudinott for 2 barrels flour	10.00
Oct. 25	Pd. Mrs. Hicks for her Negro girl for washing	2.00
	Pd. contingencies about our hogs	1.00
Nov. 4	Amt. of cash in hand	63.02
		193.52½
	[subtracted by Br. Schulz in Salem]	63.02
		130.50½

1830	Receipts	
May	Amt of cash in hand	16.90
	Recd. of E. Nicholson for tinware	1.00
June	Recd. of Sr. Chisholm for ware	1.75
	Recd. of Br. Byhan, Spr. Place	30.25
June 22	Recd. of George Hicks on acct.	3.50
	Recd. for a tin pan 0.50; 1 doz. Cher. Litanies 0.75	1.25
July	Recd. for butter 0.875; tinware $3.00	3.87½
Aug.	Recd. of G. A. Hicks on acct for cash	21.00
	Recd. for tinware	3.00
	Recd. for butter, soap & fat & wool	4.75
Sept. 18	Recd. per mail of Br. Schulz	100.00
Oct.	Recd. of D. McNair for tinware	2.50
	Recd. of Lydia Chisolm on acct.	3.37½
	Recd. for 3 lbs. fat	0.37½
		193.52½

[M 407-2: Springplace Diary.]

Nov. 9. [Spg.] Br. Clauder today returned to Ochgelogy. We heard in recent days that an Indian had shot a white man on the border of Georgia. The white man had stolen the Indian's horse, and when the latter set after him to get his horse back and the white man would not give him his horse back, he shot him down from the horse. Time will tell what the results of this incident will be.

Nov. 11. [Spg.] We finished harvesting the corn. Because of the great drought we had this summer, we got only about one-third of the corn this year than we had harvested last year. Still we are grateful to our heavenly Father for what He gave us from His gentle hand.

1830, part 3

[M 414-5-40: Translated by Julie Tomberlin Weber. Addressed to: Revd. Theodore Schulz, Salem, Stokes County, North Carolina. Postmark: Springplace, C.N., Nov. 14. Free. Gottl. Byhan, P.M. Received Nov. 29.]

Spring Place, Nov. 12, 1830

Dearly beloved Br. Shulz,

After a journey of 17 days we, my party and I, returned safe and sound to Spring Place on the 6th of this month. We had a very happy journey, as nothing eventful happened, for which we are sincerely grateful to our dear Lord!

We reached the mountains — Wards Gap — by 9 o'clock in the morning on Saturday the 23rd, and we climbed the mountain in one and a half hours. Baal carried the small wagon with the load without having to lighten the load in the little wagon, and he thus proved that he will turn out to be a good horse — if he is just fed well now!

Once again we had no rain on our return journey, except for a couple of showers in the night. Since I have been back home, however, it has often rained, to be accurate, as it rained at your place after my arrival in Salem.

On the 8th, last Monday, Br. Clauder came from Ochgeloogy to Spring Place to pick up his things and the wagon and horse which we brought along, and he returned to O______y on the 9th. I found everyone here in Spring Place healthy and well, including my dear wife, who is currently very active, for which we are very grateful to our dear Lord! On Sunday the 7th many of our Cherokee Brn. and Srs. came here to welcome us.

It is still quiet in the Nation. The Georgians have not caused any disturbances in the Cherokee Council either, although, as I was told, some officers and soldiers were present and the Council sat for only about two weeks. The U. St. troops, however, are busy chasing all of the intruders out of the country, and no one is allowed to enter the country to trade with the Indians unless he has a license, or the goods and items will be taken away from him. Thus it happened that before my return Samuel Henry, with whom we often trade, had 90 gallons of whiskey poured out and the rest of his items were taken away from him, and they arrested him in the darkness of the night. However, he escaped from them and left the wagon with the things. This happened at Mr. Gann's, between here and Ochgeloogy. The Indians and white people are not allowed to dig for gold any more either, because it is considered the Property of Georgia.

This week everyone was busy harvesting our Indian corn, because despite the fact that we complained about it, Jos. Vann's horses broke into the Indian corn fields every night and did a great deal of damage to them. Yesterday we finished with the harvest.

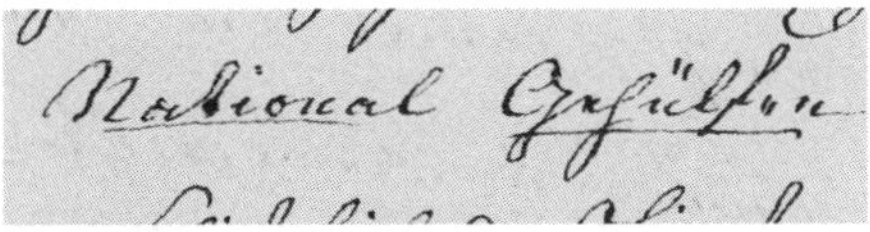

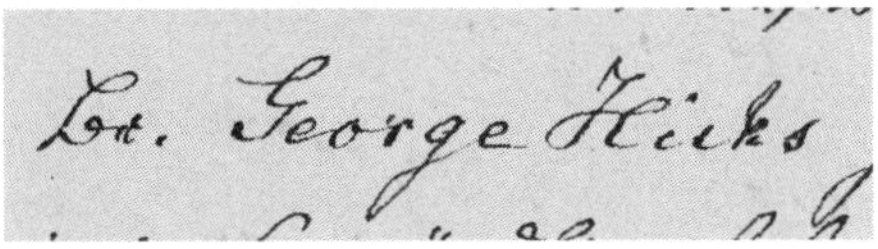

Br. Clauder asked me to mention this to you in my letter: Wouldn't it be good to have a National Helper in his Gemeine to help him, since he cannot visit the Brn. and Srs. appropriately because of his school and other business at home. He would not only visit the Brn. and Srs., but also the still unconverted Indians, and he would acquaint them with their Creator and Redeemer. In short, he would do everything that is fitting for a National Helper. He believes he has a fitting object for this office in Br. George Hicks. I myself am not so thoroughly acquainted with this Br. in any case, and in my opinion, it should be someone who has experienced grace and sought and found forgiveness for his sins in Jesus' blood and death, so that he can extol Jesus' love for sinners to others with a warm heart. However, as I said, I am not as thoroughly acquainted with him as Br. Clauder, who can also write more about him. I will not say more about Br. Clauder's suggestion; I just think it is still somewhat too early.

During my absence our Nathanael took care of the work here while I was gone as well as he could, both related to the services and holding school.

In accordance with your wishes, I inquired with Mr. Soule in Abingdon about the debt owed you by pitiful Barr. Mr. Soule told me that he had received something for you from Barr in tobacco, which he would have to sell first, and he would write to you himself around New Year and let you know how much he has taken in for you.

Mother Gambold in Ochgeloogy is currently very sickly, so that she can hardly stay out of bed.

Accept the most sincere greetings from all of us, and especially from your upright, loving Br.,

Gottlieb Byhan

[Springplace (M 407-2) and Oochgeelogy (M 409-1) Diaries. Translated by Julie Tomberlin Weber. Handwritings are Henry G. Clauder's (Ooch.) and Gottlieb Byhan's (Spg.).]

Sun., Nov. 14. [Spg.] Our Brn. and Srs. came in large numbers for the services. In the first one was a sermon on Acts 3:19 and afterward the baptism of the baby son born to our Br. and Sr. Boas with the name Lewis. In the last service we had a blessed enjoyment of the body and blood of Jesus in Holy Communion. Finally, Br. Byhan extended sincere greetings to the Brn. and Srs. on behalf of the Brn. and Srs. in Salem, most especially from the members of the Society for the Propagation of the Gospel among the Heathen. They were very happy about this. On this occasion the Indian Br. James said in everyone's name, that it was their intention to live in this world only for the Savior, and that in their current desperate situation they would hold to the One who can arrange everything for the best. The peace of God was powerfully felt during this Holy Communion and in the service.

Sun., Nov. 14. [Ooch.] Among the visitors was a young Indian who expressed his desire to become the Savior's property years ago, but he still acts indecisively and sometimes completely apathetic. We spoke privately with him after the service, during which he was very attentive. George Augustus, among others, was untiring in sharing with him from his own experience and extolling the salvation to be found with Jesus. We saw this had some success.

Nov. 16. [Spg.] The Indian Conandoah stopped in at our place on his way from McNair's. After he had asked for food and eaten it, he went on. He lives about 3½ miles from here. He told us that he had met a white man a couple of miles from here who threatened to beat him. When Conandoah realized this, he picked up a stone and threw it at the white man and hit him. As Conondoah himself said, it cost him his life.

Nov. 18. [Spg.] Conandoah returned to us, and after he had eaten he said that he was now going to the mountains we can see from our living room, and he would come back here tomorrow. However, he did not return until the 20th, when he showed us some gold he had in a little glass bottle that had been found in the mountains.

Sun., Nov. 21. [Spg.] Today we held just one service because only a few of our Brn. and Srs. had come. During the night of the 22nd we had a nice rain. We hope this will put the mills in our neighborhood back in business, since for a while only a little could be milled because the streams were unusually low.

Sun., Nov. 21. [Ooch.] In reference to the rich blessings we received this year from the gentle fatherly hand of our all gracious Lord, the sermon considered the words of Psalm 126:5-6, and challenged everyone present to give the Lord praise and thanksgiving not only for all the physical good deeds, but also most especially for allowing the seeds of His saving word to be scattered generously in so many places in this country in undisturbed peace, and that they were also beginning to produce fruit for the kingdom of heaven. In this regard we brought the Giver of all good gifts and blessings our deepest and most humble thanks.

Nov. 24. [Spg.] Late in the evening the Rev. Mr. Butrick and his wife came here on their way from Brainerd to Carmel, where they live, and spent the night. Mr. Butrick told us that they are busy rebuilding their house in Brainerd, that they would not build it as big again as the one that had been burned down, and that they were planning to take only about 30 children into the school in the future, whereas they had formerly had 50 to 60.

Nov. 25. [Spg.] Mr. David Steiner Tazizi came to our place since he had business in our neighborhood. He spent two nights with us and did not return home until early on *the 27th*. In the evening Mr. Elias Boudinot came to our place, and since it was already late in the afternoon so that he could no longer get home in the light of day, he decided to spend Sunday with us tomorrow. In the evening Br. and Sr. Samuel also arrived here already for tomorrow's services.

[M 414-5-41: Translated by Julie Tomberlin Weber. Addressed to: Revd. Theodor Schulz, Salem, Stokes County, North Carolina. Postmark: Springplace, C.N., Nov. 28. Free. Gottl. Byhan, P.M. Received Dec. 13.]

Springplace, Nov. 27, 1830

Dearly beloved Br. Schulz,

By now you will probably have received my last letter to you dated the 12th of this month, in which I reported our safe arrival in Springplace on the 6th of this month. We cannot adequately express our gratitude that the Savior led us here and there so safely. He protected us from harm and misfortune, and what kind of beautiful weather did we not have? In brief, we clearly see that He was with us and among us. With motherly hands He always leads His people. Give honor to our God!

We ask you to extend our sincere thanks to all of our friends of the mission who made efforts to delight us and our Indian children with gifts. Please greet them; and we wish for all of them rich blessings from our dear Lord for this, especially dear Br. Abr. Steiner, Sr., Srs. L. Kramsch, Bresing, yes all whom I cannot name here. Give our best greetings to Br. and Sr. Benzien, and when it's convenient ask Br. Benzien to extend sincere thanks in my name for the Tracts we received. I had the opportunity to distribute a large portion of these in Tennessee with a certain Likens, where I spent the night. The 3 adult daughters of this Likens take special care for the youth especially in this area and hold weekday and Sunday schools. They are dear people. We spent the evening talking about religion and school for the children. They live on the road from Lowrey's Ferry on the [Little] Tennessee to Columbus on the Highwassee River. They were extremely joyful that I could provide them with Tracts. I promised them I would send a number of them when I have an opportunity, which I will also do at the first chance.

Your dear letter of Oct. 21, in which you informed my dear wife of my departure from Salem on the same day, reached Spring Place on Nov. 7th, one day after my arrival. We brought Ward safely here. We are having problems with him because of his bad temper, but things will get better with time when he has settled in more.

It's a shame that I forgot to bring along writing paper, because it is much more expensive here, indeed almost double what it costs at your place. On the 14th of this month I received 10 English Daily Texts from Bethlehem with the mail. When I opened them, I decided to look up a Watchword regarding our situation for the next year. When I opened the Daily Texts, the Doctrinal Text for Feb. 9 caught my attention: When ye shall hear of wars and rumours of wars, be ye not troubled [Mark 13:7]. [Hymn:] Jesus, our Guardian, Guide, & Friend, Now thy protecting wings extend, Thy children save from harm. Since it does not seem improbable that we will perhaps hear about war and the cries of war in the future, this Text was very important to me and encouraging, and we can glance into the future looking to Him who rules all.

Currently all is still quiet in the Nation, as far as we here in Spring Place know and can find it. Br. Clauder lives in an area where one always hears and learns more than we can here in Spring Place, so perhaps he can report more, such as the general thoughts of the Cherokees and what rumors are circulating, and which are not confirmed and which can be confirmed.

This week Revd. Mr. Buttrick from Carmel spent the night with us. He told us that Mr. Evarts had written to the missionaries in Brainerd that the Govt. would not contribute any more to the schools for Indians on this side of the Mississippy, and that nothing is set aside for them. Thus we can no longer count on further support from the government. Even so, the Savior will not let His work lie undone, and He will continue to carry out His work among the Indians in a glorious manner. Revd. Mr. Buttrick paid a dollar subscription for the *Missionary Intelligencer* in my absence again. He also pays the post money himself now, because the *Missy. Intel.* is now being sent to Carmel, where he currently lives and where there is a Post Office.

We have not heard anything from our Brn. and Srs. in Ochgeloogy for 2 weeks now. The last news from there was that Sr. Gambold is now recovering.

Our Naeman Rominger seems to fit in here quite well, and we think he will tolerate things here for a while. As for Br. and Sr. Copeland in Ochgeloogy, we believe, as does Br. Clauder, that they will decide to move west, perhaps to Indiana, even if not right away. Still we do not know this for sure; it is just a guess. I personally cannot understand the man, since he still seems to be very inconsistent and does not yet know what he really wants. However, things will soon become clear.

Concerning what I wrote to you in my last letter about Br. George Hicks, I want to ask you not to interpret this as if I were opposed to Br. Clauder's making him a National Helper. I am sorry that I said as much about him as I did, and therefore I ask you not to pay any attention to my statements. Br. Clauder knows him, that is, Br. Hicks, better than I do, and whether he is an appropriate subject to assume this office or service.

Tomorrow is the first Sunday in Advent and once again we enter into the time during which our Savior's saving incarnation will be the basis of our reflections and conversations. May the Savior let our dear Cherokee Brn. and Srs. and us be especially blessed, as we reflect on His incarnation. May He awaken in all of us the desire to live on earth only for Him Who was incarnate, suffered, and died out of love for us. Our friend David Steiner Tazizi was here in recent days. He promised me he would serve as interpreter for us again at Christmas, which will be very pleasant and dear for us, and especially for our Brn. and Srs.

Three from this Nation, Richard Tayler, John Ridge, and Coodey, will go — or have already gone — to Washington as Delegates. The first and the last were in Washington in the same capacity last year. This winter the Cherokees are very anxious about the outcome of their matter in Congress as well. People believe that it will turn out more favorably for them this time, because they believe they have more friends there than they did last year. May God grant that everything turns out in their — the Cherokees' — favor. It is amazing how bravely they have acted, and are still acting, under oppression, and they are determined to continue thus until their matter is decided.

Currently a number of our Brn. and Srs. are sick with fever, but it is not dangerous. Our baptismal candidate, Br. Emanuel's wife, was also unable to come to Spring Place because of illness, and so her baptism must be postponed until she has recovered enough that she can come here.

Concerning the spiritual life of the Brn. and Srs. in our Gemeine, we can rejoice in them, although they say little about their spiritual condition. Still, especially during Holy Communion and baptism, we can see and feel that they live in grace and in the enjoyment of salvation, and in the joy of the Lord. Their daily walk also clearly shows, for most of them, that it is their desire and joy to live only for Him who has done so much for them out of love.

Our son Nathanael is holding school diligently, and it is very important to him that the children are also learning. He helps us with the outside work as much as his time between school sessions allows.

Today we heard that the President of the U. St. has given orders for the military to leave the Cherokee country. We also hear that many white people have gathered at the gold mines again to dig for gold. That's what we hear!

Praise God, we are currently all well, and everyone sends sincere greetings. Be good enough to let me know what has been paid out for Nancy Becker in Salem. Also what the cost of the things from the store was, because she would really like to have some yards of linen and such, so that I can figure it into my books for her. Along with sincere greetings to you and your dear ones, I remain your faithfully obliged Br.,

Gottlieb Byhan

[Springplace (M 407-2) and Oochgeelogy (M 409-1) Diaries.]

Sun., Nov. 28. [Spg.] On the first Sunday in Advent the Brn. and Srs. were reminded that today we once again enter into the joyful time in which we rejoice especially in the merciful birth of our Lord and Savior, and we pleaded with the Savior to let the consideration of His incarnation be blessed anew to our hearts. In the first service we prayed the Litany of the Life, Sufferings, and Death of our Lord Jesus Christ. Afterward was the sermon. In the second service the Brn. and Srs. were informed of the decision approved in our Conf. and by the Helf. Conf. in Salem that we have important reasons to let the Christmas Eve service and the lovefeast in this to be canceled this time. However, on Jan. 6th we would solemnly celebrate the Festival of the Heathen and in a lovefeast on that day we will bind ourselves with our Brn. and Srs. to new faithfulness in following Him, and entertain ourselves by reading the news from other heathen Gemeinen. The Brn. and Srs. expressed their complete satisfaction at this change and also said that they had seen things in Christmas Eve services which were extremely inappropriate. Mr. Elias Boudinott was our interpreter in all of our services today.

Sun., Nov. 28. [Ooch.] For the beginning of the richly blessed Advent season, the sermon reflected on the Gospel of Matt. 21, Christ's entry into Jerusalem. In the second service we read an uplifting text, and then Br. George Augustus gave a brief talk in the Cherokee language. He concluded with a prayer on his knees, which moved those who could understand him. We took the opportunity on this day to inform our Brn. and Srs. about the decision of the mission conference here to stop having the celebration of Christmas Eve for various reasons. They expressed their complete satisfaction with this.

Nov. 29. [Spg.] A young white man and a Negro who belongs to Mr. John Ridge came to our place to spend the night here. They had taken Mr. John Ridge, one of the three Delegates whom the Cherokee Nation sent to Washington this winter, in a carriage as far as Athens in Tenn. From there he would travel on to Washington in the mail stage. We had been recommended to them presumably primarily because they do not have to pay anything here for lodging and horse feed. This lodging and feeding horses at no cost is often very difficult for us, because everyone knows that we do not ask anything of them, so they use it twice as much and prefer to come to us than go to our neighbor Jos. Vann's, where they have to pay for everything. This free hospitality for guests also adds to the fact that this post is so very costly. At this time, however, we cannot change this and must think "other countries, other customs!" although this circumstance sometimes is a great burden for the missionaries here.

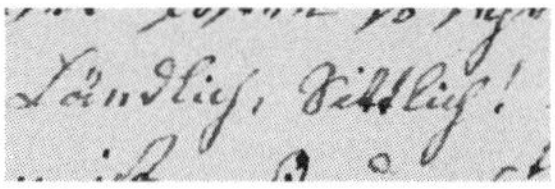

Sun., Dec. 5. [Spg.] Since it rained heavily the whole day, no one came for the Sunday services today, not even our closest neighbors, except for Br. Boas, who had already arrived yesterday evening. And so today we had only one service.

Dec. 5. [Ooch.] We had heavy rains the entire day, but were humbled when contrary to our expectations that no one would come to the service, some of our baptized friends who live close to us came on foot despite the wind and rain. We had a very pleasant and blessed hour of instruction with them in our living room.

[M 414-5-42: Translated by Julie Tomberlin Weber. Addressed to: Revd. Theodore Schulz, Salem, North Carolina. Post stamp: New-Echota, Cher. Na., Dec. 11, 18¾. Received Jan. 5, 1831.]

Ooyugillogy, C.N., Dec. 6, 1830

Dearly beloved Br. Schulz,

Although I have not yet received an answer to my last letter to you, I would like to send you a few lines and let you know that we are all well.

We are delighted and grateful that Sr. Gambold has regained her strength and that she can be active as usual in the household. All the children who are here are healthy and well and generally bring us much joy through their obedience and participation in school as well as in their free time. Our wish and the subject of our prayers is that they might all thrive for the Savior.

Otherwise, we are still in limbo with uncertainty and worry about our poor William Abraham. Oh, if only the Lord, in His grace, would give him a new, confident mind and spirit. During a conversation I recently had with him, he admitted that he often entertains thoughts of leaving his family. I made serious objections to this and with emotion I asked him not to give these thoughts any room, and to continue in humility and patience and prayer to the Lord until he enjoyed peace and quiet in his heart. He seemed to be moved and showed me several places in the Psalms of David which he found comforting regarding his own situation. However, he did not promise to give up thoughts of leaving his family. And so his family and we are very concerned about him. I will do all I can to talk him out of this. May the Lord guide my pitiful efforts with His power and blessing.

And so it brings us all the more joy to see his son George Augustus, who works faithfully for the good work among this people and especially among those who have been baptized. On one recent occasion he delivered a proper talk and prayer in Cherokee, which moved those who understood him. It is a shame he cannot read the language, because then we could use the Litany through him, but I still live in the hope of being able to read it understandably myself soon, and to read it with the children in their language, which I believe would benefit me as well.

Sr. Gann also stays away from here completely, because she has an unfounded hatred against one of the other Srs. We made an attempt to clear up this offense, but found the Indian stubbornness too strong for our admonitions to make any difference.

Such events are really discouraging, because one might fear making some problem worse when trying to correct it. Still it is my resolution to pursue with love and seriousness all who are erring thus, and not to let myself be scared away by such small impulses of the evil heart. May the Lord give me the strength for this.

During the last 2 months we had another hired hand working here to assist with the corn harvest, which with God's blessing turned out to be plentiful. We estimate it at about 500 bushels. The oats were also threshed, and we got 150 bushels from this and will offer most of it for sale. We probably will not get money for it; it is easier to get pigs or cattle. Last fall I sold 2 oxen to Mr. Henry for $25, which reduced our debt to him that much. Despite this, he gave us a request for flour, etc., for $40 against this. I had purchased a sufficient supply of this at $5 per bushel, and the prices will doubtless increase due to the general shortage of corn.

The above-mentioned worker left us today.

Would it not be advisable to pay our Br. Copeland monthly to avoid large payments? We owe him for two months again already, and I cannot pay him due to a shortage of money. Perhaps it surprised you to see a payment of $9.87½ for the Copelands in my last account, even though everything they requested was sent to them from Salem. So I would like to offer the following explanation. During the annual Council in New Town one can buy goods at perhaps 25 percent cheaper than at other times. Some articles are even cheaper than in Salem. And so we took advantage at that time. We did not yet know anyway whether or not Br. Byhan would bring anything for us, since we had not yet received any word of his arrival in Salem or about the purchase of a horse and wagon for us (which provided the opportunity to send everything we requested).

Some days ago a request came to me to marry a couple of young people, both of Cherokee descent. This was carried out at the house of one of our neighbors 4 miles from here, in the evening on the 2nd of this month. The young man did not have a license for this, which is lucky for me because according to the Georgia laws, if a missionary or preacher performs a marriage based on a license given by the Cherokees, he will be put in the Georgia penitentiary. I did not know this at the time, and so when I learned this I was all the more grateful for the guidance through which I had avoided all trouble. What do you think about this: Is it advisable to perform a marriage by virtue of a Cherokee licence? As disinclined as I am to respect just one single law of the state of Georgia, I would not intentionally subject myself to a miserable imprisonment.

I was extremely delighted to learn from the recently received *Missionary Intelligencer* that the expenditures of the missions among the North American Indians were low in comparison with others, for example Antigua or Barbados and St. Kitts, and on these two islands there are only two stations. The expenses for the year 1829 will also be more because of the construction in Spring Place and that of a church in New Fairfield.

If the only wise Ruler maintains this people and us here, then construction will also be necessary here. We are very crowded with the large numbers in school, and we must endure many inconveniences. Still under the current circumstances I sometimes have doubts about having even a new fence set. And so there is even less thought of new construction.

Since this will probably be my last letter to you for this year, I wish you the rich and revitalizing blessings from on high during the celebration of our Savior's birthday, as well as for the beginning of a new year, and we also ask for our share in this from this distance. Please greet our dear family and the dear Brn. of the P.H.C. for us all, and especially from your faithful friend and Brother,

Henry G. Clauder

[Springplace (M 407-2) and Oochgeelogy (M 409-1) Diaries.]

Dec. 7. [Spg.] We received two boys from the area of Oochgelogy into our school.

Wed., Dec. 8. [Ooch.] A young married couple visited us. They were married several days ago in this neighborhood. The young man is a member of the Presbyterian Church, but she belongs to the Methodists in this area. On this day one of our neighbors, a white man, came and asked for $16 as damage for one of his oxen he recently lost, which he claimed was the result of damage it received from one of our oxen. Through Br. George Augustus's negotiations, we settled this matter peacefully by paying the cheaper sum of $12. But this did not take place for several days.

Dec. 9. [Spg.] Mr. Butrick came to our place and spent the night here, and on the morning of *Dec. 10* he traveled on to Brainerd.

Sun., Dec. 12. [Spg.] Today we had rainy weather once again, so that no one could come to the services. This rainy weather also continued so heavily on the 13th and 14th that the streams swelled to an extraordinary level. These days we received an increase in our school size when three new scholars were brought to it.

Sun., Dec. 12. [Ooch.] It rained again very hard. Even more visitors came to the services than last Sunday. In the evening we held a Singstunde with the house Gemeinlein, during which two flutes provided pleasant accompaniment.

[M 414-5-43: Transcribed by Grace S. Robinson. Addressed to: Miss Louisa C. Kramsch, Salem, Stokes County, North Carolina. Post stamp: New-Echota, Cher. Na., Dec. 18, 18¾. Lightly edited.]

Ooyugillogy, C.N., Dec. 13, 1830

Dear Sister,

We are desirous of expressing thankfulness to the beloved members of the Female Missionary Society of Salem for the useful donations they forwarded to us by Br. Byhan for the benefit of our poor Indian scholars. For this purpose I beg leave to address these few lines to you, as the corresponding Secretary of that worthy Society; and in order to contribute my mite toward keeping alive the kind interest you have evinced in this portion of our Lord's work among the poor heathen, I will endeavour to give you some information about our school, which I must confess, is so interesting to us, that we forget in a manner the difficulties & fatiguing labours which are connected, unavoidably, therewith.

That the school is exclusively for girls you are aware of. We have at present 13 with us constantly; besides these there are about 4 at home on a visit. The most of them entered school within two years, and we have at length the satisfaction to have several readers among them. Others are making progress in spelling & writing. Sr. Copeland instructs them every afternoon in sewing, knitting, & marking.

The donation of linen, yarn, &c., is truly acceptable. But we thought it most prudent to keep the scholars in ignorance of what had been sent for them, or rather for the poorer ones, & to give them only in time of need, the articles required. Some of them are well clothed by their parents & need nothing. An indiscriminate distribution of clothing is therefore not advisable. Care must likewise be taken not to encourage their parents to indolence & carelessness, which would be the result with some, were we to make it known what had been forwarded for the poorer children. They would all be poor then! But there are some without father; others too poor to procure a change of clothing or a sufficiency thereof to be comfortable during the present season. To them your benevolence is inexpressibly welcome, while it is a source of encouragement to us to perceive such fruits of your interest in the temporal welfare to comfort of our poor, degraded, & injured Cherokees. We are convinced that our interest in behalf of the spiritual & eternal welfare of these people is fully equal thereto.

May the Lord our Saviour fit us more & more for the important work to which it pleased Him to call us. May He watch over His cause & defend us against the designs of the enemy.

The unhappy political situation of the Nation presents many discouraging aspects to our views. The efforts of the Missionaries are paralyzed to a considerable extent in consequence thereof, & yet even under these circumstances we have manifold proofs of the neverceasing attention of our merciful Lord & Saviour to the sighs & prayers of His people. To Him we recommend our distressed people, and to Him alone we look under the manifold trials incident to our pilgrimage.

Give our Love to all the beloved Sisters composing your Missionary Society & remember us in your prayers to Him who on that great day, when people & realms of every tongue shall stand before Him, shall welcome those who gave to the poor with the cheering salutation, "What you have done to one of these little ones, you have done to me, etc." May our dear Saviour accompany the laudable efforts of your Society with His blessing & increase your numbers to still greater efficiency. I remain your affectionate fr. & Brother.

Henry G. Clauder

Miss Louise C. Kramsch
Corresponding Sec. of the Female Missionary Society

[B 61-3: Provinzial Helfer Conferenz, meeting in Salem. Translated by C. Daniel Crews.]

Wed., Dec. 14. P.H.C. Minutes for 30 July and 14 Oct. were reviewed. Everything decided upon in them has been carried out, and Br. Byhan and company arrived safe and sound in Springplace on 6 Nov. A few days later on the Sunday he was welcomed back by the Cherokee people with a large number in attendance, and they found everything safe and quiet.

We had a preliminary discussion over the information or inquiry of Br. Gb. Byhan in his last letters concerning Br. Clauder's suggestion in their conferenz that they appoint a National Assistant in Oochgelogy, for which he appeared to find Br. George Hicks a suitable subject. However, we will wait to hear more details from Br. Clauder himself.

[Springplace (M 407-2) and Oochgeelogy (M 409-1) Diaries.]

Dec. 13, 14. [Ooch.] It rained unceasingly, which made all the streams in this whole country reach an unusual height. The Coosa River reached such a level that many houses in New Echota were completely surrounded by water and could only be reached by using canoes. A mill close to us was damaged so badly that it will be unusable the entire winter. Luckily another mill a little farther from here escaped the flood, so the lack of flour can be avoided. At another mill a corn house and several hundred bushels of corn were carried away, and a cotton machine was completely overturned and a significant quantity of cotton was carried away by the current.

Dec. 18. [Spg.] An Indian from the area of Chatugee came to get some medicine from us for a sick child. We gave him some herbs and some drops to strengthen the child. Already this evening our Indian Br. Israel arrived here for tomorrow's services. He lives on the other side of the Conossauga River about 10 miles from here. He said that he had waded through the Conossauga River and that the water had come up to his chest and that it was very cold. Thus he arrived at our place completely stiff and frozen through.

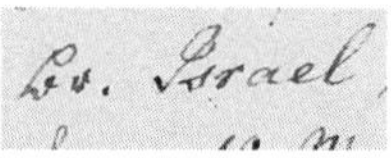

Sun., Dec. 19. [Spg.] Our services were as usual. Today we heard that a law was recently made in the Georgia Legislature that all white people should leave Indian country. But this news must be confirmed.

Sun., Dec. 19. [Ooch.] A heathen Indian woman who attended the services was asked if she had already heard about the Savior of the world, how He had also suffered for the sake of her sins. When she answered no, it was easy to see her apathy toward such things. She knew nothing about the immortal soul and a future world. We urged her to visit us often, so that she could receive instruction in these truths.

Dec. 24. [Spg.] Today Mr. Dav. Steiner Tazizi came to our place to serve us tomorrow as interpreter for Christmas Day. In the last years it happened that the service on Christmas Eve — since Christmas Eve was celebrated with a lovefeast as in the

Gemeinen — was no longer appropriate to its actual purpose, since the celebration of this caused disorder and boisterousness among the many visitors. Thus we had decided in our mission conference, with the approval of the Prov. H. Conf. in Salem, to forego the Christmas Eve celebration this time. This decision was also made known to our Brn. and Srs. some time ago. Because of the disorder which they had also seen at this Christmas Eve celebration, they had given their complete agreement to this. Instead of the Christmas Eve celebration now, it was further decided that on Jan. 6th we will have a festival celebration with all of our Brn. and Srs., about which the Brn. and Srs. also showed their satisfaction and agreement.

Dec. 25. [Spg.] Christmas Day. Almost all of our Brn. and Srs. had arrived here. In the first service, after a brief talk, the story of our Savior's birth was read from Luke 2:1-20. This was then repeated in the Cherokee language by the single Br. Solomon. Then we brought our incarnate God thanks and adoration for His inexpressible love for us poor humans, which moved Him to leave His throne of glory to redeem us through bitter sufferings and death. Then was the sermon on the birth of Jesus. Afterward was another Singstunde, in which a hymn was sung in the Cherokee language out of the hymnal published by the Presbyterians. This day was one of exceptional grace and blessing. The Savior's presence could be felt in our services.

Dec. 25. [Ooch.] After some pleasant days, the weather today was so cold that everything liquid froze even in our room. This cold, which is not unusual here, lasted for 3 days without letting up. For the celebration of Christmas on the 25th, most of our baptized Brn. and Srs. and some friends gathered here. With them we were transported in spirit to the manger of the newborn Savior of the world, and we prayed for blessings and then reflected on the great story of His birth. The second service was held completely in Cherokee, led by our Br. George Augustus and another Indian believer who belongs to the Hawies mission. The Indian singing was pleasant as usual. Many of the visitors spent the night here, and in the evening they were were entertained and instructed by our children's singing.

Sun., Dec. 26. [Spg.] Because of the unfriendly weather today only a few Brn. and Srs. came to the services.

Sun., Dec. 26. [Ooch.] In the morning one of our baptized came, who had not been here for months, since she is in a dark, unhappy spiritual state and is trying to escape our loving rebukes and admonitions as much as possible. She had barely arrived here when she saw a Sister for whom she had developed a hatred a long time ago. We had already talked with her in vain several times about controlling this. She immediately left us again in the most irritable manner before the services began. Despite this disturbance we had blessed services again in both languages, and then our guests and visitors said a loving farewell.

Tues., Dec. 28. [Ooch.] Br. Clauder visited an Indian family about 8 miles from here, accompanied by an interpreter. We informed them that the purpose of this visit was to talk to them about their salvation after this life and that they could be freed from the slavery of sin and the devil through faith in Jesus. His name was not completely unfamiliar to them. The woman, who was busy carding wool, put her work aside and listened attentively. When we were finished, she said she had heard about this matter often and had thought about it. She would like to be saved but had always come to the conclusion this was unobtainable for her. And so we explained to her that Jesus Christ died for everyone, even the greatest and most miserable sinner. She too would receive more through a simple, childlike faith in Him than she expected. During our conversation with her husband, which lasted several hours, he asked many questions about the creation of the world, the flood, and the birth of our Savior, and he asked for instruction. She tried to be present as much as possible during this. When asked if they would allow us to hold services there from time to time, they happily agreed and promised to let their neighbors know about this. After we had determined which day we would come for this purpose, we said a sincere farewell and returned home.

Dec. 28. [Spg.] Br. Byhan today went to Oochgelogy on a visit, in order to attend a gathering of all missionaries in Cherokee country in New Echota tomorrow, *Dec. 29*, where he was invited by Revd. A. S. Worcester. All the Presbyterian missionaries had arrived. The cause of this gathering was actually this: to express freely and publicly the views and thoughts of the missionaries about the current situation and circumstances of the Cherokees, primarily because it had been said that the missionaries were holding the Indians back from emigrating, which was refuted in this meeting. It was also said in this meeting that if the Indians move west, all the missionaries are of the opinion that this would cause them harm and misfortune. Also it was explained what progress the Cherokees had made the last 30 years in civilisation, religion, etc., all of which is shown in the proceedings which appear in print.

Dec. 29. [Ooch.] Brn. Byhan and Clauder were invited to attend a meeting of the Presbyterian missionaries here which was held in New Echota* ~~Since the proceedings will appear in the public newspapers, there is no point in saying more about it here~~ ([added by another hand, Br. Schulz's?:] *in which the gathered missionaries unanimously recognized their duty as follows: Due to the many incorrect explanations of the civic, moral, and religious situation of the Cherokee Nation, among which we are appointed as Jesus' servants and preachers of truth and righteousness, to present a scrupulous, unadorned testimony about the true situation of this people to the American public, especially since many have been living in the company of the Nation for 20-30 years. Afterward we prepared an essay for this purpose which was signed by everyone present and will be printed in the Cherokee newspaper, *Phönix.*)

Dec. 30. [Spg.] Br. Byhan returned today from his visit in Ochgeloogy and New Echota. He had just arrived home when a very strong storm arose which was accompanied by such heavy downpours of rain as we have never experienced here. The water in our yard stood shoe deep before it could flow away. A stream 20 feet broad and 4 feet deep ran through our field. The fences were in danger of being washed away, and since our wheat field lies somewhat low, a good deal of wheat was washed away. It was lucky that the heavy rain did not last very long. Otherwise, the water would have caused great damage to the fields and fences.

Dec. 31. [Spg.] We heard that the streams all around have swollen to an extraordinary height so that when we sent corn to the mill to be milled today, we could not get it done.

At the conclusion of the year 1830, the Gemeine in Springplace consisted of 32 baptized Brethren and Sisters. Among these are 10 complete married couples (one of these Brethren has 2 wives), 2 single Brethren, 1 boy, 1 individual man whose wife does not belong to us, 1 Widow, 5 Sisters whose husbands do not belong to us, and 1 Sister whose husband left her. Of these, 29 are communicants. In addition there are 31 baptized and unbaptized children. Total: 63 persons, 7 more than at the close of last year. The missionaries and their children add 4 more persons to this and one more single Br. who belongs to the Gemeine in Friedland, thus 68 persons altogether.

Dec. 31. [Ooch.] In the evening service at the conclusion of this year we brought the Lord our deepest gratitude for the untold proofs of His assistance and grace, which we have experienced in so many difficult and challenging circumstances throughout this year. This was very comforting to us. With remorse, we asked Him to forgive our lack of progress in so many responsibilities and pleaded with Him for new faith and courage, so we could meet the challenges of the coming year, which all appearances suggest will be a difficult one, and this was mercifully given to us.

In the year 1830, which has now ended, two adults and 5 children were baptized. The Gemeinlein here currently consists of 16 baptized adults, including 12 communicants and about 20 baptized children of our Brethren and Sisters under 12 years old. In addition 15 female scholars live here. Total: 51 souls. Because of the external pressures on this people, which make our stay here uncertain and threaten us with danger, we commend ourselves and our Gemeinlein to the special intercession of our Brethren and Sisters and all the friends of our Lord Jesus Christ, whose holy name will be proclaimed to all heathen for their eternal redemption.

Heinrich Gottlieb and Charlotte Elis. Clauder

1831, part 1

[M 415-1a-1: Translated by Julie Tomberlin Weber. Addressed to: Revd. Theodor Schulz, Salem, Stokes County, North Carolina. Post stamp: New-Echota, Cher. Na., Jan. 8, 37½, via Knoxville & Jonesboro, Tenn. Received Jan. 25.]

Ooyugillogy, Ch.N., Jan. 1, 1831

Dear Brother Schulz,

Herewith I am sending you our brief Diary through the end of the year that has just ended. From this you will see the particulars of our Christmas celebration as well as the interesting visit I had with an Indian family. On Jan. 8, the Lord willing, I am planning to hold a trial service at that house, during which our enthusiastic and beloved Br. George Augustus Hicks will accompany me as interpreter, as was also previously the case.

Last week little Copeland was seriously ill with a strong attack of St. Anthony's fire. His whole face and head were affected by this, so that both eyes were swollen shut. The Lord blessed the means used to heal him. Otherwise, we remain as busy as we can. You will see numerous things in the Diary about high streams and intense cold. Br. Byhan and the *Phönix* will have given you detailed information about the meeting of the missionaries of the American Foreign Missionary Society, held on the 29th, which Br. Byhan and I were invited to attend.

The school here is continuing as usual, and things in the country are completely peaceful. Sometimes unfortunate events take place on the Georgia frontiers, but so far they have not had widespread consequences. Br. Byhan will report to you about the success of our conversation regarding the appointment of a National Helper. For various reasons, we will postpone this for the time being.

Our friend Wheeler joined Mr. Worcester's little congregation in New Echota, because his wife has already been a member there for a long time, and he himself has been receiving instruction from the above named worker for almost two years. Despite this, he was very touched recently, and it cost him long reflection to look away from the United Brethren and to join there, where without a doubt he has the greatest duty. I have seen nothing more of Stand Watee for a long time.

Sincerest congratulations and greetings to you and your family and colleagues on today's beautiful New Year's Day. We are among you in spirit and enjoy much love and many blessings imagining this, and we commend ourselves to your prayer and intercession, your faithfully obliged Brother,

Henry G. Clauder

Please extend a sincere greeting to Henry, and also to my dear parents. Charles Ignatius is healthy and growing bigger and heavier each day. Br. and Sr. Copeland send sincere greetings.

P.S. The new horse is working out excellently for Br. Copeland. I sold the wreck of the old wagon for a new saddle valued at $20. The faithful old horse is in retirement with a full feeding trough!

[Springplace (M 407-2) and Oochgeelogy (M 409-1) Diaries. Translated by Julie Tomberlin Weber and C. Daniel Crews. Handwritings are Henry G. Clauder's (Ooch.) and Gottlieb Byhan's (Spg.).]

Jan. 1. [Spg.] We entered into this new year with praise and thanksgiving for all the benefits and blessings we have enjoyed in the passing year from our blessed Jesus. We also asked Him that in this year also that His hand will guide us in our present situation, which to all appearances is critical in regard to relations between Georgia and the Cherokees. We asked Him to be and remain our counselor and protection, and that the Word of the Cross, which we have in grace, may be made known within this poor Nation and may make its way more and more into the hearts of the inhabitants of this Land. We also ask that through the voice of the Holy Spirit yet many more may be awakened from their sleep of sin to turn to Jesus, the Friend of Sinners, and find comfort and forgiveness with Him. On account of the unfriendly weather, only a few were found in today's services.

Sun., Jan. 2. [Spg.] Several more of our Brethren and Sisters and neighbors were present for services, and a sermon was held.

Sun., Jan. 2. [Ooch.] Before our usual Sunday service began, Br. Clauder received a request from our friend Col. Adair to perform the burial service for one of his Negroes. After the service here, Br. and Sr. Clauder rode there and found a good number of people gathered. At the grave he delivered a fervent talk on Matt. 25:13, during which he urgently admonished all present to keep the warning word of our Savior constantly before their eyes and to watch, so that when He appears He will find us this way. All were quiet and attentive, which really pleased us even more, because on such occasions there is usually disorder because of the excessive crying and screaming. However, Br. Clauder had forbidden this at the very beginning.

Jan. 6. [Ooch.] For the first celebration of Epiphany many of our friends came here for the services. Many of our baptized could not come because of the distance and other circumstances. This was also the case with one baptized man who was supposed to observe as a candidate during Holy Communion. It was almost sunset when our Brn. and Srs. and friends said a sincere farewell and departed.

Jan. 6. [Spg.] The Savior made this day into a true day of blessing. Most all of our Brethren and Sisters, with their children, were present by invitation for the celebration of the day, although the streams were very swollen from the rains. In the first service there was the baptism of the Indian woman Wakee, our Br. Emanuel's wife, who was given the name Margaretha Susanna. In the second service we had the lovefeast for the gathered baptized Brethren and Sisters and their children. Since several from the first service were present at the invitation of Mr. Tazizi to serve us as translators he was present at this lovefeast. Various ones of our Brn. and Srs. of our Gemeinen gathered from among the heathen in other areas of the world were spoken about, and our people here enjoyed that very much. In the third service with our dear Lord's gift of penitence we had the enjoyment of the Holy Communion. We can say that the peace of God and the presence of our dear Lord were to be felt in a blessed manner.

Jan. 7. [Spg.] Mr. Tazizi went home again, with the promise that he was prepared at any time to serve us as translator.

Jan. 7 and 8. [Ooch.] Br. Clauder went with an interpreter to Halfbreed's, where he had received permission during a recent visit to hold services. It rained the entire morning, so only a few Indians came here; however, they were more attentive than expected. At the end of the service they were repeatedly asked to respond to what they had been told, but in vain. Yet one said they would like it if we came back again. It is common knowledge that the Indians typically do not express their thoughts about something they have heard right away. If it leaves an impression on them, they remind you about it after ages by asking questions about it.

Sun., Jan. 9. [Ooch.] It rained very heavily the entire day, but many still came for the service. Old Christian David shared the following thoughts: "I am sometimes filled with worries about my children, and I try to direct them to my Savior. I recently told my young son: You call me father, but your real Father is in heaven above. You must love Him and honor Him. He alone can help you. We encouraged him to raise his children like this, in the ways and admonitions of the Lord. We were sincerely grateful to hear the above words, since it is quite unusual to see an Indian who is concerned about the eternal well-being of his children.

Sun., Jan. 9. [Spg.] Because of today's rain no one came to us. We held a Singstunde with our house family.

Jan. 13. [Ooch.] We received a pleasant visit from the superintendent of the Methodist missions in this country, Mr. McCloud, and his wife. Since it snowed very hard the next day, they spent that night very happily in our company.

Sun., Jan. 16. [Spg.] Likewise because of the severe cold again no one was found at the service except old Mother Vann. For the last 2 weeks, because of the snow, rain, and cold, we have seen no Indians, because in respect to their clothing they are not prepared for such weather as we have recently had. We learn in these days from a newspaper which was sent to us from Georgia that the legislature there in its last sitting has made a law that all white people in the Cherokee Land as of March 1 shall swear allegiance to the Georgia Constitution and its State Laws, and if they refuse they are to be sentenced to 4 years in the penitentiary at hard labor. How our spirits were downcast at this report is not easy to describe. We see clearly that this law is aimed especially at the missionaries among the Cherokees, because it is believed that the missionaries are to blame, or are the cause, that the Cherokees will not move to the West. We will not despair, however, for God is still in control. He can turn the hearts of men and bring their onslaughts to naught, although in such circumstances as we have it cannot be denied that perhaps these circumstances might have a depressing effect on our mission in this land. In the meantime we will seek after the help of the Lord. He knows ways and means to save us in our need. If it is His will that His work here should suffer an upset, or even come to an end for a time among this people, He must have His wise purpose for this, for His work can triumph even in defeat.

[M 415-1a-2: Translated by Julie Tomberlin Weber. Addressed to: Revd. Theodor Schulz, Salem, Stokes County, North Carolina. No postmark. Received Feb. 2.]

Springplace, Jan. 15, 1831

My dear Br. Schulz,

The Georgia mail has just arrived. I did not receive anything from Salem with it, although I did receive a newspaper, the *Georgia Journal,* which the printer in Milledgeville sent me for free. The Georgia Law which they recently made concerning the Cherokee Land appears in this in full. Perhaps you have already read this in Salem as well. I cannot deny that when I read this law a strange feeling overcame me, and I have to conclude from it that we, that is we missionaries, are still in a strange situation and could really get caught between two fires. Since I do not know if you will see this Law or not, I will copy just three Sections of it here, which I believe also concern us, and I ask to hear your thoughts about it, from the H. Conf., as quickly as possible. It states in the new law:

[Br. Byhan copies the law in English:]

Sec. 7. And be it further enacted by the authority aforesaid, That all white persons residing within the limits of the Cherokee Nation, on the first day of March next, or at any time thereafter, without a license or permit, from his Excellency the Governor, or from such agent as his Excellency the Governor, shall authorize to grant such permit or license, and who shall not have taken the oath herein after required, shall be guilty of an high misdemeanor, and upon conviction thereof, shall be punished by confinement in the Penitentiary at hard labour, for a term not less than four Years: Provided that the provisions of this section shall not be so construed; as to extend to any authorized agent or agents, of the Government of the United States, or of this State, or to any person or persons, who may rent any of those improvements, which have been abandoned by Indians, who have emigrated West of the Mississippi: Provided that nothing contained in this section, shall be so construed as to extend to white females, & all male children under twenty one years of age.

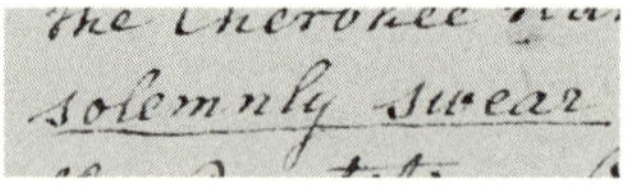

Sect. 8. And be it further enacted by the authority aforesaid, That all white persons, citizens of the State of Georgia, who have procured a license in writing, from his Excellency the Governor, or from such agent as his Excellency the Governor, shall authorise to grant such permit or license, to reside within the limits of the Cherokee Nation, & who have taken the following oath, viz: I. A. B. do solemnly swear (or affirm as the case may be) that I will support and defend the Constitution, and laws of the State of Georgia, and uprightly demean myself as a Citizen thereof, so help me God, shall be and the same are hereby

declared, exempt and free from the operation of the seventh section of this act.

Section 9. And be it further enacted, That his Excellency the Governor, be and he is hereby authorised to grant licences to reside within the limits of the Cher. Nation, according to the provisions of the eighth section of this act.

[Br. Byhan continues his letter to Br. Schulz in German:]

Once again, please let me know your thoughts and advice about this matter as quickly as possible. If we must swear allegiance to this Law, what would the Cherokees say? And if we did not swear, what would be the results of this? Even the first words in Section 7 make me believe that these laws also affect us, if I understand correctly.

Otherwise, we are all pretty well except for my dear wife, who is quite miserable at times. There are many problems. May the Lord help us manage! Accept the most sincere greetings from all of us, and you also accept a special greeting from your dear humble Br.,

G. Byhan

P.S. Please send me something else for my cashbox, because it is almost empty.

[Springplace (M 407-2) and Oochgeelogy (M 409-1) Diaries. Translated by Julie Tomberlin.]

Sun., Jan. 16. [Ooch.] About 8 persons came to the service despite the extremely cold weather we had on this day.

Jan. 19. [Spg.] Mr. David Steiner Tazizi and his brother came to our place. They had brought Mr. Jos. Vann pigs and then spent the night here. Since they had two horses, we also had to feed these for no payment, as well as an evening meal and breakfast for both of them.

Jan. 21. [Ooch.] Br. Clauder visited in New Echota, where he confirmed the truth of the disconcerting rumor that all white residents within the borders of Georgia in Cherokee Land would be required to swear an oath of loyalty and obedience to the laws of Georgia, or if they refused to face the resulting punishment. This sad news really horrified us, since no missionary who wants to be effective among the Cherokees can take the required oath in good conscience. And so we can only expect that the mission work here will suffer greatly, if it is not completely destroyed. However, the Lord has the power to protect His work against all enemies. We should trust confidently in His guidance.

Jan. 22. [Ooch.] Br. Clauder went with Br. Hicks to Halfbreed's, where a number of Indians had gone for the scheduled service despite the extreme cold. The Savior's words in Isa. 9:4 provided the basis for the reflection, and people were very attentive during this. The interpreter, Br. Hicks, concluded the meeting with a prayer in the native language.

[M 415-1a-3: Translated by Julie Tomberlin Weber; transcribed by Grace S. Robinson. Addressed to: Revd. Theodor Schulz, Salem, Stokes County, North Carolina. Postmark: Springplace, C.N., Jan. 23. Free. G. Byhan, P.M. Received Feb. 9.]

Springplace, Jan. 22, 1831

My dear Br. Shulz,

Although I just wrote to you eight days ago and informed you, or all of you, about our current situation and also about some Laws of Georgia that concern us, I cannot help but write you a few more lines.

Since my last letter to you nothing further has happened that concerns us, but I cannot deny that our situation is somewhat awkward and makes us uneasy, and so we are anxiously awaiting an answer to my last letter. We are in the Lord's hands. He will arrange things as He sees best for us! We would not have believed that things would go this far, or that the Georgians would push things so far. We almost fear that it will turn out badly. May God have mercy and soon look into this! We will trust in Him to do this in His time!

Eight days ago I wrote Revd. Mr. Worcester in New Echota and asked him to share with me his thoughts about these circumstances. Today I received his answer, as follows:

[Br. Byhan copies Worcester's reply in English:]

You ask for my thoughts on the subject of a law lately passed by the Legislature of Georgia. Some of my thoughts you will learn by the following copy of a letter which I have just written to Mr. Evarts:

"Dear Sir,

"I perceive by a number of the *Georgia Journal* sent to the Post Office here by I know not whom, I perceive that, according to a law lately passed, I must either remove from within the chartered limits of Georgia before the first of March, or procure license from the Governor of Ga. or his agent, and take an Oath of allegiance to the State, or be liable to imprisonment in the penitentiary for four years at least. Taking the oath of allegiance is out of the question. Whether to remove, or remain & risk the consequence, is the alternative. My own disposition is to remain. I am, however, subject to the direction of the Prudential Committee, and wait for instructions. I remain, etc., etc."

[Br. Byhan continues his letter to Br. Schulz in German:]

By the way, Mr. Worcester does not believe that the Georgia laws would be enforced against us if we stayed, but he also writes, "I am not, however, confident." Also he does not believe that we will stay in the penitentiary long "before we shall be rescued by order of the Supreme Court of the U. St., whose orders I do think must prevail, the resistance of the State of Georgia notwithstanding."[1]

But the question is: should we let things go that far or not? From all of this you will see that our situation, and the rest of the missionaries', is currently not easy. Accordingly you will inform us of your thoughts as soon as possible and share your advice with us. If the missionaries are not still exempted, one can believe that the mission here will not last much longer before reaching its conclusion here. And even if we were exempted and

---

[1] Quotes are in English in the original German manuscript.

were allowed to stay, then one would notice on the other side again that the Indians would not be able to — or want to — endure the treatment they have had to tolerate from the Georgians in recent times.

The Savior alone knows what lies ahead. He remains our comfort and advisor in all our problems, and we trust in him. He will not give us anything we cannot bear! We further commend ourselves to the remembrance and prayers of our dear Lord, since we need this especially in our current situation. The prayer of His children accomplishes much.

We have had very cold weather recently, as well as a good bit of snow. And so since Jan. 6 only a few Brn. and Srs. have visited us. We are all pretty healthy, except for Mother, who is occasionally overcome by her weakness. Even so, praise God, she can still be up. We greet everyone sincerely, and you, dear Br., accept another especially sincere greeting from your humble Br. who loves you constantly and uprightly,

G. Byhan

[Springplace (M 407-2) and Oochgeelogy (M 409-1) Diaries.]

Sun., Jan. 23. [Spg.] Because of the great cold, no one came for the services today. Due to rain, cold, and bad roads, we have been spared many visits this last week and for some time past, and we were disturbed little in our usual household routine.

Sun., Jan. 23. [Ooch.] As usual, there were just a few visitors here for the services. Our Brn. and Srs. are aware of the danger threatening their teachers, and today they expressed their compassion and sadness about this, more with looks and sighs than with words.

Jan. 25. [Spg.] Today Br. Clauder came from Oochgelogy to our place on a visit. We had a good deal to discuss with him concerning our current situation. We cannot decide to swear allegiance to the Georgia laws, since this would be against our conscience. We commended ourselves anew to the protection of our dear Lord.

1831, part 2

[M 415-1a-4: Translated by Julie Tomberlin Weber. Addressed to: Revd. Theodore Schulz, Salem, Stokes County, North Carolina. Postmark: Springplace, C.N., Jan. 30, paid 18¾. Received Feb. 12.]

Spring Place, C.N. Jan. 26, 1831

Dear Br. Schulz,

At the beginning of last December I wrote to you, as well as on Jan. 1, 1831. In the latter I sent you the Diary from Ooy____y till the end of the year 1830. I hope both these letters had a successful journey.

In the first you will have found my request for money to pay Copeland's salary. I now add this request in his name as well, that you might be good enough to send him his capital of $218.36½ along with interest (with the deduction of $6.00 which should be paid to Br. Foltz for a flute) as soon as possible, since he, like many other white people, would like to leave this unhappy country as soon as possible. It is his intention to move to Indiana and to buy a piece of land there. Because of this he anxiously asks you to send him at least a part of the total amount in United St. notes. He feels forced to take this step because of the new law of Georgia, with which you are without a doubt familiar, which requires all white people in Cherokee country, without exception, to take the oath of allegiance to that state, or in the case of refusal to agree to an imprisonment of at least 4 years.

As horrible and gruesome as this law might seem, I personally cannot really believe that this strictness will be carried out against the missionaries. In reality this would be something unheard of in recent times and would fill the tender emotions of all Christianity with sorrow and the deepest compassion. I believe much more that this disturbing and disruptive law is just intended first to make the Indians afraid and second, in the case of the whites who make the required oath, to carry out the rest of the laws even more oppressively, since all those without doubt would soon be appointed as court officials.

Be that as it may, no missionary will dare this, even if the consequences are this horrible. How could someone with a good conscience call something through which a weak people loses its property good and oblige himself to this? I myself cannot do this and even in the most extreme case would not agree to this. It is a matter of conscience and its voice is louder against this than all the laws, threats, and advantageous promises for it could be. Therefore, I will not deliver the required oath.

Nothing remains now but to choose between flight and imprisonment. The former is partly impossible and for many reasons would not be advisable, even if it were possible here. It would reveal a lack of trust in the strong hand of the Lord whose work we are carrying out and who can miraculously maintain us in all trials and sorrows. The faith of the Brethren and Sisters would be weakened, and I personally could never appear among them again with a cheerful expression, neither here nor anywhere else, when peace is restored.

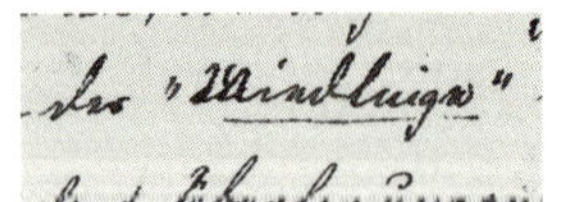

One comes too much into the hated class of the "windling" who flees when the wolf appears or just howls from afar!!

After some reflections I have made in the past days, often in the quiet midnight hours amid prayer and sighs, I feel inclined to continue on with courage and faith, and confidently waiting upon God the Almighty until I no longer have an opportunity for this and walk toward my imprisonment. I presume that your intercession with the governor of Georgia would result in my quick release, sooner than if a suit for this were started in the Sup. Court of the U.S., through which the Georgians here would just be embittered. However, it is extremely unlikely that the strictness of this law will be carried out against the missionaries, although some days ago the commanding officer of the Georgia troops passed through our neighborhood with several soldiers in full uniform and fully armed and explained that he had higher orders to take all whites as prisoners, without exception, after next March 1st.

All is in unrest. People hear nothing except talk against the oath, and I doubt if it will be generally be made. Without a doubt many will flee if actions are taken.

Now I have tried to report my simple thoughts about this sad circumstance. Br. Byhan and I can do nothing more than wait for your good advice and then follow it. Our Brn. and Srs. know that we must act in accordance with the judgment of the Directors. It is certainly sad to think of having to leave our dear Cherokee Brn. and Srs. and children. This seems to be an unavoidable consequence, but the ways and means are different. By swearing the oath, we could stay here for a while, but under such circumstances our actual purpose would be in vain and lost forever. The only thing is to wait out the storm if possible. If we are imprisoned, then the mediation of so many of our friends and Christian society would certainly bring about our quick release. May the Lord strengthen me, a weak person, for this, so that my faith will not suffer a shipwreck in the hour of distress.

But now our school will surely be ruined if Copeland moves away, which without a doubt will happen. There is also a shortage of workers again; white hired hands will not be available, so there is nothing to do but hire Indians or Negroes to do the fieldwork. If my wife can help me with the school, then no child will be sent home for sure. But if we lose help, we cannot possibly manage with the work and the school.

An overview of our entire situation sometimes allows the fearful thought: Now the end of the Cherokee Mission has surely come. And when one remembers the entire Indian mission history from the very beginning in 1737 among the Creeks near Savannah till now, one loses the courage, the desire to renew. At the same time, the few things that have been accomplished despite the almost constant unrest among this wonderful people is proof enough that no heathen is too wild to become a patient lamb in the flock of the Chief Shepherd, as can be seen from the following story.

Last Saturday I had a cold ride to Halfbreed's with my interpreter Br. George H., where I had announced a meeting once again. This time there were approximately 16 Indians present. During my first visit there 2 weeks earlier, there were only 4 present. Our dear Br. G. A. H. is also living in the daily expectation of being taken by the Georgia officers, since he recently acted as Judge for the Cherokee courts several times. Oh, if only we could expect peace, how comforted and how joyfully I would try to acquaint the dear Cherokees with their Redeemer, according to my strength and abilities, but oh, everywhere I look I find threatening danger and ruin and destruction. The night approaches when no one can do anything.

I was planning to set out again for Ooyugillogy tomorrow, but it is snowing so heavily that I might have to spend a number of days here. When I left Ooyey. yesterday morning, everyone was well.

Greet our dear parents and your dear family and dear colleagues and remember me in your prayers to the Ruler of all rulers, who strengthens the weak and comforts when affliction and sadness threaten. Excuse these hastily written lines and allow me to ask for a quick answer.

Your faithfully obliged friend and Brother,

H. G. Clauder

[M 415-1a-5: Translated by Julie Tomberlin Weber. Addressed to: Revd. Theodor Schulz, Salem, Stokes County, North Carolina. Postmark: Springplace, C.N., Jan. 30. Free. G. Byhan, P.M. Received Feb. 12.]

Springplace, Jan. 29, 1831

Dearly beloved Br. Schulz,

On the 23rd of this month I received your kind letter of the 1st of this month along with the German Watchwords, one for Springplace and one for Och_____y, and I thank you sincerely for these. I cannot understand why it took them so long to get here from Salem. Br. Schaaf's kind note of the 4th of this month arrived here on the same day. Please thank him for this and greet him and his dear wife sincerely for us.

When you receive this, my 2 letters of the 15th and 22nd of this month will surely be in your hands. From these you will have learned about our current situation, which is not the most desirable, as you can easily see. In the meantime, we trust in the Lord's help. He will not abandon us, His poor children, nor neglect us. When trouble is the greatest, help is closest.

However, we cannot deny that we are not very encouraged in the current situation, and it causes many troubling thoughts about how things will go and what the Lord has decided about us. Presumably you will want to know our thoughts about what will happen if the Georgia laws are strictly enforced, and it actually comes to the point that we had to go to the Penitentiary. During Br. Clauder's visit here a couple of days ago, we discussed the matter and considered what we would do if the worst happened. We then agreed that we did not want to swear allegiance to the Georgia laws, and could not, because this is completely against our conscience. This is why we cannot take the oath.

However, if our conscience allowed us to affirm the Georgia laws, which are unjust before God and fair-minded people, what would the Indians say to this? Would they not say: Now we see how far your friendship toward us goes. All love, all trust in us would be gone, and we accordingly would want to gather our things and go, because we would have no more enjoyable hours among them, since they would see us as the kind of people who want the Cherokees to be oppressed as much as possible and forced from their land as soon as possible.

And so we have decide to wait and see how things go and what the Lord has decided for us. However, if things should become extreme and the laws strictly enforced, then we trust that our dear Brn. would advocate for us and support us with word and deed, either that you would turn directly to the Governor of Georgia or directly to the President of the United States.

In all probability our schools will suffer under these circumstances, because if things get serious with the above laws, then the children will be taken home and our Nathl. would probably go somewhere else until the storm has perhaps passed a little. In Och____y there will probably also be difficulty in this respect, because Br. and Sr. Copeland have now decided — as Br. Clauder tells me — also to move to the northwestern states. Then the assistance they have in Sr. Copeland holding school would also be lost. Overall we must admit and we cannot deny, that when we consider the current circumstances together, we cannot avoid the troubling thought that the mission here will suffer a significant blow, if it does not lead to its complete end. Still God alone knows how He can maintain it, if it is His work.

I ask you urgently not to hold it against me if I openly present our thoughts to you, because we can assure you, dear Brn., that we live here in oppressive times and do not know what to do. We would lose courage if we did not know to Whom we hold fast in our situation.

I would like to add this: In the Georgia Law it says that the law should not extend to the Agent and Agents of the Genl. Govt.

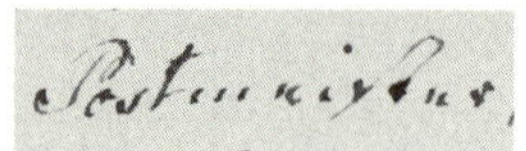

It occurred to me that as Postmaster should I not be seen as an Agent of the Genl. Govt., or if the law is enforced to its fullest, would they not consider me an Agent? If they should consider me an Agent, I would be allowed to stay here. However, Br. Clauder and our Nathl. would have to submit, or they would have to go to the Penitentiary if they did not receive permission or time to leave the country. We do not know if they would immediately take them to the Penitentiary with them or whether they would allow them time to leave the country. Now if I would be considered an Agent, I would be allowed to stay here. Then our advice would be this, that is, if we were allowed to express ourselves. That in this case there is still some hope of maintaining the mission here among the Cherokees a while longer, that Br. Clauder be named Postmaster in my place, and we would receive our recall, since then the mission place in Ochgeloogy would have trouble if Br. and Sr. Clauder moved to Spring Place. The houses in Och_____y could be given to the protection of a faithful man, perhaps Br. George Hicks, until they could perhaps be sold. I hope you dear Brn. understand what I mean by the above.

We hear that some white people near the Georgia border have already sworn allegiance to the laws. They are now considered Georgians by the Cherokees and considered their enemies.

All these circumstances cause us concern about our crops for this year. The time is approaching when we should make preparations to plant and sow, and still everything is so uncertain about whether we will be able to make use of it that we hardly know what we should do. Still we will have to go away until circumstances clear up more, or until we really see what will happen. All appearances suggest that a significant change will take place with the mission here, but how and in what manner the Lord alone knows.

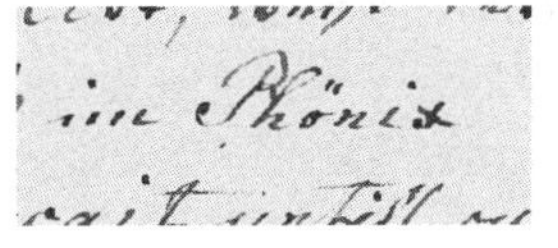

Presumably you also noted the comment in the *Phönix* of the 22nd of this month, where Mr. Boudinott says: "We will wait until our missionaries are driven away, & then we will give the alarm to all the opposers of the Union of Church & State."[1]

Our neighbor Jos. Vann also says if they knew that the other states would remain peaceful they would declare war against Georgia. From this statement one can see the thoughts of the Cherokees. These latter cannot endure much more, and it is indeed a miracle that they have remained patient this long. But it is also certain as soon as they defend themselves or act contrarily at all, their fate is sealed.

Amazingly my dear wife is able to gather herself under the current circumstances, and I am grateful to the Savior that this is so. On the other hand, things are affecting the other Srs. at both mission places more deeply, particularly Sr. Clauder. It is a great comfort to us that we know we are often and diligently remembered before our dear Lord in your prayers.

Praise God, we are currently relatively healthy, except for my dear wife who sometimes has difficulty because the work is in fact too much, and she cannot continue on as previously. She

---

1 The quote is in English in the original German manuscript.

also suffers with her feet and legs, which are swollen. She suffers from this particularly in the evening after she has worked around the house the entire day.

Br. Clauder asked me to make the following request: A certain Peggy Hicks, daughter of our Br. Wilm. Abr. Hicks who belongs to the Gemeine in Och_____y, wants to know if she could not learn to sew under a tailor in Salem if she were taken there? She went to school in Och_____y and was baptized there by Br. Clauder, and she is approximately 14 or 15 years old. She is a well-behaved girl and speaks three languages: Cherokee, English, and German. However, she is lame, because she has a twisted leg, and walks with a crutch. We believe that she would not bring dishonor to the Gemeine through her behavior. Br. Clauder has often used her as an interpreter, because she can express herself well about spiritual matters since she herself has experienced grace and her only desire in this world is to live for the Savior.

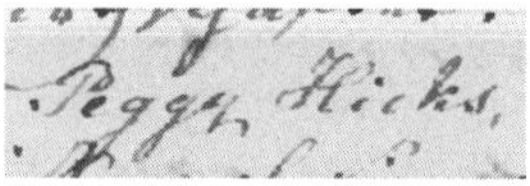

5 o'clock in the afternoon. The Georgia mail has just brought me your kind letter of the 10th of this month with the enclosed letter from the fatherland, for which I thank you sincerely. The enclosed letter was from my only sister. She reports that my father is still alive. He turned 82 years old on Aug. 22, 1830. I will answer your kind letter next week.

[Gottlieb Byhan]

[Springplace (M 407-2) and Oochgeelogy (M 409-1) Diaries. Translated by Julie Tomberlin Weber. Handwritings are Henry G. Clauder's (Ooch.) and Gottlieb Byhan's (Spg.).]

Sun., Jan. 30. [Spg.] Two travelers from Tenn., who had been at Mr. Vann's old place last night with Mr. Nicolson, Vann's Overseer, came to our Sunday services. Afterward they went back there. Today we also took the opportunity to discuss our current situation with our Cherokee Brn. and Srs., although not many of them were present. They also seemed to be very dejected and said that they also were very concerned, and that they thought the Georgians would not be so strict with them and with us, but that they are waiting impatiently for news from Washington. They heard that they might perhaps receive justice from there.

Feb. 2. [Ooch.] Br. Clauder went to the mission at Hightower for a brief visit and returned from there on *the 3rd*.

Feb. 1. [Spg.] Today we heard that the Presbyterian missionaries in Carmel and Hightower are planning to move from there to Brainerd and Candys Creek. Both places are in the state of Tennessee. If this should be the case, Spring Place and Ochgeloogy would be the only mission places still in the state of Georgia, or in that part of the Cher. Nation within the chartered limits of Georgia. We will trust in the Lord. He will see our distress and misery and will not leave us.

[B 61-3: Provinzial Helfer Conferenz, meeting in Salem. Translated by C. Daniel Crews.]

Wed., Feb. 2. The letter of our Br. Gb. Byhan dated 15 Jan. contained a copy of several articles of a law enacted last Dec. by the Georgia Assembly concerning the extension of their jurisdiction over the Cherokee Land which lies within the borders of this state, and it is indeed completely contrary to the existing treaties of this Nation with the Government of the United States. This law demands that all white inhabitants in the Cherokee Nation — with the exception of wives, minor children, and agents of the United States government — take the oath of loyalty and support to the laws of Georgia. Those who do not take this oath must vacate the Cherokee Land, or they will be arrested and sentenced by the Court to 4 years imprisonment at hard labor. Since now our missionaries, as well as the rest of the missionaries cannot fulfill this oath, Br. Byhan, with the other Brn. and Srs., is very eager to receive our advice on this as soon as possible.

The P.H.C. does not doubt that Georgia will try with all strength to put this law into effect — even though according to our view it is unconstitutional. And if they apply it to our

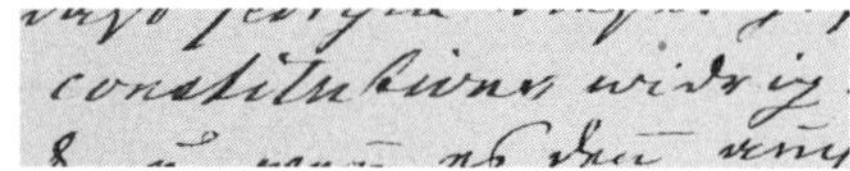

Brethren they can at first at least be freed from arrest by the Habeas Corpus Act. However, they would have to be cited before the court there before the Supreme Court of the United States has decided this significant dispute. And because its decision on this is still in doubt, they could easily lose in that dispute and be cut off from what is theirs.

After lengthy reflection before the Lord, our counsel in these most distressing circumstances is this: Br. and Sr. Byhan should and must remain quietly in Springplace since as Postmaster he is an official of the United States Government, has his commission for this from Washington, and the Post Office cannot be relinquished without incurring a large fine with his securities. In case, however, the Georgia Officials harass him, then he could decidedly and positively declare to them that he will leave only if he receives from the General Postmaster an order to do so or a successor for him is appointed. Br. Clauder, Nathl. Byhan, and Rominger will have to take refuge after the 1st of March with our friend, Captain Davd. McNair, who lives at present in the Tennessee District of the Cherokee Land 18 miles from Springplace. In the meantime, Br. Schulz will apply to him by letter.

It would be advisable for them to agree among themselves that Br. G. Byhan will visit the Indian Brn. and Srs. around Oochgelogy, and that Br. Clauder visit those near McNair's and that they undertake these visits reciprocally. As best they can, all belongings should be packed and brought together. Especially those in Oochgelogy should be delivered for safekeeping to one of their Cherokee Brn., Wm. Abr. Hicks or his sons. Because the Sisters can remain behind without danger, they are strongly advised to get help from one of the Cherokee Brn. until there is a decision from the Supreme Court in Washington, hopefully at the beginning of March. Before that, no further steps can lawfully be taken. Br. Schulz will report all this to both Brethren Gb. Byhan and Hy. Clauder by today's post.

[*Records: N.C.*, 8:3965: Salem Diary. Translated by Douglas L. Rights.]

Feb. 6. At night Br. Bechler communicated the accounts of the Unity's Mission Diacony for 1829, with an accompanying letter from the Missions Department. He commended for earnest intercession the Cherokee Mission in its ever-increasingly difficult situation.

[M 415-1a-6: Translated by Julie Tomberlin Weber. Addressed to: Revd. Theodor Schulz, Salem, Stokes County, North Carolina. Postmark: Springplace, C.N., Feb. 6. Free. Gottlieb Byhan, P.M. Received Feb. 26.]

Springplace, Feb. 2, 1831

My dearly beloved Br. Shulz,

I am hurrying to report to you receipt of your kind letter of Jan. 10, along with the enclosure, which was from my only sister. I received it on the 29th of last month, as I already informed you in my last letter to you on that same date. You will surely forgive me for not closing my last letter to you appropriately, because my mind is distracted by the things that are going to happen in our current circumstances, and in my haste I forgot. However, you will have recognized the handwriting so you knew who wrote it. We thank you most sincerely for everything you reported to us in your kind letter.

For the time being I will make it a rule to write you a few lines every eight days to let you all know immediately how things are, that is if nothing important prevents this.

Since my last letter, from which you will have seen our thoughts in the current very difficult situation, nothing else special has happened, except that we heard yesterday that the missionaries in Carmel and in Hightower wanted to return to Brainerd and Candys Creek on the Highwassee. Time will tell whether this is true. It is said that the Georgians absolutely want to have the

Yankee Missionaries out of the Nation. Now since Mr. Proctor

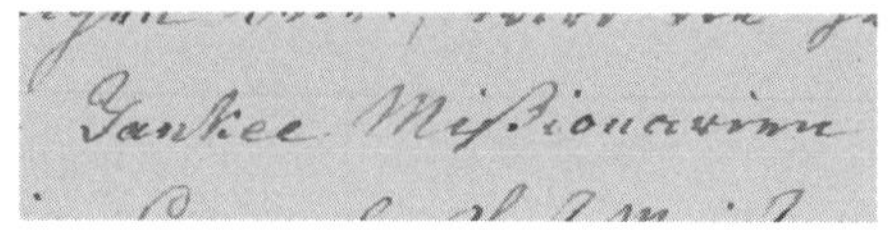
Yankee Missionarien

in Carmel is postmaster there, and he is also a missionary, or really Assistant Missionary, we are anxious to hear what he is planning to do with the Post Office there, whether he can leave it like that for so long or not. They tell me they could have nothing on me as postmaster, but I do not trust the peace at all, for the Georgians do everything to reach their goal.

I have heard nothing from Br. Clauder since my last letter to you, but I presume, if it is confirmed that they want to get the missionaries and white people out of the country, which I do not doubt in the least, then Br. and Sr. Clauder will soon appear here in Spring Place where we will further consider what we need to do. It is becoming clearer and clearer to us that our thoughts which I mentioned in my last letter, that if they leave the postmaster here in peace, are still the most acceptable, and in that case Br. Clauder will be postmaster here and we will receive our recall.

However, it is another question whether Br. and Sr. Clauder could stay until all of this could be arranged, because people say anyone who has not sworn the oath to the laws of Georgia by March 1, or is not an Agent of the Genl. Gov., should be put into the Penitentiary. Horrible!! And so I see no other way, if it should really come to the worst, than for Br. and Sr. Clauder to stay with Mr. McNair until the storm has passed and things have perhaps taken a different turn.

Still who knows how things might and should turn out? Dear God is long-suffering and allows some things that seem mysterious to us and which heavily oppress us to happen, and yet He has His wise purposes in this. I do not doubt that this entire matter and the circumstances He has allowed to happen to the Cherokees and to us are meant for the good of this Nation. We will trust in Him; we know from experience that when the trouble is greatest, help is the closest. It is clear to me and to all of us that a great change will take place in our two mission posts here among the Cherokees this year, but we are still in the dark about how and in what manner.

The 4th. We hear that there will be a gathering of the white people in New Echota tomorrow to consider what they will do in the current circumstances. As soon as I hear their results, I will report them to you. What does your old postmaster Br. G. Shober say — does he think they could take a postmaster away for long and close the Office or take possession of it without further orders from the Genl. Postmaster? I would like to hear his thoughts about this. Would the securities not have to pay the sum of the penalties in bond, which was given by me?? Please let me know his thoughts about this point, although the answer to this cannot get here before the first of March, because there are just 3 more weeks until then.

At this time I am sending something of our Diary last year. I will continue this next week. We have had to continue with our field and household work as before, because we do not know if circumstances might suddenly change so that things would remain as before. At the beginning of Jan. one of our workers, the only one whom I still had from Tenn., went home because of illness. In his place we have our single Indian Br. Niclaus Ignatius for $8 a month. I had to pay the former $10. Please send me money again so I can pay my debts. I always hate to ask for money, and yet I must, because it costs more here than at other posts.

Praise God, we are currently healthy except for Mother, who suffers from her usual afflictions. I am grateful that my dear wife can accept the current circumstances in which we find ourselves so calmly and is not fearful about the future. She shames me in this respect, although I know that without the Lord's will, not a hair will fall from our heads.

We greet you all most sincerely, and you, dear Br., accept a special greeting from your humble fellow Brother,

G. Byhan

[M 415-1a-7: Translated by Julie Tomberlin Weber. Addressed to: Revd. Theodore Schulz, Salem, Stokes County, North Carolina. Postmark: New Echota, Feb. 5, 18¾. Received Feb. 23.]

Ooyugillogy, Ch. Nat., Feb. 4, 1831

Dear Brother Schulz,

In these oppressive times it will certainly not be uninteresting to you if I write you more frequently than was previously the case in calmer times. Last week I wrote you a few lines from Spring Place, in which I informed you of Br. Copeland's decision to move away from here soon, and I expressed my hope that I would be able to continue the fieldwork through Negroes or diligent Indians if we should stay here longer. Unfortunately this hope is melting away, as I consider that among all my acquaintances in this country I cannot find a single individual suited for our work. And so this illustrates one difficulty which causes me grave concerns.

There is no thought of trying to convince Br. Copeland to stay here, because circumstances in his family require that he reach a peaceful place soon, and the longer he postpones the journey he has been planning to Indiana for a long time now, the more difficult it will be for him. It was his plan to move next fall, but now Sr. Copeland is expecting to deliver in June, and it is to be feared that there will be significant unrest in this country. Also difficulties and issues arose in our family when Br. Copeland changed his mind last Sept., so it is best for them if they move as soon as possible. Sr. Copeland would not be able to provide much help in the school or household anyway. Since Br. Copeland now has to purchase a small wagon and 2 more horses, he is planning to set out from here at the beginning of March, accompanied by one of his younger brothers.

I will now try to get a hired worker who can easily manage our work during this season. Before we begin working in the field, we will surely have learned the thoughts and instructions of the P.H.C. regarding our critical situation. If we should have to leave, even if not until next fall, we would have enough corn and other food to last until then. Perhaps you saw the comment in the *Georgia Journal*: "The late Law provides for the removal of the Missionaries,"[1] from which can clearly be seen that the actual purpose of that law is just to drive the missionaries out. Everyone here is uneasy. Many of our neighbors, tradesmen, smiths, and millers are making preparations to move. This reveals a new difficulty, because we cannot really manage without a blacksmith.

Some days ago I paid a brief visit to the missionary Thompson from Hightower. He was more than a little upset about that law. He and Mr. Worcester in New Echota are waiting for instructions from their superiors, since they can as little as myself come to a decision about what would actually be the best plan, to stay and allow oneself to be taken prisoner or to flee. Regarding the former, it is doubtful if the matter would be helped if one were freed again after a brief time. Would one then be able to carry out the Lord's work in peace here? Whatever happens, I am firmly resolved to follow the judgment and the instructions of the P.H.C. without fear or worry. Through these I will be shown the best way. Our Presbyterian colleagues have an advantage which we do not have, in that they can easily go to their other stations in Tennessee and Alabama, and in this manner flee the Georgian authorities without completely leaving the Nation. We, however, do not have any such place of refuge nearby.

Next week the Georgia surveyors are planning to begin their work in this country under the protection of 3 different companies of soldiers. In the coming weeks all the farms which have been sold by Emigrants or left behind will be publicly leased, and indeed only to citizens of Georgia. In this manner Georgia is bringing its laws and offices into this unfortunate country, because without a doubt those who occupy such places will act as magistrates.

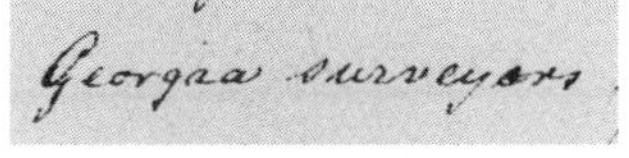

Your kind letter of Jan. 16 reached my hand on the 2nd of this month, with the very eagerly anticipated and gratefully received

[1] The quote is in English in the original German manuscript.

enclosure of $100, with which I was able to completely pay off Br. Copeland as well as Saml. Henry and to become debt free.

Yes, "the storm clouds of unrest and distress" are gathering and threatening general destruction. But perhaps they are full of grace and salvation for us and our poor Cherokee people. We entrust everything to the Lord. He will act according to His saving will, which we cannot oppose but gladly and willingly and joyfully surrender ourselves to it. Most especially comforting to me is the Text for March 1, when we will be in constant danger of being arrested, in that the Lord calls to us [Luke 12:32]: "Fear not, little flock: for it is your Father's good pleasure to give you the kingdom."

I also thank you for the notice of the new mail arrangement, since I was involved with this for so long and still take an interest in it now. It seems to me, however, that your new arrangement will not speed up the correspondence between us. Your kind letter left Salem on Jan. 13 and arrived here at the same time as a letter sent from Gettysburg, Pa., on Jan. 12.

We are all enjoying usual health. Coughs and sniffles prevail among the children, and our young Charles was not spared. Nor was I. Still there is nothing serious to fear from this, and without a doubt it comes from the changing weather, which is mostly unpleasant. I have never experienced a more severe winter here in Oo___g___ee than this one. Our cattle are suffering greatly from this, since they are vulnerable to all the weather.

I can hardly neglect to inform you of our hope that you might feel moved by our current situation to visit here soon, if the P.H.C. found it necessary. Even if our situation were less critical, a visit could certainly be beneficial and bring blessings.

Now, dear Br., excuse the brevity of this hastily written letter of greeting. Greet your dear family as well as my dear parents for all of us, and remember us, and especially your faithfully obliged Brother,

Henry G. Clauder

[Springplace (M 407-2) and Oochgeelogy (M 409-1) Diaries.]

Feb. 3. [Spg.] Five Indians came and asked for some young apple trees to plant. We very gladly gave them to them, as many as they wanted. This does not indicate that the Indians are currently inclined to move across the Mississippi.

Feb. 4. [Spg.] In the evening Doct. Bean came to our place on his way to New Echota to attend the meeting of the white people there tomorrow. They will consider what is the best thing to do in the current circumstances. This Doct. Bean lives in Sumak Town 9 miles from here and is married to Mr. McNair's eldest daughter.

Feb. 5. [Ooch.] At the service at Halfbreed's the about 90-year-old Indian attended. His wife is the elderly Sr. Hannah, who endured a lot of persecution and mistreatment from this heathen husband of hers when she was baptized in 1825. After the service today, Br. Clauder spoke with him briefly and explained to him that it was the Lord's mercy that enabled him to reach such an old age, so that before the sun of his life sets forever he could hear something about Jesus, the one who erases sins and who wanted to be his Savior as well, if he believed in Him. He was also reminded that his faithful old wife and many of his children and children's children are counted among the believers who hope confidently in an eternal and better life. He responded to these sincere words with visible emotion: "I would really like to hear more about these things; it is new to me. I have known about the great Spirit who created things since I was a child, and I have believed in him, but I did not know anything about Jesus and a future life. I hope my days will be extended so that I can come to a service here again." When we were ready to go home, he followed us alone and asked the interpreter Br. Hicks if he would have to give up his sorcery if he became a believer. When he was told that he would have to abandon everything like that, he said: "It is good. I will seriously consider what I heard today."

Sun., Feb. 6. [Spg.] Because of heavy snow only 2 Indian Brn., Joshua and Emanuel, came to our services today. They told us that in recent days an Indian in Coosawaytee had struck another Indian dead with a piece of pine wood while drunk. Further, they also told us that our Br. Israel has moved close to our place in recent days, about 3 miles from here. He used to live 10 to 11 miles from here. We were very happy to hear this, since he can now attend our services more often than previously, which he also did in the following [weeks?].

Sun., Feb. 6. [Ooch.] We had heavy snowstorms the entire day, so that only 2 of our Brn. and Srs. who live closest could come to the services. Some of the Brn. and Srs. who belong to Spring Place had arrived here late last evening, and they spent the day here. One of them, Solomon, read the Litany in the first service. They brought 2 girls along to go to our school, but we had to send them back, because we didn't have enough room.

Feb. 7. [Spg.] The old Indian Chulioa, formerly a Chief of this Nation, visited us. This Indian and the well-known James Vann were much of the reason that the Brn. were allowed to move into this country 30 years ago, because the other Chiefs were not especially willing for the Brn. to begin a mission here. He was very friendly toward us. The Methodist preacher Mr. Seales, who also lives here in this country and had married an Indian woman, also stopped in at our place on his way from Goosawaytee to hear what we are planning to do in our current situation, because he is in the same situation as we. Our Indian Br. Willm. Henry and Sr. Ester and Br. Israel's wife also visited us today.

Feb. 10. [Spg.] We received a visit from Mr. McNair and his wife, our Sr. Delila McNair. Mr. McNair offered us a place to live at his place in the event we are no longer allowed to stay here according to Georgia laws, until circumstances have improved again. We were happy and sincerely grateful to him for his generosity to us, and we assured him that in case of need we will make use of his offer. Today we heard that the Georgia Guard has captured Mr. John Martin, who is the Judge of the Courts among the Cherokees here and lives about 14 or 15 miles from here in Coosawaytee. They took him away to Georgia. We were unable to learn the reason for this action.

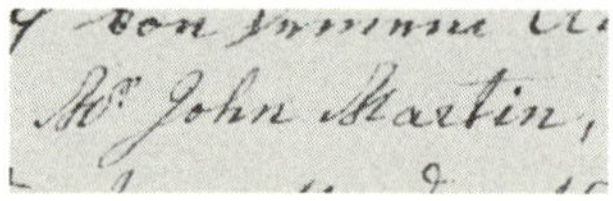

Feb. 11. [Spg.] Today we also heard that the Georgia Guard has gone to New Echota, and people have reason to believe that they want to burn the press there. Some people believe they are getting ready to arrest Mr. Boudinott, Major Ridge, or the Chief, John Ross. Time will tell what other excesses they will carry out. Trouble will soon have reached its peak in the Nation; perhaps help is also not far away anymore!

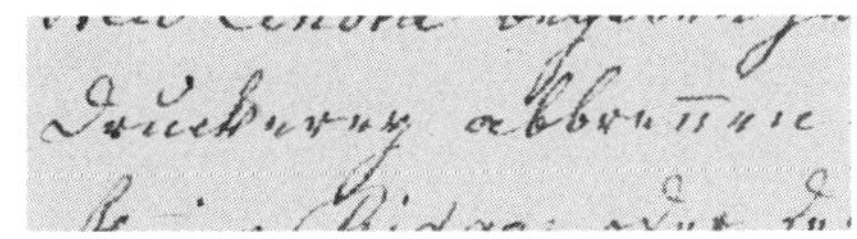

Feb. 12. [Spg.] We heard that Judge Martin was set free again by the Georgians.

[M 415-1a-8: Translated by Julie Tomberlin Weber. Addressed to: Revd. Theodore Schulz, Salem, Stokes County, North Carolina. Postmark: Springplace, C.N., Feb. 13. Free. G. Byhan, P.M. Received Feb. 23.]

Springplace, Feb. 11, 1831

My dearly beloved Br. Schulz,

Times become darker here every day. Yesterday the Georgians arrested Judge Martin and immediately took him away with them. No one knows why and it is being said that he himself does not know. This happened 14 or 15 miles from here. From there the soldiers went to New Echota, people believe and it is said, in order to burn down the Printing Office. Some believe they have already gone to arrest Mr. Boudinott, Major Ridge, or John Ross. In a couple of days it will become clear what their purpose is. God alone knows what will happen now! May He look after this oppressed Nation and not allow them to be destroyed by the burden under which they — and we with them — are currently groaning! Perhaps amidst defeat they must conquer.

Our time, that is March 1, is getting closer and closer, and since it seems as if the Georgians will take and drive all the white people out of the country with their horrible laws, and especially the missionaries, we must consider, and have done so to some extent, how we should and want to act in such circumstances.

It is a shame that we cannot get your advice in time. As things are now, we cannot see anything ahead except that we either will have to leave our mission place for a while or in fact be taken to the Georgia Penitentiary.

My advice would be this: Br. Clauder and our Nathl. should distance themselves from their respective places for some time until we see how things will really go. Capt. McNair, who is here with his wife for a visit in Spring Place just now, also believes that this is the most advisable for the 2 Brn., because we believe that the Georgians will exercise the laws they have made to the full extent. And Capt. McNair is very willing to clear a place for them to live at his place. It is true that it is difficult to leave the Brn. and Srs. in this manner, but if we stay there is no doubt the result will be that we are taken away by force. Oh, how we would like to know what you think!

The schools will also be interrupted for a while as well, both here and in Ochgeloogy. My further thoughts, as I have had no chance to talk with Br. Clauder for the past 3 weeks, are that I will stay here and wait out the storm at my post. I am counting on what everyone is saying, that they will not be able or allowed to take me away, as Postmaster. I am not leaving the Post Office until I am ordered away by the Genl. Postmaster. And so I will see how this goes and what happens to me. With tomorrow's mail I expect an answer to my letter to you dated Jan. 15th, in which I sent you the copy of the Georgia Law. I will not close this letter until the last hour when I must send it. Perhaps more will happen that I can report to you.

Feb. 12. I have just received your letter of Jan. 26, but I could not tell for sure if you had received my letter, or note, in which I copied the Georgia Laws about the white people in Cherokee country for you, because you simply informed me that you had noticed the Captions of the Law about the white people in the Milledgeville newspaper. And so I must conclude that you have not yet read my letter in which I copied it, and the newspaper itself in which the Laws concerning the white people appear in full. I have written you every week recently, and I will continue to do so for the time being, so from my following letters you will surely see what kind of situation we are currently in. It is easier to judge how things are in person and what the Georgians are doing.

Now more next week. May God advise and help us!! And we rely on Him. He will not leave us. In all of this I also consider it our responsibility to do our best not to put ourselves in danger unnecessarily, if we make a small detour — without harming too much the work for which we came here. We are eagerly awaiting your further thoughts.

I would also like to ask you to pay our Rachel $10 and put it on my account. If the interest I might have with you is not enough, then take it from the capital. I just received Rachel's dear letter of Jan. 24, and I will answer it soon.

Herewith I am sending you a page of the Diary again. Everyone sends best greetings, and you are especially greeted by your poor friend and Br.,

Gottl. Byhan

[M 407-2: Springplace Diary.]

Sun., Feb. 13. [Spg.] The sermon was on the Sunday Gospel lesson for today, and in this our Brn. and Srs. were reminded that today we once again begin the time which is so important for all believers, when we make the consideration of Jesus' Passion our main concern, and we wished that this time may also be blessed for our hearts. After this was the baptism of the baby daughter born to our Indian Br. John Jacob and Sr. Ruth, with the name Anna Caliha. The Brn. and Srs. were also informed that next Sunday we will have Holy Communion.

Feb. 14. [Spg.] Today we heard that our mission place Ochgeloogy, where Br. and Sr. Clauder live, is also seen as a place which falls into the class of those places which can be rented to whoever offers the most for it, according to the laws which have recently been made in Georgia. This is because an Indian began it and now has moved to Arkansaw. The day which has been designated for the renting of such places is March 15. If this should now really be that case that this place will be rented, then we will have a new difficulty, and we cannot see in advance what the result of this matter will be. We will also commend these circumstances to the One who commands everything.

Feb. 15. [Spg.] A circuit rider named Boot came from the Methodists and spent the night here. He told us that in the area of Ochgeloogy some white people who have married Indian women and have families want to leave their homes and go somewhere else because of the Georgia laws, because they do not want to swear allegiance to the Georgia laws. Since it rained heavily today, the streams in our area were once again very swollen.

Feb. 16. [Spg.] Mr. Nicolson, Mr. Vann's Overseer at his place about 2 miles from here, came to our place to complain about his distress and difficulty, since according to the Georgia laws, he also either must swear allegiance to them or be taken to the Penitentiary. He could not do the former, even if it cost him his life, and he could not think about going to the Penitentiary, being taken away from his many children — he is a widower — without horror and trembling. Also because he is an old man and also very sickly. His wife lies buried on our God's Acre here in Spring Place.

[M 415-1a-9: Translated by Julie Tomberlin Weber. Addressed to: Revd. Theodor Schulz, Salem, Stokes County, North Carolina. Postmark: Springplace, C.N., Feb. 20. Free. Gottl. Byhan, P.M. Received Mar. 2.]

Springplace, Feb. 17, 1831

My dear Br. Shulz,

I received your kind letter of Jan. 26 on the 12th of this month, as I already informed you in my last letter dated the 11th and 12th. Judging by your letter, you had not yet received my letter of Jan. 15th in which I told you about one of the intentions of the Georgia Law which was passed in their last General Assembly. We are anxiously awaiting an answer to this from you, because times are becoming ever more critical here and we require much advice, comfort, and encouragement from you and from the Helf. Conf. According to your letter, you have not seen the actual Laws of Georgia concerning the white people, but rather just Captions. We want to hear what you all think about it when you see the actual Law.

We were happy to hear everything contained in your dear letter, for which we are grateful. Your letter to me dated Nov. 18th turned up again. Br. Clauder, whom I had given it to read through, had it in his possession without realizing he had it. Everything concerning Nancy's frock and shoes, etc., is in order now.

Now to return to the matter of the Georgians and the Cherokees, because our minds are currently filled with this and we cannot think about anything else. Everyone thinks about our situation day and night. We are not free of it even when sleeping, and we dream about it. When you finally read the Georgia Laws, you will see that all the places where Indians who have moved to the Arkansas previously lived are considered the property of Georgia and are supposed to be rented to the highest bidder by the Agent, whom the Governor of Georgia will name. Now we have recently heard that the place where Br. and Sr. Clauder live will also be considered such a place, because an Indian started the place many years ago and later sold it to Joseph Crutchfield and moved to Arkansas. Accordingly it is liable to the current Law of Georgia to be rented to the highest bidder. If this should really be the case, we will surely hear more about this, and because of this we will get into new trouble and cannot see in advance what the results of this will be for our mission post there.

There is much movement among the white people here now. Those with entire white families, or some of them, are moving out of the country. The rest of them, along with those who have married Indian women, are looking for a place to stay either in the part of the Nation which belongs to Tennessee State or in the part that belongs to Alabama.

We have heard nothing from Br. and Sr. Clauder since Jan. 22nd. I have written him twice but have received no answer, so I do not know how the Brn. and Srs. there are doing. Presumably Br. Clauder has written you often, and he will have thoroughly informed you of their circumstances there, because the situation of the Brn. and Srs. there is serious indeed. The Lord will provide assistance!

The 19th. The Georgia mail just brought me your very kind letter in reply to the note I wrote you on Jan. 15th, in which I sent you a copy of the Georgia Law. Our view of this matter was and is just the same which you in the Helf. Conf. have of it. If I am not mistaken, I informed you in my last letter eight days ago that our neighbor and good friend Capt. McNair very happily offered to take us in as refugees. I will write to you again on the next mail day and answer your very dear letter to us.

Praise God, we are all quite well. Last night Nathl. was sick, but he is better again today. Mother continues in weakness. Everyone sends sincere greetings. And you, dear Br., accept another special greeting from your loving Br.,

Gottl. Byhan

I am sending some more of the Diary.

[Springplace (M 407-2) and Oochgeelogy (M 409-1) Diaries.]

Feb. 19. [Spg.] The post rider brought us the news from New Echota that he had heard that some United States troops would come into this country once again. Why and what they are supposed to do here were unknown to him. Time will tell if this rumor turns out to be true.

Sun., Feb. 20. [Spg.] For our first Sunday service some sentences from the *Idea Fidei Fratrum* were read and interpreted into Indian by Mr. Dav. Steiner Dazizi, who came to our place yesterday evening. In the second service we enjoyed Jesus' body and blood in Holy Communion. Today the Brn. and Srs. were officially informed that the school will have to be canceled for the current time, as they surely knew the situation in which the rest of the white people in this country and we currently find ourselves. Br. Nathl. Byhan finds it necessary to leave here for some time until circumstances concerning the Georgia laws have been changed again. Perhaps this will be the case soon. The Indians agreed with the matter and approved our measures. In response to their question, or actually to the Indian Br. Samuel's question, whether Br. Byhan, Sr., would also leave the place and whether there would be no more Sunday services held here now, he was told that Br. Byhan, Sr., will stay and wait out the storm which threatens to come over the white people, because people believe that as postmaster they cannot do anything to him. It seemed he was glad to hear this. They were advised to carry these difficult circumstances to the Savior diligently in their prayers, and ask Him to have mercy on us and them, and end this trouble in which we all find ourselves. Today we also heard once again that most of the white people in the Ochgeloogie area are moving out of the way and across the border, either into the state of Tennessee or into the state of Alabama, except for a few who are of good courage and want to wait the matter out calmly. They assure us that they will not be taken to Georgia alive.

Feb. 21. [Spg.] This morning Mr. Dazizi, who has been staying here with 2 horses since Saturday evening, returned home. Toward evening Br. and Sr. Clauder came to our place on a visit. We then had a thorough conversation with them about our current difficult and desperate situation. We thought it advisable in our current situation for Brn. Clauder and Nathl. Byhan to leave the state for a while, and go first to our friend Capt. Dav. McNair in the state of Tennessee. The thoughtful Indian Br. Wilm. Abr. Hicks had also advised this, until we see what will come of the matter. Sr. Clauder and Sr. Gambold are planning to stay in Ochgeloogy for a while to take care of the external matters. Br. and Sr. Copeland, who have served the mission in Ochgeloogy in external concerns, will begin their journey to the state of Indiana in a few days. The school there, as a result of these circumstances, has reached its conclusion for the time being, as some of the children have been taken home and some of them have been let go.

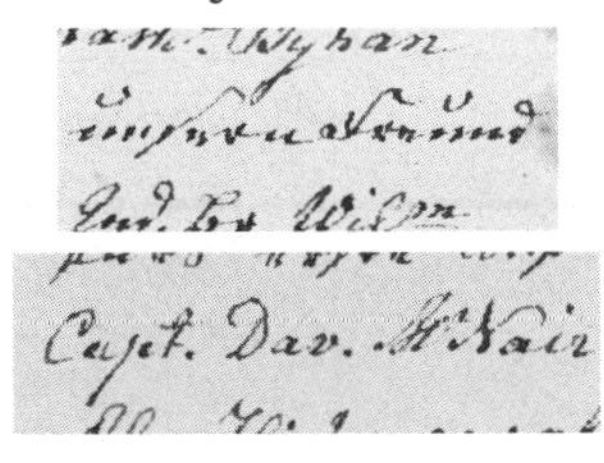

[Ooch.] During the month of February there was great turmoil in this area because of the previously mentioned law concerning white residents here who found themselves in a very sad situation as a result of this. As expected, there was an almost universal flight of all white craftsmen. This will cause the Indians significant problems in agriculture, since they will not be able to get the necessary equipment. This is affecting us as well, but it is the least of our troubles now, because like all the rest of the missionaries, we think it is necessary either to move voluntarily or to face the punishment, which would separate us from our work. In this distress, we just plead that the Lord's will might be done and that He might protect us or chasten us, as He deems best for His work.

Feb. 21. [Ooch.] Br. and Sr. Clauder went to Spring Place, where there was a joint discussion of the current circumstances. We were especially grateful to receive advice and instructions from the P.H.C. in Salem, which arrived in writing yesterday. As a result, we quickly decided that for now Br. Clauder will move to the place of refuge on the border of Tennessee offered by our friend McNair, and he will wait for further developments in this unrest.

Feb. 23. [Spg.] Br. and Sr. Clauder returned to Ochgeloogy. In recent days we heard that the Georgia Guard was going to come into our area but had received orders to go back again.

[M 415-1a-10: Translated by Julie Tomberlin Weber. Addressed to: Revd. Theodor Shulz, Salem, Stokes County, North Carolina. Postmark: Springplace, C.N., Feb. 27. Free. Gottl. Byhan, P.M. Received Mar. 9.]

Springplace, Feb. 23, 1831

Dearly beloved Br. Schulz,

In my last letter to you, dated the 19th of this month, I reported that we received your kind letter of Feb. 2, in answer to my letter to you dated the 15th of last month. In that letter, I sent you a copy of the Georgia Laws. Everything in your dear letter was important and interesting to us in our continuing difficult situation, where we hardly know forward from backward, and our thoughts actually stand still sometimes. We can hardly think any more about how things might or could go for us. The time is approaching — on March 1st — when the Laws of Georgia are supposed to be enforced.

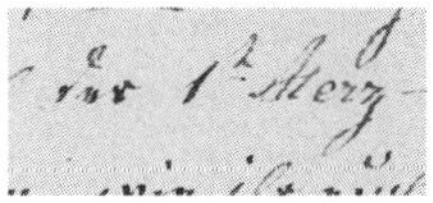

As you can imagine, fear and doubt overwhelm us. Fear, that we fear the laws will be enforced very strictly against us. Then at other times we doubt if it is really possible to carry out such laws. This then encourages us again sometimes, but these cheerful hours, or I should say minutes, do not last for long. Because immediately we remember that it is the Georgians who are supposed to carry out these laws, and I must say they have no mercy, or I might actually say they have no human feelings, because this is how they act. So we always worry again about the future. But God, who rules everything and has human hearts in His hand, will not abandon us. He will support us, we will trust in Him! He will help us through this difficult period!

Your views about the entire matter, which you shared in your dear letter, are exactly the same ones we had about the matter, and we will try to act in accordance with your advice.

Since receiving your dear letter, Br. and Sr. Clauder from Och____y were here at our place on a visit. Day before yesterday we had a very thorough conversation together about how we should act and what might be the most advisable actions in the current circumstances, and we finally came to the following conclusion: For now, Br. and Sr. Clauder will return to Och____y and Br. Clauder will pack up his things and everything there as much as possible and collect everything and find a reliable man to turn them over to, as advised in your letter. I thought perhaps Mr. Jay Hicks, Br. Wilm. Hicks's son, could keep watch over them. Br. Clauder will then come back here to Spring Place alone on the 28th of this month and then on March 1st he and Br. Nathl. Byhan will go to our true friend Mr. McNair, where they plan to wait and see how things go.

Sr. Clauder agreed to stay with Sr. Gambold in Och____y for a while. During Br. Clauder's absence Mr. Jay Hicks will live with them, and Br. Clauder will also visit from time to time, if possible, until the storm passes and we see how things will go. This is the only way we saw to escape the horrible hands of the Georgians, and it was difficult to reach this conclusion.

As you can easily imagine, this was especially true for Br. Clauder. But we have no reason at all to fear that — even if the missionaries leave for a while to avoid the mentioned laws — it would cause a sensation among the Cherokees and especially among the Brethren and Sisters. And Br. Willm. Abr. Hicks himself advised Br. Clauder that the best thing for him to do would be to leave his post for a while. So this made our deliberations somewhat easier and allowed us to reach the above conclusion more confidently. In addition, there is the fact that various Brn. and Srs. who belong to the Och____y Gemeine — I think 4 or 5 — have already moved away so that the size of the Gemeine there has already been significantly reduced. But Br. Clauder will better inform you about this, since he himself will write to the Helf. Conf. with this mail.

In your kind letter you expressed your wish for us to discuss our current situation openly with the most reasonable Indians. There is much, indeed very much, to say about this. Because this paper is too small for that, I will only say here that we have taken the opportunity to talk to our Brethren and Sisters about our current situation, and it did not seem to matter much at all to them. Through an interpreter, Br. Samuel told us: That they too were having problems — "we are in trouble too." This was all they said about the matter. Br. Clauder also says that things are the same in Och______y. The Brn. and Srs. only come out of curiosity to see what they will do in their circumstances. From this little, you will be able to conclude that they offer little comfort. Please don't think badly of me for speaking so freely, because the time has come for us to have an understanding with each other. Perhaps there will be another opportunity soon to write about this matter.

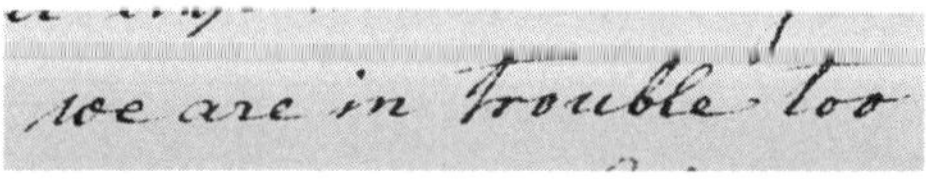

Concerning me and us in Spring Place now, I have decided, although not at all without anxious concern, what we will do or

I will do, if I wait here in Spring Place until the storm finally breaks.

I just cannot commit to simply leaving the Post Office until I receive word from the Genl. Postmaster. What kind of confusion would it cause if I left it, since this is the end of 4 mail routes? And so I will risk staying here in the hope that they will consider me an Agent of the Genl. Govt. Still we cannot deny that we are worried about whether they will leave me for the above-mentioned reason. In the meantime, we will trust in Him and commend this to Him who can work everything out for the best.

Our school has also ended now. We have one boy still here, and he will also go home in a few days. Br. and Sr. Copeland will begin their journey to Indiana day after tomorrow, which is especially difficult for them, because she is expected to deliver soon. Most of the white people have moved away now, and the ones who are still there will move out of the way before March 1. We heard today that the Georgia militia who are quartered at the gold mines were on their way to our area but received orders to go back. We do not know what their intention was.

Now we are concerned about our crops. What should we do now? Naeman Rominger, with whom we [tear in paper] have not been especially satisfied recently, will [page torn] also leave here, because one cannot trust that they — the Georgians — will not take him along as well. The time is approaching when we should be in the fields. In fact the oats should already be sown, and the workers have to leave. If missionaries remain here in Springplace, which I still doubt, they are supposed to live without buying anything. And then what will we do with our cattle next winter if nothing is planted? They have to be fed the entire winter. Thinking about this matter causes fear of the future. What is to be done? If Rominger leaves, we will have only the single Indian Br. Niclaus Ignatius, who works here for $8 a month. It is uncertain how long he will remain here, because he will have to help his father, our Indian Br. Richard Sanders, on his farm at home. And if he goes home, then I will not have anyone else to work for us. From this, you all can see that we are more than a little concerned in this regard and in this matter as well. I also wanted to add here that we currently own 35 head of cattle, large and small, and approximately 50 pigs. As mentioned, all of these must be fed throughout the winter.

Feb. 26. I just received your kind letter of the 9th of this month with the $60 which you were good enough to send me. I thank you most sincerely for this. From this you will see that we have precisely the same views about the Georgia laws that you have, and that we have reached just the same conclusions in our joint consideration as those advised us by the P.H.C. This is indeed remarkable, as you will see from this letter. Now dear God will continue to provide assistance!! I have always believed that the Georgians could do us no harm with their laws, and so I decided to wait out the matter peacefully at home, and this is what I will do as reported above. I will write again next week.

Please give our children our best greetings. We are all well except for Mother, who is frequently overcome by her great weakness. Nancy B. has recovered somewhat from a bad cold. In closing, we greet everyone and commend ourselves in our oppressive situation to your remembrance and prayer before our dear Lord. Your faithfully obliged Br.,

Gottl. Byhan

Please overlook and forgive the many errors in this letter, because it is difficult to have coherent thoughts anymore. This discouraging and oppressive matter makes one weak minded.

Please give the enclosed note to dear Br. Shaaf.

[M 415-1a-11: Translated by Julie Tomberlin Weber. Addressed to: Revd. Theodore Schulz, Salem, Stokes County, North Carolina. Post stamp: New-Echota, Cher. Na., Feb. 26, 18¾. Received Mar. 9.]

Ooyugillogy, Cherokee Nation, Feb. 25, 1831

Dear Brother Schulz,

Since my last letter to you, we have been enjoying good health, peace, and quiet, for which we thank the Lord, and we remain strong in faith in Him. Even so, the closer the danger comes, the greater it seems.

Since my last letter, almost every day has brought new events. The unrest among our white neighbors which prevailed at that time has now pretty well ended, because hardly a single one is left here! A general exodus from Georgia followed the announcement of that law, with which you are now familiar. However, it is a remarkable circumstance that only a few issues of the *Georgia Journal* included that announcement. According to all appearances, the friends of the Indians generally didn't know anything about it and therefore could not negotiate in the matter.

Our post is in a sad state in every respect, and with my lack of experience I really cannot see how it can last for long. We are losing many of our Brethren and Sisters through the flight of the white people, Mrs. Crutchfield, Chisholm, Gann, who have white husbands, all tradesmen and hired hands. The results of such circumstances are clear and easy to see. Despite all these difficulties, however, we could still maintain our courage if we could only hope that we ourselves would not fall under the strictness of the Law. But we are on the same ground as all those who have already saved themselves by fleeing.

The receipt of your dear letter of the 2nd of this month was sweet and reassuring to me and to Br. Byhan. We read it together some days ago on the occasion of my visit in Spring Place. Br. Byhan believes he is safe as Postmaster, that nothing can be done to him. After thorough consideration of all the circumstances, danger, and consequences, we decided that Nathanael and I should accept the safe haven offered us by McNair until it becomes clear if Georgia will try to enforce that Law or we have received further instructions from the P.H.C. after it has been frankly and thoroughly acquainted with internal and external circumstances of this mission, which I will try to do, as we decided.

Various things could be added regarding the actual mission work — the scattered homes of the Brethren and Sisters, their extremely infrequent church attendance, the apparent apathy of the common people toward the Gospel, etc. These circumstances existed to a small degree before the external difficulties with Georgia broke out. Now, however, they fill everyone's minds to the exclusion of all other matters, except in a few cases. Partly from this circumstance, it can be concluded that it is rare for heathen Indians to come with whom we can share a comforting word, unsolicited by them.

Actually I found somewhat more comfort during my recently begun visits and services at Halfbreed's. Our George Augustus has faithfully supported me during these, and without his help I could not accomplish anything. I doubt, however, whether this plan would last even if our external situation were better than it actually is.

Now from these changes you will become more familiar with our inner situation. Overall I believe that if peace and quiet were restored, we would in time see the fruits of tears sown in this place. Unfortunately, I long ago lost hope that the Indians could claim their rights, and I see nothing else ahead except their complete destruction, because they are not considering yielding, despite all the external pressures. Instead, companies here and there are talking about resisting. If this happens, the consequences can be clearly seen.

Regarding our external situation, it is trying in all respects. As you know, the Copelands are moving to Indiana, today in fact. Thus we are losing a reliable worker and the assistance of Sr. Copeland in the school. Unfortunately, it no longer exists now since almost all the children have already been taken home. In a few days I am planning to go away for some time, in accordance with my instructions and the advice of our Brother Wm. A. Hicks. This is a step I take with trembling and sad feelings, and still I see no other way to avoid it, because if I wanted to expose myself it would do the Cherokees no good. The only way to avoid leaving this place completely is for my wife and Sr. Gambold to remain here alone with one of Wm. Hicks's sons. The latter will plant part of our fields on the condition that if the desired peace should be restored, he would get $12 per month for his work. But if the breakup of this place follows, he should get everything he planted here himself. In the meantime, Wm. A. Hicks will take care of our things.

I just heard that the Georgia Agent, Col. Sandford, sent a notice to the missionary Thompson in Hightower that he would be arrested next Wednesday, March 2. The poor Presbyterian missionaries have been waiting in vain for a long time for instructions from their Directors. Mr. Worcester told me day before yesterday, “if I had directions to flee, I should do so.” He is

"if I had directions to flee, I should do so"

Postmaster, but he does not believe this will protect him. Thus Br. Byhan is also in danger, as am I. Now forgive me for this digression from the matter. We are threatened with another difficulty, which I must also report to you.

The large field close to us was sold to the U.S. agent 10 or more years ago by an emigrant, but along with many other places it was returned in the treaty of 1817. People say it is now being rented out like the newer emigrant places in Georgia. Now if this should actually be done, we would be in danger of getting bad neighbors.

If we believed all the rumors we hear daily, we would not feel safe for our lives, because it is unbelievable that Georgia can act in this manner for long without it leading to decisive consequences. In any case, we will pack our things and try to get them close together to be as prepared as possible. More soon. This was written in haste and with many interruptions.

Br. and Sr. Copeland send sincere greetings. They will set out from here in a few hours. They are going alone in a small wagon with one large horse.

We commend ourselves jointly to your compassion and prayer, particularly your faithfully obliged Brother,

H. G. Clauder

1831, part 3

[Springplace (M 407-2) and Oochgeelogy (M 409-1) Diaries. Translated by Julie Tomberlin Weber. Handwritings are Henry G. Clauder's (Ooch.) and Gottlieb Byhan's (Spg.).]

Feb. 25. [Ooch.] Br. and Sr. Copeland, who have assisted us with the economy and school for more than a year, began their journey to the state of Indianna, accompanied by our best wishes for blessings. On March 26th they arrived safely at the new Brethren's settlement.

Sun., Feb. 27. [Spg.] Our Brn. and Srs. came in large numbers to the Sunday services. In the second service an Indian child was baptized into Jesus' death with the name Elisabeth at the request of the parents, who do not belong to us. The father of the child is named Squirrel, brother of our Indian Brn. Israel and Emmanuel.

Sun., Feb. 27. [Ooch.] In a special meeting after the sermon, we informed the Indian Brethren and Sisters of the previously mentioned decision. They expressed their satisfaction with this, since they realized that Br. Clauder would no longer be safe here. It was their hope that the Lord would soon grant us peace again and bring us back together. On the following day Br. Clauder left his post and arrived at McNair's on

March 1st [Ooch.], where he spent his time until *March 18th* except for a four-day visit in the surrounding state of Tennessee. On that day he began his journey to Ooyugillogy for a visit, and he arrived there safely and unexpectedly on that evening. A number of the so-called Georgia Guards had passed through here some days ago and taken many white people prisoner, including three of the Presbyterian missionaries, so we were afraid that we were not safe staying here and that this would perhaps be impossible. Indeed we feared the entire mission work was approaching its end, and so Br. and Sr. Clauder decided to return together to the safe place offered them at McNair's and there await further developments in this time of trial. Sr. Gambold was willing to stay back with some of our former students and one of Wm. Abr. Hicks's sons for now.

Feb. 28. [Spg.] Br. Clauder arrived at our place on his way to Mr. McNair's, and spent the night here.

Mar. 1. [Spg.] Br. Clauder, Nathl. Byhan, and Naeman Rominger went with our farm wagon to Mr. McNair's, to stay there for some time until we see if the Georgians will really follow the laws they made in their Legislature to imprison all the white people who live here in Indian country and who do not swear allegiance to this.

Mar. 2. [Spg.] Our Br. Clement Vann returned from Head of Coosa, where he had been since the end of Dec. last year. He told us that the Georgia Guard was expected in New Echota last night but had not arrived, also that most of the Presbyterian missionaries had gathered at Mr. Worcester's in New Echota to wait for the Guard there and allow themselves to be arrested. They had received instructions from their Board of Directors that they were free to leave the Georgia territory or to stay, but they advised them to do the latter, even if it cost them everything they owned.

Mar. 4. [Spg.] In the evening at 12 o'clock we were disturbed by some drunken Indians who were going through our lane. We were happy that after they had strengthened themselves once again with their brandy wine, they went on without stopping in at our place.

Mar. 5. [Spg.] In a letter we received from Br. Nathl. Byhan, postmarked Conassauga, we learned that the Georgians are busy measuring Cherokee land and that the surveyors had already arrived at Mr. McNair's.

[*Records: N.C.*, 8:3965: Salem Diary. Translated by Douglas L. Rights.]

March 2. In Friedland, the funeral service of the married Brother, Joseph Gambold, who served for 20 years in the outer work of the Cherokee Mission in Springplace, Georgia.

[M 415-1a-12: Translated by Julie Tomberlin Weber. Addressed to: Revd. Theodor Shulz, Salem, Stokes County, North Carolina. Postmark: Springplace, C.N., Mar. 6. Free. Gottl. Byhan, P.M. Received Mar. 16.]

Springplace, March 5, 1831

Dearly beloved Br. Schulz,

On the 26th of last month, I received your dear letter of Feb. 9 with the $60 in banknotes, as I informed you in my last letter of the 23rd and 26th of last month. We are now living in the time during which the strict laws the Georgians made about the white people in Cherokee country are supposed to be carried out. Without a doubt they will do their best to follow them as much as they have the power to do so. Br. Clauder, Nathanael, and Naemen Rominger went to our friend Dav. McNair on the first of March, and they are now staying there until we see what will happen. As a result, we are living here in a very lonely manner.

All the white people have left. Our school children have all left now as well. The last one was taken away day before yesterday. We currently have the single Br. Niclous Ignatius with us. Through him we can speak with the Indians who pass by here — but there are only a few of them — and he also helps us take care of our cattle and with the housework when it is necessary. Mr. Jos. Vann has also left. People say this is because the Georgians are after him because of a debt which his father, the famous James Vann, still owes in Georgia.

Day before yesterday our Br. Clem. Vann visited us. He had just returned from Head of Coosa, where he has been staying since the end of Dec. He told us that the Georgians are expected in New Echota any hour, and that some of the Presbyterian missionaries had gathered at Mr. Worcester's to wait for the Georgians, since they received word from their Directors not to clear out of the way even if all of their possessions were taken. Still it was left up to each one whether or not to go.

This morning we heard again from one Indian that the Georgians had taken a white man in New Echota, a storekeeper who had run the store there for a certain Tarbin, who has sworn the oath to the Georgia law. It is also being said that they have divided into three companies and are looking for the whites in the country. In recent days we also heard that the U. St. troops were afoot again. Time will tell if this is true.

We, or I, have been spared thus far, but I expect them here in Spring Place — that is the Georgians — any day now, and we have to admit we wish that the worst might come soon so we would be free of the suspense in which we currently find ourselves.

We found it good and advisable to let N. Rominger leave for a time as well, because everyone told us that the Georgians would take all white people, thus also him, even though he is just a hireling. This will avoid danger and perhaps save the money to get him freed if he were taken — because people know from experience that you can accomplish a lot with them with money. I hope we agree with your thoughts and view about this as well. We are truly very sorry that most of our crops will have to lie untended because of this, since this makes the prospect for our cattle next winter very gloomy, as I already mentioned to you in one of my previous letters.

The Georgia mail has just brought us your kind letter of Feb. 12, as well as the one from the 16th with *Wöchentliche* and *Monatliche Nachrichten* and $250 for Br. Copeland, who, as I already informed you, has moved to Indiana State. Thank you most sincerely for everything. I have to postpone answering the kind letter you wrote to all missionaries on the 12th of last month until next week, since there is not enough time for that now.

But where could our letters be lying? Your letter was on the road for 20 days. I sent my Diary and hope that it is now in your hands.

Mother Byhan is currently very weak and sickly again. Praise God, the rest of us are well! We ask you to please greet our dear children and friends in the best manner. You, dear Brn. and Srs., also accept the best greetings from us and remember us further in your prayer before our dear Lord. Your faithfully obliged Br.,

Gottlieb Byhan

[M 407-2: Springplace Diary.]

Sun., Mar. 6. [Spg.] The Sunday services were as usual.

Mar. 7. [Spg.] Br. Clauder came here from McNair's on a visit. Naeman Rominger, who was also staying at McNair's so as not to fall into the hands of the Georgians, also returned from there and stayed here at Spring Place again to take care of the fieldwork, since it seems that the Georgians are not in a great hurry to take the white people away.

[J 299C-1: Aeltesten Conferenz, meeting in Salem. Translated by C. Daniel Crews. See also *Records: N.C.*, 8:3997.]

Mar. 9. Several letters from our dear Brn. Byhan and Clauder in the Cherokee Nation report their sad situation in which they have been displaced according to the laws of Georgia, and that Br. and Sr. Byhan must remain in Springplace, since he cannot leave the Post Office, and that Br. Clauder and Nathl. Byhan, according to the advice of the Prov. H. Cfz., should flee for the time being on March 1 to our friend Mr. David McNair, who lives in the Tennessee district, and that Srs. Clauder and Gambold should stay behind at Oochgelogy and come under the support of Br. Abrm. Wm. Hicks and his son Jay to keep an eye on and protect our property.

Almost all the white men have moved from Cherokee Land with their families for this reason. And so the mission in Oochgelogy has suffered a great loss of the women as well as the men belonging to the Gemeinlein, and also Br. and Sr. Copeland are thinking of moving to Indiana.

[M 415-3a-1: Translated by Julie Tomberlin Weber. Addressed to: Revd. Theodore Schulz, Salem, Stokes County, North Carolina. Postmark: Athens, Te., Mar. 11, 18¾. Received Mar. 23.]

Connesauga, C.N., March 9, 1831

Dear Brother Schulz,

On the 6th I was delighted to receive your kind letter of Feb. 16th here at our good friend McNair's, sent from Spring Place through the post. From this I learned that you had sent a joint letter on the 12th [of last month] with $250 for Br. and Sr. Copeland, but I had not yet heard anything about its arrival, so I worried it had been lost along with the money, like the letter to me of Feb. 2nd. The following morning, the 7th, I set out on the road for Spring Place, despite the heavy rains and swollen creeks, to see if the money had indeed been lost or if it had arrived. My efforts turned out well. I safely crossed the high creeks without making the horses swim for dear life or getting wet (except for the rain), and there I discovered that your kind letter and the enclosure had safely reached Spring Place on the 6th.

Yesterday I returned here to this place of refuge, where I watch the reign of terror alone with various sad reflections between fear and hope, and I plead that this might soon end. You will have seen from my last letter that Srs. Gambold and Clauder stayed behind in Ochgeelogy and that Jay Hicks has assumed the job of managing the fieldwork there, as much as he can alone. Sr. Gambold will tend the livestock there with her well-known care. Sr. Clauder could not agree to leave old Mother Gambold alone there with some children, and so she stayed too. This is even better since we have only a very small open house here in which beds stand (Nath.'s and mine), and we stay there only in the evenings and during the night.

Nonetheless, I made arrangements with good old William Ab. Hicks that if the Georgians begin using fire and sword to carry out their threats, he should immediately drive my family and all their things here with his wagon. Everything is already packed and can be loaded in a few hours, and he should then care for the things that are immoveable and the cattle.

Meanwhile, as of today, none of the movement of the military we feared has been fulfilled, although it is still expected. There are many Georgia Surveyors in the country along with a posse

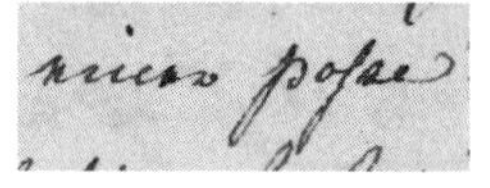

of chain carriers, packmen & horses & wagons, and we had the unenviable pleasure of hosting 10 of these people here for several days. They did behave in a very civil manner and spent the evenings singing spiritual hymns!!

As far as I know, the missionaries of the American Board remained at their post, following the advice of their Directors, which Mr. Worcester cordially shared with me, and they will stay there until the Georgians remove them by force. Mr. McLeod, the superintendant of the Methodist mission, and Nathl. Byhan and I are the only refugee missionaries, and we are all here.

I must admit the situation seems strange enough to me. I cannot understand at all how our dear Cherokee mission can exist for long under the currently prevailing circumstances. The plan to visit our dear Brethren and Sisters from here involves as many dangers as if I had just remained with them, because if it is actually true that that Law is intended to cause the expulsion of the missionaries, which one really cannot doubt, then all the plans for the continuation of the mission work will be ensnared in pretenses. We cannot expect our Brethren and Sisters to come this far to visit us; they show too little desire for encouragement and spiritual refreshment. Their minds are too filled with external concerns and pressures for them to have enough desire for comfort from their own teachers to travel 20, 30, 40 or 50 miles here alone or in company to see us.

It is known that the mission work here is very scattered, because those who have been baptized live so far apart. This makes visiting very difficult and requires a patient disposition toward all the difficulties associated with this, as I learned thoroughly this winter. I am not close to saying I am sick and tired of bearing this cross — no! If circumstances now were the same as they were last winter, I would gladly endure hunger, thirst, heat, cold, and exhaustion, as I did before. Now, however, problems are everywhere. Part of the flock has been scattered, threatening enemies are creeping around and cursing the missionaries with horrible curses and threats. Still we are not the first to have endured such trials. It was the same for our Savior. It has always been the same for His messengers and it will be the same as long as light and darkness are at war against each other.

Now trusting in the Lord God, I am planning to visit the dear ones in Ooyug_____ privately next week. I will try to take along George Augustus as interpreter and visit everyone I can find. But first I am planning to visit the U. S. Agent Montgomery 23 miles from here to see if the field attached to Ooy______y belongs to the Nation or to the U.S. Government. People say the old emigrant places were given back to the Nation in 1819. I would like to know if this is true or not. I will not close this letter until I have been there, so I can let you know what I accomplish.

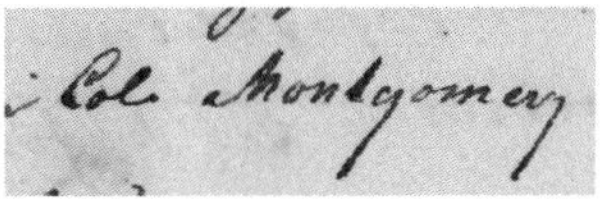

Agency, C.N., Mar. 11. Yesterday evening I arrived here and was cordially received and lodged by Col. Montgomery, with whom I had a thorough conversation. As I expected, he is completely on the side of the Genl. Government. His views regarding the Cherokees are pretty much the same already frequently expressed by Eaton, etc. If the Cherokees reached the decision to emigrate and we moved with them, our improvements would be paid for whether we went or not. However, if the Cherokees remain, as it now looks as if they will, but we missionaries found ourselves forced by the Georgia law to leave the country, Col. Montgomery does not believe we would receive compensation for the abandoned houses, etc. He believes Br. Byhan is completely safe as long as he serves as Postmaster and that I acted wisely in following your good advice, and that the field attached to Ochg____y was previously sold to the U.S. by an emigrant; it was returned to the Cherokee through the 1819 treaty, and it could not be taken from us. However, he had been instructed by the Sec. of War not to pay for improvements like this again if they were sold.

This is pretty much what he said freely without hesitation.

Concerning the support we used to receive from the U.S. Government, through him, he says that he no longer received this, and the Sec. of War had informed him that this allowance would now be used for scholars west of the Mississippi. Therefore, we could expect nothing more from the Government.

Otherwise, it is his private opinion that Georgia will not shrink from its stand, and blood will be shed. May the Lord prevent this. That's all for now, in haste. Greet my dear parents and all interested friends. Your faithfully obliged Br. and unworthy fellow Brother,

H. G. Clauder

[M 407-2: Springplace Diary.]

Mar. 11. [Spg.] Br. Nathl. Byhan, who had gone on the 1st to Mr. McNair's for safety, so as not to be taken away by the Georgians, arrived here for a visit and thought he would stay here until we heard further whether the Georgians were really planning to act according to their strict law.

Mar. 12. [Spg.] In the evening a number of our Brn. and Srs. had already arrived here for tomorrow's Sunday services.

[M 415-1a-13: Translated by Julie Tomberlin Weber. Addressed to: Revd. Theodor Schulz, Salem, Stokes County, North Carolina. Postmark: Springplace, C.N., Mar. 13. Free. G. Byhan, P.M. Received Mar. 23.]

Springplace, March 12, 1831
(10 o'clock in the morning)

Dearly beloved Br. Schulz,

Your two kind letters of Feb. 12 and 16, along with *Monatliche* and *Wöchentliche Nachrichten* and $250 for Br. Copeland, reached me on the same day as I already informed you in my last letter to you dated the 5th of this month. We thank you most sincerely for everything.

We still live in anticipation of the things that are supposed to happen to us. All is still and quiet. We have not heard about the Georgians trying to get the white people in Cherokee Country to swear the oath, and really there are none left in the country, because they have all moved away except the missionaries, who are all peacefully at home as far as we know. One might almost presume the Georgians had warning from Washington, since they are behaving so quietly, but it is more likely that the One who has power in heaven and earth and who has the hearts of humans in His hand has mercifully heard the prayers of so many children of God in the Christian world. He can guide them as He wants, and He does not give His children more than they can bear.

Still the danger might not be past yet, because the Georgia Militia is still in the country. We have heard that they must have received a certain order — but we cannot find out from where — because they are no longer buying provisions. We do not know for sure whether this is true or not, because so many rumors circulate in the country that one does not know which are true. Still the Georgians are busy measuring out or dividing the country into districts or counties, because the surveyors were at McNair's last week and had walked, measured, and drawn the border between the state of Tennessee and Georgia. The line goes approximately one mile south of McNair's.

Br. Clauder and our Nathl. have been staying at McNair's for almost 2 weeks now, but their stay there is unbearable for them. Nathl. came to Spring Place yesterday evening with the intention of staying here. Br. Clauder is also planning to return to Och____y next week, as he told us on his visit here last Monday. Currently he is on a visit at the Agent's in Tennessee.

From your kind letter I see that you believe it might be good if I inform the General Postmaster of my situation and the circumstances in which I find myself as Postmaster. At the very beginning, when I first saw the Georgia Law, it occurred to me immediately that I should inform the General Postmaster of my situation and get his thoughts and advice. I had already written a statement to send to him. But on second consideration I decided it would be more advisable not to write him about this matter, because I was convinced, as I still am, that the Georgians would not be allowed to close the Post Office here, since 4 mail routes end here, and generally they could not disturb the postal system. Therefore, I decided to see what the Georgians will do with the postmasters here in the country. As things appear to us now, I say now, it seems as if the Georgians won't bother themselves much more about the white people in the country here. Still we do not know what might perhaps happen unexpectedly that might cause them to come and enforce their Law. We thus commend ourselves further to your faithful remembrance and prayer before our dear Lord.

Br. Clauder will surely have informed you that the money you sent for Br. Alex. Copeland arrived here too late to give it to him. We cannot send it to him from here either, because we do not know where he will settle. It would not be appropriate to send it back to Salem either. And so we must use it here to finally get out of debt for once, indeed for the first time since Br. Clauder and I have been here. We want to try to remain free of debt as long as we can.

Has my Diary through Jan. 16 of this year not reached you yet? Since I am reminded anew each post day to send it, I have sent it in three sections and hope that none of it has been lost. Some days ago my dear wife had a bad attack of cramps throughout her body and especially in her chest, and it seemed as if this might be her end. Praise God, she recovered after several hours and is once again quite well, although she is very weak.

Before I close this letter, I will wait for the Georgia mail to see if it will bring us anything else from you dear ones in Salem, or if we might perhaps hear more about the proceedings of the Georgians against the white people in this country.

4 o'clock in the afternoon. The Georgia mail has just brought me your kind letter of Feb. 23, for which we thank you sincerely. We cannot learn anything about the Georgians from the post rider. He says everything was quiet on the Georgia line. Praise and thanks to God!! It seems almost as if we might soon be able to breathe freely again. We also learned from the newspapers we just received that it appears as if the Cherokee matter in Congress might turn out in favor of the Cherokees. May God grant that the matter might soon go in one direction or the other, so we know where we stand. Now God, who watches out for right and justice, will make this happen! We will continue to trust in Him.

I also just received in the New Echota mail a letter from Sr. Clauder in Och_____y, from which I share the following:

"We sit here in a blessed calm, more so than we have had in a long time. We hear many lies from time to time, but we are already so used to this that we do not pay them any attention. If we believed half of what we hear, we would have run away with all our belongings a long time ago. Last week the storekeeper in New Echota — Mr. Tarbin — was in Georgia, to swear the oath and he supposedly spent the night at Scudder's — where the Georgia soldiers are — and he said he had heard they are threatening to treat the missionaries horribly when they finally come. He also said the Georgians would take people when the Court in Georgia had ended. He says if they had taken them [earlier], their Trial would have been over right away, but this way they could hold them in Jail until the Sept. Court, and their Trial would not be until then.

"We also heard yesterday evening that one Georgian was staying with Tarbin in New Echota for a couple of days. They are supposed to have gone there — Tarbin and the Georgians — to

Worcester, and are supposed to have said: 'Well Mr. Worcester, the Georgia Officers are come here to take you. It is time you should be off or else fall into their hands.' Mr. Worcester replied: 'If they wish to see me or take me, I shall be in my house. They are welcome to come here if they want me.'

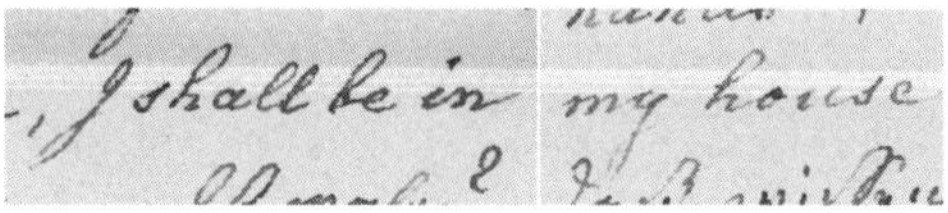

"Is this true? We do not yet know.

"We are all well and continue as well as we can. Our things are half packed and half unpacked. Sr. Gambold has not yet packed anything, and she will not do so for now. If we do not hear anything else about leaving until next week, we will begin working in the garden."

That is all from Sr. Clauder's letter.

From the letter I just received from you, I see that my Diary has not arrived at your place on time, which I was not happy to hear. I sent it in three sections — as reported above — specifically from 1 Sept. 1830 to 16 Jan. 1831. Where could it be lying? Perhaps it will still arrive. I must hurry to close this letter now. I do not know anything else to add except that we commend ourselves anew to your prayer before our dear Lord. We are confident that you remember us in your prayers — we feel it! We greet you all most sincerely — also our dear children. I remain your loving Br.,

Gottl. Byhan

[M 407-2: Springplace Diary.]

Sun., Mar. 13. [Spg.] Most of our Brn. and Srs. had gathered here. After the praying of the Church Litany was the sermon on today's Doctrinal Text [Matt. 27:56]: My God, my God, why hast thou forsaken me? After this the Brn. and Srs. sang a hymn in the Cherokee language, and Br. Samuel offered a prayer and held a talk for the congregation.

Mar. 14. [Spg.] Toward evening we finally received the extremely disturbing news that in accordance with their laws, the Georgians were in New Echota last night and this morning and had arrested Mr. Worcester, postmaster there, Mr. Wheeler, printer at the press there, Mr. Proctor, missionary in Carmel, and Mr. Gann, in the neighborhood of New Echota, whose wife belongs to the Ochgeloogy Gemeine. They have taken them to Georgia as prisoners. This news made us uneasy, as can easily be imagined, not a little because we are presumably next in line. And so we expect the Georgians here in Spring Place any day.

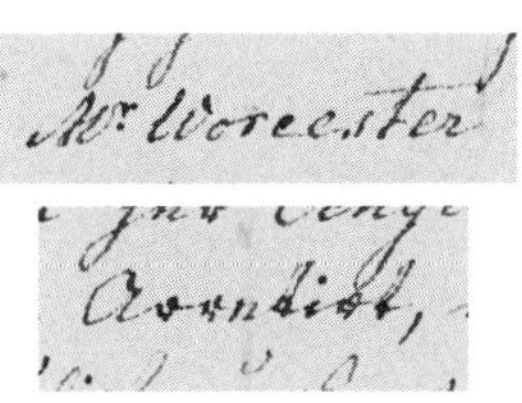

Mar. 15. [Spg.] In the morning Mr. Jay Hicks, who is staying in Ochgeloogy during Br. Clauder's absence, came to our place and confirmed the news of the arrest of the above people. Mr. Jay Hicks was an eyewitness to the whole event. Today we also received a letter from Sr. Clauder, in which she writes that she will now pack up their things, because it is now clear enough that it is not advisable at this time for Br. Clauder to return to Ochgeloogy from Mr. McNair's, and that the Srs. will also not be able to stay there much longer. At the above news, Br. Nathl. Byhan and Br. Nae. Rominger, who have been staying again at Spring Place since last week, went back to Mr. McNair's for their personal safety.

Mar. 16. [Spg.] Mr. Dazizi, who has been here since day before yesterday with three horses and a wagon, set out on the road home this morning. Since he is now setting up his own household about 10 miles from here, we will surely be able to get him more often as an interpreter now. He lived 18 miles from here until now. He promised to serve us in this way as often as we ask and his circumstances are such that he can come here.

Mar. 18. [Spg.] We had the pleasure of seeing Br. Clauder from Mr. McNair's at our place. He was on his way to Ochgeloogy to pick up his wife and child there, since it is not advisable for himself to go back there to live at this time.

[M 415-1a-14: Translated by Julie Tomberlin Weber. Addressed to: Revd. Theod. Shulz, Salem, Stokes County, North Carolina. Postmark: Springplace, Cher. Nat., Mar. 20. Free. G. Byhan, P.M. Received Mar. 30.]

Springplace, March 15, 1831

Dearly beloved Br. Schulz,

Since my last letter to you dated the 12th of this month, the danger of being taken by the Georgians has come nearer, and although I do not yet know if I will have the opportunity to put this in the mail here in Spring Place on the next mail day, I will still try to get these lines into your hands one way or another.

The following has taken place since my last letter to you. Yesterday evening we received news from New Echota that the Georgia soldiers, approximately 35 of them, moved into New Echota day before yesterday evening, the 13th, where they brought along Mr. Proctor, missionary from Carmel, as a prisoner. Early on the 14th, yesterday morning, they arrested the following persons in New Echota: Revd. Mr. Worcester — postmaster — Mr. Wheeler, printer in the press there, Mr. Gann, who lives approximately 4 or 5 miles from New Echota. His wife belongs to the Ochg_____y Gemeine. Yesterday morning they left for Georgia with these 4 persons.

This is the first case in which the postmaster was not spared, and so I already know what I should expect here. However, I cannot, and in my view am not allowed to, abandon the Post Office. Therefore, I will await my fate. These are my thoughts: They might perhaps drag me to Georgia, where I will have to endure a trial, and then I will be set free. Time will tell. The Savior is our only comfort in the current difficult situation!

Nathl. and Nae. Rominger had been staying here in Spring Place again for a number of days, because it had seemed as if the Georgians would not be as bold as they actually are, but they went back to McNair's today, so they would not fall into their hands. I do not know what will happen to our crops this year.

The future looks extremely grim, especially for our cattle. Currently I have only the single Indian Br. Niclaus Ignatius, who is supposed to take care of the crops, and I believe you know how things are with the Indians' work and their planting. Sr. Clauder will now probably go to Mr. McNair's next week as well, since Br. Clauder can no longer be seen in Ochgeloogy, at least for the time being, if he doesn't want to run the risk of being arrested. Sr. Gambold will probably stay there for a while. May God continue to help!

The 17th. Since I wrote the above, nothing else much has happened and I have not heard anything else since then about what might have happened to those who were arrested. Since the Georgians have not spared the postmaster in New Echota now, but arrested him, and I am in fact worried that they might not spare me either, I now consider it necessary to report my difficult situation to the General Postmaster, and I have accordingly done so. The only reason I did not write to him earlier was this: I could not believe that they would assault the postmasters.

And so we expect the Georgians any day, indeed any hour, and expect that they will come and take me as well. But I and my securities cannot and will not be answerable for the damage and confusion that would result if they took me away, because as long as I am postmaster here, I have no right to allow anyone else to open the mails. I will keep the mail keys in my protection until I receive orders from the General Postmaster to hand them over to someone else. Each post rider must then take his mail back with him to where he brought it from — and I cannot begin to imagine the kind of confusion this would cause, because the end of 4 mail routes is here and a kind of Distributing Office. Horrible confusion would result from this.

The 18th. This morning we had the joy of seeing Br. Clauder arrive here from Mr. McNair's. He was on the way to Ochgilloogy to get his dear wife and child from there and take them to McNair's, where they will now begin their own household for the time — because they have a little house for themselves there — until we see further what direction things will take and how things might twist and turn. In any case, it is certainly not advisable at this time for Br. Clauder to stay in Ochgillogy again, at least not for now, because the Georgians would soon have him arrested there.

He will surely have informed you in detail himself that Br. Clauder visited the Agent and others in the area near Tennessee and what he told the Agent about our situation. There is no doubt the Agent knows everything about how the Georgians are acting and what they are planning to do to oppress and torment the Indians and us as well. The Brn. at McNair's, Clauder and Byhan, are planning to begin a school for the children in the neighborhood there as long as they have to stay there, which is quite nice. Br. Clauder will probably have informed you of this himself. It almost seems as if a big change lies ahead for the Ochgiloogy mission place, but it is still somewhat too early to say more about this matter. I hope Br. Clauder writes you his thoughts, quite freely and openly, explaining what he thinks about the entire matter. The time has come when everything must be said, both the good and the bad. But I will not express myself about this point until I have more cause to do so, and this is perhaps not far away.

The 19th. I have just enough time to inform you that I received your kind letter of March 2 with the enclosed $42. Many thanks for everything! I will answer the letter itself with the next mail. I do not know anything else to add except that we greet you all sincerely and also our dear children. The Savior will continue to help! I remain your loving, humble Br.,

Gottl. Byhan

N.B. I can send this letter with the mail from here after all, as I hardly expected on the 15th, last Tuesday.

G. B.

1831, part 4

[Springplace (M 407-2) and Oochgeelogy (M 409-1) Diaries. Translated by Julie Tomberlin Weber. Handwritings are Henry G. Clauder's (Ooch.) and Gottlieb Byhan's (Spg.).]

Sun., Mar. 20. [Spg.] The services were as usual. When our Br. Israel read the news in the *Cherokee Phönix* in the Cherokee language about the imprisonment of Mr. Worcester and some of the other white people, it led to a discussion with our Brn. and Srs. who were present about our current situation. During this we saw that the Indian Brethren and Sisters have compassion with our current difficult situation. We told them that we and they can do nothing in this situation in which we find ourselves except to turn diligently in prayer to Him, our Savior, the helper in all trouble, and ask Him to be and remain our comfort and our helper in these desperate times. They seemed to be very dejected when they heard that the Georgians had arrested the above-mentioned people, and they promised to present these circumstances and our and their trouble to the Savior in prayer. The Indian Connondoah, who does not belong to us, seemed to become somewhat upset about the way the Georgians acted, and said in a pretty serious tone that they would do something if the Georgians should take Br. Byhan away from here. He was thanked and asked to act calmly, because God would not give us more than we could bear, and besides it could also harm them, the Cherokees, if they do not behave quietly. Besides we believe that everything that happens to us and is decided about us must serve our best interests, because no hair falls from our heads unless it is God's will.

Mar. 21. [Ooch.] Br. and Sr. Clauder left this post which was so dear to them, after they very sincerely bade farewell to the Indian Brn. and Srs. the previous day. Our request to the Lord, for whom nothing is impossible, was that He would soon grant us peace and quiet again, and that He would allow us to carry out his work here in this place. We brought Him our humble thanks for hearing our pleas immediately, because the very next morning after we arrived at McNair's, a messenger brought us a letter from our friend Elias Boudinott with the news that all the missionaries who recently were imprisoned had been declared free in Georgia during their interrogation. The rest of the missionaries would not be allowed to be disturbed, since the Government of the United States supported and protected the missionaries here through subsidies. Now we were able to begin our return journey to Ooyugillogy in safety, with praise and thanks. We did this on the 25th after bidding farewell to our friend McNair, with whom Br. Clauder had lived for 3 weeks, grateful for all the love and friendship we had enjoyed.

Mon., Mar. 28. [Ooch.] Br. and Sr. Clauder returned safely to Oochgillogy and rejoiced to find those who had remained there in good health. The previous day, Sunday, 22 persons had gathered here and Brn. William Abr. and George Hicks had served them with talks. In the night of *the 29th*, we had a strong storm which made the streams impassable. We were happy and grateful that we had reached home before this.

Mar. 21. [Spg.] Toward evening Br. and Sr. Clauder arrived here with their child in their single span wagon.

Mar. 22. [Spg.] They went on to Mr. McNair's, where they have their first stop and will run their own household until we see what the fate of the rest of the missionaries in this country, and especially of those who were recently arrested by the Georgians, will be. In the afternoon Br. Byhan received a letter from Mr. Elias Boudinott in which he reported that the missionaries, Mr. Worcester, Proctor, and Thomson, had had their hearing in Georgia and that they, the missionaries, were to be seen as Agents of the government of the United States. As a result they would be released again. Also that Mr. Worcester will be back at his post in New Echota in a few days. We ourselves hardly knew what to say for astonishment and joy, and what to do. We could not keep back the tears of gratitude and joy, because we saw the immediate assistance of the Lord here. He has seen our trouble, our worry, and our confusion, and has heard our prayers and taken mercy on us, and when the trouble was greatest, He, our dear Lord, was closest. Praise and thanks be brought to Him for His merciful assistance! Br. Byhan immediately sent the above-mentioned letter from Mr. Boudinott with the Indian Br. Niclous Ignatius to Br. Clauder at Mr. McNair's, and he received it early on *the 23rd*. As a result of this news, Br. Nathl. Byhan also returned from there today.

Mar. 24. [Spg.] Today the missionary Elsworth and his wife stopped in at our place on their way from New Echota to Brainerd and spent the night here. Mr. Elsworth confirmed everything that Mr. Boudinott had reported in his letter several days ago, and that Mr. Worcester is already back at his post in New Echota. Mr. Elsworth also told us that Judge Clayton, who was the presiding Judge in the Court in which those who were arrested had their hearing, and who by the way is not very inclined toward the Indians, is supposed to have explained that Mr. Worcester was excepted from the famous Law first as postmaster and then as missionary, because the missionaries are under the Protection of the Genl. Government. It has also been decided that the missionaries will be able to carry out their calling in the future without being disturbed.

Mar. 25. [Spg.] Early today Brn. Nathl. Byhan and Naeman Rominger went by wagon to Mr. McNair's, and Sr. Byhan went along for a visit, to bring back the rest of the things the Brn. had taken there when they fled. Mr. and Mrs. Elsworth also set out on the road to Brainerd today. Toward evening Br. and Sr. Clauder also arrived here on their way back to Ochgeloogy from Mr. McNair's. We had a strong storm during the night, but little rain.

Mar. 26. [Spg.] Toward evening Sr. Byhan and Nathl. Byhan and Naeman Rominger returned with the wagon from McNair's. They brought all the household equipment back with them that they had taken there when they fled. We all were very happy and thankful that after the unrest and flight of almost four weeks, we can hope that we can now perhaps live in peace for the most part.

[M 415-1a-15: Translated by Julie Tomberlin Weber. Addressed to: Revd. Theodor Schulz, Salem, Stokes County, North Carolina. Postmark: Springplace, Mar. 27. Free. G. Byhan, P.M. Received Apr. 6.]

Springplace, March 24, 1831

Dearly beloved Br. Schulz,

Full of praise and gratitude toward our dear Lord and Savior, I can now inform you that circumstances since my last concerned letter, dated the 15th, 17th, and 19th of this month, have changed greatly and have improved considerably. In the last letter mentioned to you, I informed you that the Georgians had finally arrested Revd. Mr. Worcester, missionary in New Echota, and postmaster there, Mr. Proctor, missionary in Carmel, and Mr. Thomson, missionary in Hightower, and a couple of other white persons in the neighborhood around New Echota, and they took them with them to Georgia to be questioned there. These people have now faced their interrogation and indeed in the Supreme Court in Gwinnett County, Georgia. Judge Clayten, who is not cherished by the Cherokees, was the presiding Judge. He explained in the Court that the well-known Law concerning the white people in Cherokee country does not concern the missionaries at all, because they are under the protection of the Genl. Government. Thus they were exempted from this Law. Mr. Worcester, as postmaster, was free anyway because as postmaster he was an Agent of the Genl. Government. Judge Clayton is supposed to have said that this Law is a wretched, or as he expressed himself — a miserable Law — and he hopes that it will be repealed in their next Legislature.

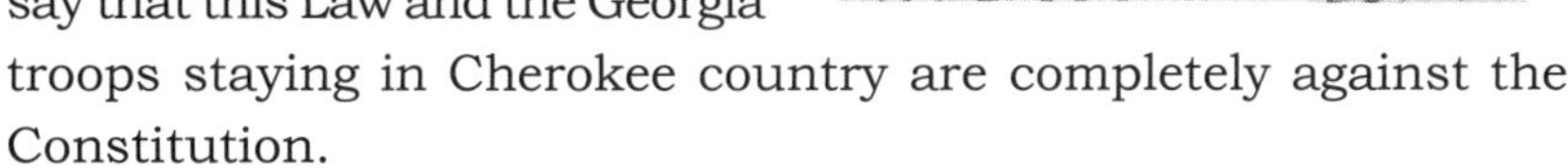

Many people in Georgia also say that this Law and the Georgia troops staying in Cherokee country are completely against the Constitution.

Praise God! We now know where we stand and can now breathe more freely. When trouble is the greatest, the Lord's help is certainly closest. He, the helper in all distress, can guide the hearts of humans as He wants to. The Savior looked upon His children and heard our tears and sighs, which were sent up for the poor Cherokees and us to the throne of grace, and He did not withhold His assistance. All praise and adoration belongs to Him for this!

Last Monday the 21st Br. and Sr. Clauder came to our place in their wagon, and early on Tuesday the 22nd they continued their journey on to Mr. McNair's, where they will set up their own household in a small house. At 4 o'clock in the afternoon on the latter day, the 22nd, I received a letter from our friend Elias Boudinott in which he informed me of the outcome of the matter with Mr. Worcester and the others who had been arrested. That same hour I sent this letter and the single Indian Brother Nicl. Ignatius to Br. Clauder at McNair's, and I hear he will return here to Springplace tomorrow, the 25th. Our Nathl. returned yesterday already with Br. Ignatius. Mr. Elsworth, missionary in Brainerd, is just arriving here with his wife. He confirmed everything Mr. Boudinott reported to us in his letter, since he had just been visiting Mr. Worcester in New Echota and now is returning to Brainerd. This entire matter will cost the Presbyterian missionaries about $200.

Despite all this, however, the Georgia soldiers will continue taking all the white people in the country according to this miserable Law, to cause them difficulties and expenses even if they can't do anything else with them. But there are almost no more in the country or in the Georgia area, because they have all moved away.

March 26th. Yesterday evening Br. and Sr. Clauder arrived back here at our place in Spring Place with their belongings on their way back to Och______y. And yesterday Nathl. and Rominger and my wife also went to Mr. McNair's with our wagon to pick up the rest of the things left there. But now I am worried about our Rominger, because everyone believes that the Georgians will not spare him, and I myself do not believe it. But how should our very extensive fieldwork be continued if we are not allowed to keep any white workers? We do still have our single Br. Nicl. Ignatius, and we could also perhaps get a couple of other young Indians to work, but I must admit not much will come of this, because our work is an unfamiliar thing to the Indians. So the outlook for our crops is bad indeed. We have already been set back considerably in our fieldwork because of this miserable Georgia Law.

Now perhaps things will become even clearer regarding the Rommingers [Clauders], and in any case my next letter will explain more matters for serious consideration which I cannot mention yet at this time.

Your kind letter of March 2 and the enclosed $42 arrived on the 19th of this month, as I already reported in my last letter. Sincere thanks for this. It was just a rumor that the Georgians would put an attachment on our mission place and improvements, and there was nothing to the matter, as Br. Clauder himself will surely write. We still do not know where Br. and Sr. Copeland are at this time. Br. Clauder will also have reported that Br. Copeland could not receive the money you sent him, because he was already gone.

You will probably have to allow us some time to estimate the value of our mission places, because this is not such an easy matter for us. We will try to make a rough calculation of our property here as soon as possible. I am expecting the Georgia mail any minute, so I will not close this letter until I see if I receive something from your dear hand.

4 o'clock in the afternoon. The Georgia mail just arrived, but it brings me nothing from you, which makes me uneasy. Perhaps something will come tomorrow by way of Knoxville, Tenn. I just received a letter from Mr. Proctor, missionary in Carmel, in which he writes among other things:

[Br. Byhan copies Mr. Proctor's letter in English:]

"You will be pleased to hear that the Georgia Law does not affect your missionaries & ours. The judge decided, that the missionaries who have received money from the Genl. Government were Government Agents, & therefore might remain at their work unmolested, & I furthermore heard Col. Montgomery ask Col. Sandford if Br. Clauder could return to his family, & his Labors, & remain unmolested, & he answered him that he could, in as much as that he had received money from the Genl. Government."

[Br. Byhan continues his letter to Br. Schulz in German:]

Br. Clauder just received your letter of the 10th of this month. Continue to remember us with love, and commend us in your thoughts and prayers before our dear Lord. All send their best greetings. Most especially your poor, familiar Br.

Gottl. Byhan

[M 415-1a-16: Translated by Julie Tomberlin Weber. Addressed to: Revd. Theodore Schulz, Salem, Stokes County, North Carolina. Postmark: Springplace, C.N., Mar. 27, paid 18¾. Received Apr. 6. Br. Schulz has penciled in: $6 to be debited from Copeland & paid to Geo. Foltz.]

Spring Place, March 26, 1831

Dear Brother Schulz,

I received your kind letter of Feb. 2 last week when I visited in Ooy_____y, after it had probably spent 6 weeks on the road. Luckily your letter to Br. Byhan of that same date arrived in good time. It contained almost the same thing as the one to me. I also received your dear letter of Feb. 16 in good time; it was sent here in Br. Byhan's pack along with $250. I thank you sincerely for this communication which is so encouraging in these trying times.

It is a shame that Br. and Sr. Copeland had already begun their journey to Indiana before the money designated for them had arrived. In the meantime Br. Byhan will already have reported to you that he and I are using part of it to get completely out of debt. For this I need approximately $16.75 for Ooy_____y. Regarding Br. Copeland, I made an agreement with him that if he really reaches the Brethren and Sisters in Indiana he would send you news of this so that you can send him his money next fall through Brethren who are moving there, perhaps Philip Blum or others.

In an earlier letter to you I reported that Br. Copeland wants you to pay a debt of $6 to Br. George Folz for him. But I see from your statement of the principal & content due Alex. Copeland that no such deduction of $6 has been made. From this I conclude that Br. Folz has not yet been paid. Perhaps you will take the opportunity to satisfy Br. Folz.

Copeland had a heavy load on his small wagon and left with it rather pitiably. We learned that he had to have a new wagon wheel made in the first days of his journey, and he sold various articles for a low price to reduce the load.

Perhaps I do not know where and how to begin describing our circumstances and prospects to you, because almost every day brings new and unexpected things. On the 18th of this month I left McNair's before daybreak and in the evening arrived safely to my loved ones, who were not expecting me in Ooy_____y. So that I would not be seen by spies who are scattered around the country, I went through the bush off the road part of the time, just guiding myself by the sun. After our Brethren and Sisters had arrived for the service on the 20th, and we spent a blessed hour in the awareness of Jesus' presence, I informed them of my decision to go back to McNair's the following day since I saw no other option than to stay there the entire summer, and I would visit them infrequently since the country was unsafe and I would be seen as a resident of the Cherokee Nation. The Brethren and Sisters decided to meet as usual on Sundays for their mutual edification. Both Brother Hickses — George Augustus especially — will be active in this. I must add just parenthetically here that old Wm. Ab. is gradually getting stronger and is continuing his previous quiet, contented walk. May God grant that new troubles do not mislead him to unfaithfulness.

Sr. Gambold received Margaret Mary as a companion and was very hopeful of managing everything with the Lord's assistance. She explained that she would not leave Oochgelogy until she could return to Salem, or the entire matter was closed. At that time it really seemed as if this would be soon, and we assumed it would be. On the following day, we said farewell to Ooy_____y with feelings that I cannot describe. We had loaded the small wagon with some clothes and bedding. Br. Hicks's wagon was supposed to bring the rest of our necessary items the following week, primarily foodstuff. Tuesday the 22nd we arrived safely at McNair's and moved into the little house which Nathl. and I had already occupied 3 weeks earlier. But the following day brought unexpected good news.

Early in the morning Nicholaus, an express messenger sent by Br. Byhan, came with a letter from Elias Boudinott containing the happy news that the arrested missionaries, Proctor, Worcester and Thompson, had been declared free by Judge Clayton (a bitter enemy of the Cherokees) and that under the protection of the Genl. Government they could not be disturbed by the Law. Although the reason for this favorable decision is inexplicable, it is absolutely a matter worthy of gratitude that all the missionaries were immediately declared free. However, the Law still exists and another Judge might perhaps have other views and act more strictly. Still that is not to be expected. And so we are on the return journey now, with grateful hearts.

We are planning to spend the day here tomorrow and on the following day, Monday ([penciled in:] viz. 28th), return to the beloved, quasi-abandoned Ooyugillogy.

But there are admittedly gloomier prospects to face there. We are eagerly awaiting your advice.

Should we start the school anew? Without help it is almost impossible — but many of the Brn. and Srs. are pressing for this.

Sr. Gambold, who served so faithfully, is getting increasingly weak as she grows older, and she cannot continue in her accustomed way. However, as long as she can stand she will be active. We have almost decided not to begin a school, at least not at this time. We have to tell those Brn. and Srs. who are pressing for this no, and explain that it is not possible. We are too weak.

What should I do about the grain that is being grown by Jay Hicks this year? I think you know from my previous letter that he is working on condition — $12 per month if the mission needs the grain. If, however, changes have taken place so that we do not need it, then it is his. He is also taking care of the cattle and all the various other jobs. But it is better to know as soon as possible which of these conditions will be followed. You, dear Brother, will be able to decide this best. By the way, Jay Hicks is a diligent young man with whom one can get along well. He is planning to plant all of our fields so that none, I presume, will lie fallow.

His father, William Abr., acted very fatherly toward the Sisters left behind during my absence of 3 weeks, and he will continue to treat us like this. The same with friendly McNair, with whom I lived for 3 weeks along with my horse. When I asked him for my bill before moving out day before yesterday and I wanted to pay him, he did not ask for a single cent from us. He was happy and grateful that we paid him such a pleasant visit.

I posted my last letter to you in Athens, Ten. It was probably surprising to you. It happened like this. When I had time and opportunity I went over from the Agency to the heavily populated McMinn County just to distribute comforting texts (tracts). I had about 300 of them along and found many who were willing and grateful to receive them and read them. The people were somewhat amazed that they could have little booklets like these at no cost. By accident I met the company of an Agent of the American Sunday School Union who is traveling around in eastern Tennessee to support Sunday schools and with great success. I spent more than a day with him and had the opportunity to participate in his services. Among others, I spent one night with a Mr. Patton, who gave you lodging in 1826 and still remembers you.[1] He is a Presbyterian. My 3-day visit in Tennessee was very instructive. I forgot my own difficult situation. My tracts acquainted me with many friends and followers of our Lord Jesus Christ, with whom I spent pleasant edifying hours. It is almost not necessary to add that I was lovingly provided lodging everywhere for no money.

I hear that Mr. Worcester is back with his family in New Echota, where I am planning to see him and speak with him next Monday. It is said the expenses of his arrest and trial added up to $200. However, I cannot believe that he had to pay this. It is amazing enough that those who became refugees, as I myself did, spent 3 weeks away from loved ones; however, those who were arrested were separated for only 10 days!

Nothing was done for the poor Cherokees in Congress. I have little hope that the Supreme Court will issue a prompt decision through which rapid assistance might be managed. It is obviously the intention of the Genl. Government to sacrifice the poor Cherokees to the destructive laws of Georgia, and it is impossible for them to tolerate them. But the intention of thus forcing the Indians to emigrate will probably fail, because they will await their sad demise here. Perhaps in the end, in desperation and blind anger, they might still attempt bloody revenge against all who are white. May God protect us from this and prevent this land covered in sin from becoming a stage for war and bloodshed, although it is in need of a humbling discipline. Enough about this. I harbor no hope for the situation of the Cherokees!

gar keine Hoffnung für die Sache der Cherok.!

Greet all who are interested, especially my dear parents and your dear family. We are all well. Ignatius is difficult to the point of exhaustion. I remain always your faithfully obliged Br.,

Henry G. Clauder

[1] See *Records: Cherokees*, 7:3448, 3465.

[M 407-2: Springplace Diary.]

Mar. 27. [Spg.] Palm Sunday. In the first service was a talk and prayer, in which we pleaded with the Savior once again to be close to us during the consideration of His bitter sufferings and His death on the cross, and that this would be blessed anew for us and the impression of His bitter suffering in death might never leave our hearts. Then we began reading the story of the Passion Week, which we continued in the second service. Br. Clauder led the services here in Spring Place today.

M*ar. 28.* [Spg.] Br. and Sr. Clauder left here to return to their post in Ochgeloogy. Toward evening a Presbyterian preacher named Hall came to our place and spent the night.

Mar. 29. [Spg.] Mrs. Vann visited us and told us that the Georgia Guard would come into our area in the next few days. A traveler had brought the news that they, the Georgia Guard, wanted to set out yesterday from Fort Gilmer where they were quartered, to go through this area and the border of Alabama. Thus we can now expect them in our area. This news caused us concern once again about Br. Nathl. Byhan and Nae. Rominger. Concerning the former, we would hope that this pretext that he is assistant or clerk in the Post Office will serve to protect him. Concerning Naeman Rominger, however, we were somewhat worried, since we do not know if they will permit us to have a white man as a worker. Naeman Rominger decided to stay and wait for them here, but to be careful that the Georgia Guard does not immediately apprehend him until Br. Byhan, Sr., has asked the commanding officer if we are allowed to keep him as a worker. If they do not permit him to be here, then he must leave here as quickly as possible. This will admittedly put us in a bad position concerning our agriculture. We must have help in any case, and if the fieldwork is done by Indians, who do not know anything about this, then the outlook for the future of our cattle is in fact sad.

[M 415-1a-17: Translated by Julie Tomberlin Weber. Addressed to: Revd. Theodor Shulz, Salem, Stokes County, North Carolina. Postmark: Springplace, C.N., Apr. 3. Free. G. Byhan, P.M. Received Apr. 13. Br. Schulz writes in the address: Answer of the Dept. of War about Springplace's new building, by McKenny.]

Springplace, March 29, 1831

My dear Br. Schulz,

As I already reported, I received your kind letter dated the 2nd of this month on the 19th and now I want to try to reply to various things you mentioned in it.

First, I just wanted to say that since my last letters to you, dated the 24th and 26th, nothing else noteworthy has taken place except that today we heard that the Georgia soldiers are now planning to enter our area and further toward the West Tennessee road as far as Mr. Richard Tayler's, about 24 or 26 miles from here, and then further toward the border of Tennessee and down to the Alabama border. It is still not known what their purpose is. However, we are concerned about our Rominger now, because we do not know if the Georgians will allow him to work for us. I still hope they will allow us to have him, because we have always informed the Genl. Government that we have white people who take care of the fieldwork. So I think they might not have a problem with it. When the Georgians come into our area I hope to get an opportunity to discuss this matter properly and reasonably with the commanding officer. But if they insist that we were no longer allowed to have any white men working for us, then we would truly be in a very bad situation, and the prospects for next winter would be extremely gloomy, especially for our cattle.

Rominger says he will not leave until he actually knows if he is allowed to stay or not, but he will remain on guard so that when they come he does not let them see him until I have learned from them if I can have a white man working for me or not. We will see what happens.

Yesterday Br. and Sr. Clauder moved back to Och____y from here, so that each of us is now back at his post again.

Now to respond to some of the points in your last letter to me. The Georgians have not put an attachment on our improvement in Och____y. We are not hearing any more comments about this, so it was just meaningless talk. The Genl. Government did not pay anything for the construction of our house in Spring Place, although we built it with the knowledge of the Agent, Col. Montgomery, and I had also informed Col. McKenney in Washington about it. The latter just wrote to me that they had no objection to it. He wrote:

[Br. Byhan copies from Col. McKenney's letter in English:]

"In regard to your purpose of erecting a new building, there can be no objection to it — and if the fund will authorize it, some aid may be afforded during the next year."[1]

[Br. Byhan continues his letter to Br. Schulz in German:]

However, nothing ever came. McKenney's letter is dated Dec. 13, 1828.

In the past few days I have taken the time to look through Br. John Gambold's accounts, and as far as I can tell from this, the mission here has received $2,721 since Aug. 1809, from the Genl. Government or from the Genl. Government's Col. Meigs and McMinn, and from Col. Montgomery since I have been here. However, I believe that Br. and Sr. Gambold sometimes received some from Col. Meigs, which was not given by the Genl. Govrt., but the account books do not show how much. I can still remember that — when we lived in Salem — in the years between 1812 and 1820 — I heard they had received a gift[2] from Col. Meigs — so I do not believe that the entire sum noted above was paid by the Genl. Government. This cannot be determined from the books, as I said, because it just says that so much was received from this person or that one.

---

1 See Br. Byhan's copy of Col. McKenney's letter in *Records: Cherokees*, 8:3962.

2 Perhaps, for example, *Records: Cherokees*, 3:1430.

You also expressed your wish that I report to you the value of our houses and improvements. This is a matter which seems

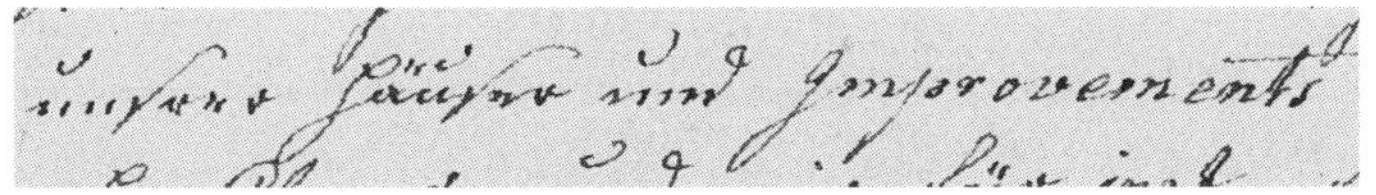
unsere Häuser und Improvements

very complicated to Br. Clauder and me at this time. For example, are we allowed in good conscience to list our houses for what they cost us? We had to pay more, I would say about 50% more, for everything here, and we still have to. And so our establishments are very expensive, indeed higher than we could ever expect to receive for them. It is the same case with our fields. If we valued them according to what I had to pay Jos. Vann for the field I got from him 2 years ago, then our fields would be of considerable expense and value. And if we estimated the entire business too low, we would lose a lot. And so it seems to us that it is still too early to make estimates of both of our establishments. Also we cannot ask anyone for advice in the current circumstances, not even a reasonable man like Mr. McNair, because this would give the immediate impression that we all wanted to move away, and this would be very disadvantageous for the Brn. and Srs. here. ([Margin note:] The Indians would also have their own thoughts about this.) Therefore, we really would like to postpone this matter a while longer, especially since it seems that our departure from here is not so close, although we never know how long we will be able to stay.

I have already informed you that Br. and Sr. Copeland had left before his money reached my hands, and since we do not know where he currently is, we still have the money in our hands. Br. Clauder and I have taken the freedom to use it to pay all of our old debts for once. This is the first time we have been debt free as long as we have been here. We hope there will be no objections to this.

Those would be the main things to reply to your kind letter dated the 2nd of this month. We did not receive a single line from Salem on the last mail day.

Br. and Sr. Clauder moved back to their post in Och_____y last Monday, as previously reported, and Sunday evening we had a joint discussion concerning our schools and how our prospects look overall for the mission work in the future, or from now on. Br. Clauder said that it has always been a pleasure for him to take care of the school in Och_____y, as long as there is help from the Sisters in the household. But Sr. Copeland is gone now, and since his dear wife now has a small child she cannot manage as much in the household any more as in the beginning, although she will certainly not be inactive. Old Mother Gambold is also beginning to get weak and tired, so that she cannot get around as well as she used to anymore, etc, as Br. Clauder will also have written about in detail.

The situation is the same here in Spring Place and even more so, because we have only boys here to help with the housekeeping. Our Nathl. is willing to continue holding school and taking care of it, but since there is too little help, just the same as in Och_____y, we do not see how we can manage. It is impossible for my wife to continue as she used to, and how is she supposed to take care of the housework when she sometimes is so weak that she cannot walk and can hardly sit, and then she is supposed to cook, bake, and do all that is necessary for the work the entire day. Nancy Becker has her hands full with milking, washing, mending and sewing for the children. The latter often takes her 2 days' time each week — and then they must work until 11 in the evening. It has happened that Nancy Becker has sat until midnight mending for the children.

And so we do not see how we can take care of the work and the household with the help we currently have, either here or in Och_____y. Our common decision, therefore, was this: for the time being, until we have learned the thoughts of the H. Conf. in Salem about this matter or until we get more help in the household, we cannot take any more children into the school. It is flat out impossible for us to feed and care for children in our current circumstances.

It can perhaps be said: Get help. Perhaps you can get an Indian girl. We have experienced sufficiently what kind of help this is. We have had Indian girls, and they stayed with us only until they had new shoes, new frocks, etc. Then they said they wanted to go home for a visit, perhaps to see an old grandmother once more, promised to return in 2 or 3 days. In perhaps 2 or 3 months they come and ask if we don't need them again, when the shoes and the clothing they have received from us are torn. This is a true description of what happens with the help of Indian girls. So we can hardly decide to take such help anymore.

Br. Clauder also mentioned that he lost 6 Brn. and Srs. or Gemein members due to the Georgia Law, so that their Gemeine consists of only 11 Brn. and Srs., and he complains that most of them have seldom attended services since Br. and Sr. Clauder have been there. Here in Spring Place, the Brn. and Srs. attend services quite regularly when you consider that most of them live so far from here and are so scattered. Still there are some who seldom come, in whom one would wish for more life from God.

So these would be the main things I have to report for now. Br. Clauder will surely also write a thorough report. We will wait for the thoughts and suggestions of the H. Conf. in Salem, and by the time that reaches us we will also have heard how the Cherokees' matter has turned out in the Supreme Court. Things must be decided in their favor there.

Apr. 2nd. I just received your letter of the 16th of last month. Sincere thanks for this. We also received the *Nat. Intel.* from March 19 with today's mail. Since I have not yet had time to read it carefully, I have nothing more to say about it except this. Things did not turn out as I personally had thought. Now God will help further!

We are very surprised that we have heard nothing more from our children! We greet each of you most sincerely. I greet you especially, your loving friend and Brother,

Gottl. Byhan

1831, part 5

[B 61-3: Provinzial Helfer Conferenz, meeting in Salem. Translated by C. Daniel Crews.]

Wed., Mar. 30. We received a letter from Br. Byhan dated the 19th [15th, etc.] of this month reporting that the State of Georgia indeed through military force not only has imprisoned the whites living in the Cherokee Nation but also on the 14th took two Presbyterian Missionaries, one of whom is Mr. Worcester the Postmaster in New Echota, as prisoners into Georgia. Br. Gb. Byhan is now expecting the same fate at any moment, but is patiently and with trust in God's help continuing on with his office as postmaster in accord with our advice and his own conviction. At the same time he indicated that the other Brethren are undisturbed at Mr. McNair's, and Sr. Clauder is planning to follow them there also from Oochgelogy as soon as possible. The widowed Sr. Gambold is of a mind to remain there alone with the assistance of her neighbor Br. Wm. Abr. Hicks, who has left his son Jay at her house to support her.

This disturbing report was completely contrary to our expectations, since according to the Constitution of the United States, and even in respect to the last harsh laws of Georgia, one can believe and maintain that officials of the United States Government are to remain without challenge. We decided accordingly that by today's post — as Directors of the Missionaries here — to write to Gov. George R. Gilmer in Milledgeville and apply for protection for Br. Gb. Byhan until he receives an answer to his report to the General Postmaster in Washington or until he is relieved, and that he be allowed to remain free.

Since the Supreme Court of the United States also has now dismissed the lawsuit of the Cherokee Nation against the State of Georgia, since it was set forth in the name of the Cherokee Nation as a foreign state and they are not recognized as that, and therefore did not stand under their jurisdiction, we must therefore wait and see to what decision the poor Cherokee Nation will now come.

[Springplace (M 407-2) and Oochgeelogy (M 409-1) Diaries. Translated by Julie Tomberlin Weber. Handwritings are Henry G. Clauder's (Ooch.) and Gottlieb Byhan's (Spg.).]

Mar. 30th. [Ooch.] Br. Clauder visited the Brn. and Srs. in the neighborhood.

Mar. 31. [Spg.] In the evening a number of Brn. and Srs. had already arrived here for tomorrow's observance of Good Friday. Mr. Dav. Steiner Dazizi also came here today. Tomorrow and on Easter Sunday he will serve us as interpreter in our services.

Apr. 1. [Spg.] Good Friday. Most all of our Brn. and Srs., some Indians who do not belong to us, and our closest neighbors gathered for the services. During the consideration of His bitter sufferings and death, we could feel the Savior in our midst, especially in the last service. The tears shed by those present also testify to this. Today we had storms and strong downpours of rain the entire day, so that many of our Brn. and Srs. could not go home and had to stay here.

Apr. 1. [Ooch.] On Good Friday we had heavy rains the entire day, so only those who had been baptized could come to the service. A remarkable thing happened during the reading of the story of Jesus' Passion, when such a dark rain cloud passed above that we barely got enough light through the window to read.

Apr. 2. [Spg.] We had beautiful warm weather again, but on

Apr. 3. [Spg.] Easter Sunday it looked like rain again. Thus it happened that at 10 o'clock, after the Brn. and Srs. who had gone home on Good Friday had come again, we prayed the Easter Litany in the Saal, or in the church. We had a strong storm, and it was accompanied by heavier rains than we have had yet this spring. At half past 11 was the sermon on the words: The Lord is risen indeed [Luke 24:34]. At 1 o'clock we had the blessed enjoyment of the body and blood of Jesus in Holy Communion. The married Br. Emanuel and the married Sr. Lydia Elisabeth, Br. Boas's wife, observed as candidates during this. After this the Brn. and Srs. were informed in a discussion that we would currently not be able to take any children into the school because of lack of help in the household, and that we will also report this to the Directors in Salem, in the hope that perhaps they will send help and support. We hope and wish for this, so that at least we will be able to take the children of our Brn. and Srs. into the school. The Brn. and Srs. agreed that under these circumstances in which we currently find ourselves, we cannot take in any children, and they promised to wait contentedly until we have received answer from the Conf. in Salem. From the newspapers we received yesterday we were sorry to learn that the Indians cannot expect any help from the Supreme Court of the United States at this time. Time will tell what the results of this will be and how things will develop. We must commend it to Him who can arrange everything for the best.

Sun., Apr. 3. [Ooch.] 15 persons came for the Easter sermon. The continuing rain prevented us from praying the Easter Morning Litany on our God's Acre; we did this in the Saal. We also informed the Brn. and Srs. that we will not be able to hold school for now, since we were very far behind with the field and garden work. With our small number we were not able to manage the school and the work associated with it. This was plain and clear to the Brn. and Srs., so they agreed to manage without the school.

Tues., Apr. 5. [Ooch.] We visited Sr. Susanna Charity Watee, who has been ill with consumption for more than 2 months. A number of days ago she had improved somewhat, so that she was able to be out of bed some during our visit of several hours. As in her healthy days, now during her long and painful illness she found the presence of Jesus especially comforting, and she waited with an obedient mind for her release from all sufferings and for her journey home to peace, which is available to the redeemed people of God.

[M 415-1a-18: Translated by Julie Tomberlin Weber. Addressed to: Revd. Theodore Schulz, Salem, Stokes County, North Carolina. Post stamp: New-Echota, Cher. Na., Apr. 9, 18¾. Received Apr. 24. Br. Schulz writes in the address: O______y building cash.]

Ooyugillogy, Ch. Nation, Apr. 7, 1831

Dearly beloved Br. Schulz,

It is a special pleasure for me to write my letters to you from here once again, and with a grateful heart I remember the goodness of the One who allowed my return to come so quickly and unexpectedly, which enabled me to return to the appointed post. Praise and thanks to the Lord. Nothing is impossible for Him. The enemies of His kingdom on earth have no power against Him and the poor, weak messengers who trust in Him. The worldly judges who try to slow His work and with proud hearts boldly attempt to destroy it must be surrounded by fear and doubt in the decisive hour of judgment, because they cannot achieve their evil intentions and will have to put down the sword of judgment with shame and dishonor and declare the poor, innocent criminals free.

Judge Clayton, whose notoriety is known far and wide, will now learn through experience the truth of the words our beloved Savior spoke before Pilate's seat of judgment [John 19:11]: Thou couldst have no power at all against me, except it were given thee from above. The experience he has had will perhaps be as instructive for him as it has been comforting to the missionaries set free and the rest of us. The decision the said Judge made regarding the missionaries is inconceivable. Only a Judge like

Clayton can pronounce a judgment like this. In his opinion we are Agents of the Government. We have unfortunately not received financial support from the government for a number of years. This remarkable decision can only be understood as a fruit of fear. Fear was the reason for it, because it is quite well known that if the missionaries had been condemned to the penitentiary, there would have been a general uprising in the North.

This sign of fear on the side of the Georgians makes the Cherokees and the rest of the white adopted citizens, who thus far are still unprotected, even more resolved, since it gives them more hope to assert their just matter. This hope rests solely on the favorable decision of the Supreme Court of the U.S. which is expected soon, and which may already be known. Everyone is waiting with fear and trembling or hope for this news. If it is unfavorable, then things are over for the Cherokees. The scene that would take place then cannot be foreseen, but without a doubt it will be extremely sad.

The current situation is already causing disadvantages for the people. A great shortage of food prevails among the common Indians because of the drought last summer. As a result of the long, extremely cold winter, they are losing many cattle. In our neighborhood one person alone lost 24 head of livestock. Robberies occur frequently, and fighting follows, as well as the more frequent drunkenness, since the whites here and there in the country who have taken the required oath are now carrying out the destructive whisky trade as citizens of Georgia. The Cherokee laws against the introduction of brandy are strict, and as long as these were in force only a little of it came into the country. Now, however, this wall of protection has been destroyed, and the destructive current of this flowing fire brings distress and death everywhere. This is now a brief glimpse of the current situation in our neighborhood.

On the 28th of last month, we returned safely here after I had been gone for 4 weeks, but together just one week. We had just arrived here when it began to rain so heavily and persistently that all the streams became impassable, and it is still like this now since it has stormed every day and night. We are glad that we did not allow the rain clouds on the 28th to scare us away from returning home. Otherwise, we would have had to spend one more week, if not more, in Spring Place.

I was very happy to hear that our Brn. and Srs. and others, 22 of them, had come here the day before, Sunday the 27th, for mutual encouragement. During this both Brn. Hickses, George and Wm. Abr., as well as Christian David, were active in both languages, English and Cherokee. Sr. Gambold was present here and speaks about the sense of Jesus' presence that prevailed during this. Praise and thanks to the Lord. Is it not a matter for gratitude to see a good number of converted Cherokees gathered for their common improvement? Certainly it is more encouragement than we poor servants, who often try to carry out our work so apathetically, have earned. If I myself could have had the pleasure of attending this meeting as a stranger in a corner, even if I could not have understood much or anything in it, the sight would have been rich in blessings, just as the thought of it alone makes me happy now.

Sr. Susan Charity, Christian David's wife, has been ill for more than 2 months already with consumption. Several days ago we heard that she was close to her end, and so we visited her on the 5th and found her much better than we had expected. The extreme cold [page torn], and since spring is now bringing beautiful and mild weather, which delights us all, our ill Sr. also feels somewhat better and can remain for a number of years in our pond of human affliction. In the meantime, it seems that she has not forgotten her final, blessed ending, her journey home to the Lord in the kingdom of health. Mary Margaret accompanied us to help as interpreter, a service she has already provided us well. When we go visiting in the country here there are naturally always events that come up, if we only could get a tongue to serve as a translator. It is good not to pay attention to all the rest of the difficulties. Such a move admittedly seems quite formidable.

Br. Byhan will already have informed you that we cannot hold school for now; this will surely not be surprising to you, since you are aware of our difficult and lamentable circumstances. Otherwise, things would almost have been the same if Br. and Sr. Copeland had stayed here longer, because of the sad emotional state of Sr. Copeland, who suffered greatly as a result of her fits. Last Sunday I announced to the Brn. and Srs. that the school must necessarily be canceled for now (I personally believe forever) and explained our situation. They understood this well and declared they were satisfied since there is no other way. Until now 4 children have still been here, but they will go home as soon as possible.

From one of your recent letters to Br. Byhan I saw your wish to have a copy of the accounts of our construction expenses here. The blessed Br. Gambold made the following entries, which I presume include everything you want. I am copying them verbatim.

1823 Jan. 1	Pd. Joseph Crutchfield for the House — except the chimney — and other improvements, purchased of him for a missionary establishment	$497.00
	Pd. ditto for fencing the yard around the house	15.00
Sept. 6	Pd. Austin Copeland for fencing the garden	25.00
Oct. 3	Pd. for 8 lbs. of nails $2.00; for laying the hearths $2.12½	4.125
1824		
Jan. 4	Pd. Samuel Adair for work on the chimney	4.50
Feb 5	Pd. John McCartney for carpenter & joiners work as per bill, including plank, etc., furnished	211.02
Mar. 13	Pd. Saml. Copeland for his pile of plank & scantling	40.00
	Pd. Austin Copeland for 2600 lap shingles @ $6 per 1000	15.60
Mar. 16	Pd. McCoy for 50 lbs. nails $9.50; 6 pairs of H hinges and 2 locks 3.25	12.75
	Pd. Joseph Crutchfield his bill for brickmaking, erecting the chimney, etc	111.50
1825		
Feb. 26	Pd. Lavender for nails received in Jan. $1.50; March 30 Lavender nails 5.25	6.75
	Pd. McCoy & Harnage for nails $14; window glass $12	$26.00
	Pd. for planks $4.75; 10 July pd. Alex Copeland for 3,200 lap shingles $21.00	24.75
Sept. 9	Pd. Jerem. Horn for building 2 Chimneys (schoolhouse)	20.00
Oct. 1	Pd. Austin Copeland for plank $10; John Ross for 51½ lbs. nails $10.30	20.30
	Pd. Alexander Copeland for work in schoolhouse $2.50	2.50
	Pd. Austin Copeland for plank [in schoolhouse]	6.35

1826

Jan. 3 Pd. Joseph Copeland for flooring & doors in the schoolhouse & for benches in the chapel 38.05

June 5 Pd. Elijah Hicks for 60 lbs. of nails [in the schoolhouse & chapel].............. 10.10

Aug. 23 Pd. Joseph Copeland for carpenters work [in the schoolhouse & chapel]................ 9.00

Dec. 15 Pd. Jeremy Horn for making a new roof on our house....................... 18.00

1827

Mar. 19 Pd. Elijah Hicks for 80 lbs. of nails 12.80 [in the schoolhouse & chapel].............. 12.80

193.10
[187.85]

Dec. 7 Pd. Aust Copeland for 1000 brick $5.00; pd. Jos Crutchfield for sundry & timber $76.915..81.915

1828

Feb. 4 Pd. Jos. Crutchfield for nails & weatherboarding 3.22

$1,221.475
[$1,221.48]

This is an exact copy of the account by blessed Br. Gambold. I cannot include the expenditures for both the stalls and barn, because they were built by hired workers who received salary. I will write again soon.

Greet my dear parents. I will write them very soon. We are all well physically, but we have to admit that our drive for mission work is somewhat flat due to the prevailing difficult external circumstances. In the meantime, the Lord, who is full of grace and love, will gently strengthen this sooner or later. Let us trust in Him and commend ourselves to His gracious assistance. We sincerely ask for your prayers for this and the prayers of all who are interested. Your faithfully obliged, unworthy coworkers in the Lord's vineyard,

H. G. Clauder

N.B. New Echota, the 7th. Completely unexpectedly today I found the Cherokee Delegates here. They had arrived here yesterday evening. I saw the anxiously awaited decision of the Supreme Court. It includes nothing on which hope for better times could be based. Georgia will not be prevented from the execution of her laws, and as a result the Cherokees will not be able to tolerate things here much longer without taking decisive steps. I wish we could remain in the status quo until the Cherokees indicate what they plan to do now. Our moving alone would arouse attention and many bad results for the work we have tried to further here. May the Lord guide us to act in accordance with His wishes. Yours,

H. G. Clauder

[Springplace (M 407-2) and Oochgeelogy (M 409-1) Diaries.]

Sun., Apr. 10. [Ooch.] After the sermon we celebrated the memorial meal of our Savior Jesus with a small number of our communicants to strengthen our souls.

Mon., Apr. 11. [Ooch.] It was unusually cold for this time of year. The following night a heavy frost killed all the fruit blossoms.

Apr. 15. [Ooch.] Once again we received a pleasant visit from Mr. McCloud, whom, as we mentioned earlier, is in charge of the Methodists' mission work in this country. The next day Br. Clauder accompanied him, at his invitation, to one of his preaching places, where meetings were supposed to be held on this day and the next. Mr. McCloud first delivered a moving sermon on 2 Cor. 4:17-18, with special reference to the sufferings which are currently taking place. As requested, Br. Clauder concluded with a brief talk on Isa. 49:14-15, with reference to the preceding sermon. During the entire service there was a quiet reverence among the listeners. That evening our neighborhood was once again disrupted by the sudden appearance of a number of Georgia Guards, who searched various houses at the same time to imprison those white men who had not taken the required oath. They had as little success achieving their goal this time as on the following day, when they attacked the meeting of the Methodists in the expectation of arresting these stubborn white people. However, they had watchmen at the doors of the meeting house who gave them a sign as soon as they saw the Guards in the distance, and they had enough time to run into the underbrush nearby.

[*Sun., Apr. 17.* Ooch.] Our Sunday service was not disturbed, but strengthened our wisdom and faith through reflection on the words of Rom. 8:18.

Sun., Apr. 10 and *Sun., Apr. 17.* [Spg.] The Sunday services were held as usual. The listeners gathered in scarce numbers for these. Otherwise, it is currently very still and quiet in the Nation, and we see Indians only every now and again, and those whom we see go very quietly past our houses without stopping in, and it seems to us as if we are completely cut off from all people. All seems dead and barren, and, so to say, as if there is no more life in the Nation.

[M 415-1a-19: Translated by Julie Tomberlin Weber. Addressed to: Revd. Theod. Schulz, Salem, Stokes County, North Carolina. Postmark: Springplace, C.N., Apr. 17. Free. Gottl. Byhan, P.M. Received Apr. 27.]

Spring Place, Apr. 16, 1831

My dear Br. Shulz,

I just received your kind letter of the 30th of last month in reply to mine to you dated the 19th [M 415-1a-14] of last month, from which you will have seen that the Georgians will carry out their strict laws. From my letters that followed you will have seen that the missionaries have been released. I now have 3 letters before me from your dear hand, because 8 days ago I had no time to write, and this would also have been the case again today if I had not considered it necessary to report to you immediately the receipt of your dear letter of the 30th.

Since my last letter to you, not the slightest has happened here, neither on the side of the Georgians nor the Cherokees. All is quiet, and we are living in undisturbed peace, so that there is nothing new to write about.

I also just received the Genl. Postmaster's reply to my letter to him, dated March 19, which says:

[Br. Byhan copies S. R. Hobbie's letter in English:]

I am directed by the Postmaster General to acknowledge the receipt of your letter of the 16 of last month, and to assure you that your enquiries will be answered in a short time.

S. R. Hobbie

[Br. Byhan continues his letter to Br. Schulz in German:]

This letter arrived from Washington in 14 days. Why do our letters go so slowly then?

Next week I will write again. Please greet our children for us. We have been waiting a long time for a letter from them. We all greet you sincerely. For now, accept these few lines. The Delegates have come home, but we have not heard or seen anything of them.

Your familiar Br.,

Gottl. Byhan

[M 411-1-31: Transcribed by Grace S. Robinson. Addressed to: Rev. Theodore Shultz, Salem, Stokes County, North Carolina. Postmark: Columbus, In., Apr. 7, 25. Received May 3. Handwriting is Mary Gambold Copeland's. Lightly edited.]

Columbus, Bartholomew County,
State of Indiana, Apr. 3, 1831

Dear Friend & Brother Shulz,

You have undoubtedly been informed by Mr. Clauder that we left Oochgelogy on the 25th of Feb. in order to move to the State of Indiana and after a long and tedious Journey we arrived here at Mr. Clayton's on the 26th of March, and they are kind enough to let us stay with them until we can build a little hut to move into, & my husband has pickt out a piece of land and is working on it but is not able to pay for it yet. We would therefore thank you kindly if you would send us our Money by the first opportunity, as we stand very much in need of it. We would be very glad if you could let us have it in U. States money, as no other paper money is current.

We never would have went such a distance without the [vicinity?] of some of our own society where there was hopes of a little congregation being gathered again, and to our great joy we found it so. Mr. M. Houser keeps meeting most every Sunday. He kept Meeting too on Good Friday, and several evenings before. He seems to be very anxious to see a congregation flourish here.

I found a great many of our old acquaintances from the neighborhood of Salem, all poor beginners as well as ourselves. Everyone tries to help his neighbour as much as is in his power. Brotherly love & union reign among them. I understood that our Salem friends have contributed their part too toward buying a piece of land & building a Church & Schoolhouse here. I hope they may see the time that they can say it was not done in vain. I hope and wish that our good Lord may crown all the efforts which have been made for this purpose with a blessing, and I have no doubt He will do it too, if we only rely on His Mercy & Faithfulness. I should be very glad if some of our Brethren in Salem would pay us a visit once.

Please to give my best respects to all in your family, and all my good Friends and acquaintances in Salem if they should happen to inquire after me. Although I cannot correspond with them by letters I think of them often and wish to see them all.

I should like to know how my poor old father is coming on. I suppose it goes very hard with him to be confined so much to the house, as he is getting very old and can't get about as he would wish to. If you should happen to see him once I would thank you to give our best respects to him and tell him where we are and that we enjoy good health.

We remain yours affectionately,

Alexander & Mary Copeland

[M 411-1-32: Transcribed by Grace S. Robinson. Addressed to: The Board of Directors of the United Brethren's Missions, Salem, N. Carolina. Post stamped: Mille., Ga., Apr. 13, paid 18¾. Received Apr. 24.]

Executive Department Georgia
Milledgeville, 13 Apr. 1831

Gentlemen,

Your letter of the 30th Ulto upon the subject of the Missionaries employed by the Board of Directors of the United Brethren's Missions among the Cherokee Indians residing in Georgia has been received.

I have the highest respect for the general character of the United Brethren and entire confidence that the Board of Missions have in its efforts to improve & christianize the heathen and savage Aborigines of our country been directed by the most pious & benevolent motives. I regret that your Missionaries should have found any difficulty in complying with the requirements of the laws of the State. The principal object of those laws have been to remove from the Cherokees, white men of bad character and those who from mistaken views of the rights & powers of the state have been engaged in exciting the Indians to sedition & opposition to the policy of the Government.

The officer of the Guard which had been stationed among the Cherokees to protect the public property from trespass and to arrest violaters of the law has been directed specially to bring to trial every white man who in any manner commits an injury upon our Cherokee population. And it is a source of high satisfaction to believe that under the present Administration of the laws of the State the rights of liberty, personal security & private property belonging to the Indians are far better protected than they have been heretofore.

According to your request and in full confidence that your Missionaries will conform to your directions, the Commanding Officer of the Guard will be directed to wait with them until they can conveniently remove from the State or take the oath required by law.

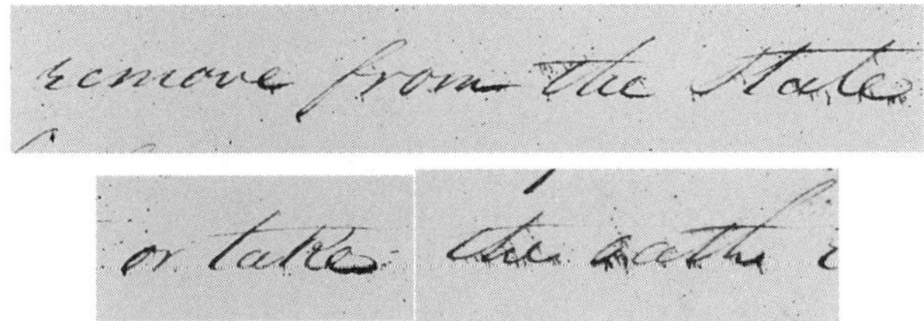
remove from the State

or take the oath

I cannot close this letter without expressing the fullest conviction that the removal of the Cherokees to the west of the Mississippi will result to their advantage & the hope that such removal instead of embarrassing the efforts of Christians in communicating to them the light & saving influences of the Gospel will prove the efficient mean of obtaining for them the most satisfactory success.

Very Respectfully Yours &c,

George R. Gilmer

The Board of Directors of the United Brethren's Missions

[Springplace (M 407-2) and Oochgeelogy (M 409-1) Diaries.]

Apr. 18. [Spg.] We heard that the G. Guard is busy again arresting white people in the Ochgeloogy area. People believe that they are now after the Methodist preachers, but these are only guesses here. We also heard that several days ago they arrested and took to Georgia Mr. John Bell, a native-born man in Goosawaytee who formerly served in the Cherokee law as Constable. It is not known why they arrested him.

Mon., Apr. 18. [Ooch.] Br. Clauder and Sr. Gambold visited in New Echota, where they found many friends and acquaintances sick in bed.

Apr. 20. [Spg.] Two Methodist preachers who held services in the Ochgeloogy area, Mr. McLoed and Mr. Frott, stopped in at our place. They told us that the Georgia Guard surrounded the house in which they were holding services during worship to imprison some white persons they believed they would find in the service. But the white people saw the Ga. Guard before they came into the meeting house, and thus they had gotten away in time. The Georgia Guard, however, had not made any disturbance in the service, but had quietly attended it. The Methodist preachers had afterward told the commanding Officer that they believed they had perhaps come to arrest them, the preachers, to which they replied that they had no orders to bother the missionaries. The Cherokee Delegates had returned from Washington some time ago, and the Indians are being informed of their actions there in their towns, because the Georgia Law forbids them from gathering for a Council in New Echota. We heard further today that the Georgia Guard will be quartered in New Echota for some time. People believe this is so they can arrest some white people who live in the neighborhood there. Some people believe they also want to stay in New Echota so that the Indians cannot hold a Council there.

Apr. 21. [Spg.] Some surveyors from Georgia stopped in at our place and wanted to buy Indian cornmeal, but we could not provide them with this. Also two young gentlemen from Georgia, students as it seemed, stopped in at our place. After they had put a letter in the Post Office and looked at our spring they went on.

Sun., Apr. 24. [Spg.] Mr. Dav. Steiner Dazizi served us as interpreter in our services today. Recently we heard that the Indians in the area of Pine Log, below Ochgeloogy, are supposed to have said that they wanted to kill the Chief, Mr. John Ross, because they believe that in 1828 he had made a secret treaty with the Genl. Government concerning their land, and so they want to oppose the Georgians with force. Since they have to die sometime after all, they would rather die defending their land, because this would be a more glorious death. We hear that Mr. John Ross, along with some other respected men, will visit the Indians in their towns and try to calm them down.

Sun., Apr. 24. [Ooch.] We had very few listeners at the usual services, which is all the more unusual because no other worship services were being held close to us.

[M 415-1a-20: Translated by Julie Tomberlin Weber. Addressed to: Revd. Theod. Schulz, Salem, Stokes County, North Carolina. Postmark: Springplace, C.N., Apr. 24. Free. G. Byhan, P.M. Received May 4.]

Springplace, Apr. 24, 1831

Dear Br. Schulz,

Your kind letter of the 6th of this month, as well as the report of the Directors for the Spread of the Gospel among the Heathen, as well as a *Mission Intel.* finally arrived here yesterday evening with the Georgia mail. We thank you most sincerely for everything. Since I cannot thoroughly answer your 2 last letters due to a lack of time, I will hastily report that everything is quite quiet right now, although the Georgia Guards — as they call themselves — are trying to find and arrest all the white people in the country. Still, praise God, we live in peace and quiet.

From a letter I received from Br. Clauder yesterday evening, we learned that the Indians at Pine Log and Hickiry Log, not very far from Och____y, are becoming somewhat dissatisfied, and they have said that they would no longer tolerate the treatment of the Georgians, and that they are threatening to kill the Chief, Mr. John Ross, because they believe that he privately sold the land to the United States in 1828. Br. Clauder will probably write you various things about this as well, and has probably already written you, since he has more opportunity to hear details about the matter in context. Generally, I believe that the Indians will hardly remain quiet any longer in these circumstances. They are also supposed to be saying in the above-mentioned areas: They see that they must die, and to die in war, taking revenge against their enemies, is honorable. God help us! All will go as He has decided for the inhabitants of this country.

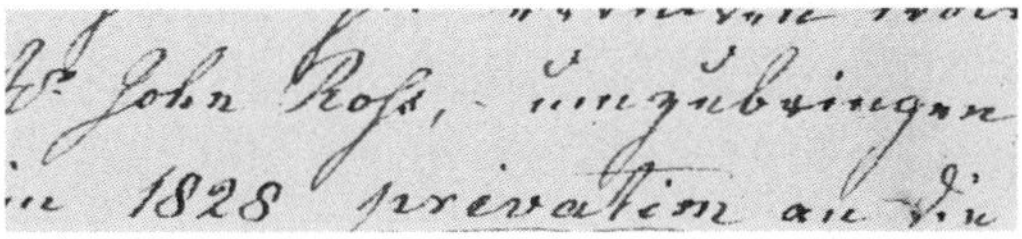

From your letter which I received yesterday, we saw the desire of the Conf. for us to start the school again. For now I can only say that I refer to my explanations and all of our explanations included in one of my previous letters, which now will be in your hands. I must also say now that we cannot feed and care for any children in our current situation without more help in the household.

My dear wife is very weak, and Nancy Becker has not been healthy for a number of weeks now. I still have Rominger working for me. People believe that they will not disturb him. I have often given him the choice to go if he believes he is not safe, but he wants to wait for the worst.

Everyone greets you most sincerely. Your faithfully obliged Br.
Gottl. Byhan

[Springplace (M 407-2) and Oochgeelogy (M 409-1) Diaries.]

Mon., Apr. 24 [*25*]. [Ooch.] Br. Clauder, accompanied by Br. George Hicks, left here to look for one of our horses, which had run away several nights ago. After much effort and many tests of their patience, they finally found it again on *the 29th*.

Apr. 29. [Spg.] To our joy we heard that Chief John Ross and some other Indians had visited the above-mentioned dissatisfied Indians, but could not find out where the above rumor had arisen or who had started it. He was told, however, that in a meeting of the Indians there had been talk about this. Others said that they had also heard this but no longer knew from whom. May God prevent there being more serious incidents between the Georgians and the Cherokees, because in this case it would have led inevitably to the downfall and destruction of the latter. We heard further that the Georgia Guard had set Mr. John Bell — see the 18th — free again. The Georgia Guard also left New Echota after they had stayed there for several weeks.

[M 415-1a-21: Translated by Julie Tomberlin Weber. Addressed to: Revd. Theodore Schulz, Salem, North Carolina. Post stamp: New-Echota, Cher. Na., May. 7, 18¾. Received May 18.]

Ooyugillogy, Cherokee Nation, May 5, 1831

Dear Brother Schulz,

Several days ago I received your kind letter of the 6th of last month. It brought us pleasure and encouragement. Since my last letter to you, we have enjoyed our usual good health and quiet, and are grateful to the Lord for this. In the meantime, a number of interesting events have taken place which I will describe to you here briefly, although Br. Byhan might have beaten me to this already.

First, our neighborhood had a visit from the now well-known Georgia Guard, whose purpose, like the first time, was to arrest the white people. To this end, all the houses and buildings in this area were carefully investigated, some of them during the night, and the Methodists' gathering place was disturbed by this horde on Sunday during the worship service. However, their repeated attempts remained fruitless each time. Only one single boy fell into their hands in New Echota. He was dragged off to headquarters, and finally after he had proved his minority, he was set free again. During their stay around here we enjoyed undisturbed peace, and we saw nothing of them.

As a result of another circumstance, I made a small journey to Georgia last week! And actually in the company of our George Hicks. During the night of Apr. 20th, our best horse, which might well be worth $90, escaped. From a number of tracks we determined that it had not been stolen but had run away. On the 25th I got Br. G. H. to go with me in pursuit of it. We followed the tracks to Pinelog and Sa,le,ko,ee, 12 miles east from here, which confirmed our suspicion that the horse will run back to its former home in South Carolina. In the evening of the 2nd day we received the news through a traveler that a horse like ours had crossed the Chestatee River near Leathersford the previous day.

And so we continued our journey most hastily on the following day and arrived there before noon, but we found we were deceived in our expectations. No one could give us news. We were also not prepared to go on, although we were only 60 miles from the border of South Carolina. And so we returned by a different road, and had the luck! of getting lost for one day and spending one cold night under the open sky and getting off of our intended path. On the 4th day of our journey, after we had crossed the most horrible mountains, we finally reached the mission station Carmel, some 30 miles southeast of Springplace. And in this neighborhood, completely unexpectedly, we found the horse we had worked so hard to find. We thus saw that the road which had seemed like a wrong way to us was in fact the right way, and that we had reached our goal on an unplanned road, led by an unseen hand, and we found what we had lost!

As usual I will now include my semi-annual account of expenditures and income.

From my letters, as well as Br. Byhan's earlier ones, you will have seen that we are not in a position to hold school for the time being due to a lack of help. The Indian Brethren and Sisters and others in this area understand very well that we cannot hold school in our current difficulties as much as they wish it were otherwise. When we still had Sr. Copeland's help, we were able to carry out the many necessary tasks only with difficulty, and visit. Now, however, our hands are full, and I cannot see how it is possible to manage with a small number of young school girls, from whom little help could be expected.

In order to explain this even more clearly, I will describe what keeps us busy on a daily basis. Sr. Gambold spends most of the time at the springhouse, where she is busy with pots, milk, cream, and butter. We both help her milk the 11 cows. In the meantime, my wife takes care of the kitchen and the rest of the domestic work. I myself am here and there, on the fields, in the garden, in the house, or even in the bush looking for cows! Our hired worker Jay Hicks had his hands full in the fields. We are actually finished planting the corn. Now, however, we will soon start plowing and chopping, which also belonged to his work and will have to wait for me to do it.

We really wish to continue here "as if the stay of the Cherokee Nation were certain" and to serve them with a school as previously. But for reasons and causes which will now be clear to the dear Brethren, we find it impossible to turn our wish, your wish, and that of the Indians into a reality. And so nothing else remains for us except to ask urgently for help. To that end we want to turn first to the Lord, who can order all things, and ask that He so guide the hearts of His faithful maids that they might increase their strength to help promote His work here despite the trials and sorrow.

I doubt that I can give you a clear view through my description of the circumstances that prevail here. How desirable it is, then, for a Brother from Salem to visit here and see our internal and external circumstances. And how encouraging this would be for us and our oppressed Cherokees! It is indeed only a short stretch between us! I still hope that you, dear Brother, will visit the dear Cherokees once again.

Praise God, the Cherokees are still united among themselves, although some traces of dissatisfaction and suspicion are appearing toward John Ross and the other heads in 2 remote districts. Ross, Ridge, and Lowry are now on a tour through the entire Nation and are holding small Councils to preserve their union and to resist the jibes of the Georgia intriguers! May God, the Lord, preserve us from internal unrest.

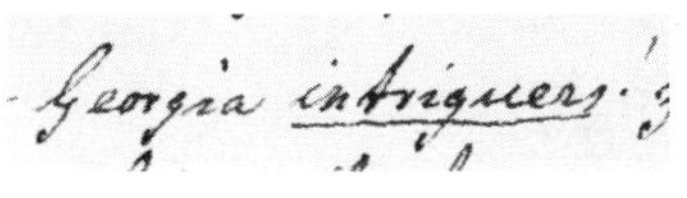

Mr. McNair had received your letter of Feb. 9th before we arrived there. We have not yet heard anything from Br. Alexander Copeland. It was his intention to move to Bartholow County in the area where Martin Hauser and Clayton live. The U.S. notes which were intended for him and which Br. Byhan did not think it would be good to send back to Salem through me, were exchanged in Tennessee for Georgia and South Carolina notes at 1½ percent premium. Br. Byhan has the entire sum on hand and can easily exchange it for U.S. notes again. Such bank notes do not seem to be so rare here and in Tennessee. At least they are not particularly sought after. There is no other opportunity from here to Indiana except by mail, and it seems too unsafe to me to send a significant amount of money that way.

Sally Ridge was joined to Christ's Church through holy baptism some weeks ago in Creekpath. Her father has not visited us for a long time, but he is always very friendly. Last week I saw him in the company of Ross and Lowry in Pinelog. He asked about you and Br. Steiner. I gave a copy of our Cherokee Litany to the 2 latter gentlemen, and they accepted them gratefully.

Yesterday we visited at Wm. Hicks's. He still continues to talk in a very friendly manner. Among other things, he said yesterday that he is now enjoying peace and quiet in his heart and he can believe that the Savior has forgiven his sins and that he cannot praise and thank him enough for all the patience and mercy He has shown him, a poor sinner. He is here for the service every Sunday, as are George and his family, who attend church in an exemplary manner.

Mrs. Worcester in Echota has already been ill for 8 months, and there is little hope for her recovery. Sr. Watee is well again. Next week we are planning to visit our Sr. Ridge. There is a great shortage of corn in this country. Every day we have visits from hungry Indians. Many offer to work, but they are rumored to be thieves, and no one wants to have anything to do with them. We are still having very cool nights, and last week had frost several times.

Greetings to my dear parents, Henry Aug. Schulz, and all the rest of my friends. Your faithfully obliged friend and Br.,

H. G. Clauder

[M 419-B-7-a: Transcribed by Richard W. Starbuck.]

Cash receipts and expenditures at Ooyugillogy Mission
from Nov. 5, 1830, to May 5, 1831

[1830] [Receipts]

Nov. 5 Amt of cash in hand 63.02

To tinnery: 0.50; expenses: for butter 0.25; wine 0.375....... 1.12½

Dec. 24	To expenses: recd. for loan of wagon $1.00; tinnery 0.50	1.50
	To expenses: for soap & butter $1.225; knitting 0.375	1.60
1831		
Feb. 26	To: George A. Hicks in full	2.25
	To expenses: recd. for oats, butter, & potatoes	4.75
Feb. 2	To Diacony of Missions: recd. of Br. Schulz per mail	100.00
Mar. 26	To Spring Place: recd. of Br. Byhan	20.00
	To expenses: for butter & potatoes	2.62½
	To: E. Nicholson recd. on acct.	1.00
	To expenses: recd. for oats & butter	1.50
	To: Elias Boudinott recd. on acct.	1.50
	To expenses: recd. for dried peaches, eggs, & butter	1.75
Apr.	To expenses: recd. of Saml. Worcester for a cow & calf	12.00
	To expenses: recd. for 5 lbs. butter	0.37½
		214.99½

[Br. Schulz writes in Salem:]

214.99½
63.02
151.97½
193.52½
345.50

[Expenditures]

[1830]		
Nov. 8	Pd. Jno. Adams for work	10.50
	Pd. ferriage 0.50; basket 0.50; venison 0.50	1.50
Dec. 3	Pd. barrel salt $12.90; venison 0.75	13.65
	Pd. Saml. Henry on acct. for flour, coffee, & iron	20.00
Dec. 7	Pd. Jno. Adams in full: 7.40; Austin Copeland 3.00	10.40
Dec. 20	Pd. assistant in hog killing 0.625; gloves 0.75; ferriage 0.25	1.62½
Jan. 1	Pd. postage of letters & papers	0.45
Feb.	Pd. horseshoeing 0.25; seamstress for sewing 2.00	2.25
	Pd. Alexander Copeland for 4 mos. work @ $12 per mo.	48.00
Mar.	Pd. Negro Simon for 17 days work	5.50
	Pd. ferriage 0.625; shoeing horse 0.25	0.87½
	Pd. Saml. Henry on acct. for flour, coffee, tea, rice, misc.	40.00
	Pd. ferriage 0.75; horseshoeing 1.50; stirrups 0.50	2.75
	Pd. 2 bottles snuff 1.25; blacksmith .125	1.37½
Apr. 1	Pd. postage last quarter	0.85½
	Pd. hire of a Negro 5 days	1.93
	Pd. for 10 lbs. iron 1.00; 3 yds. calico 1.3125	2.31¼
	George A. Hicks cash lent him	7.00
Apr. 30	Pd. part of exp. in procuring stray horse	1.93¾
	Pd. for ferriage Feb. 22	0.50
May 5	Amt. of cash in hand	41.58½
		214.99½
	[subtracted by Br. Schulz in Salem]	41.58½
		173.41

[Springplace (M 407-2) and Oochgeelogy (M 409-1) Diaries.]

Sun., May 1. [Ooch.] The sermon was on John 16:31. More listeners were present for this than last Sunday.

Sun., May 1. [Spg.] Only a few came for the services because of the high streams, but they were well attended again on. . .

. . .*Sun., May 8.* [Spg.] Some misunderstandings have taken place among the Brn. and Srs. in the recent past, and today they were put aside in a community discussion in the presence of Br. and Sr. Byhan. In conclusion they shook hands as a sign that such things should not be thought of again.

May 6. [Ooch.] After a long drought, we had a soaking rain today. Some surveyors from Georgia who were close to our place came here for protection from the storm, which continued into the night. *On the 7th* they went on, for which we were grateful. Once again in the afternoon we had a strong storm, accompanied by hail. The rain showers at this time of year are really unusually heavy. They completely washed away the young field and garden plants along with the loose dirt, especially on new cultivation places, and they had to be planted over 2 or 3 times.

Sun., May 8. [Ooch.] The sermon was on Rom. 13:3-4. The main points of this were repeated in Cherokee by Br. Hicks. In conclusion, Br. Wm. Abr. read and interpreted part of John 6. Jesse Halfbreed, an Indian, attends the services here regularly and shows that he still has some good impressions from last winter when Br. Clauder often held meetings at his house. For now he cannot get an interpreter to continue, as he would like to do.

Tues., May 10. [Ooch.] We visited our Sr. Sussannah Ridge, who lives 20 miles from here. Margaret Mary Hicks accompanied us as interpreter. Since her husband, the well-known Major Ridge, was away from home on business for the Nation, our visit was especially encouraging to her. She really regretted that she cannot come to the services here for various reasons, such as the distance, the infirmities of old age, etc. Nonetheless, she maintains a daily relationship with her Lord and Savior whose presence she can feel, although He is invisible. He is everything to her. We were very happy to see her motherly joy over her only daughter Sarah, who recently joined the visible Church of Christ in Creekpath through holy baptism.

Wed., May 11. [Ooch.] We returned home. On the way home we visited Sr. Fields 18 miles from here. Her husband, who was a baptismal candidate here some years ago but who later joined the Methodists, now lives in his previous sinful ways. Since he was not at home, Br. Clauder could not carry out intention of sincerely admonishing him.

Fri., May 13. [Ooch.] We visited Sr. Catharine Maria Gann, whose husband, a white man, was imprisoned by the Georgians last March. At his hearing he was ordered to leave this country by May 1st. He is not planning to follow this order and leave his large business and large family, so he expects to be taken in again. On the way home a storm drove us into an Indian hut of the poorer class, where we found scanty shelter. Here there were none of the better ways of life more common among the Indians, and even less desire for the knowledge of the One Thing Needful [Luke 10:42].

Sun., May 15. [Spg.] We made up the celebration of Ascension Day. Today there were some Indians in our services who allow themselves to be seen here only very seldom. We were thus very happy that Mr. Dav. Steiner Dazizi was here today, who served us as interpreter. Perhaps they also took the impression of what they heard in the services home with them.

Sun., May 15. [Ooch.] During the sermon, which was better attended than usual, we considered the words of Mark 9:24: Lord, I believe; help thou mine unbelief.

May 18. [Spg.] Br. Byhan, Sr., went to Ochgeloogy on a visit to discuss various matters concerning our mission with the Brn. and Srs. there and he returned here to Spring Place on *the 19th.*

Wed., May 18. [Ooch.] We were delighted by a brief visit from our dear Br. Byhan in Spring Place. On this occasion we had a joint discussion about the current circumstances of both posts in this country.

Sun., May 22. [Spg.] Pentecost. In the first service was the sermon on the festival material, and in the second we enjoyed the body and blood of our Lord in Holy Communion. The married

Br. Emanuel watched as a confirmand, and his wife, the Indian Sr. Marg. Susanna as a candidate. Afterward we informed the Brn. and Srs. that now, despite the lack of help in the household, we will begin the school again. Mr. Dav. Steiner Dazizi was our interpreter again today.

Sun., May 22. [Ooch.] It was holy Pentecost and we began with the sermon, which was repeated by an Indian Brother in his language as usual. In the following service, mission newsletters were read. We also announced publicly that the school will be resumed here in a few days. Among the outsiders visiting here today was Georg Vann, a former scholar of the blessed Br. Wohlfarth in Spring Place.

Mon., May 23. [Ooch.] Toward evening the same land surveyors who were here some weeks ago came here. They were on their way home after completing their work. One of their company had already arrived here some days ago. He had been helping us in the fields, where we had a lot of work at the moment. On the following morning they all went on.

May 27. [Spg.] Early in the day we found that thieves had been at our springhouse during the night and had tried to break open the door of it, which they had not managed to do, however. Still they had taken along a couple articles of clothing which were outside the springhouse. They had also stolen various small articles which they were able to pull out from the cracks between the logs.

[M 415-1a-22: Translated by Julie Tomberlin Weber. Addressed to: Revd. Theodor Schulz, Salem, Stokes County, North Carolina. Postmark: Springplace, C.N., May 29. Free. G. Byhan, P.M. Received June 11.]

Springplace, May 28, 1831

My dear Br. Schulz,

Since my last letter to you, dated Apr. 24, nothing else has happened here in the Nation that would be particularly noteworthy. And so I have become somewhat negligent in my writing.

On Apr. 23rd I received your letter of March 30th, on May 7th the one dated Apr. 14th, and on May 14th the one dated Apr. 27th. We thank you most sincerely for all of them.

Now to answer your letter of Apr. 14, which included the reply to my announcement, actually our announcement, that we had reached the decision not to accept any children in our current situation, since we do not really see any way the Srs. here and in Ochgeloogy can manage the work without more help in the household. My dear wife is getting weaker and weaker, and Nancy Becker has not been healthy for a number of months now, although it seems that she will gradually recover her health again, which is our hope and desire.

At this time, I also need to state and openly admit that we do not yet see how we will be able to manage the main work without more help. We must believe that you cannot imagine the circumstances here and the situation in which we currently find ourselves. One must be present, one must see the work with his own eyes, indeed I might say experience everything personally — and who wants to do this? — in order to get a correct understanding of the situation here and the way things really are, because they cannot be described.

We were amazed that our explanation — of why we cannot hold school for now because of a lack of help with the household — has strengthened your opinion that we might start the school. We must therefore conclude that for now we cannot count on any assistance in that respect, and so we have no more hope of getting that kind of help in the future.

Since the Prov. Helf. Conf. cannot approve our suggestion and strongly advises that we hold school, when I paid a visit to Br. and Sr. Clauder in Och_____y last week we decided to start the school again next week, and we informed our Brn. and Srs. last Sunday that they could bring their children back. God, who is wise in all things, will also know how to help us in this regard! Even if there is no human help in sight, we have entrusted ourselves to Him alone.

There is no thought at all of the school children helping in the household and in the fieldwork as you suggested, as they should certainly do. Concerning help in the kitchen, we know what has happened previously and what the results were, and most of the fieldwork is really too hard for them. Furthermore, 3¾ years ago we were advised to keep the mission things closed off from the schoolchildren and not let them go everywhere, which we followed. In fact we have found this very necessary, although we were accused of being greedy and strange people. Even in the kitchen there is no work for boys 6-10 years old except fetching some water and perhaps picking up chips, and then it would immediately be said that the children have no school and are just supposed to help in the kitchen, as was the case before.

They also say to our faces that the children are being spoiled here. Then there is also the fact that if they are fattened up here, so to speak, and go home plump and fat, they still tell their people that they get rotten meat to eat here — which their relatives naturally believe is the gospel truth — also that their children are not well bathed here, etc. We could add many things to this which in fact are very annoying to us, but I will not do so at this time. Then others say they were tired of preparing food for their children and washing for them at home, so they wanted to send them to school.

The ingratitude is indescribably great. Nothing we do is enough for them, and the more we do, the more is asked of us. This is most especially true with the children of our neighbors who are wealthy and would be in a position to pay school fees and also for the food their children eat here. Instead, they complain and mock the missionaries and accuse them of being greedy people. There is much like this to say, but enough of this here.

We are currently living in peace from outside; we hear nothing or little now about the Georgia soldiers — or Guards as they are improperly called. Here I must note, however, that one statement made by the Governor of Georgia in his reply, "To the Board of Directors of the U. Brn. Mission," was not very comforting. He writes: "According to your request & in full Confidence that your Missionaries will conform to your directions, <u>the Commanding Officer of the Guard will be directed to wait with them, untill</u>

they can conveniently remove from the State, or take the oath required by law."[1] In my opinion this makes it clear enough that we either must leave the state or swear allegiance to their Law. We would never do the latter. We urgently ask you to tell us your thoughts about this statement.

In your letters you have often mentioned that your considerations concerning the Cherokee Mission must depend on what the Cherokees decide to do. So in reply: They are not at all thinking about moving, and we would be in an especially bad situation if we gave even the slightest indication that we were thinking it would be good for them to move west. As far as we have heard and know at the present time, since they have learned about the opinion of the Supreme Court they have decided to act according to their own laws again, and they are planning to tolerate and accept everything that the Georgians might do to them for this, even if they are all arrested. Accordingly, they have begun to hold Courts again, and the Chief, Mr. J. Ross, has sent word to the Judges and the other officers that they should take up their duties to carry out the Cherokee laws again. However, anyone among them who did not want to do this should inform him so that he could name someone else to their position.

That is how things here look now, and so there is no thought of moving west and the mission here could exist for many more years if Georgia tolerates missionaries in the state, since the Cherokees have now reached the above decision. And the Conf. can guide its deliberations accordingly.

And so we ask you once again to release us from this post. Br. Theod. Schulz will still remember that when we accepted the call here we were promised that we could return as soon as another Br. and Sr. could be found for this place, but we believe they have never been sought. At that time, the Conf. also believed and agreed that my wife is too old and weak for this post, which is difficult in all respects. Concerning me personally, there is no need to look far, because anyone who is willing to serve the

---

[1] The quotes are in English in the original German manuscript.

Savior here, no matter who he is, would be more beneficial to the work here than I am. We helped the Brn. out of a predicament at that time, and we have faith in them that they will not leave us stuck in a bad situation now. In addition, we were not given a new call here through the Lot, so we are even happier to ask urgently for our release and to receive it. The Savior will provide for our support and assistance. He has never left us, and He will continue to take care of us.

In your kind letter dated Apr. 14, you wish that we would consider what measures should be or would be taken regarding our property. What should be considered mission costs and what belongs to it. As I have already reported above, we think it is premature to do this now, since the Cherokees are not yet thinking about moving away. However, we will take the time to put everything on paper as well as we can, so that it can be used no matter what happens. In any case, we cannot drive the cattle and the pigs to Salem, as you asked in your letter. Otherwise, it seems to us that the formal departure from here is still very far away, although we cannot know this. It is perhaps closer than we think.

Last Sunday I received a letter from Br. and Sr. Copeland in Indiana. They arrived at the Claytons in Bartholomew County on March 26. Br. Copeland had claimed a piece of land next to the Claytons, but he wrote that he could not pay for it until he had received his money from Salem. Perhaps you will succeed in having it sent to him through Br. Schweiniz. Regarding the money which was sent here for him, we had to use it, since Copeland was gone.

On Pentecost last Sunday we had a blessed enjoyment of Holy Communion. The Indian Br. Emanuel watched during this as a confirmand, and his wife Margareth Susanna as a candidate. Mr. Dazizi served as interpreter in our services. The two Sisters, Felicitas Hicks, Charles Renatus Hicks's widow, and Sr. Delila McNair, had also come for it this time. They live 18 to 20 miles from here. The peace of God could be powerfully felt in all of our services.

Night before last thieves got into our springhouse. After they had tried to break open the lock to the doors and then the doors themselves, they climbed onto the roof, as we could see from their footprints, and they tried to get in there. They did not succeed at this either, because the shingles were nailed on. Finally, they had to be satisfied with taking whatever they could get through a small crack between the logs. This included about 8 or 10 pounds of veal, a knife, some salt, an apron which was wrapped over the meat, a frock which belongs to Nancy Becker, and some other small things. We found no trace of who they might have been.

Recently the Georgians took a missionary in Wills Valley under arrest — Doct. Butler — and took him away with them. When they had been traveling about one day they came to Head of Coosa, where Major Ridge lives, and they set him free — but they made him promise that he would come to Scudders at Headquarters at his leisure. Is that not ridiculous?

We are having very unpleasant weather here, cool but at the same time so dry that the field and garden crops cannot grow. Otherwise, there is a great shortage of bread among the Indians because they have no more corn. Indians often come to us just to get something to eat. We cannot imagine what will happen to them before the new corn has grown. Our corn is also pretty wilted, so that we would probably have to buy some if we did not have hope that the wheat we have in the field might help out to a good extent. Everything in the field and in the gardens is about 3 or 4 weeks behind because of the cool and dry weather. We did make some hay this week from mountain grass and clover. Oats will be very short this year, so that prospects for the cattle next winter are bad. Perhaps we will get more favorable weather so that everything might still turn out well. We will have few peaches this year or perhaps none, because the few that are there are usually found and eaten by the Indians when they are half grown. There is a pretty good crop of apples.

Recently we had a visit from the missionary Revd. D. Buttrick from Carmel about 30 miles toward the border of Georgia. He told us that he was planning to remove his family to that part of the Nation which lies in the state of Tennessee, because he does not believe they are completely safe from the Georgians in Carmel.

Perhaps I can report whether I have received anything from you with today's mail from Georgia before I post this letter in the mail.

Since the Georgia mail did not bring us anything from Salem today, I will close this letter. Everyone here sends greetings. And you also accept a special greeting from your poor fellow Brother,

Gottl. Byhan

[Br. Schulz writes:] Is there an answer from the Genl. Postmaster?

[Springplace (M 407-2) and Oochgeelogy (M 409-1) Diaries.]

Sun., May 29. [Spg.] In our Sunday service we prayed the Church Litany and read some from the *Idea Fidei Fratrum.* Only a few Brn. and Srs. came today. Today 2 children were brought to our school, with whom we will begin school once again. Most of the Indians have no more corn, and the need for bread is starting to become great among them, so we currently have a good many visitors who either want to buy corn or just beg for it. We are mostly approached by the latter. We must also help them as well as we can then. Otherwise, things look sad for the corn crop, because the weather is so cold and harsh that the planted corn cannot sprout, and what is able to sprout is eaten up by the so-called cutworms. Many people have had to plow their fields under and plant anew.

Sun., May 29. [Ooch.] Services were as usual.

Mon., May 30. [Ooch.] We heard that Judge Clayton's recent decision made in Georgia in favor of the missionaries among the Cherokees had been declared invalid by the governor of that state, and that they would receive official notice of this, so they could use the appointed period of time to move away.

1831, part 6

[Springplace (M 407-2) and Oochgeelogy (M 409-1) Diaries. Translated by Julie Tomberlin Weber. Handwritings are Henry G. Clauder's (Ooch.) and Gottlieb Byhan's (Spg.).]

May 31. [Ooch.] The taking prisoner of Br. Clauder in the

Die Gefangennehmung des Br. Clauder
seit mehreren Monaten unter dem

morning by the well-known Guards was completely unexpected. For many months, under the pretense of carrying out the laws of the state here, they have committed some unbelievable horrors. Br. Clauder was immediately taken by horse to the quarters of the commanding officer at Br. Wm. Hicks's, and they indicated that he would be let go after a brief conversation. But when he arrived there things seemed completely otherwise, because he was put in offending leg irons and ordered to the other prisoners, including a Methodist missionary, Mr. Trott, whom we know. During the night he and the others were bound with a chain around his leg attached to a rail, so he had to endure his time in painful circumstances. After an hour, Br. Clauder finally succeeded in making some explanations that satisfied the captain and secured his release, with the condition that Br. Clauder and the rest of the missionaries would leave the country within a short period of time.

[M 415-1a-23: Translated by Julie Tomberlin Weber. No address; no postmark.]

Oyugillogy, C.N., May 29, 1831

Dear Br. Schulz,

On the 26th of this month I received your dear letter dated the 30th of last month, 8 days later than one from my dear parents dated May 3. Your kind interest in our well-being provided me with special encouragement in these gloomy days of trials.

I am happy to be able to report to you that our school will finally begin again tomorrow. Many of our former students arrived here for this today. It is our decision to continue with this as well as we can under the current circumstances. This cannot last long, however, because I, as well as the rest of the missionaries, expect an official notice from the Georgia agent to leave the country by a designated time, or perhaps even to be taken to prison. From the following facts you can see what the basis for my expectations is.

Through the mediation of some person in Georgia (presumably the Governor) Mr. Worcester has been released from the Post Office job in New Echota, and it has been given to a Georgian who lives there. Furthermore, Doct. Butler, a missionary of the American Board, was arrested by the well-known Guards some weeks ago with the explanation that the missionaries were not agents of the U.S., and therefore they were not exempted from that law which is too familiar to us. Col. Nelson repeated this explanation to the missionary Thompson in Hightower and added that he would soon receive notice of this, and he might be subject to a second arrest. For this reason Mr. Worcester was relieved of his office so that his commission would not provide him safety.

Gov. Gilmore's point in his letter to the P.H.C. in Salem might easily be overlooked. He promises protection for Br. Byhan only until he has a successor in the Post Office and can move. [in English:] He does not refer, by the most distant allusion, to Judge

Clayton's decision, which recognized us indiscriminately as agents of the U.S. His otherwise ambiguous letter is at least plain in this point. The favorable decision of Judge Clayton will doubtlessly be repealed ere long — if that is not already the case.

These are the current signs of the time, which do not indicate anything good can be expected. In the meantime, we will wait patiently for your advice about what we should do in these circumstances.

I cannot neglect to share my frank thoughts about this matter. I am still of the opinion that we should not leave this post before we endure a brief imprisonment, or if this were to last for long — which would lead to our complete departure from here — then the blame would rest on Georgia. The blame obviously belongs to Georgia, but this is not how the Indians would see it if we tried to save ourselves by fleeing. The purpose and intention of the Georgians are too clear and firmly entrenched than to allow hope that the threatening storm might soon pass over. Their law must be enforced, and those who cannot submit to it for reasons of conscience will joyfully endure the penalty. It is certainly our sincere desire that the drawn-out, pitiful matter with the Cherokees and with this mission would soon come to an end, and in my opinion only the Georgians themselves can hasten this, as soon as we are not in their way.

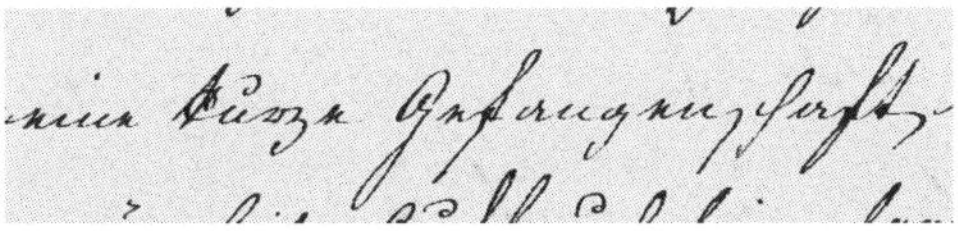

It is nearly impossible and pointless for me to move back to McNair's, because nothing offers hope for more peaceful times if we wait. Our stay there could turn out to be very long, and I do not feel any joy about doing this now. Sr. Gambold would not be able to remain behind alone here this time, since she has been very unwell for several weeks already and needs quiet, which cannot be found here. I do not even need to add that I will follow your instructions faithfully, even if they are contrary to those previously stated.

May the Lord arrange everything so that it works out best for us and for the poor oppressed Cherokees. They will hardly be able to find peace again here, and I fear their stubbornness is thrusting them into deeper misery. I would be sincerely happy if they would move like the Choctaws, who are emigrating to the west en masse along with some of their teachers.

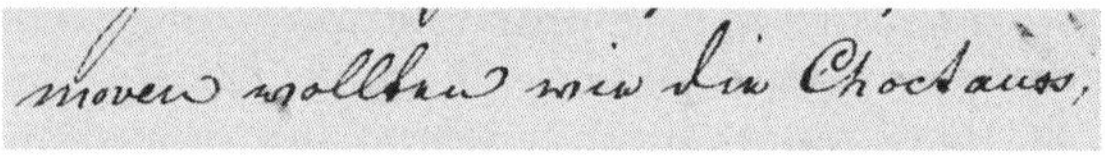

The Post Office in New Echota is now in bad hands, but we want to try to continue our correspondence further through it as before, except in such cases where letters of special value are sent. Then it is safer to send them to Spring Place (as long as Br. Byhan is postmaster).

Next Sunday Christian David is supposed to join us as a member in Holy Communion for the first time. Wm. Hicks is planning to travel to the Vally Towns in North Carolina this week, to see if he can profitably establish a store at the gold mines there. He is in debt and must find ways to free himself. Gann and his family are moving to Alabama. Once again, our little church is losing a member. Services are now better attended here by Methodists. There are not as many of their preachers and exhorters as before.

Three weeks ago we visited at Ridge's at Head of Coosa and had a good time there. Sr. Ridge was home alone. Margaret Hicks was along to interpret.

Thank you very much for the items of news included in your kind letter, which are of great interest to us. I would wish for a better name for the volunteer company. Their name (Guard) has a bad reputation here! The postal service has grown a lot. I am amazed that Shober, Sr., and Zevelly can manage it alone.

Have Br. and Sr. Newby arrived in Salem? Salem will soon be the largest town in western North Carolina, won't it?

A letter from Br. Alex. Copeland finally arrived from Indiana, where he has settled close to Clayton, Hauser, and the other Brethren. There is no opportunity to send him his money from here. Where you are, you will surely be able to find a good way to send it. He spent one month on the journey, which was fortunate, and 40 miles from here he had to stay a while because of a broken wagon wheel.

Our fields are suffering greatly from the drought and from frost we had during the nights of May 24-27. The so-called cut worms have also caused damage among the young corn plants. Last week we had to transplant ½ of our entire crop.

We were visited by the Georgia surveyors twice recently. They asked for lodging here and were taken into the schoolhouse. They behaved respectably. One of them spent 3 days here before his company came. In the meantime, he was quite helpful to us in the fields. They are now finished with this area.

Greetings to your dear family, Henry especially (he owes me a letter), Br. Bechler and Br. Schaaf. Finally I commend myself to your further loving remembrance and remain your faithfully obliged Brother,

H. G. Clauder

The 31st. Yesterday evening I saw Revd. Mr. Thompson, who had received 2 letters from Gilmore and Sanford with the order to go beyond the limits within 10 days. I read both letters. Gilmore's letter is extremely abusive. He writes that the Genl. Government did not see us as Agents, and that in his view we were here only to civilize the Indians, to prevent and move their stubbornness, and that if he (Thompson) did not pay attention to this notice he would be treated most severely. The rest of the Presbyterian missionaries have received the same notice and without a doubt will move. Late yesterday evening, we were somewhat disturbed by drumming which came from the Georgia guards who were camping nearby with many prisoners. I am expecting them here this morning. Now our stay is surely at an end. If our colleagues flee there is no point in our staying either. But I will remain until I receive instructions from you or Sanford to go. If only we had not started the school again.

The 31st. 12 o'clock. 3 hours ago I was taken prisoner by 3 soldiers and led to Wm. Hicks's, where Col. Nelson has been staying since yesterday evening. I was taken in briefly and brought to the other prisoners. After an hour I sent word to Col. Nelson asking if I could have an interview with him, to which he gladly agreed. After hearing my explanations, during which I referred to Gov. Gilmore's letter to you and to the official notice given to the rest of the missionaries, he let me go in a friendly manner with the stipulation that I use the time period of 10 days designated for the others to leave. He spoke very flatteringly about the United Brethren, but he could not grant a longer time period. He regretted that we could not use the provision of the Law to stay here (take the oath). He is being very strict with the rest of the prisoners, among whom there is a Methodist missionary who will be guarded in chains with the rest of them during the night, and he is not being allowed to ride his horse, but must go by foot in this horrible heat.

It is possible and also perhaps appropriate that I will use my deportation from here to travel to Salem by way of the Vally towns and Morganton (which I could do in 7 days) to give a thorough report about the state of affairs here, which is now perhaps necessary to be able to finally reach a decision. Surely this could not happen too soon now. Tomorrow I will go to Spring Place to consult with Br. Byhan. All is in great confusion again.

8 o'clock P.M. May 31. I just received your dear letter dated May 19, which arrived in New Echota on the 29th. Faster than ever! One would not expect that it would arrive in the midst of such agitation. Mission work is now at an end, but for reasons different than what you would presume. Mr. Thompson spent the night here and will move, as will Butrick and Proctor.

Spring Place, June 1. I arrived here at noon. 2 hours later the Guard (20 men) marched past here in full ranks on the way to Sumack, but they did not stop in here. Naeman Rominger had gone to McNair's one hour earlier. Without a doubt Br. Byhan will soon receive his dismissal from the Post Office. I would like to ask the P.H.C. to let me use the time of my deportation for a trip to Salem to avoid depression of spirits, which would result from a long stay alone at McNair's. Please answer soon regarding my request. Your inquiries regarding N. R. will now surely be pointless. If not, I hope to be able to answer them point by point.

This letter has grown long. Please excuse my small scrawl and all the confusion, which is just a sign of the confusion here! Br. Byhan will write personally. Your faithfully obliged Brother,

H. G. Clauder

[Springplace (M 407-2) and Oochgeelogy (M 409-1) Diaries.]

June 1. [Spg.] Br. Byhan, Sr., went to Mr. McNair's on business. When he arrived there he heard that the Georgia Guard had received new orders to arrest all missionaries and white people at once if they did not want to swear allegiance to follow the Georgia laws. And that they were already busy below Ochgeloogy arresting white people and had actually arrested some. There was also various other disquieting news of what the Georgia Guard had already done. This news upset Br. Byhan more than a little, and so after he had stayed at McNair's a couple of hours, he set out on the return journey to Spring Place. When he had already ridden about 6 or 7 miles he met Br. Naeman Rominger from Spring Place with the news that Br. Clauder was at Spring Place on a visit and that the Georgia Guard had arrested him yesterday but set him free again with the announcement that he had to get his things in order within 10 days and leave the state of Georgia. This afternoon 12 to 14 men from the Georgia Guard with the officer, Col. Nelson, went past our house through our lane in full gallop, without calling, to arrest some white people in Sumak Town. Late in the evening Br. Byhan arrived at Spring Place.

June 1. [Ooch.] Br. Clauder went to Spring Place, and he returned from there the following day. At home he found a brief letter from the Commandant of the previously mentioned Guard with the happy news that for the time being Br. Clauder could stay peacefully at his work; if a higher authority orders us to move away, we would be given enough time to do so.

June 2. [Spg.] Early in the day old Mother Vann and Jos. Vann's wife herself came to our place. They said that the Georgia Guard had just picked up Mr. Jos. Vann to go to Sumak, because the commanding officer, Col. Nelson, wanted to discuss some things with him. Mr. Vann then had to go with them with no further ado. Toward noon Br. Clauder left here again on the way to Ochgeloogy. Two hours afterward Mr. Vann sent word to us asking Brn. Byhan and Clauder to go to him, since he had something to tell us. But since Br. Clauder had already left here,

Brn. G. Byhan and Nathl. Byhan went over. Mr. Vann then told them that Col. Nelson had appointed him to tell us that for the time being we could stay here in peace until further orders, and then we would receive 10 days to move out of the area of Georgia, and that he had left the same instructions with Mr. Willm. Abr. Hicks for Br. Clauder. We also hear that the Post Office will be taken away from Spring Place, so that when he is no longer postmaster they will be free to treat Br. Byhan the same as the other missionaries who are allowed only 10 days to leave the state of Georgia. All the rest of the missionaries will now leave the state of Georgia except Mr. Worcester, who currently cannot move because of illness in his family.

June 3. [Spg.] After a long drought we received a beautiful soaking rain, for which we were sincerely grateful to our dear heavenly Father. A traveler from the area close to Pfaff Town, Stokes County, N. Carolina, named Johns, stopped in at our place today. Because of continuous rainy weather he stayed with us until early on the 4th, when he continued his journey.

[M 415-1a-24: Translated by Julie Tomberlin Weber. Addressed to: Revd. Theodor Schulz, Salem, Stokes County, North Carolina. Postmark: Spring Place, C.N., June 5. Free. G. Byhan, P.M. Received June 15.]

Springplace, June 3, 1831

Dear Br. Schulz,

Since my last letter to you, dated May 28, various things have taken place from which one might conclude that the mission here will soon have reached its end, and all of us will be released from the extremely unpleasant and uncertain situation in which we have existed since the beginning of January already. The following has happened here this week.

Already at the end of last week and the beginning of this week, we heard a rumor from afar that the Georgia soldiers had received a new order that the missionaries in the country should be arrested if they would not take the oath to the laws of Georgia, because the decision of Judge Clayton, that the missionaries were to be considered Agents of the U. St. G. because they had received its support, has been declared null and void. This news did not bother us, and accordingly, trusting in the help of the Lord, we began our school again last Monday. Since I had business at McNair's, I rode there on Monday. But when I arrived there I heard many things about the Georgia soldiers and what they were now planning to do and that the missionaries would no longer be spared now. Also they were already at the Head of Coosa several days ago and had arrested some there, and now they would come into our area. This and other things unsettled me, so I set out to return to Spring Place after a visit there.

When I had ridden 6 or 7 miles, Naem. Rominger came riding toward me with the announcement that Br. Clauder was at Spring Place for a visit. He had been arrested by the Georgians yesterday but was set free but told that he had to leave the state of Georgia within 10 days. I cannot describe how I felt upon hearing this news.

Before I could reach Spring Place, the soldiers had already reached Spring Place, and 12 to 14 of them sprang through our Lane without stopping or calling out, and they made their way to Sumack Town to catch more white people. They had the Methodist preacher, Mr. Trott, with them, and they were leading him around the country. Supposedly they even had him in chains, because it is said he had verbally attacked the Georgians.

On Wednesday evening I returned to Spring Place. In a joint discussion with Br. Clauder, we decided that given the current situation, it was best for Br. Clauder to flee to Mr. McNair's once again and that Sr. Clauder and Sr. Gambold, who are very willing to do this, should remain in Och_____y with Mr. Jay Hicks until we see what will happen and what our further fate will be. Sr. Gambold stated that she would not move away from there until her complete move to Salem.

Now further: Early Thursday morning, Mother Vann and Mrs. Vann came to our place and told us that the soldiers had just taken Jos. Vann to Sumack because the commanding officer, Col. Nelson, wanted to talk with him. At 12 noon Br. Clauder returned to his post in Och_____y. At 2 o'clock in the afternoon

Mr. Vann sent word to us, to Br. Clauder and me, that we should come over to his place, since the soldiers had set him free again, and he had something to tell us. Br. Clauder was already gone, so Nathl. and I went over.

Mr. Vann told us then that Col. Nelson had appointed him to tell us, Br. Clauder and me, that we could remain peacefully at our places until further orders, and that he, Col. Nelson, had also left a note with the same message for Br. Clauder at Willm. Abr. Hicks's, which he will surely receive when he returns from Spring Place. Col. Nelson also asked us very specifically if I was still the postmaster, and since I was an old man who was the young man they had seen here, etc. I also heard recently that I will soon be released from the Post Office, that it was already known in Milledgeville that I was no longer postmaster. And so now I am awaiting the dismissal from the office of postmaster each mail day, and when I am no longer postmaster, then the order Col. Nelson mentioned above will surely come anew. I forgot to mention above that Col. Nelson had also told Mr. Vann that we would also have 10 days to remove after we had received the next order.

I personally assume that as soon as I am no longer postmaster, this new order will appear, and that we then will have to remove in 10 days.

You can surely imagine what our current situation is like, and now we leave it up to the Conf. to decide what can be done about the mission here. Before I send this letter, I will wait for tomorrow's mail. If I receive my dismissal from the Post Office, our stay here will not last much longer. Br. Clauder, who wrote to the Conf. this week, will have reported in detail what happened to him and how his current situation and ours are.

So now we anxiously await an answer to our letters. Br. Clauder was almost ready — since he cannot stay at his post — to make a visit to Salem to be present for your further deliberations about the mission. However, I presume that upon his return to Och_____y when he has received the above-mentioned instructions and time limit from Col. Nelson he will decide not to travel to Salem.

Now it is clear, to us at least, that we can no longer maintain our posts here and in Och____y, because it is impossible for us to be useful any longer in the circumstances we have been in for almost half a year now. It would have been very desirable if a Br. from among you could have paid a visit here to see our situation personally and to judge it. But now since I suppose this cannot be, we ask even more urgently for a quick answer from the Conf. and instructions about what should be done in these difficult circumstances that touch body and mind.

June 4, 4 o'clock in the afternoon. I just received your dear note from May 18th, along with the 3rd booklet of printed and handwritten *Nachrichten*, which we gladly received and thank you sincerely for them. I can only reply the following to your kind note. We ask you and Mother Schulz to see that, if our Rachel cannot tolerate her current situation because of her health, please have her give up her service there. We will be happy to pay for her board. We know how she is; when she has a lot of work before her she does more than she is able. At least that is how she was here. And so we would prefer that she leave there before it is too late.

You are correct when you write that the mission work is paralyzed in the situation we and it currently exist, as you will see above. May God have mercy and continue to help!! I will send the income and expenditures by the desired time, if I am still here. I have not heard anything new since yesterday except that the soldiers are at Headquarters again. Sincere greetings from all of us to all of you, and a special greeting from your poor Br.,

Gottlieb Byhan

[Springplace (M 407-2) and Oochgeelogy (M 409-1) Diaries.]

Sun., June 5. [Spg.] The services were as usual. Otherwise, we noticed today that our Indian Brn. and Srs. were very touched when they heard and saw that our presence here will probably not be allowed to continue much longer, and especially the Srs. could not keep back their tears. We advised them to continue behaving calmly and to take this matter to our dear Lord diligently in prayer.

Sun., June 5. [Ooch.] After the usual Sunday sermon, one of our Sr. Gann's children was baptized into Jesus' death with the name Maria. Christian David participated in Holy Communion for the first time after confirmation, and a heart-rending awareness of Jesus' presence prevailed during this.

[M 415-1a-25: Translated by Julie Tomberlin Weber. Addressed to: Revd. Theod. Schulz, Salem, Stokes County, North Carolina. Postmark: Springplace, C.N., June 5. Free. G. Byhan, P.M. Received June 18. Br. Schulz writes in the address: End of March: governor's answer & Judge Clayton's decision. June 15: of the reversal of the latter & our results.]

Springplace, C.N., June 5, 1831

My dear Br. Schulz,

In my letter to you yesterday, I wrote that we had received orders from the commanding officer, Col. Nelson, that we could remain at our post until further orders. Yesterday evening, after I had already closed my letter to you and it was in the mail, I received a letter from Br. Clauder with the New Echota mail, in which he gave me a copy of the order he received from Col. Nelson when he arrived in Och_____y last Thursday, and he requested that I send it on to you immediately. It says:

[Br. Byhan copies Col. Nelson's letter in English:]

Hixes, May 31, 1831

Dear Sir:

The character which you have sustained, being contrary to that of others, I have determined to make you a distinguished object of our forbearance. You will therefore remain with your family in quiet, or pursue your own inclination untill further directed.

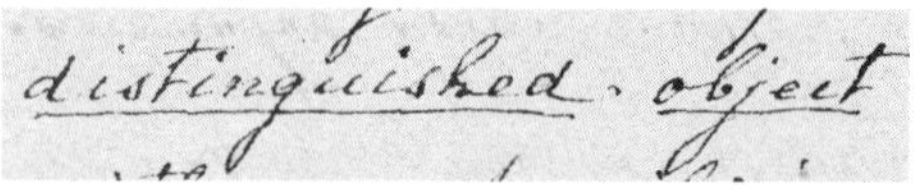

Should you be in future directed to comply with the Laws or

leave the territory, time will be given you to comply with at least as much convenience to you as at this time. With my best wishes for your success in the cause which you are labouring in, be pleased to accept my personal respect & esteem. Respectfully,

C. H. Nelson, Sub. Com. Ga. Gd.

[Br. Byhan continues his letter to Br. Schulz in German:]

This indicates that Br. Clauder can stay at home in peace for now. This gives him time to move away conveniently, which is what will have to happen in the end. Everyone here believes that as soon as I have received my farewell or dismissal from the Post Office, our final notice to remove will be given. As we hear, the Georgians are making great efforts to find a postmaster to take my place. However, as far as we know, they have not yet succeeded in this. Personally, I do not know of anyone in the neighborhood here who could be postmaster except for a certain Wacaasee in Sumak Town, who lives at a place vacated when its previous residents moved to Arkansas. It is believed that he will become postmaster. Thus I am expecting my dismissal every mail day.

We sincerely wish that the *Phönix* of June 4 reaches your hands properly. There are letters from the Governor of Georgia to Mr. Worcester in it, from which one can see the attitude of the Georgians toward the Presbyterian missionaries. Please let me know if you have received it.

I sent my letter yesterday by way of Georgia. This one is supposed to go through Knoxville. We will see which reaches Salem first. The former left already this morning. Everyone greets you all, and I especially greet you as your friend and Br.,

Gottlieb Byhan

[Springplace (M 407-2) and Oochgeelogy (M 409-1) Diaries.]

June 9. [Spg.] Rev. Mr. Thomson, missionary in Hightower, arrived at our place with his family on his flight to Brainerd and spent the night here. He had temporarily given his house and the rest of his property in Hightower to an Indian, a member of his congregation. Afterward the Georgia Guard had taken possession of it. Mr. Thomson is planning to live in Brainerd and visit his congregation in Hightower from time to time and serve them with word and sacrament. On the same plan Rev. Mr. Buttrick from Carmel wanted to go to Willstown in the state of Alabama, but he then moved to Candys Creek in the state of Tennessee. Mr. Proctor, also a missionary in Carmel, will set up a tent about 8 miles from Mr. McNair's in the state of Tennessee, in a Settlement of Indians, as it is called, and live there and hold school for the Indian children there until further orders from their Directors. So at this time most of the mission places of the Presbyterians have been closed by the laws of Georgia in this part of the Nation which belongs to the state of Georgia. As far as we are concerned, we here in Spring Place and Ochgeloogy cannot be grateful enough to our dear Lord for arranging things so that we are still allowed to stay at our posts until further orders. How long we will maintain this permission, however, we admittedly cannot know, because presumably as soon as the Post Office is taken from Br. Byhan — and we hear the Georgians are really trying to have it taken away from him — instructions will also come for us to leave the state of Georgia.

June 10. [Spg.] After heat of 98° Fahr., a strong storm arose in the northeast accompanied by very heavy rains and wind. Luckily the strong wind, which could have been very disadvantageous for our wheat and oats, did not last long. At our invitation Mr. Jos. Vann and a certain Mr. Howel visited us today. The former bled Sr. Byhan, who has been sickly for a long time already. Indians now come to our place almost every day to beg for corn, since there is almost none left to be had in the country. The need for bread is currently very great among the Indians. We are helping them as well as we can from our little bit as long as we still have some. This year we have some wheat to harvest, and it will be very useful to us this year.

Sun., June 12. [Spg.] After the sermon was the baptism into Jesus' death of the baby daughter born to our Br. and Sr. William

Henry and his wife Martha, with the name Sarah Jane. Mr. Dav. Steiner Dazizi was here today and served us as interpreter, so we took advantage of the opportunity to explain our current situation clearly to our Brn. and Srs. and tell them that we did not know how long we would still be allowed to stay here. We could tell they had great compassion for our situation, but did not say much more about it. They just said: We are in the same situation. They were asked to commend this matter and the difficult situation in which we all find ourselves diligently in prayer to the Savior, who can arrange everything, even our difficult and desperate circumstances, for the best.

Sun., June 12. [Ooch.] After a long drought, a pleasant rain refreshed the thirsty earth, and during the sermon we brought the Lord our humble gratitude for this.

Mon., June 13. [Ooch.] We received a brief visit from the missionaries Butler and Chamberlin. They were on their return journey from the Georgia Agency where the former was told to leave the country. The latter lives within the borders of another state.

June 14. [Spg.] Toward evening a traveler came to us whom Mr. Vann sent to us because he had no more feed for the horses. He spent the night here. This man was from N. Carolina, from Hertford County. Since he was planning to go through Salem, he promised to tell our Brn. and Srs. there thoroughly about our situation.

June 17. [Spg.] Once again two travelers came whom Mr. Vann sent to us, and they spent the night.

[*Records: N.C.*, 8:3969: Salem Diary. Translated by Douglas L. Rights.]

June 15. Letters from our Brethren Byhan and Clauder, missionaries in the Cherokee country, advised us they could no longer remain at their stations unless they took the oath of allegiance to the State of Georgia. Br. Clauder had already been apprehended, but was released after a conversation with the officer — with the intimation that he would have to leave the state after a period of respite.

[B 61-3: Provinzial Helfer Conferenz, meeting in Salem. Translated by C. Daniel Crews.]

June 15. After we received on the 24th of Apr. a polite answer[1] from Governor Gilmer in Georgia to our letter, in which he stated that he had ordered the Georgia officers in the Cherokee Land not to disturb our missionaries until they could move at their leisure, and had also instructed them to free the arrested Presbyterian missionaries from the law court in Georgia, and that they were to be regarded as agents of the United States Government, our Brethren who had fled to Mr. McNair's could return to their posts to await what the Cherokees will finally decide.

Letters received today from the Brethren Byhan and Clauder unfortunately report that the Governor in Georgia has declared the declaration of the judge there incorrect. This judgment was that the Missionaries should be regarded as Agents of the Genl. Government. The Presbyterian and other Missionaries there, through order of the commanding officer of the Georgia Guards, have received word to leave the Cherokee Land in 10 days. Otherwise, they will be dealt with according to Georgia laws. Also Br. Clauder was brought as a prisoner by the soldiers to Br. Hicks's, but (after he appealed to Colonel Nelson on the basis of the letter of protection of the Governor) he was released with the explanation to leave in 10 days. The abovementioned officer softened this in a couple of days, and allowed him and Br. Gb. Byhan to remain for the time being at their places undisturbed with their families until they get new orders. But then they will have to leave the Cherokee Land.

Accordingly, the other Missionaries thought to withdraw gradually, and because the respite given to our Brethren can hardly

[1] Governor Gilmer's April 13, 1831, letter is M 411-1-32, pages 4444-45 above.

last longer than Br. Byhan's being given a successor as Postmaster by the Genl. Postmaster in Washington, of which this Brother has already heard tentative rumors, our Brethren and Sisters there in this distressing time are craving advice as soon as possible from the Prov. H. Conferenz.

In that there is now no prospect that our Missionaries can continue their work undisturbed, and therefore their true purpose and calling cannot proceed as wished, and we also do not dare take on ourselves the responsibility to place them in inevitable misery, danger, and imprisonment to no avail, there was nothing left for us to do than offer to bring them here for the time being, until the circumstances of this Nation have developed further.

In the meantime, our Brn. and Srs. should remain there until Br. Gb. Byhan is relieved as Postmaster or until they are ordered out by force. As soon as one of those two things happens they should immediately report it to us by post and the two four-horse wagons will be sent to pick up their things. In case the Brethren are not allowed to wait there for the transport they will have to move again to Mr. McNair's and wait for the wagons there. In the meantime they must pack their transportable furniture and gear, and what cannot be taken along, such as the cattle, they should leave with Mr. McNair or other friends to be sold — and they should get the said friend's advice on this. Br. Schulz is asked to write him on this account and to communicate all these decisions to our Brn. and Srs.

As soon as the Brn. and Srs. must move, the War Department of the United States in Washington will be contacted about the houses and improvements there at the earliest opportunity.

1831, part 7

[M 415-1a-26: Translated by Julie Tomberlin Weber. Addressed to: Revd. Theodor Schulz, Salem, Stokes County, North Carolina. Postmark: Springplace, C.N., June 19. Free. G. Byhan, P.M. Received June 29.]

Springplace, June 17, 1831

Dear Br. Schulz,

On the last mail day, I received your letter of the 25th of last month along with the 4th booklet of printed *Gem. Nachr.* I received the 3rd booklet 8 days earlier, as I already reported. I sent the note regarding the inheritance of Br. Rüde to Br. Clauder 8 days ago.

What you wrote to me in your last letter about the mission work in East India and about their institutions and schools is certainly good news. However, they have presumably been put in a position to be able to pay for this good work; presumably the external circumstances are also completely different from those among our Cherokees.

My last letter to you was dated the 5th of this month. Since then nothing else has happened that concerned us, except that, as we hear from time to time, it is more and more certain that the Georgians will tolerate absolutely no more missionaries in the country. We hear that the Georgians are doing everything to take the Post Office from me, and as soon as I have been discharged, which I expect every mail day, we will receive orders to leave the State of Georgia within 10 days. Today we heard that Mr. Wakassy — a Georgian in Sumak town — inquired at Mr. Vann's whether we would move away as soon as the Post Office is taken from me. One can almost presume that the Georgians will immediately move into our house as soon as we have left it, which one can pretty well conclude from the following.

Doct. Buttler, missionary in Wills Valey, and Mr. Chamberlane, missionary at another mission place, visited the commanding officer in headquarters, Col. Sanford, in order to ask for protection and patience for Mr. Buttler and Mr. Worcester, because his wife's health does not allow him to move out of the state just now, and the 10 days they were given to move are now over. However, Col. Sandford treated Doct. Buttler very rudely and told him that the sooner he leaves the better, or things would not go well for him, because they, the soldiers, have had more trouble taking the missionaries away than all the rest of the white people. Doct. Buttler and Mr. Worcester had not been allowed to leave other families in the houses. If everyone did not go, the soldiers would clear the houses and put someone else into the houses. This last is admittedly contrary to their own Law, but the Georgians can do anything, so I fear this might also be the case with us.

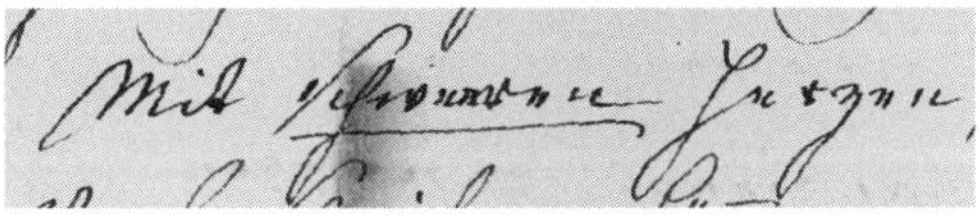

With heavy hearts and with concern we cannot describe, we await the time — and it is not far off — when we will have to make our departure. The loss will be great for the mission diacony both here and in Och_____y. So far we have worked our fields as usual, and yet we must believe that we will not harvest the fruits. One can expect little from the people here if we cannot harvest the wheat, oats, corn, potatoes, etc., for all of this, and yet it was impossible to leave the fields lying fallow. Sometimes we truly do not know what we should think or say about our current situation. We will soon become weak spirited, and it would not be surprising if we actually did. Therefore, we are waiting eagerly for further advice from the Conf.

In the last two weeks we have made some arrangements to get the necessary items, such as papers, etc., in order so that we can pack up quickly when the 10-day order comes, because we hear and note that there is no hope of mercy with these B____n. Now may God continue to help us! Last Sunday we took the opportunity to explain our current situation to our Brn. and Srs. It seemed to really touch them, but they had little or nothing to say about it, because they are also in an awkward situation.

The Presbyterian missionaries are all gone except for Worcester and Doct. Buttler. The former wants to see whether they will take him or not.

Currently, there is great famine among the Indians, because they have no more corn, and so to speak, there is no more to buy in the Nation. And so hungry Indians visit us daily either for food or for corn. We help them as much as we can.

We have heard nothing this week from Br. and Sr. Clauder. Currently we are having beautiful, productive weather. The field and garden crops look good. The question, however, is always with us: Who will harvest it all?

Now may the Savior who has helped us and advised us thus far continue to provide counsel. Even when we do not see what to do we will continue to trust in Him! Everyone here sends best greetings. Your loving, poor Br.,

Gottlieb Byhan

N.B. June 18. I just received Br. Shaaf's note from June 1st and the news from June 4.

[Springplace (M 407-2) and Oochgeelogy (M 409-1) Diaries. Translated by Julie Tomberlin Weber. Handwritings are Henry G. Clauder's (Ooch.) and Gottlieb Byhan's (Spg.).]

June 18. [Spg.] Sr. Delila McNair arrived at our place toward evening on her way to Head of Coosa to visit her daughter there, and she went on further early on *Sun., June 19.* Since it rained incessantly this morning, only a few Brn. and Srs. came for the services.

Sun., June 19. [Ooch.] After the sermon we shared some parts of the *Missionary Inteligencer* with those who were present. Toward evening we had the unexpected pleasure of welcoming our Sr. Delila McNair here at our place. On the following morning she continued on her journey to her children in the southern part of the Nation.

During this time, we had a lot of visits from Indians asking for food in exchange for blueberries. We received one or more bushels of them daily! In some cases, they even offered their silver jewelry and clothing for a little hominy or bread. We gave it to them without accepting the payment offered.

[M 415-1a-27: Translated by Julie Tomberlin Weber. Addressed to: Revd. Theodor Schulz, Salem, Stokes County, North Carolina. Postmark: Spring Place, C.N., June 19, paid 18¾. Received July 2.]

Springplace, June 19, 1831

My dear Br. Schulz,

Yesterday evening after my letter to you dated the 17th of this month was already in the mail, I received a letter with the New Echota mail from Br. Clauder. In this he wrote me that the Georgia soldiers have made an appearance in the area around Ochgeloogy once again, and plan to arrest all white people without exception. He writes me that he will not write to you this week, so I will share with you an excerpt from his letter to me. He writes:

"In your last letter you commented, 'It seems all is quiet again.' But this is just an appearance. The peace is not to be trusted, because each disruption by the Georgians is worse than the previous one. Last Monday I saw Mr. Butler who had just returned from Scudders — headquarters — where he had promised to appear. There he was told that before long the soldiers would be back in the country to catch all the white men who were supposed to be caught, and he and Mr. Worcester would be in big trouble if they did not move, which is certain.

"Col. Sanford also told him that those white families who were left here whose men had fled would have to clear out of the houses soon and that 'completely different' people from the current ones would move into them. So if I am instructed by the P.H. Conf. to move to Mr. McNair's for months, sooner or later the Sisters left behind here could be thrown out of here with all their things. Your situation would be the same. And so the P.H. Conf. cannot consider instructing us to go to a temporary place outside the limits of Georgia, with or without our families, in hope of better times.

"In addition to that, the P.H. Conf. promised Gov. Gilmore to remove us as soon as possible, and Col. Nelson promises to spare us until we can conveniently move. However, what can be expected if the Georgians see that we have not made even the slightest preparations to fulfill the promise of our Directors? The results will not be pleasant or desirable. If no promise or anything to this end had been given, we would know where we stood. But now I feel forced to do everything to fulfill this promise even to an enemy."

This statement by Br. Clauder will give the P.H. Conf. a clear insight into our current indescribably difficult situation. We here in Spring Place agree completely with his thoughts, and we ask and deeply hope that we might soon be released from this uncertain and immeasurably oppressive situation.

The Savior alone comforts us in our current circumstances. If He were not our Comfort, our Help, and Counsel, we would have lost courage long ago. But He helps us manage from day to day with His strong Jesus-Hand. All thanks to Him for this!

The above comments from Br. Clauder's letter were written on the 16th of this month. In the evening on the 17th he added:

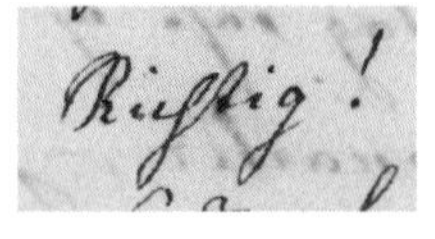

"Correct! The peace was not to be trusted, because the soldiers are in this area once again, but as far as I know they do not have anyone yet."

We cannot describe the sorrow we felt at the thought that we should let our cultivated fields, our cattle, etc., leave our hands, and yet it seems this will be the case. Admittedly, we do not yet have the promised new Order, according to which we will have 10 days to move away. Nor have they taken the Post Office from me yet. But all this can happen in a few days, and then there is no more mercy from the Georgians. Then we have to move. And so we are anxiously awaiting instructions from the P.H. Conf. We also consider it to be the best thing and advisable in our current situation to go ahead and pack the things we do not use on a daily basis.

But you cannot believe how difficult it will be for us and with what feelings we will start this work, when we know in advance that we will have to completely leave the little flock of gathered believers, and yet, as it seems to us, this will be the case. Now the Savior knows what is best and why He has allowed these difficult circumstances to happen to us and to the inhabitants of this country!

You will find Br. Clauder's receipt enclosed. With the most sincere greetings to you, I remain your faithfully obliged Br.,

Gottl. Byhan

[Springplace (M 407-2) and Oochgeelogy (M 409-1) Diaries.]

June 20. [Spg.] Early in the day we discovered that an attempt had been made during the night to steal a beehive from our bee house. The entrance to the beehive was stopped up with dirt and the hive itself was moved from its place. We could not tell if they were disturbed while committing the robbery or if the hive was too heavy, because it was the heaviest of all the beehives. We also discovered that the thieves had been in the barn and had cut off the straps from some horse bridles and taken with them all the straps and ropes they could find. It seems as if the Indians in the current situation in which they find themselves are falling back into their old ways of living habits and customs, since disorderly conduct, drinking, dancing and gambling, and stealing are setting in among them again. It is also not surprising, since they are not allowed to follow their own laws and are declared to be worthless by the Georgians, and they are even punished by the latter for following them. Although it is said that they have extended their laws to the Indians, they themselves, the Georgians, do nothing in this respect. And so the disorder in the country here is really beginning to be habitual. God alone knows what the end of this whole matter will be! Many Indians who were with the Methodists or Baptists when the missionaries were still living peacefully in this country are now falling away and saying that religion is nothing, because they tried it and there was nothing to it. May God have mercy on them! God does not let anything happen by chance, and who knows why this current punishment had to come upon them. If they would only repent and consider what will contribute to their peace instead of all letting the former heathen customs become habits among them. Now the Lord knows His time when the light of the Gospel will find entry into their hearts and they will be turned from the darkness to the light! In the meantime we can do nothing but pray for them, and commend them to the One who also redeemed them from eternal ruin with His bitter sufferings and death.

June 25. [Ooch.] We received a pleasant visit from the previously mentioned Methodist missionary Trott, who recently suffered so much at the hands of the Guards. After 12 days of imprisonment he was released for now after he posted assurance that he would appear before the court next September. Through him we received the troubling news that the mission station at Hightower has been taken by the Georgians, since it, like all the rest, had been declared public property of the State. The missionary who lived there, Thompson, was led to Georgia under guard. This news caused us to worry that the same thing would happen to us and that we could not spend a single day in peace and certainty, because further consequences of this matter could be expected.

Sun., June 26. [Spg.] A good number of our Brn. and Srs. gathered for the services. In the second one Br. Samuel offered a prayer and address to the Brethren and Sisters in the Cherokee language. On this occasion it must be noted with gratitude toward our dear Lord that our Indian Brn. and Srs. currently are in a pleasing spiritual condition. We can see in them that they have experienced grace in their hearts, and their walk shows what children of the Spirit they are. May the Savior keep them with Him and His wounds!

Sun., June 26. [Ooch.] Because of the continuing rain, only a few of our Brethren and Sisters came for the service in the afternoon. We held a prayer service with them, in which we looked in faith to our only Helper and Protector, and we were strengthened and comforted.

June 28 and 29. [Ooch.] Br. Clauder visited the Brethren and Sisters in the neighborhood. The question about the Cherokees moving is approaching a final decision, which people are anxiously awaiting. The last hope of the Indians to receive protection against the oppression of individual states, promised in the end by the authorities of the United States, is now almost gone. So there is nothing left for them to do but give in and seek peace in a different place. Many of them expect to find this place in the Mexican provinces, since the news that recently appeared in the Cherokee newspaper about the closed nature of the country and the political circumstances of that area give them reason to expect this and offered the happy prospect that they not only could expect a friendly reception and attain the rights of citizens, but that they could also avoid forever oppression like that which their property here has forced upon them. Even some of our Brethren and Sisters talk a lot about moving there and clearly express their desire for us to move with them. In this matter we direct them to the Lord, for whom all things are possible, that He might arrange everything according to His wise counsel, remove all obstacles, and Himself open the door for this.

Sun., July 3. [Spg.] Today we once again received a letter from our dear Br. Theod. Schulz, as we had already received one with the mail yesterday from the P.H. Conf. in Salem. From this we learned that the P.H. Conf. in Salem has decided to recall the Brn. and Srs. from the two mission places here for the time being. This is because in the current situation between the Georgians and the Cherokees, the missionaries cannot be of much use here, because they are constantly oppressed by the Georgians and threatened with prison if they do not leave the country or the state of Georgia. This decision was then solemnly reported to our Brethren and Sisters today after our Sunday services. This news aroused such deep compassion and regret among them that some of them could not hold back their tears, and the rest were quiet and seemed dejected. All of them asked us to let them know when we hear something more precise from the Georgians or when the time is designated when we will move away. Our Sr. Delila McNair, who stopped in at our place this morning from a visit at her daughter's at Head of Coosa and spent Sunday here, served us as interpreter. Today we also heard that the Indians about ¾ of a mile from here, formerly called Mountjoy, had had a dance last night. It seems as if the evil enemy is now especially busy bringing the Indians completely under his dominion, as all the former heathen entertainment as well as drinking, fighting, gambling, and stealing are the normal order of the day again. May God have mercy on them!

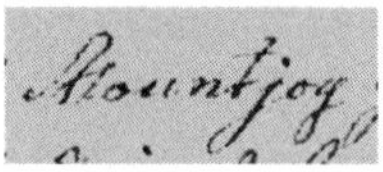

July 4. [Spg.] We received a pleasant visit from Br. Clauder. Since we now know that our stay here in this country will probably not last much longer, we considered together how we should prepare ourselves for the coming journey and how we should best sell the things belonging to the mission which cannot be taken along, or how we could leave behind with a friend to sell for us if an opportunity arises, etc.

July 4. [Ooch.] Br. Clauder went to Spring Place, where letters from our dear Br. Schulz in Salem had arrived. They contained the P.H.C.'s decision to close the mission here for now under the current circumstances, as soon as we get instructions from the authorities of the State of Georgia to leave this country.

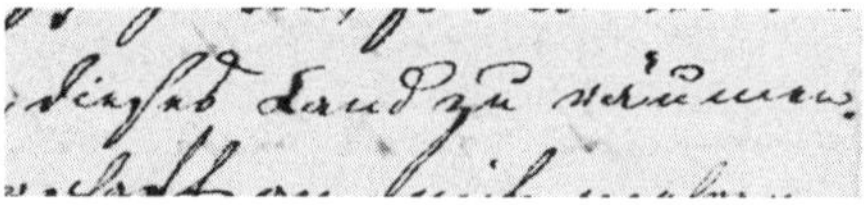

[M 415-1a-28: Transcribed by Grace S. Robinson. Addressed to: Revd. Theodore Schulz, Salem, North Carolina. Postmark: Springplace, C.N., July 10, paid 18¾. Received July 20. Lightly edited.]

Spring Place, July 4, 1831

Dear Br. Schulz,

On my arrival here this afternoon I had the pleasure to receive your welcome letter of June 18th, the contents of which have, in various respects, terminated the painful suspense in which we have lived for the last 5 weeks. In other respects we still remain in suspense, as to the probable lenity or severity which we may expect from the hands of the Officers of Georgia. We have, to our astonishment, not yet recd. the expected official warning to remove from the limits of the Charter of Georgia, which was intimated in Col. Nelson's note to me, a copy of which Br. Byhan forwarded to you some weeks ago. How long we may yet share this forbearance we cannot say. And it would be, I think, rather preposterous to indulge the hope that the United Brethren's Missionaries should be entirely excepted from the operation of a law, under the influence of which several of our most esteemed fellow labourers have suffered so much. We have no grounds to expect such a distinction & it is perhaps owing to the difficulty in the contemplated dismission of Br. Byhan from the postmastership & the consequent alterations of several mail routes that he & myself, as his fellow labourer, have escaped so far further molestation. Taking it, therefore, for granted that the proscriptive notice will sooner or later reach us, I am heartily thankful for the definitive directions your letter contained by which we all know the steps to be pursued on our part in the expected emergency.

In the meantime we shall make the preliminary preparations for a final remove, & indeed we have done so already in various cases.

I have a prospect to dispose of my little stock of tin ware for cash. Many articles could be sold at home if the Indians had money. I have made a small beginning in taking the article of hides in exchange. Hides are purchased by the Tennessee traders at 10¢ per lb. cash. Thus if I should even not meet with a trader here I could sell the whole on the way in Tennessee.

Another suggestion I would offer. I shall probably have an opportunity to get two or three saleable horses, partly for debts due the Mission & partly for house furniture. Extra horses can be of much service on our long & hilly road, & can then perhaps be easily disposed of. This is only a prospective plan, but in which Br. Byhan coincides with me.

Should this plan succeed it would obviate the difficult & protracted plans of consigning the effects of the Mission to other persons. They could perhaps in a short time hereafter effect no sales at all, by reason of a more unsettled state of affairs, or get nothing in payment. It shall be my effort to render the unavoidable losses to which we will be subject as small as possible.

My delay in writing no sooner to you must have perhaps given cause of surprise & deserves explanation. For several weeks after the arrest of myself & others we enjoyed tranquility, nothing of importance occurred. The delay was still extended for the purpose of enclosing the Diary from 1st Jan. to end of June, which I was in the meantime engaged in transcribing. I have the same with me, but shall not enclose it, as it consists of several sheets & would cost at least 56¼ cents to send per mail, an expense which can be saved, I hope, to deliver it together with Records & mss. in person.

Gratefully acknowledging the goodness of our Lord & Saviour, it gives me pleasure to announce our perfect & continued health. Mother Gambold has entirely recovered her usual health. Our little Charles is a stranger to sickness or indisposition, thanks to the Lord for this & all other blessings. His Mother enjoys her accustomed good health. May the Spirit of all grace give us wisdom & continued reliance upon our heavenly Father's aid. May He comfort us in the hour of sore affliction and teach us more & more that all things work together for good to them that love the Lord.

With my best wishes for your health, believe me to be your affectionate fr. & Br. in Jesus,

H. G. Clauder

[Springplace (M 407-2) and Oochgeelogy (M 409-1) Diaries.]

July 5. [Spg.] Br. Clauder returned to Ochgeloogy. Today we also finished driving in our wheat. Since Indian corn is currently very scarce here, our wheat will be of great use to us.

July 7. [Ooch.] The well-known Guards arrived in our neighborhood once again with many white missionaries as prisoners. The following day Br. Clauder received a couple of lines from the commandant, Nelson, with the news that the protection we had previously enjoyed through his earlier letter of May 31st has now been withdrawn. In other words these are definite instructions to leave the country. Leaving the poor, faithful Cherokees is a painful thought, which we cannot express in words. The Lord alone can and will comfort them and us through this difficult trial and bring everything to a glorious conclusion. As a result of this news, we immediately began disposing of those articles that would not be good to take along.

[M 415-1a-29: Translated by Julie Tomberlin Weber. Addressed to: Revd. Theodor Schulz, Salem, Stokes County, North Carolina. Postmark: Springplace, C.N., July 10. Free. G. Byhan, P.M. Received July 20.]

Springplace, July 8, 1831

Dearly beloved Br. Schulz,

Your two kind letters of the 15th and 18th of last month arrived here, the former on the 2nd and the latter on the 3rd.

From these we saw that the Prov. Helf. Conf. has decided to recall us and Br. and Sr. Clauder from the post here for now, and that as soon as I have my dismissal from the Post Office, which is not yet the case, we will get ready for our return journey to Salem. We all consider it best to distance ourselves from here until the circumstances and times have perhaps improved, to a place where the missionaries are not in danger day after day of being arrested and sentenced to the punishment of imprisonment. We are happy that we have hope of escaping from this almost unbearable suspense, because every day and every evening we must wonder: Perhaps today or tonight we will lose our freedom. And it will not be taken by Indians or savages who have little knowledge of God and Civilisation, but by white people who pretend to be civilized and religious. As one of the surveyors said, he was a Methodist preacher.

Now we will look to Him, the Helper in all distress. He can save all who come to Him. He knows best why He allowed this situation to happen to us and to the inhabitants of this country.

The Indians are starting their heathen ways again, ballplays, drunkenness, etc. But theft has especially become the order of the day. Nothing is safe from them anymore. Even the cattle in the bush are not safe from them any longer, and they steal these only in order to get the hides, since they get money for these. When they sell them, they buy themselves brandy with it.

Last Monday Br. Clauder was here in Spring Place on a visit, and we considered together how we could best inventory and sell things so that we would forfeit as little of it as possible, although we will lose enough despite all of our best efforts not to lose anything. As soon as I am dismissed as postmaster and we have received orders to remove in 10 days, we will turn to the commanding officer and request to allow us to remain at our place until the wagon from N.C. picks us up, so that we don't have to move twice. It would be very difficult for us to move to Mr. McNair's first. We do not doubt that our request will be granted by the officer.

Driving our livestock to Salem is not really feasible, although without a doubt it could be sold well there, because our livestock looks really good and is much better than all the rest of it in this area. The reason for this is that it has been well cared for and fed throughout the winter and it received appropriate salt.

We thought we might perhaps get a horse for our pigs, which we could hitch with one of ours, and we might sell it in Carolina, although I believe horses are not as easy to sell at your place as cattle. We want to do all we can so that we lose as little property as possible.

Our Sr. Delila McNair sent word from afar that her son Niclaus wanted to take our place and move into our house. We would like it if this were the case, and I will do my best to work it out if possible. In my next letter I can perhaps give you more information about this matter.

After we had seen from your two kind letters the decision of the Prov. H. Conf. about our departure, we informed our dear Indian Brn. and Srs. of this last Sunday. They were admittedly all very surprised, but they also understand that given the current circumstances and under the pressure in which we and they currently live, we cannot stay here longer. The best thing for us is to distance ourselves for now in the hope that times and circumstances will soon change. Some of them seemed to be greatly touched by this, but they said little or nothing about it. They asked us to let them know immediately as soon as something happened between us and the Georgians, and we promised them this.

On this occasion I just wanted to add one thought we had when we — Br. Clauder and we — were considering and talking about this matter. That is: Would it not be good and helpful if the Prov. H. Conf. wrote some kind of farewell letter to our Brn. and Srs. and read it to them in the service when it comes time to leave and had it interpreted? We are convinced they would all consider it an honor, and it would make a deep impression on them. This was what we thought; we will leave it up to the Prov. H. Conf. to do what it thinks is best in this matter.

Currently we are having lots of wet weather, so our oat harvest is looking quite poor, since it has now rained more or less every day this entire week.

Otherwise, we are gradually preparing for our departure, since we do not know what day we will receive new orders to remove. Today we heard that the Georgia Guard will appear here in our neighborhood in a couple of days. I will not close this letter until the mail from Georgia arrives here tomorrow, so I can see if I will receive anything from Washington and report this to you right away.

I would just add that Mr. Worcester, missionary in New Echota, has decided not to remove. I would not want to be in his position if he is arrested again, which will happen sooner or later.

July 9. The Georgia mail has just arrived, but again brought me nothing from Washington, so we must continue to live in suspense. What do you think, dear Br., if it takes too long for my dismissal from the Post Office, should I not resign to escape this awkward uncertainty? But for now I will await your answer to this question.

All send their best greetings, and especially your poor Br.,

Gottl. Byhan

[M 407-2: Springplace Diary.]

Sun., July 10. [Spg.] Almost all of our Indian Brn. and Srs. came for the services. We learned from a letter we received yesterday evening from Br. Clauder with the New Echota mail that he once again received orders from the commanding officer that he should leave this country, so we reported this to our Brn. and Srs. today in a community discussion. They were very touched by this, although they did not have much to say to it. Still we could see in them that they are very sorry that we have to leave them. The Indian Br. Samuel said they would now have to think their teachers had died and they, the Brn. and Srs., would seem like sheep who have no shepherd. On this occasion they were advised and asked if this should really be the case that we had to leave them, to walk worthily of the grace they have received and to build each other up in the Word of God. Currently a mournful feeling prevails among the Brn. and Srs., and we can clearly see that some of them take it as their duty to diligently carry their and our desperate situation to the Savior in prayer. It is especially important to our Indian Br. Samuel, whom we have often mentioned, that the members of our Gemeine now hold together, so that they could build each other up in God's word from time to time. All of this and other quite Christian-minded expressions by them serve as a true comfort to us. This whole conversation was accompanied by the tears of our Brn. and Srs., as well as by ours. Although a painful feeling prevailed among us, we were still aware in a comforting manner of a feeling of the presence of our unseen Friend.

[M 415-1a-30: Translated by Julie Tomberlin Weber. Addressed to: Rev. Theodor Schulz, Salem, Stokes County, North Carolina. Postmark: Springplace, C.N., July 10, by Knoxville, etc. Free. G. Byhan, P.M. Received July 22.]

Spring Place, July 10, 1831

Dear Br. Schulz,

Since my last letter to you the page has turned once more, and our circumstances have suddenly changed. Late yesterday evening, after my letter to you was already in the Georgia mail, a certain Copeland arrived here — a white man who was fleeing with his small family — with Br. Clauder's wagon, and brings me a letter from Br. Clauder in which he informs me that he has now received the expected new order from Col. Nelson, commanding officer of the Georgia Guard, in the following words:

[Br. Byhan copies Col. Nelson's note in English:]

Dear Sir,

Any protection that my Note of May last may have given you is withdrawn. Very respectfully,

C. H. Nelson,
Sub. Com. G.G.

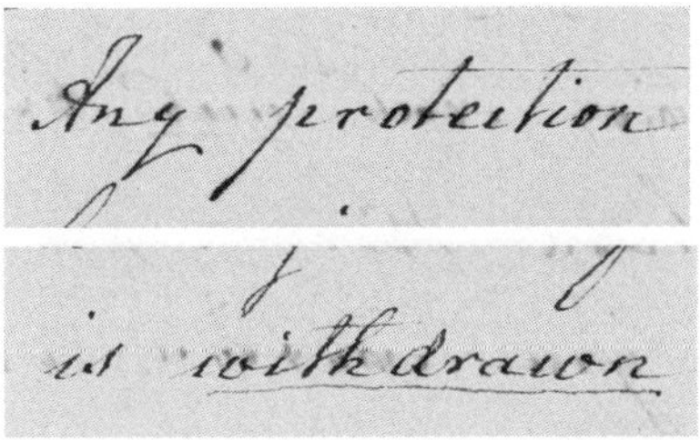

[Br. Byhan continues his letter to Br. Schulz in German:]

At the same time, Br. Clauder sent me an article and request to Col. Sanford, at Headquarters, asking if he would be good enough to let us live at our places until our wagons from Salem have arrived to pick us up. I immediately sent this request off with the Georgia mail — and I am now awaiting the answer to this.

Also late yesterday evening I received something from the Genl. Post Office in Washington, but not yet my departure from the Post Office. The letter just contained questions concerning some mail routes. The letter includes one expression which suggests a change, that is: "& direct the mail carriers to perform accordingly till farther advised from the Dept." I immediately replied, so as not to lose any time.

So this is how the matter stands now. If we receive a negative answer from Col. Sanford to our request, which we can expect this week or at least next Saturday, then Br. Clauder & family will go to our friend and benefactor Capt. David McNair. However, we here in Spring Place cannot leave yet, because I am not free of the postal service yet. Since the soldiers under Col. Nelson are expected in this area this week, we believe we will be able to learn more concerning us. I will write again with the next mail. It is a difficult question whether it will be advisable to send the wagons right away, since I am not yet free, or to wait until I am free of the Post Office, but I think by the time the wagons come I will also be adrift. May the Lord have mercy on all of us and protect us!

I also wanted to add that due to certain circumstances in Br. Clauder's family, there is no time to lose in sending the wagons, as he himself — Br. Clauder — will surely write.

They arrested Mr. Worcester in New Echota again last week, and also the Methodist preacher Mr. Trott. We fear things will go very badly for them this time, since they were very lenient with them and allowed them time to remove.

Now, dear Brn. and Srs., pray for us that the Lord will grant us power and strength to bear all that He has considered good and has imposed upon us. We trust in Him that He will assist us. Your familiar Br.,

G. Byhan

In great haste!

1831, part 8

[M 415-1b-31: Translated by Julie Tomberlin Weber. Addressed to: Revd. Theodore Schulz, Salem, Stokes County, North Carolina. Postmark: Spring Place, C.N., July 17, paid 18¾. Received July 30.]

Ooyugillogy, C.N., July 13, 1831

Dear Br. Schulz,

Since my last English letter to you from Spring Place, I have received a greeting from Col. Nelson as I expected, which Br. Byhan has reported to you. We could see the few words from the Col. as nothing other than a notice to submit, and that his earlier note of May 31st would not provide me with the slightest protection. Therefore, we are busy packing and taking care of the external preparations for our complete move.

Immediately after I had received Nelson's note, I wrote several polite lines to the superior commanding officer, Sandford, with the request to spare us until the wagons, which were ready to pick us up at any time, could arrive here from Salem, and that he might inform Br. Byhan if he approved the requested time period of 35 to 40 days. However, I doubt whether he will do this. He has a spiteful disposition and would perhaps prefer to punish me and bother me for my impudence, as is the sad case with Mr. Worcster, Prott, and McCloud.

The Lord willing, we might perhaps leave this place next week. What we cannot sell here we are planning to transport to McNair's, provided it is transportable. But cattle and pigs cannot be driven there, because there is a bad river on the road between here and Springplace, and the young livestock — the calves and pigs — cannot be taken through it. There would also be significant expenses associated with this. And so we were happy to find in our faithful old William Hicks a purchaser of the entire stock of cattle, consisting of 50 pigs, mostly small, and 31 head of beef cattle, along with calves, for $224.50, for which he gave us 2 of his most beautiful and best horses. After they have receive somewhat more corn to eat, they can be sold in Salem. In addition, he remains in debt $19.50.

Tomorrow I am planning to make an arrangement with Br. Hicks about the standing crop. No one wants to buy it, out of fear the Georgians might want to make it their own, and this worry is not without reason. As you perhaps have seen from the *Phönix*, they declared the buildings and all the fields belonging to them and grain from this year the property of the State during a visit to the Hightower mission. Now nothing else remains except to make a conditional agreement, which just depends on whether a seizure of the crops actually takes place or not. Perhaps I will be able to add to the terms Br. Hicks has agreed, since I have several days before this letter must be in Newtown. I also have prospects of getting Br. Christian David's ox cart to drive all of our things to Spring Place. This will be a little help for the other wagons and will at least save expenses for one week. He accepts payment here in property which has not been easy to remove so far.

Oh, may the Lord help us through these narrow straits! I am filled with anxious worry every day, and even during the night, about storing the things here. Everywhere I look I see useful property, but there is no prospect of selling it even for a low price, and there is much that cannot be taken to McNair's. Now I hope Wm. Hicks, who will place part of his large family into the buildings here, will do his best with the articles left behind on consignment.

Oh, dear Brother, you can hardly understand the difficult, oppressive times which prevail in this unfortunate land. Letters and newspapers do not tell half of it and don't give most readers the impression that fills a witness with trembling for the well-being of the entire country. How gladly we would have welcomed you here once, especially in these recent times when your advice, your views about everything would have been necessary and encouraging. Now this is the way things are, and I ask for patience and indulgence in all of the many difficult circumstances, which are indeed useful lessons of experience for me but which also require experience to be dealt with appropriately.

The evening of the 13th. Since I have an opportunity to send this to Spring Place tomorrow, I want to use my little remaining strength this evening to add a few lines to it. For a number of days now, I have had a bad sore throat which has forced me to fast. In addition to this there are the billions of complaints that are common in summer, but I am [taking measure] immediately to counter these. Today we were fortunate enough to finish packing a load, and tomorrow expect the wagon that is supposed to drive it to Spring Place. The road between here and Spring Place is horrible, so that only a small load can be taken. The drivers from Salem will be very happy that they do not have to drive the road to here.

I have not yet reached any agreement with Wm. Hicks about the crops. The deal with him for the pigs was also canceled. If we only had the opportunity, or even more the possibility, to drive them to McNair's, perhaps I can sell them there.

Next Sunday we are planning to enjoy Holy Communion with our Brn. and Srs. for the last time. May the Lord reveal Himself to us in grace and comfort. I doubt whether I will find it necessary to write you again before our departure. In the meantime, greet the dear Brethren of the P.H.C. sincerely from us. May the Lord be our guide during our journey and protect and comfort us until the blessed end of our earthly pilgrimage. I remain your familiar, obliged friend and Brother,

H. G. Clauder

Confidential

My wife's condition is such that, as far as we can tell, she will hardly be able to travel to Salem by the middle of September. Under these conditions we cannot even think about her remaining behind at McNair's. Staying anywhere during the journey should also be avoided if possible. And so there is nothing else to do but to get everything here in order as quickly as possible and to start the journey to Salem without delay. Next week we will discuss this thoroughly with Br. and Sr. Byhan and hear their advice. Unfortunately, however, necessity leaves hardly any other options.

Even Sr. Gambold feels very pressured to hurry because of her daughter's repeated urgent requests, so that after an absence of 8 years, perhaps she can embrace her once again in this life. Dear Brother, there you see almost unchanging reasons for us to get there as quickly as possible. We are planning to go by way of Jonesboro and Wilksboro.

H. G. Clauder

[M 407-2: Springplace Diary. Translated by Julie Tomberlin Weber.]

July 12. [Spg.] Br. Byhan, Sr., went to our friend Capt. McNair on business. The latter promised to serve us in our current situation wherever and whenever we are in need of his assistance. He is also very willing to give Br. and Sr. Clauder and Br. and Sr. Byhan temporary lodging until circumstances have changed or we can be picked up. This man and his family do much for us. May the Savior reward them for it! In recent days we heard that the Georgians have once again arrested Mr. Worcester, Doct. Buttler, Mr. Trott and Mr. McLeod, and taken them to Georgia. People fear that this time it will be more difficult for them to be set free. From the following we can see that the Georgians are not treating those they have arrested in the best manner: When they arrested Doct. Buttler, they tied him to a horse with a rope and he had to follow on foot, because the prisoners were not allowed to ride as long as it is possible for them to go on foot. Now when the horse stumbled and fell down, because it was pitch dark night, it also pulled Doct. Buttler down. It jumped a good deal when it got up again, so it also pulled him with it over fallen down trees and through thick bushes. People say that Doct. Buttler almost lost his life. The soldier who was riding the horse to which Doct. B. was tied broke a rib when the horse fell. It is horrible how the Georgia Guard treats those arrested. The treatment they have to endure before their guilt is legally established is much worse than the punishment which they have to tolerate after their sentencing.

July 13. [Spg.] Br. Byhan, Sr., returned to Spring Place from his visit at Mr. McNair's. Today the Indian Connondoha and his wife, our Sr. Hanna, were busy gleaning wheat from our fields.

July 14. [Spg.] They finished. When they wanted to go home we gave them another half dozen sheaves of wheat, which they also threshed before they went home. There is really famine among the Indians. We have visits every day from hungry Indians whom we must help as far as we are able. We suspect that the above-mentioned Indian Connondoha, who gleaned wheat from us, was the one who has already robbed our springhouse a couple of times. Still we must treat him well so that he does not do us greater harm.

[M 415-1b-32: Translated by Julie Tomberlin Weber; transcribed by Grace S. Robinson. Addressed to: Revd. Theod. Schulz, Salem, Stokes County, North Carolina. Postmark: Springplace, C.N., July 17. Free. G. Byhan, P.M. Received July 30.]

Springplace, July 16, 1831

My dear Br. Schulz,

In my last letter to you dated the 10th of this month, I informed you that Br. Clauder is now leaving the territory of Georgia in accordance with the new order, or the command he received from the Georgia Guards. Obeying this command, he will set out on the road to our friend Dav. McNair's in a couple of days now. He himself will surely have written you about this, since he wrote a letter to you that I will send tomorrow morning along with this one by way of Georgia.

Since my last letter to you, nothing else of note has happened here. I still have the Post Office, and it almost seems as if I must stay here longer, because I cannot leave the Post Office if it is not taken from me here. In that case, we will send our things back with the wagons from Salem, and as soon as I am free of the postal service I will follow with my wife in the small stage wagon. It is not yet clear who all will return from Spring Place with the wagons. If I am free of the Post Office before the wagons come, then we will all come. I do not know if I informed you in my last letter that we asked the commanding officer, Col. Sanford, to allow us to wait at our respective places for the wagons from Salem. But since we have not yet received an answer from him Br. Clauder and his family will move to McNair's next week and wait for the wagons there.

This week I paid a visit at McNair's. He asked me to thank you and the Helf. Conf. for the letter to him and to greet you all in the best way, and also to inform you that since he is bad at writing, he will not be able to answer the letter to him just now. Furthermore, he asks me to assure you that we will be welcome to stay at his place when we flee, and that he sincerely wants to do all that is within his powers to help ease our situation. He is our true friend; may God reward him for this!! During my last visit there, Sr. Delila McNair told me the following, which she

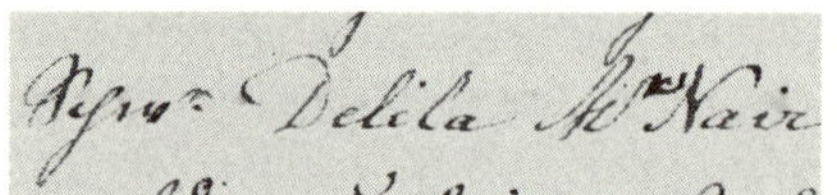

asked me to report to the Prov. Helf. Conf. and to learn their thoughts about it.

The fact that we will leave our Brn. and Srs. in this area has really touched them and hurts them very much. Now they have had the following idea. They want to stay together and build a house for a Br. and Sr., missionaries, on the Tennessee side so that the school for their children could be started again. However, in their current circumstances the missionaries cannot feed the schoolchildren now — as previously — and then they could not go home to eat either, so each one of them who has children in the school will contribute to their food, or as Sr. McNair expressed it, "Each shall throw something in."[1] I do not have time to express my thoughts about this plan just now, because there would be

[1] The quote is in English in the original German manuscript.

much to say about it. It seems to me it is an important matter, which must be well and thoroughly considered, especially in the current circumstances.

I was amazed to hear today that I was also accused at the headquarters of the Georgia Guard of having held a political sermon, and that this was the only thing they had against me. Now this is obviously blatant slander, because any person who has heard my sermons and can speak English really must realize immediately that I cannot express myself adequately in English, and therefore I am not in a position to hold a political sermon. So this false accusation is more laughable than troubling. I have done this, however: I have always directed my listeners and the inhabitants of this country to the Lord for assistance in the current oppressed times. He can guide any circumstances, no matter how difficult they are, so that they work for our best. I have always been careful about saying the slightest thing about the behavior of the Georgians, both in private conversations and — even more so — in public gatherings. If all people had been so fearful and careful about discussing the behavior of the Georgians, little or nothing would be said about them. However, I must admit that this news does not upset me and seems laughable to me, as I have said. Anyone who knows me will know that I cannot deliver political sermons! In the meantime, we can pretty well figure out who was good enough to do us this favor. It seems that even when one thinks he is surrounded by friends, he must still be on guard about speaking about things to avoid being slandered. One must keep learning.

In my last letter, I informed you that the Georgians had arrested Doct. Butler and then bound him to a horse's tail; this was incorrect. They chained him to the horse's neck. People say he was badly hurt when the horse fell.

Before I close this letter, I will wait for the mail from Georgia, which is expected in a couple of hours. Perhaps there will be various things to report then.

5 o'clock in the afternoon. In the Georgia mail I just received an answer from Col. Nelson to the above inquiry of Col. Sanford. It says:

[Br. Byhan copies Col. Nelson's letter in English:]

Camp Gilmer, July 15, 1831

Dear Sir,

The Letter of Mr. Clauder of the 8th int. has just arrived to Col. Sandford, in his absence has fallen into my hands. I feel the greatest Cheerfulness in saying to you, that I have no doubt, but that Col. Sanford will without the least hesitation grant to each of you the fullest time as for that you may make your arrangements and leave the Territory. Our Object is not to oppress any who may manifest a determination to comply with our Laws.

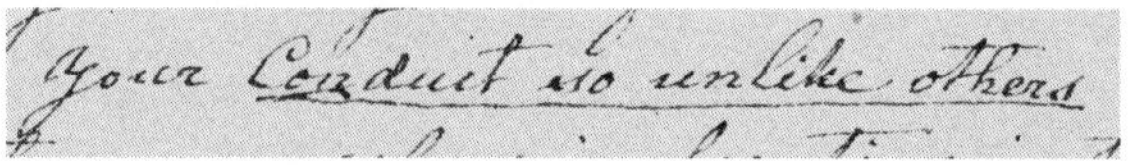

Your Conduct so unlike others who professed no other Motives than yourselves in locating in the Country has created with us the most hearty Reciprocity of feelings, which you were pleased to Express for the our own individual Welfare & that of our State in wishing you and the cause you have so honorably Supported, prosperity wherever you may go.

Please Except my Respect, personal Regard, etc. Respectfully,

F. M. Nelson, Sub. Comd.

Rvd. Byhan, Springplace, C.T., Ga.

[Br. Byhan continues his letter to Br. Schulz in German:]

According to this letter Br. Clauder could patiently await the wagons from Salem in Och_____y. But what will happen to us?? Since I didn't receive anything from Washington again today, I must continue to maintain the postal service. It seems to me and to all of us that there is extreme confusion everywhere. I just received a letter from our Rachel, from June 25, which I will answer with the next mail. Accept the most sincere greetings from all of us, and you especially from your humble fellow Brother,

Gottl. Byhan

[Springplace (M 407-2) and Oochgeelogy (M 409-1) Diaries. Translated by Julie Tomberlin Weber. Handwritings are Henry G. Clauder's (Ooch.) and Gottlieb Byhan's (Spg.).]

July 16. [Ooch.] At noon Christian David's wagon arrived here to take our things to Spring Place. But it got late before the load was ready, so he stayed with us until Monday, the 18th.

July 16. [Spg.] Toward evening 10 soldiers from the Georgia Guard under the orders of Lieutenant Brooks arrived here completely unexpected. They rode up to our gate hastily and stopped. When Br. Byhan, Sr., who was busy in the Post Office, since the Georgia mail had just arrived, saw them he hurried out to them. He was greeted very cordially and asked if we had a lot or pasture for their horses and if we would allow them to spend the night with us. This was all answered affirmatively. Then they unsaddled their horses and brought all of their things, provisions, etc., which they were driving with them in a small wagon and their flint guns with bayonettes into our house. After the unease and confusion this visit and event caused us had passed somewhat, Br. Byhan took the opportunity to explain our current situation to the commanding officer, that we are also planning to leave as soon as we receive notification that we have to leave the country, and that as soon as we notify our Directors in Salem, N.C., of this, they will immediately send a wagon to pick us up, etc. Now he said it was a shame that we could not decide to swear the oath. We were so well settled in. We would experience great loss upon leaving our places. We should consider better. In brief, he tried everything possible to move us to take the oath. When he saw that he could do nothing, he finally said: "Well, you will not be molested here, because we are convinced that you have not meddled with our political affairs like other Missionaries. They, for their impertinence, will have to abide by the consequences." When they

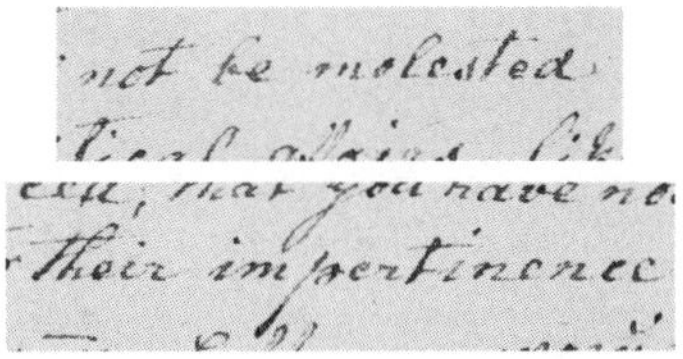
not be molested
tical affairs like
that you have no
their impertinence

had eaten their evening meal, for which at their request we had given them milk, pickles, cabbage, etc., they settled down on our porch, which looked kind of like a bedroom but at the same time also somewhat warlike.

Sun., July 17. [Spg.] Early in the day they set out on their way to Rossville, as it seemed and as they also said, to seek out some white people there. They said they would call in here again in 4 days to spend the night here, which was admittedly not the most pleasant news to us. Today most of our Brn. and Srs. came for our services as well as Dav. Steiner Dazizi, who served us as interpreter. In the first service was the sermon on the words of our dear Lord [Mark 16:15]: Go ye into all the world, and preach the gospel to every creature. Afterward was the baptism of the baby boy born to our Indian Br. and Sr. Jeremias and Rebecca, with the name Ephraim Walter. In the last service we had a blessed enjoyment of the body and blood of Jesus in Holy Communion. The Indian Br. Emmanuel joined us as a participant for the first time, after previously receiving the confirmation blessing. His wife, the Indian Sr. Margaretha Susanna, watched during this as a confirmand for the last time. We could sense the Savior in our midst and we were aware of his comforting presence in a sweet way in all of our services today.

In the evening a white man with three horses and a Negro came and spent the night here. Mr. Vann had told them that he had nothing for people to eat nor feed for their horses, which is also unfortunately true, as his whole large enterprise is currently going strongly backward instead of forward. He himself is likely the cause for this, because he has not been leading the most honorable life recently.

Sun., July 17. [Ooch.] Since this was the last Sunday we would be here, an unusually large number of people gathered for the sermon. Attentively and emotionally, we considered the words of Heb. 13:8: Jesus Christ the same yesterday, and today, and forever. After the sermon, we gathered with our fellow communicants for the last time, deeply bowed, to enjoy the meal of our Lord and Savior. The melancholy feeling which prevailed during this can be experienced in similar situations but not described. Still our hearts were comforted and strengthened by our Savior's dear presence. Most of our Brn. and Srs. were present, as well as Elias Boudinott and his wife.

Afterward the elderly Br. Christian David said that he had told Br. Clauder to extend his sincere greetings to various Brn. and Srs. in Salem, and then he told him: "Tell them an old heathen turned to God after he had grown old in the service of sin. He heard God's word and experienced it as a saving power."

[M 415-1b-33: Translated by Julie Tomberlin Weber. Addressed to: Revd. Theod. Schulz, Salem, Stokes County, North Carolina. Postmark: Springplace, C.N., July 17. Free. G. Byhan, P.M. Received July 27.]

Springplace, July 17, 1831

Dear Br. Schulz,

Yesterday evening after I had already closed my letter to you dated yesterday and had put it in the Georgia mail, our people suddenly yelled out to me: The soldiers are coming! And before we could be affrighted they were already in our yard. They immediately asked if there was a field here where they could put their horses. When we told them there was one, the commanding officer Lieutenant Brooks said: "Halt, boys, we will stay all night here." Now we had them on our backs. They camped out on our porch the entire night. There were 10 soldiers and 11 horses. From Lt. Brooks's talk we concluded that nothing has yet been done by the Georgians to remove the Post Office from here. He even told me that he — Brooks — would do his best to leave the Post Office for me here, because they — the Georgians — were convinced that we would not get involved in their political affairs. He also encouraged me to take the oath of allegiance, to which I replied, however, that my conscience would not allow me to do this. He also said it was a shame that we now had to leave a place that we had furnished so nicely, which had cost us so much effort and expense. And so he would do his best to see that we were not disturbed. The question now is: Did he mean it frankly and honestly? I must say that I feel doubtful — but one cannot know.

When the soldiers arrived I ordered Rominger to stay hidden at first so I could ask Lt. Brooks about his stay with us. I immediately took the opportunity to name all the individuals here at Spring Place — and especially Rominger. He assured us that no one here should be molested, and then Rominger appeared again.

Now, dear Brn., our situation is indeed strange, actually I might say confused. What is to be done now? For now there is no indication that I will be free of the postal service soon, and so I cannot leave Spring Place until I have a successor. According to my letter to you dated the 10th of this month, the wagons from Salem are presumably being sent to fetch all of us from here, and I cannot leave because of the Post Office, so only Br. and Sr. Clauder will be able to return with the wagon. And still it seems impossible to us that if Spring Place preserved itself through the postal service, the young, energetic Brn. and Srs. would be returning and relieving us old people here.

These matters are extremely complicated, and I hope that this letter might reach your hands more quickly than usual, so we can learn the thoughts and advice of the Helf. Conf. soon. I have not yet had the opportunity to discuss the current state of affairs with Br. Clauder, and I will not be able to do this until tomorrow. And so we cannot report our joint thoughts for 8 days, but by then the 2 wagons will probably have left Salem already. God knows what will happen! He has helped us thus far, and we trust that He will continue to help us!

You will understand that we are in a miserable situation not only regarding whether to move or stay, but also concerning our external existence if we do stay, since we have not been able to cultivate our fields as we should have because of the constant unrest and fear. And so we will not be able to get our livestock — that is, not all of our livestock — through next winter. And how are we supposed to feed all the Indians, and perhaps also a group of schoolchildren, and who will do the work for the Sisters and in the household??

I could add more, but the time is too short for now, and you will be able to see our situation from what is written above. May the Lord be with us and also with you!

Everyone sends greetings, and especially your faithfully obliged Br.,

Gottl. Byhan

N.B. When the soldiers left this morning they said they would come back here next Wednesday evening, and they would spend the night here.

One more thing: I am wondering if it would be good for the Conf. or the Directors to write to the Genl. Postmaster to see if another postmaster has been assigned to my post, or if Br. Clauder could not become postmaster here, since the Directors were planning to take me away from here? In the first case, it might perhaps happen that a Georgian would be placed in our house as postmaster, which should of course be considered.

When Br. Clauder and I spoke about this some time ago, he said it seemed strange to him that the postal service should be maintained here. And I must admit it is the same for me.

I can only say that it is extremely difficult for a missionary here if he has to deal with the mail when services are supposed to be held, since it really scatters a preacher's mind.

[Springplace (M 407-2) and Oochgeelogy (M 409-1) Diaries.]

July 18. [Spg.] Today we again had a number of hungry Indian women to feed. They came here only to still their hunger. They asked for permission to glean wheat from our wheat fields. Since they had already been gleaned, however, and we now have put our cattle into the field, they would not have found any more grains. And so we gave them each a sheaf of wheat, from which they immediately rubbed the wheat with their hands in our lane and took it with them.

July 19. [Spg.] This morning we became aware that many apples had been stolen from our orchard again. In the afternoon a wagon arrived here from Ochgeloogy with part of Br. and Sr.

Clauder's and Sr. Gambold's things, which were packed for Salem. Toward evening the above-mentioned soldiers arrived here again and spent the night here again. Brooks, the commanding officer assured us once again that he would do his best so that we are not required to leave Indian country. However, only time will tell how far his influence will work in our favor.

July 20. [Spg.] Early in the day the soldiers left us again and hurried back to their headquarters, Camp Gilmer.

July 20. [Ooch.] In the evening we gathered once again in our Saal with a number of Brn. and Srs. and friends, whom Br. Clauder fervently admonished to remain faithful to the Lord until the end. During the concluding prayer, which was offered by an Indian Brother in the English language, tears flowed from almost all eyes. On the following day the last wagon loaded with our belongings was sent to Spring Place. In the afternoon we visited some of our friends and neighbors and experienced some proofs of their love and compassion. We spent the night with our Br. and Sr. Wm. A. Hicks.

July 22. [Ooch.] With a wistful feeling, we returned to our post for the last time to prepare for our departure, which took place at noon after an unforgettable farewell from our dear Brethren and Sisters. In the evening we arrived at our dear Boudinott's in Echota, where we were most cordially received and given shelter. We also had the unexpected pleasure there of seeing many residents of this town gathered together. They shared their best wishes for our journey and their hope that we would return soon.

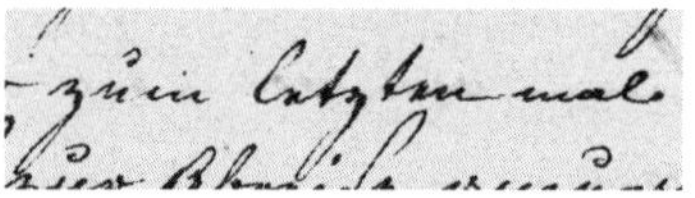

July 23. [Ooch.] In the morning our dear friend and host commended us in a sincere prayer to the Lord's guidance and merciful protection, and then we said a grateful farewell. We continued our journey to Spring Place, where we arrived in the evening, full of praise and gratitude for the Lord's merciful protection.

July 23. [Spg.] Br. and Sr. Clauder and the widowed Sr. Gambold arrived here with the rest of their things. They will now stay with us for a while in Spring Place, since Br. Clauder has received the promise from Col. Nelson that he can stay in Georgia Territory until the arrival of the wagon from Salem, and to wait here for the advice of the Helf. Conf. in Salem about our current situation. In the evening two travelers came again whom we had to keep overnight.

[M 415-1b-34: Translated by Julie Tomberlin Weber. Addressed to: Revd. Theod. Schulz, Salem, Stokes County, North Carolina. Postmark: Springplace, C.N., July 24, via Salisbury. Free. G. Byhan, P.M.]

Springplace, July 22, 1831

My dear Br. Schulz,

I had just put my last letter to you, dated the 17th of this month, into the mail when I received your kind letter of July 2nd by way of Knoxville on the said day. Sincere thanks for this. I still have the Post Office, and who knows when I will be free of it. From your letter we learned that the wagons are not being sent from Salem until I am free of the Post Office. This is appropriate, because what would the second wagon carry if my family and I cannot leave? I cannot possibly leave here until the Post Office has been taken from me.

Given all this, we are in a situation which causes us more than a little worry. Br. and Sr. Clauder are moving now, and they have already sent part of their things here this week, and another full wagon is expected here today. Tomorrow he himself and his entire house family will arrive here, as he writes, in order to wait for the wagon here or at McNair's. But the wagons are not coming until I am free. Then there is also the fact that Sr. Clauder — as Br. Clauder wrote me — cannot travel anymore after the beginning of September because of family circumstances.

All of this taken together makes us more than a little concerned. The commanding officier, Brooks, who was here once again on the 19th of this month with a party of soldiers and spent the night with us, said that he would do his best, both with Col. Sanford and with Gov. Gilmer, to see that the Post Office would not be removed from here and I remain postmaster. We surely cannot count on this, because I believe it was just flattery.

Now if it takes a long time before I get free and before the wagons could come, where would Br. and Sr. Clauder stay during that time? I almost think — and I must say, I fear — that Br. Clauder might decide to begin the journey to Salem with his small wagon without waiting. I would really not be happy about it if he left us alone here. Since I have not yet had an opportunity to discuss this matter with him, I do not yet know his thoughts.

Please do not think badly of me for expressing my private thoughts here. This is what I was thinking. If it should really happen that the Post Office is not taken away from me here and I should remain postmaster — which seems to be possible after all, because a postmaster is an Agent of the United States Government after all — and because the mission place in Ochgeloogy has been closed for now, it seems to me it would be more advisable if Br. Clauder were postmaster in my place and we went back, because Br. and Sr. Clauder are younger and much more fit than we. However, it is another question whether Br. Clauder will agree to this, if it is said that the Post Office was the reason he was allowed to stay here.

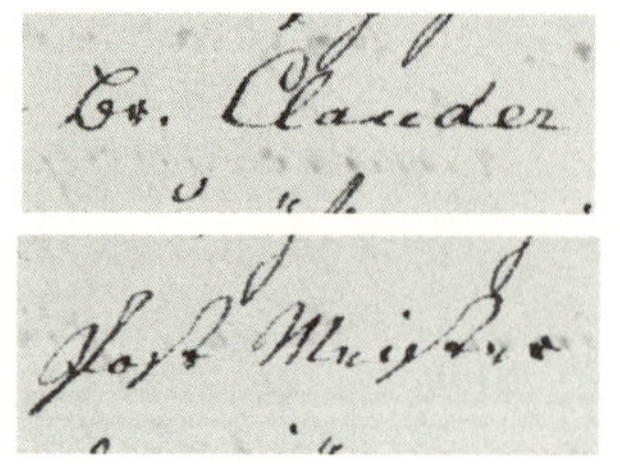

These were my initial thoughts. God knows what will take place! Humans plan and God acts!

You would like to know what kind of an arrangement we have made for our livestock. I hear that Br. Clauder has traded all of his for a horse. We still have ours here in Spring Place, but some cattle buyers have already contacted us. We ourselves wish we could bring them along, if a departure ever actually takes place, but it might be too far them. Our livestock looks glorious and good, and if it could be brought there it would certainly sell for a good price, but it would also cost something.

You would also like to know how our finances are. If I paid all my debts or could pay them now, I would have approximately $90 in the cashbox. I do not know how things are for Br. Clauder.

We sincerely wish that our circumstances might change in one way or another.

In addition to our other distress, worry, and concern, there is also the fact that our neighbor Jos. Vann is not taking in any more traders or travelers, though he is still operating a "house of Entertainment." He is now sending every traveler to us, and says to them that we are a "house of Entertainment," so that we are much plagued by travelers, which really is not pleasant for us.

house of Entertainment

And since we have little feed anyway — or I should say none — for our livestock, if a Br. and Sr. must be here next winter we have not been able to make any because of the situation in Georgia. In that case as well we would have to get rid of most of our livestock, because we cannot over-winter them.

One can also see that it does not reflect well on us — or, as people say, it is held against us — that we had the Georgia Guard spend the night twice. But could we help it? Could we say: We are not taking in any people like you? The Scripture says: Love your enemies, bless those who curse you, treat well those who hate you, etc. In brief, it seems to us that our neighbors would have preferred it if the Georgians had arrested us and treated us like Mr. Worcester and Doct. Butler, who are still under arrest and are being treated very badly. Our Brn. and Srs., however, do not think this way.

By the way, our neighbor is living in misery and vice; he now has <u>three</u> wives — his household is going severely backward.

What a shame you cannot visit us because of all of your business! It would provide amazing relief for us, and you would get a clear insight into our situation. When you are finished in Wilkesboro, come quickly over here!!

As far as we know, the Cherokees are still quiet, but it cannot be predicted how long they will remain so.

Last Sunday we had a very blessed Holy Communion with our Cherokee Brn. and Srs. The Indian Br. Emanuel was confirmed and was a member for the first time, and his wife watched as a confirmand for the last time. It was a day of true refreshment!

The 23rd. The Georgia mail has just arrived here, but it did not bring us anything from Salem. We all greet you most sincerely, and special greetings from your loving Br.,

Gottl. Byhan

5 o'clock in the afternoon. The rest of Br. and Sr. Clauder's things have just arrived here, and in one hour we expect them as well.

G. B.

[M 415-1b-35: Translated by Julie Tomberlin Weber. Addressed to: Revd. Theod. Schulz, Salem, Stokes County, North Carolina. Postmark: Springplace, C.N., July 24, via Knoxville, Jonesboro, Ten., Wilkesboro, N.C. Free. G. Byhan, P.M. Received Aug. 3.]

Springplace, July 24, 1831

Dear Br. Schulz,

After I had already put my letter to you dated yesterday into the Georgia mail, Br. and Sr. Clauder and Sr. Gambold arrived here from Ochgeloogy with the rest of their things. Br. Clauder was extremely weak and had to go to bed right away, but this morning he is noticeably better. The mission place in Ochgeloogy has thus been abandoned now.

The actual reason that I am writing once again today is primarily to explain our current situation to the dear Prov. Helf. Conf. for your special consideration. From the last letter from Br. Schulz, dated July 2, we saw that the wagons from Salem were not being sent until I am free of the Post Office. Yesterday evening I received news from headquarters, delivered orally and from the commanding officer, Col. Sandford, that we here in Spring Place should not be interrupted and that we could stay. He sent us this word through Lt. Brook, who was here 8 days ago. The reason we were allowed to stay is without about a doubt because they have not been able to get a postmaster to take my place.

I know nothing to reply to this except that I have no faith in this oral assurance that we would remain unchallenged, since I continue to hear that they are still secretly looking for another postmaster to take my place. And even if they cannot get another one, then I must honestly admit and explain that — if the postal service is the only reason we are allowed to stay here — we here in Spring Place, including myself, do not want to stay. I do not want to stay at any mission post because of a Post Office alone. The actual purpose will be missed and neglected through this. In addition to this, the mail arrives here on Sundays just before the services are supposed to begin, and sometimes during the services. Who can focus his thoughts on giving a talk then? I cannot. Therefore, it seems to all of us that the time has come to decide what we will do, whether I should resign or not.

In addition there is the extremely unpleasant matter, which absolutely should not be the case, that we are plagued and tortured with travelers almost every day who want to eat here and spend the night, because our miserable Jos. Vann has not wanted to take people in for a long time now, and so he sends them all to us so that our house often looks little different than a Tavern.

We ask the Helf. Conf. to consider all of these circumstances and let us know the result as quickly as possible. We also ask you to consider the circumstances of Br. and Sr. Clauder — and especially of Sr. Clauder — who indeed cannot agree to a longer postponement of a final decision.

Our situation is indeed extremely difficult and it often makes us plead to the Lord to release us from it soon! Furthermore, I must express my concern that we believe two wagons will not be able to load all of our things and so various things must be left behind at McNair's.

It also occurs to me that if the Helf. Conf. should decide that I might resign, would it not be good if this were done directly by Br. Schulz in Salem? Because my appointment as postmaster was also arranged by Salem and it would significantly help with this matter.

Everyone sends sincere greetings, and especially your faithfully obliged Br.,

Gottl. Byhan

In haste.

[M 407-2: Springplace Diary.]

Sun., July 24. [Spg.] In the first service a sermon was read since we had no interpreter here today. In the second was Bible reading, which was repeated in the Cherokee language by the Indian Br. Niclaus Ignatius, after which they sang another hymn in the Cherokee language. Br. Clauder led this service. In the evening Mr. Dav. Steiner Dazizi came to our place and spent the night here.

July 25. [Spg.] Toward evening 2 white people from S.C. also came and spent the night.

July 30. [Spg.] We heard that some soldiers were in our neighborhood again, as people said, to arrest Mr. Bean, Mr. McNair's daughter's husband, and a white miller in Sumak Town. They were not able to get the former, but had arrested the latter and, as we later heard, had treated him very badly and taken him to Camp Gilmer with them. Today we also heard that Mr. Worcester and the rest of the Presbyterian missionaries who were arrested in the middle of last month had been set free again, but are obliged to appear at the next Court. Despite this, however, they are in danger every day in the meantime of being arrested anew if they do not leave Georgia territory. We hear that Mr. Worcester has now also decided to leave Georgia Territory with his family and go to Brainerd. But this did not happen then. In the evening the Georgia post rider brought us the news that Sergeant Brooks had told him to tell us that Col. Nelson sent word that we can live here peacefully and that we and our families would not be disturbed.

1831, part 9

[M 415-1b-36: Translated by Julie Tomberlin Weber. Addressed to: Revd. Theodore Schulz, Salem, North Carolina. Postmark: Springplace, C.N., July 31, paid 18¾. Received Aug. 13. Br. Schulz writes in the address: $110.50 to Br. Reichel for Maj. Ridge's acct.]

Spring Place, July 30, 1831

Dear Br. Schulz,

Br. Byhan's last letter to you will have informed you of our arrival here last Saturday the 23rd. Our things had already been brought safely here over the horrible road from Oo______y. The road from there to here was awful, but we managed to pass safely through all the mud holes and swamps. We also experienced merciful protection from physical harm when one of the wagons tipped over on a bad place in the road.

Now we find ourselves in a new school of patience here, since Br. Byhan still has not received his expected release from the Post Office and the wagons from Salem are not being sent until that has actually been done. We cannot predict when we will be able to travel on, because my plan to begin the journey with my family, as I wrote you in my last letter, did not agree with the views of the rest of the Brn. and Srs., and I myself was secretly opposed to it. I will gladly remain in the dear Cherokee country as long as possible.

The oral notification which Br. Byhan received last week through the post rider — from the Col. of the Georgia Guards — is really favorable enough, but since we have already experienced how long such promises last, we cannot really rely on this, especially since the Georgians expect that we will move as soon as possible. Unfortunately, I have packed away the copy of my letter to Col. Sandford dated July 8th, otherwise I would send you a copy of it. It would show you what kind of relationship we have with him. As soon as I had received the few lines from Col. Nelson on July 8th, which contained a retraction of the protection given in his earlier letter, I wrote to Sandford, as far as I know, the following, among other things: "I beg leave, respectfully, to state that my continuance here to this date, was in consequence of Col. Nelson's note of May 31st —— According to the determination of my Directors at Salem N.C. I shall now remove, & as our removal will be final & some time required to make the necessary preparations, I would crave a still further indulgence of 35 or 40 days. Waggons are in readiness at Salem, N.C., & will be dispatched for us as soon as the notice of the withdrawal of protection can reach there."[1]

In answer to this letter, Sub Commander Nelson, in Sandford's absence, wrote to Br. Byhan, who has sent you a copy of this in accordance with my wishes. Now if we consider the letter from the P.H.C. to Gov. Gilmer, and mine to his Agent Col. Sandford, we cannot disappoint the Georgians' expectation that we will move as soon as possible. If it were not for the wretched postal service, then Br. Byhan would also be ready soon.

There are also other things to note about the postal service here. It used to be a secondary matter for the convenience of the mission; however, in the current situation it is an oppressive burden, since Sunday is the primary day for activity in the central work for which the mission here exists, and 2 mail deliveries arrive here and 3 have to be prepared in all haste on precisely the same day, in precisely the same hour, when one should really be busy with other matters, when one should be preparing for services. In addition 2 post riders must be lodged, and since we have been here I have noted that all travelers from Tennessee or Georgia — who expected to find lodging at Vann's but do not

[1] The quote is in English in the original German manuscript.

find it because of his cursed living habits — come here as the only place where they must be taken in out of mercy. Every night there are travelers here. In this regard, it is extremely difficult here —we were spared of this burden in Oo______gy, praise God — and confidentially I am not surprised that Br. Byhan has asked so long and urgently for his release.

The burden of external matters which do not have the slightest connection with the mission work but are just brought about by local causes is enough to dampen the strongest spirit and the most fervent drive. It is true that the commission as postmaster protects Br. Byhan from the Georgia law, but how little use this is to him in his actual mission calling. In the current situation, it is much more of an obstacle and harm to the mission than it was previously a benefit. I agree completely with your recent thoughts in a letter to Br. Byhan, that you could request Br. Byhan's release from the General Postmaster or instruct him to resign, if only he received the agreement of the P.H.C. to do this.

Sr. Gambold is also here with us and asks that if our stay here might last long and the health of her daughter Dorel has not yet improved, her brother in Bethania might come with a one-span wagon to pick her up from here at her own expense. She has not heard from her sick daughter for several weeks now. I personally do not doubt that we will all be picked up soon, perhaps as quickly as a special wagon for Sr. Gambold could arrive here.

You will have learned various things about the imprisonment of the missionaries Worcester, Butler, and Trott through the *Phönix*. For several weeks they lay in the most horrible prison at the headquarters of the guard before they were taken before a civil magistrate in Lawrenceville. Yesterday, we here learned that they were all free again after they had posted bail for their appearance at court this coming Sept. and they had been ordered to leave the country. I doubt whether Worcester will go. Butler was treated cruelly when he was arrested. He was bound to one of the soldier's horses with a chain around his neck. He walked beside it like this for several miles in the dark night. He could not stop until the rider finally took him behind him on the horse.

The chain around his neck was almost unbearable. Unfortunately the horse fell and actually on both of his riders. Butler was severely harmed by the chain and was picked up for dead. He finally recovered, however, and was dragged away. This event and the other suffering which he endured led him to become seriously ill, and it is said people doubt whether he will recover. No Turks treat their prisoners like this, only the cruel Georgians.

Before I left Ooyu_____y I received Major Ridge's note payable to Benj. Reichel, the principal & interest amounting to $110.50, which I have on hand, partly in U.S. notes. Be so good and submit this amount to Br. Reichel.

Wm. Hicks became the purchaser of the entire stock of livestock, also the standing fields and many articles from the household. In return I received 2 good, salable horses and notes of hand which amounted to $150, payable 12 months after date. He received many items which could not be properly removed into his protection for future sale for the benefit of the mission. I kept a list of these.

I see that I have failed once again in my intention — to write well and clearly — forgive my miserable scrawl.

Br. Byhan sends his sincere greetings. Since his last letter to you everything here has remained quiet, so he is not planning to write this week. Greet my dear parents when you get the chance, as well as the dear Brethren of the P.H.C. and your dear family from all of us, and especially from your faithfully obliged friend and Brother,

H. G. Clauder

[M 407-2: Springplace Diary. Translated by Julie Tomberlin Weber. Handwriting is Gottlieb Byhan's.]

Sun., July 31. Br. Clauder gave today's sermon, which Mr. Dav. Steiner Dazizi, who came here today, interpreted into Indian. Afterward Br. Byhan, Sr., prayed the Church Litany, which was repeated in the Cherokee language by our single Indian Br. Solomon.

[M 415-1b-37: Translated by Julie Tomberlin Weber. Addressed to: Revd. Theodore Shulz, Salem, Stokes County, North Carolina. Postmark: Springplace, C.N., July 31. Free. G. Byhan, P.M. Received Aug. 13.]

Springplace, July 31, 1831

My dearly beloved Br. Schulz,

I was not planning to write you on this mail day, first of all because nothing significant has happened here since my last letter to you dated the 24th of this month, and also because Br. Clauder wrote to you from here this week, and that letter has already left with the Georgia mail this morning. However, since we learned and heard all sorts of things yesterday evening which were previously unknown to us, both from the New Echota *Phönix* and also through the post rider, I thought I would write you a few hasty lines with the Knoxville mail.

From yesterday's *Phönix*, dated the 30th of this month — if it reaches you safely, and oh, how we hope it reaches your hands soon — you will learn about the treatment which Mr. Worcester and some other missionaries experienced from the Georgia Guard in Camp Gilmer. One might ask if they were Christians? — or those who call themselves Christians? — who could do this to their fellow humans. Humanity shudders at such things! Let us know if you have received it. Mr. Worcester and the other missionaries were set free after they were bound to appear at the Supreme Court. However, according to Gov. Gilmer's letter, as soon as they allow themselves to be seen on this side of the Chatahutchy they are in daily danger of being arrested anew, and there is no doubt that they will be arrested again soon. Yesterday another division of the Georgia Guard came close to us, actually to Sumak Town, and people believe they will attend the Methodist services there, which have been held on this side of Mr. McNair's in recent days and again today, in order to catch white people there.

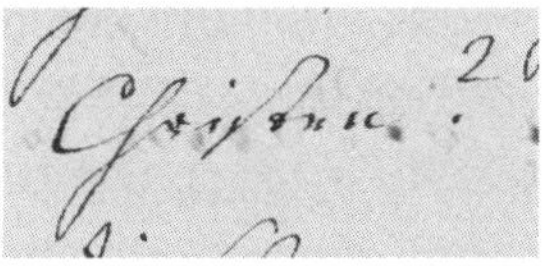

Times are becoming increasingly sad and ever more difficult. Because of oppressive circumstances and due to the situation in which we find ourselves, I once again feel compelled to ask quite fervently and urgently to help us out of this disconcerting situation if at all possible. The only way this will happen is if I resign, so that I am free of the miserable Post Office. Then we can get out of the way of these B——n. Ochgeloogy has been deserted, and Spring Place, as circumstances are, is also, so to speak, ruined and ended, and we all agree that it would be good if we made a formal departure.

If the Helf. Conf. considers it good for me to resign, I might ask that this might be arranged directly from Salem with the General Postmaster, as I have explained in one of my previous letters, so that I am free of the matter.

However, there is no more time to lose.

It is impossible to stay here for another winter, because the fieldwork has gotten so far behind due to the circumstances that have lasted for 5 months now, and if it continues to go like this for 2 more months that we have so many horses to feed — currently we have 6 of them, because those from Och_____y must be kept here, and have to take in all the travelers who come here and feed their horses — then we will have no winter feed for our own cattle left over for winter. And since nothing like this can be purchased here — and what would it cost even if we could get it? — there is no prospect of making it through the next winter. Therefore, it is best if the work here is concluded for the time being. If this mission is started again and renewed, then it would be advisable to start it again on a completely different footing than things have been thus far.

Now may the Savior continue to assist us and keep us in His care and protection, because not a single hair falls from our heads without His knowledge.

Everyone sends best greetings. And you are especially greeted by your poor, familiar Br.,

Gottlieb Byhan

[M 407-2: Springplace Diary.]

Aug. 1. In the morning a young man came past here with his stepmother and 5 of his siblings and some servants on his way from Georgia to Tennessee. We had to give them breakfast, because, as already explained, Jos. Vann has not wanted to take in any travelers for some time. This man told us that he had been appointed by Col. Nelson to tell us that he had been appointed by Col. Sanford, the Sub Commanding Officer, to inform us that we and Br. and Sr. Clauder could stay at our mission places undisturbed, and that we should not be bothered in our calling, and that Col. Sanford, who is currently ill, will write to us himself about this when he is well again. Now since these are orders we do not put too much stock in them, since we have already gotten to know the Georgians somewhat in that respect. In the meantime this helps calm Br. and Sr. Clauder somewhat that they will not have to move on from here after 10 days, which they were allowed in Georgia Territory by Col. Nelson, but will be able to stay here in Spring Place. All of us here are currently really experiencing and learning what it means: Take therefore no thought for the morrow: for the morrow shall take thought for the things of itself [Matt. 6:34], since in the current confused times we can in fact see nothing in front of us, so to say, because each day brings us alternately either quieting or upsetting news concerning our situation here. [Hymn:] See nothing at all and plead as a child, and trust in the One who promised, that is our strength from day to day! In the evening two more persons came whom we had to keep overnight, as was also the case on the 2nd, when we also had two travelers overnight.

Aug. 3. Three people came with five horses. They stayed here, so that our house looked more like a guesthouse than a mission house.

[M 415-1b-39: Translated by Julie Tomberlin Weber. Addressed to: Revd. Theodore Schulz, Salem, Stokes County, North Carolina. Postmark: Spring Place, C.N., Aug. 7, via Knoxville, T., paid 18¾. Received Aug. 20.]

Spring Place, Aug. 6, 1831

Dear Br. Schulz,

I have time and opportunity this week to send you a written greeting once again, along with various remarks regarding our current situation. In my last letter to you, dated July 30, I mentioned some things about the particular difficulties here, partly due to reasons beyond our control and which are an almost intolerable burden for the Brn. and Srs. living here, and which are also in direct opposition to the actual mission work here. It is hardly possible to give you an accurate view of the circumstances here at this place, although it is always our desire to do so. In the current crisis it is especially desirable.

The constant visits by travelers are a very particular burden here in Spring Place. Mr. Vann, who used to lodge all travelers, has adopted an unfortunate way of life. He is rarely at home, and even when he is there he sends all the travelers here. Usually they arrive here in the dark of night and ask for lodging. On the way to Georgia there is no inn closer than 12 miles; on the West Tennessee road there is nothing closer than 12 miles; and on the road to Head of Coosa & South Alabama there is nothing closer than New Echota 20 miles from here. Now considering this, it is impossible, indeed it would be inhumane, to turn away tired travelers. In this way, this post has become like an inn, even if we do not want to use this name.

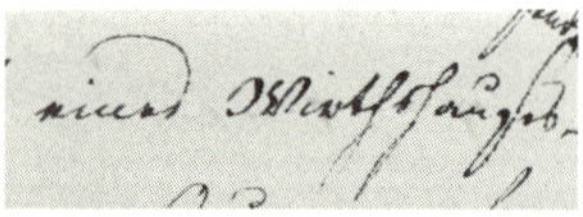

For our mutual satisfaction, we are adding the following list of visitors. Br. Warner would be happy to have such a large number of customers:

Monday, Aug. 1: For breakfast 5 persons, 2 servants, 3 horses; evening 2 travelers from Tennessee to Georgia, 2 horses. Aug. 2 late at night: 2 travelers from South Carolina to W. Tennessee, 2 horses. Aug. 3 late at night: 3 travelers from West Tennessee to Georgia, 5 horses. Aug. 4 evening: 1 man & horse, supper and breakfast.[1]

The accusation against missionaries, which has already appeared in the public press, is that they came into this country to seek their fortune by lodging travelers; therefore, this is difficult to deny. Such facts give hostile people the best opportunity to make accusations like the one stated.

You will have seen from my last letter to you, as well as from the *Phönix*, that Mr. Worcester was set free on bail. He has also removed now, like all the rest. As far as I know, we are the only missionaries who are still living within the borders of Georgia in Cherokee country.

I do not know what the Georgians are planning; their behavior is beyond understanding. Last Monday we received an oral message from Sandford and Nelson, through a traveler we know, that we could stay here in peace! Br. Byhan would be postmaster and I would be a pensioner of the U.S. Nelson would visit Br. Byhan in several days and Sandford would write to me. This was the point of the message received. I hope, dear Brother, the repeated ambiguities which were revealed already by the Governor and his agents will serve as a warning to all of us not to trust anything and not to go back on any decision already made. They knew very well that I made hasty preparations to leave immediately after receiving Nelson's note of July 8, and now that they know that we are here and cannot start the household in Ochg_____y again since everything has been sold, they want to allow us to remain! Miserable deceit! If I had remained quiet after July 8 and not made any preparations to move, it would have been seen by them as disrespect for their laws and notices, and I could have expected to be in prison very soon. By the way, I personally do not want any distinct favor from them, since all the other worthy and active missionaries had to leave the country. Who knows how soon their inconstant favor might be withdrawn, and we like the others would have to tolerate their persecution.

---

[1] The paragraph is in English in the original German manuscript.

Otherwise, things concerning the Cherokees are peaceful, as far as can be expected given the limitless oppression. We hear nothing about moving or about making a treaty. Their decision to continue with their laws, courts, and councils has not been carried out. Their magistrates are afraid of the punishment. The laws of the Cherokees will not be used against criminals any more, and those of the Georgians are by far not carried out and very incomplete to protect rights and justice. The results of this matter have often already been mentioned: robbery, drunkenness, and murder. The country is filled with whisky traders who carry out this ruinous trade everywhere.

It is said that Tennessee will extend its laws to the Cherokees within its borders in the coming legislature, the same with Alabama, as has already been the case with the Creeks within its borders.

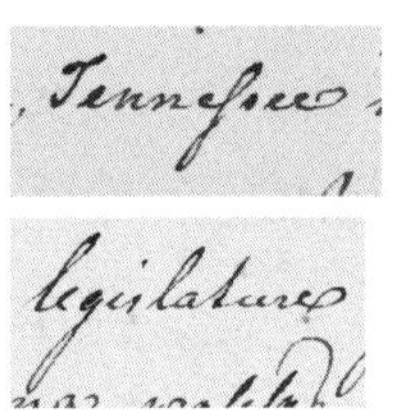

We were painfully disappointed in our eager expectation of receiving a letter from you in today's mail. It has been 3 weeks now since Br. Byhan received the last letters from you. (Another traveler has just arrived to spend the night.) In this distress and tension it is really a great trial to have to live in uncertainty for so long. Still there is one small hope that the Knoxville mail will delight us with letters from you tomorrow. Br. Byhan has still not been released from the post service. We have now been sitting here for 2 weeks and waiting for him to be able to get everything here ready to travel. But there is still no sign of this.

Meanwhile, the fall is approaching, and then we will not be able to travel. Because of the special circumstances of my family, Br. and Sr. Byhan also agree more and more that a longer postponement here is unnecessary, and they agree with the plans we first reported to you in my last letter from Oochgelogy, to begin the journey to Salem immediately with my family and Sr. Gambold. We are planning to set out from here at the beginning of next week, if nothing unexpected in these times of change prevents us from this decision.

Sunday the 7th. Once again, nothing from Salem with the Knoxville mail. It is impossible that you have not written to Br.

Byhan or me since July 2nd. Your kind letters have been taken or held up somewhere. Neither can we presume that someone from Salem is on the way here, since a letter from D. Ruede dated July 19 does not contain anything of this kind, which would give us reason for such hope. Now the Lord will arrange everything for the best. May we always look to Him and willingly allow ourselves to be guided according to His will.

Our decision to set out in several days is not firm. It is therefore not certain whether and when we will go on from here. On Aug. 17, the 40 days within which I had hoped to clear the Georgia borders will be over. There is new danger again of being dislocated by the Guard. Greetings to my dear parents and your dear family from your faithfully obliged Brother,

H. G. Clauder

[M 415-1b-38: Translated by Julie Tomberlin Weber. Addressed to: Rev. Theod. Schulz, Salem, Stokes County, North Carolina. Postmark: Springplace, C.N., Aug. 7. Free. G. Byhan, P.M. Received Aug. 20.]

Spring Place, Aug. 6, 1831

My dear Br. Schulz,

On the 17th we were very delighted to receive your last letter to me, dated July 2, via Wythe Courthouse. Since then we have received nothing else from you dear people. From your kind letter, we learned that the wagons will not be sent from Salem until I am free of the Post Office, and we approve of this. But dear Brn., we are in fact in a very awkward and truly very difficult situation. What are Br. and Sr. Clauder supposed to do? Because upon receiving the order from Col. Nelson — dated July 8th — Br. Clauder got his things in Och_____y in order and moved here to Spring Place with all his belongings to wait here for the wagons from Salem, according to permission granted by Col. Nelson. Last Monday, the 1st of this month, we received the oral assurance from Col. Nelson, through a traveler, that we could remain at our post undisturbed, Br. Clauder as Pensioner and I as postmaster.

Is this not absurd? The U. St. Govt. declared, first, that the missionaries, who had previously received the assistance of the Genl. Govt., would not be protected from the laws of Georgia. Why is an exception being made for us now? It is impossible to believe that Col. Nelson did not know that Br. Clauder had left with everything. Why did Col. Sanford not send the orders before Br. Clauder had moved away from Och_____y and before the mission place was completely deserted, because the promise comes from Sanford through Nelson to us? And so it is nothing but a certain policy which they have down.

And then it cannot be denied that if we remain — especially Br. Clauder — that the people will view us with a suspicious eye, because all the missionaries have now left the Georgia Territory. So people wonder — and we have in fact already seen traces of this — why is it that the Moravian missionaries are allowed to stay, but no others can? They must have a good relationship with the Georgians! We have already realized that they took note when we provided lodging for the Georgia Guard 2 times. And how could we do otherwise? We could not turn them away or treat them rudely. Their work is of no concern to us, and we are supposed to submit to the authority that has power over us. The Savior also says: love your enemies, bless those who curse you, etc. Even if we do not approve of their behavior, it is not our place to quarrel with them about this.

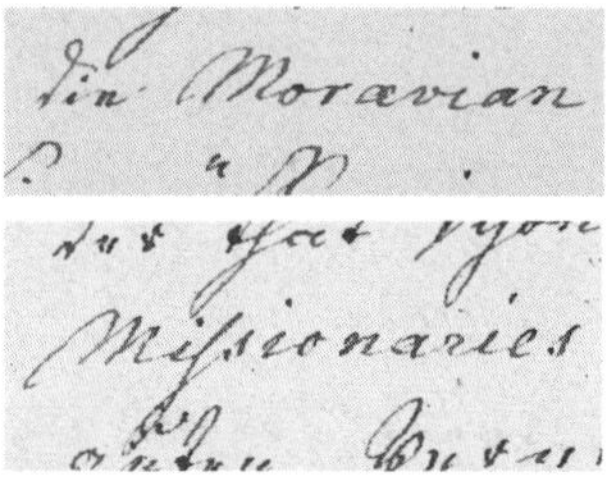

The greatest trouble we are having currently is that — if it should be a while before the wagons come from Salem — Br. and Sr. Clauder will not be able to travel because of his wife's condition, and if they do not set out from here within week or at most two, they will not be able to travel for now. Therefore, we have already thought about and discussed whether it would not be advisable for Br. and Sr. Clauder, along with Sr. Gambold, to set out with their small wagon on the journey to Salem without waiting for the large wagon from Salem? Still we want to wait for a letter from you dear people in Salem first, which we expect tomorrow, before it is really decided if Br. and Sr. Clauder precede us to Salem.

Furthermore, for some time there has been this difficult and unbearable circumstance that we have to host all those who are traveling through and past here, because our neighbor — who has recently been leading a depraved life — does not want to host any more strangers, and he sends all of them to us. We cannot turn them away, because there is not a house closer than 12 or 15 and 20 miles from here where they could stay. This is why our house looks like an actual Tavern. And so we ask you, for God's sake, to put an end to the work here — as it now is — in one way or another. Also those who have claimed that the missionaries are only trying to make money in this country are strengthened in this belief — or actually in the slander — when Spring Place takes in strangers and has to lodge them. Prospects of being able to get our livestock through the next winter have also vanished, because in 3 or 4 weeks — if things continue as they have been going — we will have no more oats and no hay for our own livestock.

All of these circumstances together make it extremely necessary for a change to be made at this mission post, and if you were here you would see this even more. The best is naturally that we all return to Salem for the time, as decided in the Helf. Conf., even if it is only for the time being, and perhaps after some time Brn. and Srs. would be sent back here. Then the layout, circumstances, and set-up would take on a different form.

And so my dear wife and I repeat this statement and the explanation that we will not and cannot remain in this confusion any longer. It is necessary that I get free of the Post Office to enable our recall or departure, and I ask that the Helf. Conf., through Br. Theod. Schulz, ask the Postmaster General for this, because I am being recalled from my mission post, since I also received the postal service through the negotiations of the Directors. However, if the Helf. Conf. has hesitations about taking this step, I will be required to do it and resign. Still I would prefer for the Directors to do it for me, because I feel no inclination to stay here any longer on account of the Post Office.

All of the circumstances here seem to come together so that a complete change of all the circumstances makes it essential for our missionaries to distance themselves from here for a time.

Stealing is currently getting the upper hand here, so that hardly anything can be kept unless it is locked in the houses, or everything is taken away. Our springhouse has already been robbed several times. All the straps are cut off of the horses' harnesses and wagons and taken away. They even try to steal beehives, which was the case here a couple of weeks ago. They did not succeed here, however. The cattle are shot down in the bush and skinned to get money for the hides in order to buy brandy. Since there are really no laws in the land anymore — neither the Georgians' laws nor the Cherokees' — everyone feels free and does exactly what he wants.

Sunday the 7th. I wrote this far yesterday, expecting that a letter would arrive from you dear people with the Georgia mail, but nothing came. Then we had hope of receiving something with the Knoxville mail. It arrived at 11 o'clock in the morning but behold, again nothing. What should we think about this silence?? Have you really forgotten us? We do not want to believe this. Since your last letter to me — from July 2nd — we have heard nothing else from Salem. Has the Post Office been robbed perhaps and your letters to us have thus been lost? We do not want to believe this, and we believe it is more likely that we can now look forward to a visit from you. And how important it would be if you advised us and helped us in our current increasingly troublesome and oppressive situation, especially since it seems pretty certain that this mission is now approaching its end.

Oh, dear Brn., write us again, because we need comfort and encouragement! Did my accounts reach your hands? This is the 8th or 9th letter in which I am uncertain if it has arrived at your place or will arrive. Everyone sends best greetings. And you, dear Br., accept another special greeting from your loving friend & Br.,

G. Byhan

In haste

[M 407-2: Springplace Diary.]

Sun., Aug. 7. Br. Byhan, Sr., led the first service and Br. Clauder the second, in which what was read from the Bible was repeated by the single Indian Br. Nicl. Ignatius in the Cherokee language. Finally there was singing in the Cherokee language.

Aug. 8. Br. Clauder went to Mr. McNair's on business.

Sun., Aug. 14. Br. Clauder gave the sermon and Br. Byhan the Bible reading. Mr. Dav. St. Dazizi served us again today as interpreter.

[M 415-1b-40: Translated by Julie Tomberlin Weber. Addressed to: Rev. Theodor Schulz, Salem, Stokes County, North Carolina. Postmark: Springplace, C.N., Aug. 14. Free. G. Byhan, P.M. Received Aug. 29.]

Springplace, Aug. 14, 1831

My dear Br. Schulz,

Since I have a little time just now before the Knoxville mail comes, I will hastily report the receipt yesterday evening — after a long drought — of your two kind letters, dated July 20 and 27, as well as the farewell letter from the Helf. Conf. to the Indian Brn. and Srs. We thank you most sincerely for everything in these. Next week I will write more thoroughly. I still have the Post Office, and there is no hope — as it currently seems — that I will soon be free of it.

Now may the Lord guide us further with His faithful hand, as He has done thus far! It must serve for the good of all of us! He will help us through all the difficulties that might be ahead of us! When ye shall hear of wars and rumours of war, be ye not troubled (Text from Feb. 9 [Mark 13:7]). This really comforts us sometimes!

Day after tomorrow I will make a trip to Camp Gilmer to discuss with Col. Sandford various matters concerning Br. and Sr. Clauder.

Sr. Clauder will now wait here in Spring Place for her confinement, and it seems the delivery is not far off anymore. Br. and Sr. Clauder and Sr. Gambold believe that Sr. Clauder will no longer be able to tolerate the journey to Salem.

Everyone here greets you all most sincerely. Special greetings to you from your faithfully obliged, humble Br.,

Gottl. Byhan

[M 407-2: Springplace Diary.]

Aug. 15. Genl. Newnan from Georgia stopped in at our place. After he had eaten lunch with us and his horse had been fed, he continued on his journey to New Echota. Genl. Newnan greatly disapproved of the way the Georgia Guard treated prisoners, especially the missionaries, and said that presumably the officers will be legally prosecuted for this. We did not get involved in any discussion about this subject with him. Generally we must be as careful as possible not to make the slightest comment in political matters, because the less said about the current circumstances between the Georgians and the Cherokees, whether it is said to someone from Georgia or from Tennessee, the better it is for us.

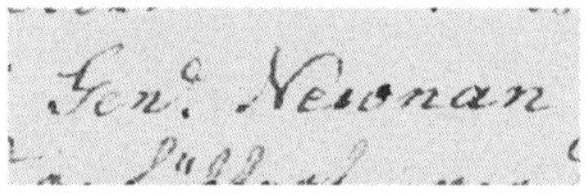

Aug. 17. Br. and Sr. Clauder, who have stayed with us since July 23rd, began their further journey from here to Salem today with the widowed Sr. Gambold, accompanied by our best wishes for blessings. Since we are now alone at our post in these desperate times, we commended ourselves especially to the Savior for His protection and safekeeping. He has already helped us through many difficulties. He will also remain with us further and continue to be our advisor, comfort, and help!

[M 415-1b-41: Translated by Julie Tomberlin Weber. Addressed to: Revd. Theodore Schulz, Salem, Stokes County, North Carolina. Postmark: Springplace, C.N., Aug. 21. Free. G. Byhan, P.M. Received Sept. 7.]

Springplace, Aug. 20, 1831

My dear Br. Schulz,

On the 13th of this month we received your two kind letters dated the 20th and 27th of last month, as well as the farewell letter from the Helfer Conf. to our Indian Brn. and Srs., which will be shared with them and delivered in its time. This will certainly be very important to them, if it should come to that. We thank you most sincerely for everything in your two kind letters, and we will try to act in accordance with it as far as circumstances here allow.

Last Wednesday, the 17th, Br. and Sr. Clauder began their journey from here to Salem with their little wagon hitched to two horses — accompanied by our best wishes for blessings. Sr. A. M. Gambold is also going with them. Br. Nae. Rominger is also coming with them with two more horses. With the latter, I must ask you to pay him for work that he has done here. I still owe him $36.45¾. Since he still had to pay another 12½ cents to the post rider and 75 cents to Polly Vann for making clothes, his credit in my book is $35.58¼, which I ask you to pay him.

I also ask you to tell Sr. A. Maria Gambold that our single Indian Br. Niclaus Ignatius bought her chest of drawers, which she had left behind here in Spring Place, for $17. You will also be good enough here and pay Sr. Gambold this $17. I will then enter these two sums you have paid off for me, of $52.58¼, in my book, as if I had received the money from you.

The Georgia mail just arrived here, but it did not bring us anything from Salem.

Everyone here sends best greetings, and so does your dear, familiar, poor Br.,

Gottlieb Byhan

[B 61-3: Provinzial Helfer Conferenz, meeting in Salem. Translated by C. Daniel Crews.]

Sat., Aug. 20. The letters received today from the Brn. Gb. Byhan and Clauder, dated the 7th [6th], report that Br. and Sr. Clauder and the widowed Sr. Gambold find themselves again in Springplace where all the things they are to take with them are also piled up. The latter planned to begin their return journey here soon.

The situation of the Brn. and Srs. in Springplace becomes more trying as time goes on. This was especially true after their neighbor Jos. Vann quit giving lodging to anyone at all, so that all travelers approach Br. and Sr. Byhan in Springplace, and every day, both day and night, they not only entertain themselves exceedingly, but they also eat up their scanty supplies of animal feed and groceries, and this is not only costing them a lot, but will also bring them into the greatest privation. Since there is no guesthouse anywhere near them, the demands of travelers on them are unceasing, as are those of the Georgia Militia who are roaming around in the Land.

This is causing all sorts of mistrust, since it makes it appear that the Brethren are holding with the Georgians because all the other missionaries have left the Cherokee Land of the Georgia District. Br. Byhan begs that we allow him to resign his Post Office position, or better that we ourselves deal with the Postmaster Genl. in Washington on his behalf. After the deepest consideration, we felt that the latter course would not be advisable, but did allow Br. Byhan to resign the office himself, given the very peculiar circumstances, but not to refer to us in the slightest as the Board of Directors of this Mission. Br. Schulz will send Br. Byhan this answer today with a draft for his resignation for the Postmaster Genl. in Washington.

[M 407-2: Springplace Diary.]

Sun., Aug. 21. Since it rained heavily almost the whole day, only a few of our Brn. and Srs. came to the services. Thus we prayed the Church Litany, first in English and then, since the single Indian Br. Solomon was present, in the Cherokee language. Finally a couple of hymns were sung in the Cherokee language.

Sun., Aug. 28 and Sept. 4. The services were held as usual. Otherwise, nothing noteworthy happened in the time in between, and we lived very quietly and to ourselves, and undisturbed.

[M 414-5-32: Translated by Julie Tomberlin Weber. Addressed to: Revd. Theodor Schulz, Salem, Stokes County, North Carolina. Postmark: Springplace, C.N., Aug. 28. Free. G. Byhan, P.M. Received Sept. 10.]

Springplace, Aug. 27, 1830 [1831]

Dear Br. Schulz,

The Georgia mail brought us nothing from Salem again today, which seems somewhat strange to us. Maybe next week's mail will bring something. We have not received a *National Intelligencer* from Washington for 2 weeks now either. Have you perhaps canceled it? If this is the case, we will be very sorry indeed. Then we would learn nothing else about how things look in the rest of the world, since it sometimes seems to us anyway as if we have been abandoned by all Christian people. Still dear God is our Comforter!! And we rely confidently on Him. He will not leave us!

This week we have had excessive amounts of rain. The streams everywhere have reached an unusual height, and currently, as I am writing this, it looks like rain again. How did the journey go for our Br. and Sr. Clauder? We thought about them a lot and often, and hope our dear Lord will assist them. On the 20th of this month I already informed you of their departure from here on the 17th by way of Knoxville, Abingdon, etc.

Br. Clauder wrote me back from Tennessee that Mr. McNair had bought Sr. Gambold's chest of drawers and paid her for this, so only Naem. Rominger needs to be paid by you.

Otherwise, nothing has happened since Br. Clauder's departure from here. However, the more time passes, the less likely that I will get free of the postal duties.

Everyone sends greetings, as does your poor fellow Brother,

G. Byhan

Please greet our children for us.

P.S. Last week I forwarded 2 letters to Br. Clauder from here to Salem with the mail. When this reaches your hands, he should safely have received them. I wish so very much that he would write me. Greet him and his travel companions for us.

G. B.

[M 415-1b-42: Translated by Julie Tomberlin Weber. Addressed to: Rev. Theodor Schulz, Salem, Stokes County, North Carolina. Postmark: Springplace, C.N., Sept. 4. Free. G. Byhan, P.M. Received Sept. 17.]

Springplace, Sept. 2, 1831

My dear Br. Schulz,

We received your kind letter of Aug. 13th on Aug. 28, and we thank you sincerely for this. Br. and Sr. Clauder and Sr. Gambold and Nae. Rominger had already set out from here to Salem on Aug. 17th. And so the wishes of the Conf. that Br. and Sr. Clauder remain here now could not be followed, because a previous letter from you had encouraged them to come to Salem — which they seemed to be very glad about — although they would have stayed here if they had still been here when your last letter arrived. On Aug. 30th I received two letters for Br. Clauder with the mail. However, I sent them to Salem since he had already left, and he will then surely receive them when he arrives there — or will already have received. Since then I heard that one of the letters was supposed to be from either Col. Sanford or Col. Nelson, with the announcement that he could remain in the country undisturbed, or something like this, which Br. Clauder will be able to say better. Since Br. Clauder's departure from here, nothing the least bit interesting has happened here except that we are having constant rain, and there is no sign of the weather changing.

So now we are alone at our posts here — but the Savior is still with us. He will not abandon us, which we often sense in a blessed manner. The Lord is with us, what can humans do to us? Another great encouragement for us is that we notice and feel that our Indian Brn. and Srs. are glad we have not left them yet or will not have to leave them.

However, from your kind letters I see that you have canceled our *National Intelligencer*, which really seemed very strange to us. Please allow us this as long as we are here, since it does not appear that we would ever completely leave this post, and we would also like it if we could hear frequently news about Congress next winter. We had already been suspicious for some time before you reported to us about whether it had been canceled or not, because we have not received an *Intelligencer* for a good while now. I have also already written to Gales & Seaton and asked why none was being sent to us anymore.

Please give Br. Clauder our sincere greetings and tell him that I have received his two letters from Maryville and Dandridge, along with the $20 bill. I will show the bill to Mr. Tarvin as soon as possible.

We are very eager to hear how Br. and Sr. Clauder managed in the mountains with all the rainy weather, crossing all the rivers — we hope safely.

We also see from your letter that we will not receive any more *Wöchentliche Nachrichten*, because you have canceled these. I can say nothing in reply to this except that this hurts us a great, great deal.

Now we will try to continue on and follow our call as much as grace allows, because everything He does and allows to happen will certainly have a good end. May He maintain our confidence in Him; then everything will go well, and in the end we will see that everything had to happen precisely as it happens. We build on a firm foundation in Him, full of hope that does not wane.

Since the Georgia mail did not bring us anything from Salem today, I just want to send our sincere greetings from all of us, and also from your familiar friend and lowly Br.,

Gottl. Byhan

[*Records: N.C.*, 8:3971: Salem Diary. Translated by Douglas L. Rights.]

Sept. 2. Br. and Sr. Henry Gottlieb Clauder with their little son, and the widow Anna Maria Gambold and the Single Br. Naaman Rominger, arrived here safely after a difficult journey from the country of the Cherokees. Since Br. Clauder could not take the prescribed oath of allegiance to the State of Georgia, he was compelled to quit the state and, therefore, his station. The farewell of the Clauders and Sr. Gambold from the little Indian congregation Oochgeelogy was sorrowful on both sides. Br. Byhan, holding his commission as postmaster of Springplace from the Federal government, until he is relieved of the same, or resigns, will visit Oochgeelogy from time to time. Sr. Gambold will retire here and Br. and Sr. Clauder will have their temporary home here also.

Clauders' Journey Home, 1831

[M 409-1: Oochgeelogy Diary. Translated by Julie Tomberlin Weber. Handwriting is Heinrich Gottlieb Clauder's. The travel diary of Br. and Sr. Clauder concludes the Oochgeelogy Diary.]

After spending almost 4 weeks in Spring Place with our dear Br. and Sr. Byhan, we began our journey to Salem on Aug. 17. That same day we drove to the home of our acquaintance McNair, where we spent the night.

Aug. 18. About 9 in the morning we said a tearful farewell to these friends and continued our journey. In the afternoon we arrived at the river Amoee, which was quite swollen from all the rain. However, we crossed it safely and kept dry by raising the body of our wagon with some supports. Around 4 o'clock we crossed the Hiwassee River, which is the border between the Indian country and the state of Tennessee. Here we saw the last Cherokees. In the evening we found lodging with a farmer we know named Cobb. Both he and his wife seemed to be thoroughly awakened. The early and blessed death of an 18-year-old son had the blessed effect on these old people of awakening them. We discussed religious things together until late in the night.

Aug. 20. In the morning we successfully crossed the beautiful and wide [Little] Tennessee River. The road was excellent, so we covered 15 miles before breakfast. Toward evening we drove through the beautiful little town of Maryville, where there is a theological seminary with about 60 students.

Aug. 21. At noon we had a heavy storm. We continued our journey without stopping until evening when we once again had to endure a heavy rain. We reached a place to lodge on the banks of the French Broad River where we spent the night.

Aug. 22. Despite the rain, which was unceasing, we continued our journey. However, because of the extremely bad road we could make only slow progress. We were happy and grateful after a trip of 15 miles in relentless rain to reach the village of Dandridge, where we found an excellent lodging and friendly and accommodating hosts. Our hope that the rain was over now and that the next day would be pleasant was disappointed on

Aug. 23, when we covered 18 miles in heavy downpours on horrible roads. We spent the night with very friendly people who are Baptists. Br. Clauder was asked to lead the family devotions, which he joyfully did. By the way, these old people are the parents of the well-known speaker and member of the Senate in Congress of the United States, Mr. Barton from Missouri.

Aug. 24. We learned that the streams on our road past Greenville and Jonesboro were impassable. And so we were happy to follow our host's advice and drive toward Rodgersville, where we reached the large post road on which there is no fear of being stopped by high streams. We had some rain showers today, as we have had for many days. Despite all the difficulties on the road, as well as the continuing sickliness of our young Charles, we were sincerely happy and grateful that we could continue our journey.

Aug. 25. Rain the entire day. We saw the beautiful river Holston several times in the distance. We ate our breakfast with a man named Fourgey, who is known in Salem and used to have a daughter in the boarding school there. In the evening we crossed the northern branch of the previously mentioned river on a beautiful bridge near the little village of Kingsport, where we spent the night.

Aug. 26. After we had driven on in the rain for several hours, we finally had the joy of seeing the dear sunshine around noon. In the afternoon we successfully crossed the so-called Chesnut Mountain. The beautiful view from it was somewhat obscured by low clouds. When the weather is clear you can clearly see the Cumberland Mountains in the state of Kentucky, as well as all the mountains between the states of North Carolina and Tennesee, which appear to tower very close by.

Aug. 27. We had to drive until 11 o'clock in the morning before we could get feed for our horses and food for ourselves. In the afternoon we once again had to endure 8 miles in heavy rains. The road was almost impassable because of the heavy wagons and large herds of cattle which are driven on it to the northern markets. Toward evening we drove through the little city of Abingdon in the state of Virginia, where there is an important salt trade, which is often carried out near here.

Aug. 28. We were extremely joyful to have beautiful weather today, since the road would also dry out soon. In the evening we reached a German inn whose owner visited Salem many years ago, and who still spoke negatively of the place. My efforts to give him a better impression were in vain. The rough and rocky road we passed today left us unusually tired. There is now a suggested project to lay a railroad over this road, which promises to be of great use for this area and eastern Tennessee.

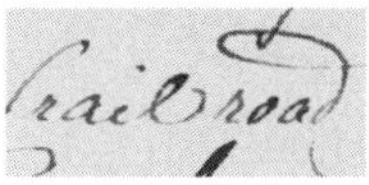

Aug. 29. At daybreak we continued our journey through an extremely beautiful and fruitful area. On both sides of the road, almost without interruption, there were the most beautiful farms, most owned by German farmers. In the evening we crossed through a beautiful and bustling village named Wythe.

Aug. 30. We left the big road we had been following since the 24th. In the morning we successfully crossed the New River, which has flat banks. Some miles on this side we climbed the mountains, known by the name Blue Ridge, without any trouble. In this mountain area you seldom find good inns, and so we had to drive until late in the night before we found a shelter where we could stay.

Aug. 31. 5 miles from our camp we finally reached the place where our road led us back down the mountains we had climbed yesterday. This was a dangerous undertaking since the road had been almost completely destroyed by the recent rains. By locking both of the back wheels on the wagon, we reached the bottom slowly and safely, and we silently gave our Lord our thanks for this.

Sept. 1. Once again we had heavy downpours of rain. We were happy and grateful that our difficult journey was almost over now. In the evening we reached the first Gemein town, Bethania, and on the next day,

Sept. 2, we finally reached the place where we have been instructed to live for now, with our dear parents in Salem. We had spent 16½ days on the journey from Spring Place. Finally, we commend ourselves and the poor Cherokee Brethren and Sisters we had left behind to the remembrance and prayer of all friends and followers of our Lord Jesus Christ.

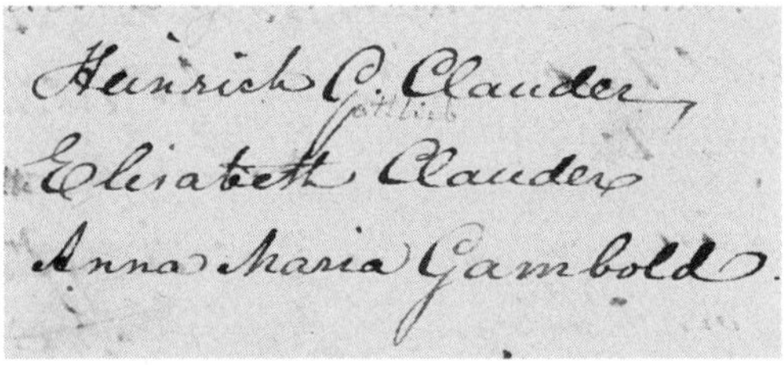

Heinrich G. Clauder
Elisabeth Clauder
Anna Maria Gambold

1831, part 10

[M 407-2: Springplace Diary. Translated by Julie Tomberlin Weber. Handwriting is Gottlieb Byhan's.]

Sept. 7. Br. Byhan went to Mr. McNair's on business and returned on *the 8th*. In recent days we began making Indian corn feed, although the weather was not very favorable for this. Today a young Indian came and offered to help us making feed. Since he seemed to be a very orderly Indian, we took him in to work for several days. Today we also heard that Judge Clayton in Georgia is supposed to have said that the Cherokee Indians had just as much right to dig for gold on their land as they have to plant corn. As a result of this declaration by Judge Clayton, the Commander, Col. Sanford, had written to the Governor of Georgia about the Georgia Guard to get more help, or soldiers, because he and his 40 men would not be able to prevent the Indians from digging for gold. The Governor of Georgia answered him that if 40 men cannot keep the Indians from the gold, then 10,000 can do it. Time will tell what the end of this will be, and what the consequences will be. Today we also heard that the Cherokees are planning to hold their annual Council in Oct. in New Echota, as previously. Presumably this will lead to more unrest between the Georgians and the Cherokees.

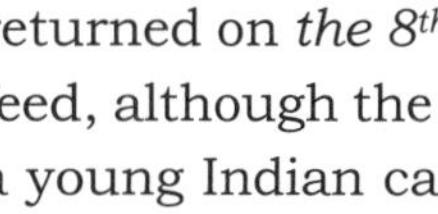

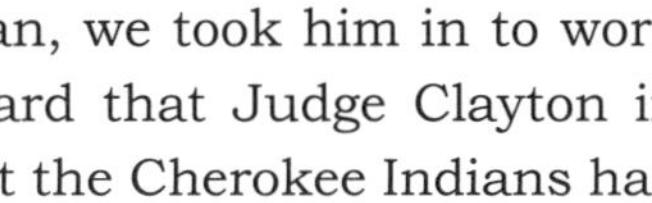

[M 415-1b-43: Translated by Julie Tomberlin Weber. Addressed to: Revd. Theodore Schulz, Salem, Stokes County, North Carolina. Postmark: Springplace, C.N., Sept. 11. Free. Gottlieb Byhan, P.M. Received Sept. 24.]

Springplace, Sept. 10, 1831

Dearly beloved Br. Schulz,

I received your kind letter of Aug. 20 on the 4th of this month. It included instructions from the Helf. Conf. that I should return the Post Office to the hands of the General Postmaster and resign. I have done this now, and I will send the resignation to Washington with tomorrow's mail. It is a shame I did not receive your letter of eight days ago one hour sooner, since I would have been able to write immediately, but it was just time for the service and so it had to be postponed for eight days. I was not able to name a successor for the General Postmaster, because one might say that people are very rare here right now. I did not want to suggest a certain Wacasser, who lives in Sumak and is a Georgian, because the General Postmaster knows that such a person exists in Sumak, and so I did not name any successor. We will see then in approximately 5 weeks what the results will be.

This week I visited our friend McNair, and I had no choice but to share our decision with him in confidence, partly because I believed I might be able to recommend his son Niclaus as my successor, or might be allowed to. However, Mr. McNair did not seem willing for his son to become postmaster in Spring Place, although his wife had no objection to this. And then his son Niclaus was not home just then, and he could not be asked if he would like to accept it or not, and if he wanted to move into our house. And so I decided to send in the resignation without naming a successor. Even so, I still believe that the General Postmaster, the postmaster in New Echota, and Wacasser in Sumak wish to find even the slightest reason to make a different arrangement with the postal service here and get me out. Mr. Wacasser in Sumak is supposed to have said I had now become rich enough in the Post Office, because otherwise we would not manage here as well as we do, and so it was time for someone else here to get the Post Office.

Everything else in your dear letter is certainly to be feared: that we would be negatively viewed by unkind or otherwise adversely inclined people in our difficult situation for the acts of love and service we carry out for fellow humans in distress, and as if we had harbored a special affection for the enemies of the Cherokee. We have already seen signs of this, and once someone has thought an idea like against us, it would be very difficult to get rid of it. Indeed there are even signs that some people wonder why the Georgians leave me unchallenged, since all the white people without exception have had to leave the Georgia Territory. It is particularly incomprehensible to some of them that they leave our Nathanael here so undisturbed, and one sees in them that they wonder about this, although they do not say much about it — that is, not to us personally, but they are just surprised that the Georgians do not touch us. And so it will be good if we distance ourselves for a while as soon as we can.

The latest thing here is that Judge Clayton in Georgia is supposed to have declared as his opinion that the Cherokees really have as much right to dig for and seek gold in their country as they have to plant corn. This prompted the commander, Col. Sanford, to write to Gov. Gilmore that he might send him more soldiers, because his 40 men who are here in the country are not sufficient to prevent the Indians from digging for gold. Gov. Gilmore supposedly answered him that if 40 men were not sufficient to prevent the Indians, then 10,000 could certainly do it. That is what people here are saying.

Furthermore, the Indians are planning and have decided to hold their annual Council in October in New Echota again, and if all the head men should be taken as prisoners, they believe that the more severely the Georgians treat the Cherokees, the better their matter will turn out with the Government. So they are always happy when the poor missionaries have to suffer righteously from the Georgians, because they then believe those white people who are on the Indians' side will make more efforts to help the Indians get justice. And when they hear that this or that white man has been very badly treated by the Georgians, they say: "That's well, it is all for our best."[1]

Br. and Sr. Clauder have probably been with you for several weeks now and will already have given you a thorough report about all of this. We would like to hear when they arrived in Salem. Greet them for us and tell Br. Clauder that I have received his two letters from Marysville and Dandridge, the latter with the $20 bank note.

Please greet our children for us as well, and tell Sophia that we received her letter of Aug. 4th and that I will answer it soon.

Now may the Lord continue to help us. He has helped thus far. He must be our help, comfort, and counsel. We are facing remarkable times here, because it can be presumed that the Cherokees will not be able to remain quiet much longer. Perhaps something will happen at the Council they are holding in Oct. God is still sitting in the seat of power. Nothing will happen and can happen to us without His knowledge.

All the bad things that typically happen among heathen Nations are happening here again and becoming the norm, most specially theft. Nothing is safe from them anymore. One would like to keep everything locked up if one could, so that it is not stolen. No law exists here any longer. The Georgians do not enforce, theirs and the Cherokees are not allowed to enforce theirs, so we are actually living in a free country here where each person can do as he pleases.

The Georgia mail brought me nothing from Salem today. Everyone here sends you his best greetings. And you, accept another special greeting from your familiar friend and Br.,

Gottlieb Byhan

[M 407-2: Springplace Diary.]

Sun., Sept. 11. In the first service was the sermon on Luke 4:18-19. At the conclusion of this was the baptism of the baby daughter born to Mr. Charles Buttler and his wife Anna Johanna

---

[1] The quote is in English in the original German manuscript.

with the name Mary. In the second service we enjoyed the body and blood of Jesus in Holy Communion. The Indian Sr. Magdalena Susanna, wife of our Indian Br. Emanuel, joined us in participating for the first time, after first receiving the confirmation blessing. After the service we spoke thoroughly with the Indian Br. Emanuel concerning an offense which annoyed a number of Brn. and Srs. Mr. Dav. St. Dazizi was here today and served us as interpreter.

[M 415-1b-44: Translated by Julie Tomberlin Weber. Addressed to: Revd. Theod. Schulz, Salem, Stokes County, North Carolina. Postmark: Springplace, C.N., Sept. 18. Free. Gottl. Byhan, P.M. Received Sept. 30.]

Spring Place, Sept. 17, 1831

My dear Br. Schulz,

On Sept. 4th I received your last letter to me dated Aug. 20th, as I already informed you in my last letter to you, dated the 10th of this month, and at your advice, I sent my resignation from the postal system to the General Postmaster in Washington, and I am now waiting for an answer.

Since nothing special has happened here since my last letter to you, I have only the following to add at this time, and I want to learn the thoughts of the Pr. Helf. Conf. and what they think about it. When I visited at Mr. McNair's last week, we also discussed who would probably occupy our house if we returned to Salem as well. Mr. McNair told me that Joseph Vann, our neighbor had already told them that he did not want to put Georgians into it when we left, and that in that case he would prefer to take it over himself. Now the question is, if things go that far, how and in what manner and on what conditions do we give it to Jos. Vann now? Do we put a specific price on the house, or the houses and improvements, or do we just let him take possession of it until we see if we should expect something from the Government for the improvements? Admittedly it is certain that we will never get back what it has cost us. Now if

Jos. Vann purchased it, he would not be able to pay for it right away in any case, and he would have to give me a bond, and if this happens Mr. McNair promised me that he would provide security for the payment. I would really like to know the thoughts and advice of the Pr. Helf. Conf. about this matter.

We will not be able to avoid a loss in any case if we should leave here, despite all care and caution; and I must admit that this matter has caused me much worry and concern and has caused me many sleepless hours. Oh, how we wish — if it were possible — for the mission to remain here in the Land of the Cherokees. Or if it should be interrupted for a while and then renewed, it could be established on a completely different footing as far as the external work! The place where this could be started again should also be very carefully considered. Still these are just my preliminary thoughts.

We have heard recently that the Indians want to hold Court in Chatooga District, and at the same time we heard that 8 soldiers have already marched there, either to prevent the Indians from holding Court or to arrest them right away. We will surely hear the results in time.

The Indians also want to hold their annual Council on the 2nd Monday in Oct. in New Echota, which is completely against the Georgia laws. We will have to see what the results of this will be.

I have one more request of you. Could you let me know how long John Hein's wagon box is, except for the place in front which the drivers always like to have, so I can plan the boxes I have to make for our things accordingly if we are picked up.

Concerning the Georgia money that you write me you have put aside for me, I will do what I can to exchange it if you send it along. Are the South Carolina notes not accepted in Salem either?

Now the Presbyterians have also begun holding Camp Meetings in this country. Yesterday, today, and tomorrow they have one on Candys Creek in the part of the Cherokee Nation which lies in the state of Tennessee, not far from Highwassee River. We heard that many preachers from Tennessee will go there.

I just received Br. Clauder's letter of Aug. 28, via Augusta, Ga. I still cannot grasp how it found its way from Abingdon to Georgia. In addition, there was 25 cents postage on it, despite the fact that Br. Clauder had written P.M. on it, which I corrected. I saw in this that he and his company had a relatively difficult journey to Abingdon because of the rain and bad roads. Hopefully the Savior brought them safely all the way to Salem. Give him our best greetings. I will write him with the next mail. I received nothing from Salem today. Perhaps tomorrow's Knoxville mail will bring us something.

Everyone sends best greetings, especially your friend and Br.,

Gottl. Byhan

[M 407-2: Springplace Diary.]

Sun., Sept. 18. Only a few of our Brn. and Srs. came for the Sunday services.

Sept. 19. Three Methodist preachers stopped in at our place. They brought us the news that the white people who were arrested some time ago by the Georgia Guard and had received permission to go home to their relatives again upon the security that they would appear before the Court in Georgia, which was held last week, had now been found guilty at that Court and according to the law had been sentenced to four years in prison. Their names are as follows: the Rev. Mr. Worcester, missionary in New Echota, Doct. Buttler, missionary in Wills Valley, two Messrs. Thomson, both from Hightower, one of them missionary there, Mr. Wheeler, printer of the *Cher. Phoenix*, Mr. Gann, Br. Austin Copeland, who belongs to the Oochgeloogy congregation, Mays, Delozier, Eaton, and Trott, a Methodist preacher. This situation aroused general compassion among the residents here. But it is also generally believed that all is for the best in the Cherokees' affairs with the Georgians and must be useful for the former. We could do nothing but wish them comfort and help from the One who does not leave anyone without comfort if he turns to Him in a childlike way.

Sept. 21. Br. Byhan today went to New Echota on business. On this occasion he also paid a visit in Och_____y at Br. and Sr. Wllm. Abr. Hicks's, who were very happy about this visit. Br. Hicks said that the few Brn. and Srs. who are still in Och_____y since Br. and Sr. Clauder left meet from time to time in their meeting house to encourage each other and to strengthen themselves with the Word of God. During this they are aware of God's peace in a comforting way. In case Br. Byhan also returns to Salem, they asked that they might be served Holy Communion one more time. This was promised them. Our deep wish is that the Savior will not leave these abandoned sheep but keep them with Him and His wounds, so that they might remain faithful to the grace they have experienced in their hearts.

Sept. 22. Br. Byhan returned to Spring Place.

[M 415-1b-45: Translated by Julie Tomberlin Weber. Addressed to: Revd. Theodore Schulz, Salem, Stokes County, North Carolina. Postmark: Springplace, C.N., Sept. 25. Free. Gottlieb Byhan, P.M. Received Oct. 8.]

Springplace, Sept. 24, 1831

Dear Br. Schulz,

Last Sunday I received your kind letter of the 7th of this month, from which we learned of the arrival of Br. and Sr. Clauder & Co. in Salem. We join them in expressing gratitude to our dear Lord for guiding them so quickly and safely to you despite all the rain and the bad roads. Br. Clauder will probably have given you a thorough report about everything here, so I can limit myself in this letter to what has happened since Br. Clauder's departure from here and what is still taking place.

The most important thing at this time is this: You will probably remember that the Georgia Guard have arrested various white people throughout this summer; however, they were set free since they gave security to appear in the Sept. Court, which was to be held in Gainesville. These white people then stood trial in the Gainesville Court, and they were found — <u>Guilty</u> — and accordingly must go to the Penitentiary. Their names are: Rev. S. A. Worcester, Doct. Butler, Trott, two Thomsons from Hightower, Mr. Wheeler, Mr. Gann, Austin Copeland, Mr. Hays, Mr. Delozier, and a Mr. Eaton. Time will tell what the consequences of this will be now. People believe that all of this must serve the best interests of the Indian matter. Only time will tell if this turns out to be true.

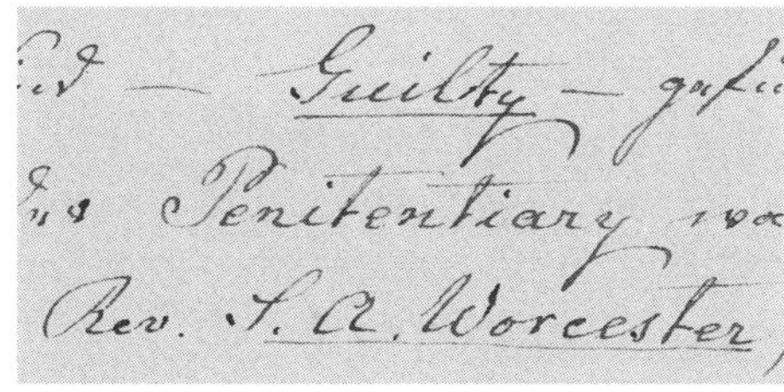

Guilty

Penitentiary

Rev. S. A. Worcester,

I think I had already informed you in a previous letter that the Indians want to hold their annual Council on the second Monday in October this year. The Georgia Guard, however, will probably throw a wrench into this plan.

I see from your letter that things did not turn out so well with the sale of one of the horses Br. Clauder brought to Salem. Since there was a pretty substantial loss from this, it makes me somewhat hesitant to trade livestock for horses. Yet if it gets to the point we need to move, we would also need two more horses to hitch 3 to our small farm wagon, because we will really need our wagon to bring along the things that cannot be sold here. And since the wagon is very strong, we can load it pretty well so that we can hitch at least 3 horses to it. And so I think it would be best if 2 horses could be sent along — excluding the 8 horses in the two large wagons — to hitch them in front of the small wagon.

Naem. Rominger had expressed his willingness to come back out here and to drive the small wagon to Salem; he will also be able to give you a complete report about this matter. Naturally we have to have a driver for the small wagon, but there is still time to talk and to write about this matter. If it actually happens that we can get away from here this year, we will not arrive in Salem much before Christmas.

This week I visited Br. and Sr. Wm. Abr. Hicks in Ochgeloogy, which really delighted them. They said that the few Brethren and Sisters who are there sometimes meet, and then they comfort each other and instruct and encourage each other to remain with the Savior, and to live for Him alone in this world. They are really longing to celebrate Holy Communion, which I promised to hold for them as soon as it is feasible. Nathl. and Alexander Sander are now busy making corn feed. The weather is admittedly not the most favorable, but we will get a nice quantity of feed.

In our neighborhood many people are ill. Primarily a cold fever is spreading among the people, especially among the Negroes.

The 25th. I did not close this letter in the hope that the Knoxville mail might bring something from Salem, so that I could immediately report receiving it if we happened to get anything. But we found ourselves disappointed; we did not receive anything.

Everyone here sends greetings. Your humble fellow Brother,

Gottl. Byhan

[M 407-2: Springplace Diary.]

Sun., Sept. 25. Only a few of our Brn. and Srs. came here. We spoke today with the Indian Sr. Rosanna about an offense she had been accused of through unfaithfulness, and through which she had really hurt a number of our Brn. and Srs. She did not seem to be especially remorseful about this, and so she was seriously admonished to think about what she had promised the Savior upon her baptism and asked through His grace to keep her walk such that she would not be an embarrassment to the Savior and the Gemeine. She was further admonished to be careful in her manner of talking, so that she would not be offensive to the Brn. and Srs. But unfortunately we noted that she really tried to help herself with untruths.

Sept. 28. Two Indians who had killed a wolf in the neighborhood came to our place today and showed us its ears. They asked for 6¼ cents from us, because, as they said, every neighbor is giving them this much for their efforts. So we gave them the 6¼ cents they requested.

Sept. 30. In the evening Mrs. Bean, Mrs. Vann, Dav. Vann's wife, and their children and a Negro woman came to our place and spent the night. The Indian Brn. Joshua and Israel, who looked for cattle in the bush for us this week, also came and brought us a small deer which they shot today. They also spent the night here. Our house was thus pretty full. In addition we had 5 more horses to feed overnight.

Oct. 1. Early in the day our Br. Clement and his wife, old Mother Vann, and also Niclaus McNair came to our place. All of them had their breakfast here, so that there were 20 persons at breakfast. This did not bother us, however, because it happens often here. It is always hardest on the Sisters with the house-keeping. Today we heard that the Governor of Georgia has declared the following about the above-mentioned persons who were sentenced to go to prison: They must do one of three things. They must go to the Penitentiary, or they must swear the oath that they will support the Georgians in their laws, or third, they could go home, put their things together, and leave the Georgia Territory as soon as they have harvested their corn. Everyone promised to do the latter, except for Rev. S. A. Worcester and Doct. Elizur Buttler, Presbyterian missionaries who chose the first option. It is said they were then immediately put into the penitentiary.

Sun., Oct. 2. Since it looked as if it would rain the entire day today, only a few Brn. and Srs. came to the services. In the afternoon the weather cleared up again.

Oct. 5. Toward evening Mr. and Mrs. Rodgers came to our place with our Sr. Delila McNair and spent the night here. The former then went on early on the 6th. Sr. McNair, however, stayed here and did not leave on the road for home until early on the 7th. Mr. Vann told us today that the Indians will not have their Council in New Echota this year, but rather in Chattooga District, because they feared they would be disturbed in the former place. Chattooga District lies in the state of Alabama, where they believe they will be safe from the Georgians.

[*Records: N.C.*, 8:3973: Salem Diary. Translated by Douglas L. Rights.]

Oct. 6. The Wachovia Society For the Spread of the Gospel had its annual general meeting with a blessed sense of the Lord's presence. The mission among the Cherokees in its present critical situation was especially remembered in prayer.

[M 415-1b-46: Translated by Julie Tomberlin Weber. Addressed to: Revd. Theodor Schulz, Salem, Stokes County, North Carolina. Postmark: Springplace, C.N., Oct. 9. Free. G. Byhan, P.M. Received Oct. 22.]

Springplace, Oct. 8, 1831

Dear Br. Schulz,

I already reported to you on the 24th of last month that your kind letter to me dated Sept. 7th arrived here on the 18th. Since then nothing else special has taken place here. Everything is still and quiet except that a certain Mr. Carey from West Tenn. is traveling around in the country as an Agent of President Jackson and persuading the Indians to move to the west and registering the ones who are willing to move. But we hear that few are willing to let themselves be registered as emigrants.

In my last letter I informed you that 11 or 12 of the white people who were arrested throughout the summer here by the Georgia Guard and bound at Court have had their trial and were found guilty, and as a result of this they had to go to the penitentiary. Among these were also Mr. Worcester and Doct. Buttler, two missionaries. These people are now all being sent to Milledgeville in Georgia. But before they went to the penitentiary, Gov. Gilmer gave them the choice of doing one of the following three things: First, if they really wanted to they could go to the penitentiary; second, they could take the oath of allegiance; and third, they could go home, get their things together — we also heard that he had allowed them to harvest their corn, which is not certain, however, — and then leave the Georgia Territory. All of them decided to do the latter except Mr. Worcester and Doct. Butler, who chose the first. They were then immediately led to the penitentiary and put to work.

Many of the Indians, especially the Halfbreeds, believe now that this circumstance, that these two people are in the penitentiary, will be very beneficial to them with respect to their land, and that this will especially help make the Georgians leave them in peace in the future. It is not yet clear to me that this will be the case. They are already practically considered the saviors of the Cherokees and seen as martyrs. However, those who were set free and want to leave the Georgia Territory are receiving little respect from most people, although they do not really talk about them much.

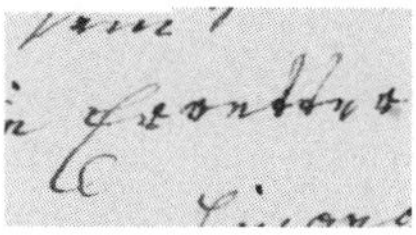

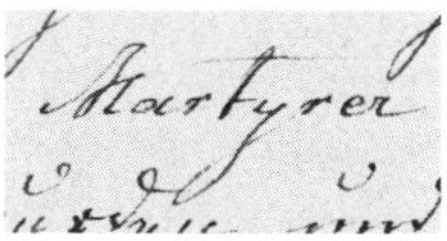

Day before yesterday I received a letter from Rev. Mr. Buttrick, who used to be a missionary in Carmel about 30 miles from here, also from the Foreign Board of Missions just like Mr. Worcester and Doct. Butler, in which he wrote, among other things:

[Br. Byhan copies Mr. Butrick's letter in English:]

We rejoice to think that you & your family are still in the Nation, unmolested. As yet, I must consider the course your Society took, to be judicious. Our blessed Saviour has never promised to secure to us our rights in this world; nor can we as missionaries to the heathen engage to defend their temporal interests. By divine assistance, we will love them & pray for them, that all the dealings of divine Providence may be subservient to their good. But our heavenly Father governs the temporal & political interests of the world by another set of men, over whom, we, as missionaries, cannot control. As yet I feel that the Lord has good in store for the Cherokees, etc.

[Br. Byhan continues his letter to Br. Schulz in German:]

From this one can see that he does not completely share the opinion of his fellow Brethren, the missionaries named above. I would just like to add that we were told that the missionaries should not flee, but should allow everything to happen to them that the Georgians, or our enemies, considered good, because

Paul and Silas were also put into prison. The reason Paul and Silas were put into prison, Acts 16, is certainly not the same reason Worcester and Butler are in the penitentiary. Now we will see if their imprisonment will help them at all in regard to their land and what kind of effect it will have on their work between them and the Georgians and the Genl. Government. The missionaries in the penitentiary are confident in their belief that their imprisonment will be of great benefit for the Cherokees' matter.

In 8 days I expect a reply from the general postmaster to my resignation. We are very curious to see how this will turn out. By orders received from the General Postmaster, in the future all 4 mails are supposed to arrive here on Saturday evening and leave again Sunday morning.

5 o'clock in the evening. The Georgia mail has just brought me your kind letter of Sept. 24, for which we thank you sincerely. The letter asked if it would not be possible to send the wagons from Salem in Oct., and we wondered if we should consider writing for the wagons before I have received an answer from the Post Office. We then considered the matter right away and agreed on the following. You could send the wagons as soon as you receive this to hasten the departure from here as much as possible, so that the journey does not get pushed too far into winter. And if the answer from the Post Office should turn out, so that I might perhaps remain alone until January, then I could follow alone, although I hope this will not be the case. But then we would need to ask for a driver and 2 horses for our small farm wagon. Br. Naeman Rominger has offered to come back here with the wagons to drive our small wagon.

For various reasons, we could not accept your suggestion that Mother and Nathl. go ahead alone first.

Be so good and do not forget to send the tent with the wagons. Also 2 new coffee burners, one for Sr. Delila McNair and one for her daughter. Our Rachel also has something to send; please let her know. Please let us know by post when the wagons set out from Salem. I will not neglect to write again on the next mail day, and to inform you if the answer has arrived and how it turned out. I hope it might be such that I also will be free right away, since we have to leave and are no longer living in peace here, and we cannot pursue our calling any more as we should until times get better.

Along with sincere greetings to you all, I remain your faithfully obliged Br.,

Gottl. Byhan

[M 415-1b-47: Translated by Julie Tomberlin Weber. Addressed to: Rev. Theodor Schulz, Salem, Stokes County, North Carolina. Postmark: Springplace, C.N., Oct. 16. Free. G, Byhan, P.M. Received Oct. 26.]

Springplace, Oct. 16, 1831

My dear Br. Schulz,

Our expectation and the hope that yesterday's Georgia mail would bring an answer from the Genl. Postmaster in Washington to my resignation 5 weeks ago was not fulfilled, and so I must spend 8 days longer in the almost unbearable uncertainty in which we have lived for almost 9 months now to wonder what will finally happen to us. Now the Savior has helped thus far; He will not leave us in the future! Despite all this uncertainty, however, in my last letter, dated the 8th of this month, I wrote to you that you might send the wagons, but if it should be the case that I cannot immediately leave when the wagons arrive here because of the P.O., my wife and I will remain here alone until I am the free of the P.O., and then we will follow afterward in our small stage wagon.

I think I also mentioned this in my last letter, if the Conf. should have any objections to this, please let us know right away.

Since my last letter of the 8th of this month, nothing of note has happened here, except that 30 soldiers under the command of Col. Nelson appeared in New Echota last Monday in the expectation that the Council would gather there this week. They found themselves disappointed because the Council will not be held until the 24th of this month in Chatooga — in the state of Alabama.

Along with sincere greetings to Br. and Sr. Clauder from all of us, share with them the news that Mr. Thomas Gann died last week. He got a fever in Milledgeville when he was supposed to enter the penitentiary. He could not get rid of it after he returned home, and he then died of it.

Half past 11 in the morning. The Knoxville mail has just brought me your kind letter dated Oct. 5, thus in 11 days. Since I do not have time to answer it now, I must postpone it until the next mail. In the meantime, please accept many thanks for it.

Everyone greets you most sincerely, especially your faithful friend and Br.,

Gottl. Byhan

[M 415-1b-48: Translated by Julie Tomberlin Weber. Addressed to: Rev. Theod. Schulz, Salem, Stokes County, North Carolina. Postmark: Springplace, C.N., Oct. 23. Free. G. Byhan, P.M. Received Nov. 5.]

Springplace, Oct. 22, 1831

My dear Br. Schulz,

I received your kind letter of the 5th of this month, as I already reported to you on the 16th of this month — on that day, thus in 11 days. It seems the letters via Knoxville go the quickest, because they usually take 16 days via Georgia.

Nothing especially interesting has happened since my last letter. We continue to live in relative peace and quiet, and we are slowly preparing for our departure, although I still have no answer to my resignation from the Genl. P.M. Still I hope that I will receive an answer with the Georgia mail today, since it has been 6 weeks now since I resigned. I will not close this letter until I can report whether I received an answer today or not.

I wrote you 2 weeks ago now that you should send the wagons, because we believed that the answer from the Genl. P.M. would certainly not take much longer, and thus we would not lose any time and could travel before winter begins. And if the answer does not follow as quickly as we would like, then the work could still be continued for now, and my wife and I would then stay here as long as it takes to get free of the wretched Post Office story, and we would then follow with our little stage wagon. Currently we presume the latter will be the case. We would certainly prefer it if we could all begin the journey together. The situation in which we currently are living — and it becomes more oppressive every day — is indescribable. God alone can help us endure it!

Since Mr. Jos. Vann is leaving for the Council today — which is supposed to be held next week in Chatooga in the state of Alabama — yesterday I took the opportunity to speak freely with him about our situation, because he is, after all, one of the Head men of the Nation. He promised that during our absence he would have our house occupied so that no stranger can settle here, and that if missionaries from our Society returned to that country, he would immediately give them back possession of the little house. He did not want to make any use of our church either, but it should serve only for "Members of our Church" who wanted to gather in it for worship; it would always be free and available to them.

5 o'clock in the afternoon. The Georgia post has just arrived, but we were all amazed that once again it brought us nothing from Washington.

I already regret that I wrote so prematurely and hastily for the wagons, but everything is very confused, as it has been throughout the entire year, and so this must be as well. My wife and I will probably have to spend the winter here. Now the Savior knows best what will be good and saving for us!

All here join me in greeting you, your loving friend and Br.,

Gottl. Byhan

N.B. I just received Br. Clauder's letter of Oct. 8. Remember us diligently in your prayers before our dear Lord. We really need this!!

G. B.

[B 61-3: Provinzial Helfer Conferenz, meeting in Salem. Translated by C. Daniel Crews.]

Sat., Oct. 22. Although Br. Byhan has still not received a successor as postmaster at Springplace, he is expecting with every post-day an answer from Washington, and he states in his letter received here today his wish that the wagons to pick up his things be sent from here, and because this will require more than 2 wagons, and they have only one wagon there, he therefore asks us to send another 2 horses with Naeman Rominger, who can then drive the 3rd wagon back here.

In that winter is drawing near, and the road will be much worse the longer the return journey of Br. Byhan is put off, the Oochgelogy as well as the greater part of the Springplace things are packed, and the former may suffer damage, Br. and Sr. Clauder and Sister Gambold, who on 2 Sept. arrived here from Ochgelogy, are really wanting their winter clothing and bedding. And so we decided that Br. Schulz make arrangements with the carter and propose that they set out at the beginning of November. By the time they reach Springplace Br. Byhan should have been relieved as postmaster, and if not, Br. Rominger can remain there until this occurs in order to return with Br. and Sr. Byhan and their things, even if this takes until the beginning of the new year.

[M 407-2: Springplace Diary.]

Sun., Oct. 23. And the two previous Sundays, few of our Brn. and Srs. came to the Sunday services. Thus only one service was held each Sunday. In the time in between, nothing else of note took place except that we heard that some Indians had also found gold in the mountains about 6 or 7 miles from here. But they want to keep this very quiet, so that the Georgians do not learn of it. Otherwise everything has been very peaceful in the Nation recently.

Oct. 26. We heard from a traveler who had spent the night at Mr. Vann's that Genl. Jackson, President of the U. St., is supposed to have died. The future will tell if this news is confirmed or not. [This entry is lined out by pencil.]

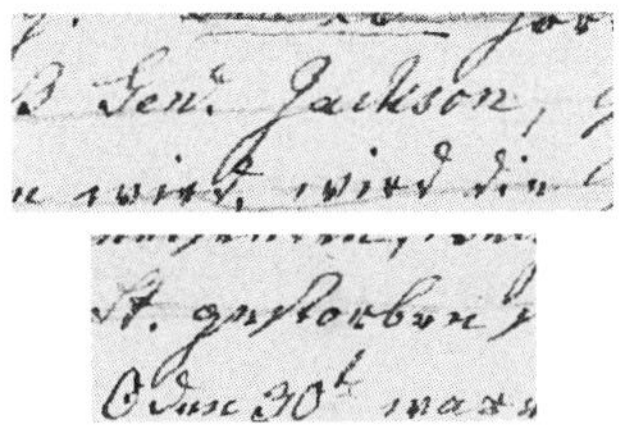

Sun., Oct. 30. The Sunday services were as usual. Only a few Brn. and Srs. were here again.

[M 415-1b-49: Translated by Julie Tomberlin Weber. Addressed to: Rev. Theod. Schulz, Salem, Stokes County, North Carolina. Postmark: Springplace, C.N., Oct. 30. Free. Gottl. Byhan, P.M. Received Nov. 12.]

Springplace, Oct. 30, 1831

Dear Br. Shulz,

Since I have a little more time before the Knoxville post arrives, I just wanted to report quickly that the Georgia mail still has not brought a reply to my resignation from the Genl. P.M., and so we do not know what we should think about the entire matter. Yesterday I sent my resignation off once again with the Georgia mail.

Since we can now expect the wagons from Salem in approximately 14 days, I have decided if I have not received any answer from the Genl. P.M. by then that the entire family will return to Salem with the wagons and I will remain here alone until I am free of the miserable postal service, and then I can follow alone, because once the wagons are here they must have a load to carry on the return journey. At first we thought my wife and I would remain behind, but we decided this is not practical, first, because we would have to keep more things here than we can later get into the stage wagon to transport, and second, Nancy and Nathl. will not leave unless Mother goes along as well. Therefore, we have decided that if I am not free of the Post Office before the wagons set out from here again, I will remain here alone.

On the one hand I am already sorry that — at your instigation — I wrote so early for the wagons.

On the other hand this is not really so, because the journey would have been postponed until winter — and it is already late enough and we certainly have to expect bad traveling weather.

So this is our position now, if I am not released from the Post Office by then.

I have now sold our livestock. I got one horse for $80; it is 6 years old, a very beautiful, tame horse, and I hope that it will sell well in Salem.

May God grant that the matter here takes one direction or another now! Because of how things are now, we do not have a pleasant hour and not only is this not good for the mission work, but it is very harmful to it. And so it is certainly good if we — as a certain bishop in church history said — can go off to the side a little until circumstances here have improved again.

The mail from Knoxville has just arrived, but it has not brought us a single line from Salem.

Everyone here sends best greetings, especially your familiar friend and Br.,

Gottl. Byhan

In great haste

[M 407-2: Springplace Diary.]

Nov. 2. Br. Byhan went to Mr. McNair's on business and to Columbus in Tennessee.

Nov. 4. He returned from there. Today Mr. Jos. Vann returned from the Council which was held in the last weeks in Chatooga District in the state of Alabama. Br. Byhan visited him early on Nov. 5th, since he was very ill with fever when he came home. We did not learn anything else from him about what was dealt with or settled in their Council, except that they will send 3 Delegates to Washington again this winter, John Ridge, Wm. S. Coody, and John Martin.

Sun., Nov. 6. After the services today the Brn. and Srs. were informed that Holy Communion will be held next Sunday, the 13th of this month, and they were advised to examine their hearts before the enjoyment of this high good to see if they had come further in grace and in depending on the One who purchased their souls with blood, or if they have become lukewarm and sluggish in their love for Him. They were asked to surrender themselves anew to the One to whom they pledged faithfulness at their baptism, and who shed His blood out of love for them and died for them, to free them from the rule of sin. Mr. Dav. St. Dazizi was the interpreter, since he arrived here unexpectedly during the services.

Nov. 10. We had strong storms and heavy downpours of rain.

[M 415-1b-50: Translated by Julie Tomberlin Weber. Addressed to: Rev. Theod. Schulz, Salem, Stokes County, North Carolina. Postmark: Springplace, C.N., Nov. 13. Free. G. Byhan, P.M. Received Nov. 26.]

Springplace, Nov. 12, 1831

Dear Br. Schulz,

I received your kind letter of Oct. 22nd on the 6th of this month. Thank you very much for this. Everything contained in it was very interesting to us, although it could not ease our situation — which continues to become more distressing — or even less, release us from it. Because it will remain truly distressing until we finally know where we stand, whether we have to stay here or if it might be possible for us to finally depart. God alone knows what will happen. He alone can comfort us in our current situation. With the last post eight days ago today, I once again did not receive an answer from the Genl. P.M. to my resignation. If I should receive an answer with the mail today, I will let you know before I close this letter.

By the way, we agree that it was premature for me to write for the wagon on Oct. 8th — at your suggestion — because if the wagon should come now, the confusion — which is already indescribably great even apart from this — will become much greater — unless Br. and Sr. Clauder return with the wagon in our place, since we can see something like this from your last letter — or if I were free of the postal service. Worries, concern, and irritation are constants at our place day and night. Even so, why am I writing so much about this? God, who has helped thus far, will continue to help!

I must also report that all of our cattle have been sold and that I have accepted a horse for one part of the payment for $80, so we now have no more cattle here except 2 milk cows. Mr. Dazizi bought these, but he wants to leave them with us as long as we are here, and if we remain here he will give them completely back to us.

I wanted to add one more thing. If we should have to stay here, the school should and must be started again in order to satisfy our Brn. and Srs. and the rest of the Indians. But how can we do this, since everything here has been shattered and is in the greatest state of confusion? We cannot do it since certain circumstances — which I do not want to mention here — absolutely do not allow it. And so there would still be a number of things to consider, if we could discuss this work in person, which have caused us much worry and concern. The burden bows us to the ground.

Our neighbor Jos. Vann returned home from the Council sick eight days ago, but I cannot learn anything from him about what they arranged or decided, except that they want to send John Ridge, Wm. S. Coody, and John Martin to Washington this winter as Delegates. Perhaps today's *Phönix* will give us more information. Otherwise, all is quiet in the Nation. We hear and see hardly anything more of the Georgia Guard. We just hear that they occasionally arrest an Indian man or woman who has been caught digging for gold. What will the Georgia Legislature, which is now in session, arrange now?

4 o'clock in the afternoon. The Georgia mail has just arrived here, but it brought nothing from Washington once again. We

are thus still in the dark and do not know what will happen now. God knows!!

Everyone here sends greetings, and you, accept another special greeting from your familiar friend and Br.,

Gottl. Byhan

[M 407-2: Springplace Diary.]

Sun., Nov. 13. Most of our Brn. and Srs. gathered here. In the first service was the sermon on the words [Gal. 6:14]: God forbid that I should glory, save in the cross of our Lord Jesus Christ. In the second service we enjoyed the body and blood of our Lord in Holy Communion. During this the Indian Sr. Lidia Elisabeth watched as a confirmand and the Indian Sr. Sophia Carolina as a candidate. The Savior could be sensed in our midst. Mr. Dav. St. Dazizi was here once again today and served us as interpreter.

Nov. 17. In the evening, completely unexpectedly, Naeman Rominger arrived here from Salem and brought us the news that the two wagons which will pick up the rest of Br. and Sr. Clauder's and Sr. Gambold's things here will be here tomorrow. Accordingly these wagons then arrived here late in the evening of *the 18th*. With these two wagons Br. and Sr. Byhan will also send part of their things to Salem, since as soon as Br. Byhan is let go from his postal position, they will probably have to go to Salem as soon as possible, in accordance with the advice of the Helf. Conf. in Salem.

1831, part 11

[M 415-1b-51: Translated by Julie Tomberlin Weber. Addressed to: Rev. Theodor Shulz, Salem, Stokes County, North Carolina. Postmark: Springplace, C.N., Nov. 20. Free. Gottl. Byhan, P.M. Received Dec. 2.]

Springplace, Nov. 19, 1831

Dearly beloved Br. Shulz,

On the evening of the 17th, day before yesterday, Naeman Rominger arrived at our place completely unexpectedly with 2 horses, and he brought us the news that the two wagons driven by Hine and G. Nething were just one day's journey from here. They then arrived here safely yesterday evening at 8 o'clock. Now if I were free of the postal service we would be able to return with the wagons. But since this is not the case, my family and I must remain behind until I am also free. We are very happy that Nae. Rominger has permission from you all to remain here until we can leave too, to drive our farmer's wagon back. If I do not hear or receive anything with today's mail concerning the postal service, the drivers are planning to begin the return journey next Wednesday, or Thursday the 24th at the latest.

I received your kind letter of the 2nd along with the enclosed $100 from Geo. Nething. Of the $50 you gave Br. Rominger for his use on the journey, he gave G. Nething $20, and he gave me the rest, which is $22.48¾.

The Georgia mail just arrived and it brought me a letter from the Genl. P.M. concerning mail routes but nothing about my resignation. At this point I can only think that my letter with the resignation must have been lost. I really think that if he had received it, he would have given me some reply to it. I am glad that I sent the resignation once again if the first has been lost, so that I might perhaps receive an answer with the next mail eight days from now.

Today we almost decided that my wife, Nathl., and Nancy Becker would begin the journey to Salem, with all of our other belongings and wagons, with the 2 wagons from Salem, because winter is at the door, and bad weather is certainly to be expected soon. However, we met some difficulties with the drivers, and thus this plan was given up again. We want to wait out the matter patiently. Nae. Rominger and I were planning to follow later on horse.

Please greet our children for us, and please tell our Sophia that I have just received her letter of the 6th of this month, and I will answer it with the drivers if possible.

In your kind letters of the 2nd you say something about a German Daily Texts book, but none has arrived.

Our old friend Rev. Mr. Buttrick also asks you to remember him again with an English Daily Texts book for next year. Please send him one. He is a dear man, and he gets one every year. I will write again with the drivers. Everyone here sends you best greetings. You are especially greeted by your loving, poor Br.,

Gottl. Byhan

[M 415-1b-52: Translated by Julie Tomberlin Weber. Addressed to: Rev. Theod. Shulz, Salem, Stokes County, North Carolina. Postmark: Springplace, C.N., Nov. 20. Free. G. Byhan, P.M.]

Springplace, Nov. 20, 1831

Dear Br. Schulz,

Mr. Nöthing asked me to tell you that there is a letter from him to his wife with this post, and he asks that you please send her word so that she gets it as soon as possible from the office. This morning N. Rominger brought me the Tracts with the German Daily Texts. We are very grateful for the latter. We are still considering whether or not one way or another we can transport my dear wife to Salem before Christmas, and Rominger and I would remain here and follow on horse as soon as I am free of the postal service. However, I might not be rid of it before next summer, when Br. and Sr. Clauder would have to take my place, which would be the best thing.

It's a shame that the mission work will be so totally and completely ended all of a sudden, since everything is currently peaceful. It sometimes hurts us, but we cannot change it now. We cannot endure things here. Br. and Sr. Clauder would be the people [for the task]. Your familiar

G. Byhan

[M 415-1b-53: Translated by Julie Tomberlin Weber. Addressed to: Rev. Theod. Schulz, Salem, Stokes County, North Carolina. Postmark: Favd. by Mr. George Nöthing. Received Dec. 10 by Nething & Hine.]

Springplace, Nov. 21, 1831

Dear Br. Schulz,

I have already informed you by mail that the wagons arrived here very unexpectedly on the 18th of this month in the evening. They are planning to set out on the return journey tomorrow morning. Since we had no idea at all that the wagons were coming, we were very busy last Saturday and today.

The boxes and barrels are all numbered. No. 3 belongs to the mission and contains mostly iron goods, primarily tools belonging to Br. Clauder. There are shavings on top to fill in the spaces. A small barrel of honey is intended for Br. and Sr. Theod. Schulz and is marked.

Otherwise, there are a few things here and there belonging to the mission, but only very few, and they can wait until we ourselves return. We would really like to know where our things will be unloaded. I am sure you will inform us.

My wife just told me that there are no mission items except in No. 3.

In No. 7 are the mission books and writings, as well as Br. Clauder's books, a couple of pillows that belong to our Rachel, a couple of blankets that belong to us, and all sorts of other things that would be best kept together until we come, except what belongs to Rachel. You can also do what you would like to with the books.

We hope and wish that everything will arrive safely in Salem.

Concerning the money, I already informed you day before yesterday by mail that Naem. Rominger has paid me \$22.48¾ from his travel money. He had paid the drivers Hein and Nöthing \$20 on the way. And today I paid John Hein \$5 for his return journey. George Nöthing believed he had enough travel money, so I did not pay him anything.

Time will tell how much longer we will stay here. We are just happy now to be discharged soon and to be able to leave soon and that Naem. Rominger is allowed to stay this long. Admittedly the wind and weather will determine whether we can set out right away.

Now the Savior has helped thus far; He will continue to help!

Everyone sends best greetings, and especially your loving friend and Br.,

Gottl. Byhan

(In haste.)

[M 407-2: Springplace Diary. Translated by Julie Tomberlin Weber. Handwriting is Gottlieb Byhan's .]

Sun., Nov. 20. Only two Indian Sisters came to the services here today. We held only one service and in this we read some from the *Idea Fidei Fratrum.* Since the above-mentioned two wagoneers from Salem want to begin their return journey tomorrow, we were still busy in the afternoon packing, as well as on

Nov., 21. The weather today got very cold and inclement, as it snowed at times and sleeted, but the wagons still set out from here back to Salem in the morning on *the* 22nd. The single Nae. Rominger from Friedland, who had come with the wagons, stayed with us to give us a hand with the household and to drive the wagon for us on the journey to Salem.

Nov. 26. We had strong storms and heavy downpours of rain, from which the streams in our area really rose. And so on

Sun., Nov. 27, only our closest neighbors and Brethren and Sisters were able to come to the Sunday services. It now appears that we will stay here through the winter, so we have decided to begin a small school again at least for the children of our Brethren and Sisters. This was announced to the few Brn. who were here today. They seemed to be very happy about this.

[M 415-1b-54: Translated by Julie Tomberlin Weber. Addressed to: Rev. Theodor Schulz, Salem, Stokes County, North Carolina. Postmark: Springplace, C.N., Nov. 2~~3~~7. Free. G. Byhan, P.M.]

Springplace, Nov. 28 [27], 1831

Dear Br. Schulz,

Yesterday your letter of Oct. 26 finally arrived here; it took 4 weeks and 3 days to get here via Greenville, S.C., so it seems that the mail via Greenville, S.C., does not go as quickly as people believe.

From your letter I learned that my letter of Oct. 16 arrived in Salem via Knoxville in 10 days. And so I will send my letters via Tennessee in the future. We also learned from your letters that the wagons which are supposed to pick up Br. and Sr. Clauder's and our things were planning to set out from Bethabara on the 3rd of this month — and I can inform you that they set out from here already on the 22nd of this month. Perhaps this note will reach Salem before the wagons return there.

Once again I did not receive anything from the Genl. P.M. with yesterday's mail, and we now see no chance of avoiding spending the winter here. And Praise God! we are feeling content and we have surrendered to this so far, and we see that it is the

Savior's will that we old people should endure here. We understand more and more that it is a pitiful shame to leave the Indian Brn. and Srs. Perhaps it is just for a brief time, yet we want things done however the Lord arranges them.

I will write again with the next mail and answer your letter, since there is not enough time with this post. Please let us know where our things are put when they reach Salem. We also ask that the correspondence between us not be interrupted, because we are alone here.

Everyone here sends best greetings. Especially your friend and lowly Br.,

Gottlieb Byhan

[M 415-1b-55: Translated by Julie Tomberlin Weber. Addressed to: Rev. Theod. Schulz, Salem, Stokes County, North Carolina. Postmark: Springplace, C.N., Dec. 4. Free. G. Byhan, P.M. Received Dec. 17.]

Springplace, Dec. 1, 1831

Dear Br. Schulz,

I already informed you eight days ago that your Oct. 26 letter finally arrived here on Nov. 26th, and also that the wagons had already set out from here on the return journey on Nov. 22nd and will probably have arrived in Salem long before this reaches you. Since I had not yet received my farewell from the postal service — and still have not — I was forced to remain here longer and wait for my dismissal. The next day — after the wagons had arrived here — we considered — the entire house family — what should be done now — since I cannot leave Spring Place in any case. We all agreed that the entire family should return to Salem with the wagons. Nae. Rominger should drive our farm wagon, and Mother and Nathl. in the stage wagon, and I would remain here alone with one horse, since I would follow alone as soon as I am free of the postal service.

We announced this decision to the two drivers and asked to hear their thoughts about it and whether they thought we could go with them. But they had all kinds of hesitations and difficulties, primarily this: There would not be enough people with the wagons, since they might have to ask us, especially in difficult places and going up mountains, to assist, so they might be held up and not be able to get home as quickly as they wished. In short, we noted and saw that they preferred that we — or the family — should not go along unless I also went right away. Therefore, we let the entire matter rest and decided we would all remain here until I can go as well.

I am explaining this so thoroughly here, because it does not really harmonize with a particular statement in your dear letter. You write: "The most critical things are the 2 horses that Rominger is supposed to bring along. The drivers had taken these horses along, and since someone else is going with them, the latter should see that the wagon is driven here with 3 horses." They did not want Rominger to drive the wagon back, and they were afraid of staying.

Now no matter what the case, all appearances suggest that we can no longer come before spring. First, it is winter now; and second, we do not know when I will be free of the postal service. The best thing now is this. We can come as soon as time and circumstances allow without waiting for the wagons from Salem. Here I would just like to add that we announced to our Brn. and Srs. last Sunday — to as many of them as were here, that is — that we will remain here this winter, and as long as we are staying here we will start the school again. But we are planning to take only the children of our Brn. and Srs.

We are happy and grateful that Nae. Rominger has been allowed to remain with us until we can also leave. Many troubling thoughts have occurred to us. If we or another Br. and Sr. should be here after the next spring, what will happen with the farming. We still cannot make any preparations for this in the uncertainty in which we currently find ourselves. Still when the time comes, so will the advice!

I think I have already informed you that our cattle have all been sold and that I have also accepted a horse for part of the payment. We have not yet sold the pigs; we are very happy about this now — since we will perhaps not be able to leave this winter, — because we will have something to slaughter after all.

On Nov. 13 we celebrated Holy Communion with most of our Indian Brn. and Srs. One Indian Sr. was watching during this as a confirmand, and one as a candidate, so we will have a confirmation at our next Holy Communion, which we are planning to hold on Jan. 1, 1832, the Lord willing.

On the above date, Nov. 13th, an unusual event took place which I cannot neglect to share with you. During the sermon I used the expression, according to the words of our Lord [Matt. 14:6]: I am the way, the truth and the life; no man cometh to the Father, but by me. That those who want to teach and preach other words must direct their listeners to Jesus Christ as the mediator between God and humans, and whoever does not do this is himself in error and is leading others astray. This was, as it seemed, too much for our Indian Br. Samuel, because as soon as we left the church after Holy Communion in the 2nd service, the Brn. gathered in the yard and had a serious discussion, and we did not know what the cause of their conversation was. Finally they entered our house, where they once again discussed the matter thoroughly, as it seemed, without our understanding what the cause of it was. Finally they called in Mr. Steiner Dazizi, who had interpreted for me today, who explained the matter to them, as he told me later.

The way the matter stands now is that Br. Samuel has not been here since then. However, I presume that when he comes back I will have to explain to him what I meant by this expression, and I will be glad to do so. This Br. Samuel, along with his wives, mother, and daughter, seems to have strong attachments to the Methodists, and it seems to us he is trying to find a way to use this as a pretext to go over to the Methodists

Being poor, wretched, and sinful is very bitter for these poor people. It will be clear what he is thinking when he visits here again. On Nov. 12th the eldest of his wives — Br. Samuel's — the mother of the second wife, came here in the evening with 2 adult girls, and one adult boy, and 3 horses, and stayed here till Monday morning. Then she left, seemingly very irritated and dissatisfied, without saying farewell or expressing gratitude for all that she had enjoyed here.

You ask in your letter if I have found someone to occupy the house. I think I already informed you in my previous letter that Jos. Vann will take possession of the house and place with the stipulation that we, if one of us returns here as missionary, should regain possession of everything, because the Georgians will not get possession of this place with his permission.

Dec. 3rd. Today the Delegates — I have already sent you their names — left from Judge Martin's 15 miles from here to go to Washington. Presumably they had a so-called Frolick the last night, as John Ridge had last year or arranged before he set off. Instead of asking God to grant them fortune in their undertakings, the devil was served. How can God have mercy on them when they want to serve another? May God have mercy!!

If we should ever actually move away from here, I would really like to know what our church bell cost, if I could perhaps sell it. Perhaps you can find it in your books and let me know. If another should be brought here, the bell from Ochgeloogy is still at Mr. McNair's, and it is hardly conceivable that it will be needed again in Ochgeloogy. Please let me know also how much the 2 coffee burners cost.

The mail today brought me nothing from Washington once again.

Everyone here sends best greetings, and especially your friend and Br.,

Gottl. Byhan

[M 407-2: Springplace Diary.]

Sun., Dec. 4. Only a few Brn. and Srs. came again. After the services we had an open, and confidential heart-to-heart talk with our Indian Brn. about a misunderstanding which took place 3 weeks ago. Everything was put aside in love. Br. Samuel, who was not here today, also sent word that he was completely comforted and satisfied. We were glad to hear this. Mr. Dav. St.

Dazizi was our interpreter. He came here early today. Otherwise we can clearly see and note that our Indian Brn. and Srs. are very glad that we will stay with them this winter, although they did not say much about it, according to their usual manner.

Dec. 8. Toward evening Mr. Buttrick and his interpreter, Mr. Thomas Bigbee, came to our place on their way from Candys Creek to Carmel and spent the night here. This evening a pretty deep snow for the climate here fell again. Since the beginning of this month we have already had very cold and inclement weather, so that we have seen only a few Indians these days.

[M 415-1b-56: Translated by Julie Tomberlin Weber. Addressed to: Rev. Theodor Schulz, Salem, Stokes County, North Carolina. Postmark: Springplace, C.N., Dec. 11. Free. Gottl. Byhan, P.M. Received Dec. 24; responded Dec. 28.]

Springplace, Dec. 10, 1831

Dear Br. Schulz,

I just received an answer from the Postmaster Genl. in reply to the resignation I submitted, which reads as follows:

[Br. Byhan copies the Postmaster General's letter in English:]

Your communication tending your resignation of the Office of Postmaster of Spring Place is received. You are requested to recommend a Successor. If the Postmaster General accepts your resignation now, no person being named to succeed you, the office must be discontinued. This is a result which it is desirable to avoid, and therefore you are earnestly solicited to propose a candidate for the appointment.

[Br. Byhan continues his letter to Br. Schulz in German:]

So I have gotten this far, really not further than before. In the meantime, we know where we stand now. I ask for the thoughts of the Conf. about this. I know of no one here to recommend except Mr. Wacasser, the only white man in this area, who lives in Sumak 7 miles from here. But since people say his character is not supposed to be the best, I have some hesitations about this. I will talk with Mr. Vann about it for now. I will not do anything further in this matter until I receive an answer to these few lines from the Conf. Perhaps later I can recommend Br. Clauder. Please answer as soon as possible.

Another concern is that if I suggest Mr. Wacasser as my successor, he must attend here and might even take possession of the house and yard, which Mr. Vann is not likely to allow — since he himself, as I have already reported, wants to take possession of the house until we need it again ourselves.

Everyone sends greetings, including your familiar

Gottl. Byhan

I wonder where the wagons are in the horrible weather we have had throughout the week? I am enclosing a part of the Springplace Diary.
In haste.

[M 407-2: Springplace Diary.]

Sun., Dec. 11. It was so cold again and the roads so bad that our services were attended by only a few people. Since no one was here who could speak English and Indian, we could speak only a little with those present.

Dec. 12. Mr. Buttrick and his interpreter returned from Carmel, as well as Mr. Thomson, who was formerly a missionary in Hightower and now lives in Brainerd. All three spent the night here. The Presbyterians have given our place, Spring Place, the name Pilgrims Rest. Through them we learned that the Georgia Guard is getting ready to leave Cherokee country. It was not yet known if others would come in their place. They also said that the Cherokees are now busy digging for gold again, and the Georgia Guard is not preventing them from this.

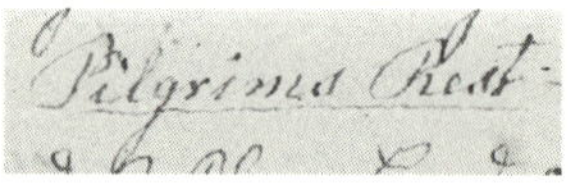

[M 415-1b-57: Translated by Julie Tomberlin Weber. Addressed to: Rev. Theod. Schulz, Salem, Stokes County, North Carolina. Postmark: Springplace, C.N., Dec. 18, via Athens, Ga., Greenville, Morgenton, N.C. Free. G. Byhan, P.M. Received Dec. 31.]

Springplace, Dec. 16, 1831

My dear Br. Schulz,

I received your kind letter of Nov. 26th on the 10th of this month, when I informed you eight days ago that I finally received an answer from the Genl. Postmaster to my resignation, of which I sent you a copy. The Genl. Postmaster asks that I should name my successor or suggest one. This worries me now, since in fact I do not know anyone to name or to suggest. It is true there is a certain Wacasser in Shumak, a Georgian, previously a peddler, a man who does not have the most honest character. I could name him as successor, but I must admit my conscience does not yet allow me to suggest him.

In recent days I spoke with Mr. Jos. Vann about this matter, when he asked me if I had received an answer from the Genl. P.M. And so I was forced to tell him about the matter as it stands now. I asked him if I should recommend the above-named Wacasser as P.M., and if he believed he would be fit for this. He replied, however, that he could not recommend him because he was a deceiver. And if I recommended him as the P.M. here, he would get possession of our house — at least one room in the house — and we would never get him out of it again. It seems then as if the Genl. P.M. was not willing to take the Post Office away from here. Mr. Jos. Vann says that as long as he is here he will do his best and everything possible to prevent a Georgian from getting a hold on our house and improvements.

I could make one other suggestion to the P.M. Genl., that he could join this P. Office with the one at Mr. McNair's, which might cause various changes in the routes and perhaps dissatisfaction among the various contractors. One other means: If the P.O. should not be removed from here, then I suggest Mr. Niclaus McNair as Successor, if he were willing, which I would have to be certain of first. He would then have to come here every eight days and take care of the post and mails, which admittedly would be somewhat difficult for him. I believe Mr. Vann would have nothing against this arrangement.

Now all these circumstances taken together — including the fact that we cannot possibly travel before spring, and we also noticed from your kind letter the expression that it might perhaps get to the point that if there is any prospect of the Cherokees remaining, an offer should be made for Br. and Sr. Clauder to return again — now as already said, these circumstances taken together have led us to decide to wait until we have considered the thoughts and the advice of the Conf. in Salem before I do anything further about the issue of the Post Office. We therefore ask for a quick reply.

In answer to the remark in your kind letter — if there is any prospect of the Cherokees staying — I must note that at this time there is not the slightest appearance that the Cherokees would move, since Mr. Vann, who sits in their Council after all, told me just yesterday that they would never move west because currently they were more committed than ever not to remove. They cannot chase the Georgians away with force. Admittedly every year some of them move west — those who allow themselves to be persuaded and who perhaps are in debt here, or those who have high hopes of the money they will get for their improvements — but it is inconceivable that they would all move, at least not for now.

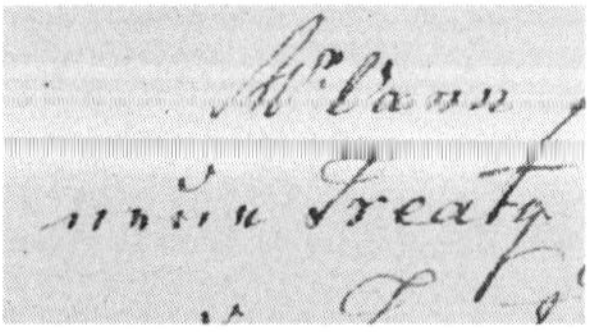

Mr. Vann also told me that the U. St. was planning to make a new Treaty with them. He said the Indians would not make a new Treaty, because if the old Treaty is not supposed to be valid, then the new one would not be valid either.

We cannot deny that it seems regrettable to us that our Indian Brn. and Srs. are supposed to be left now, since we can stay in peace among them, and yet we do not see how we can endure the various circumstances here any longer. We, along with everyone here, regret that Br. and Sr. Clauder have gone back.

Day before yesterday we heard that the Georgia Guard arrested a certain Rodgers, who lives between here and New Echota, and they have taken him to Georgia. Otherwise, everything in the Nation is quiet. We hear that the Indians are digging for gold again without being disturbed by the Georgia Guard.

We have been having very cold and inhospitable weather. In addition there was a snow of 4-5 inches. Presumably it was even deeper at your place. On the 5th of this month the Therm. was at 5½° in the morning. This morning it was at 12°.

We are very eager to hear how and when the drivers arrived in Salem. We hope you will let us know as soon as they have arrived there.

We announced to our Brn. and Srs. 3 weeks ago that we want to take children into the school again now, and to hold school throughout the winter as long as we are here, but none have brought a single one here. Presumably the cold weather is also the reason that they are not bringing any children.

In one of my previous letters I reported that I had offended our Br. Samuel with a certain expression in one of my sermons, and this has now been put aside and taken care of. I have not actually seen and spoken with Br. Samuel personally since then, but he sent me word that he now understood how I meant it and that he was completely satisfied with it.

Dec. 17th. On your birthday today, we wish you much grace and many blessings from our dear Lord. May He be very near today as well, and may He be your powerful protector, advisor, and comforter in all of your duties and work, which is certainly often not easy. We pray for this most especially for you today. Remember us lovingly as well in our loneliness.

I will send this letter via Georgia. Perhaps it will go quickly, which I hope and desire.

I would like to ask the Brn. of the Conf. sincerely once more, although I might perhaps be annoying you, but I can't help it! Please consider thoroughly the above matter concerning the occupation of Spring Place, and answer me as soon as possible. I hope the Brn. understand me. The 3 primary questions are:

1. Can an offer be made for Br. Clauder to return and take my place. In this case it would perhaps be good if the Post Office remained in our hands, because to a certain extent this would protect the missionaries from the attacks of the Georgians.

2. Should I suggest a successor in my place, perhaps the above-mentioned Wacasser, who then, if the P.O. is not removed from Spring Place, would, so to say, get possession of our house? And it would not be clear in advance how we could get him out of it again if the mission here is continued, or should be, because he would claim a right here on account of the Post Office. In my opinion, this point deserves thorough consideration. It seems to me that we should in any case prevent the Georgians from rejoicing that they had gotten hold of our house and place through this change.

Or 3. Should I write the Genl. P.M. that I did not know a successor to name or to suggest, and he then, against his will — as he writes — would have to take the P.O. away from here.

One of these three points must happen! In any case it would be good if Spring Place should not be discontinued, that the Post Office remains in our hands, not because of the profit the P.O. makes, but on account of the mission work.

By the way, I can assure you that the Cherokee will not move west very soon. It could be eight or ten years before they all go.

Everyone sends best greetings, as does your faithful friend and poor fellow Brother,

Gottlieb Byhan

4 o'clock in the afternoon.

The Georgia mail just brought me a letter to the commanding officier of the Georgia Guard, Col. Nelson, from the Genl. Postmaster. Time will tell if it might be about the Post Office here. As soon as I hear something, I will report this.

G. B.

I am sending another Diary from March 20 to May 29, 1831.

[M 407-2: Springplace Diary.]

Sun., Dec. 18. After our Sunday services, the Indian Br. Samuel gave another talk to the Brn. and Srs. in the Cherokee language.

Sun., Dec. 25. A pretty large number of people came here for the celebration of Christmas Day. In the service at 12 o'clock the listeners were first told of the purpose and why we celebrate Christmas Day today. Then the story of the birth of Jesus Christ was read. The single Br. Solomon then repeated it in the Cherokee language. Then we brought our incarnate God thanks and adoration for His inexpressible love for us poor, fallen humans, being born into this world to redeem us through suffering and death. Then there was the sermon on the holy day, which was interpreted into Indian sentence for sentence by Mr. Dav. St. Dazizi. A certain Rily Thornton, who lived among the Choctaw for a couple of years and held school there, was present in our service. Since this Thornton used to live in this Nation, he had come to visit his friends here. After the service Mr. Curry, who was sent by the Genl. Govt. to enroll the Indians who want to move to Arkansaw, came to visit at our place. This Mr. Curry, Mr. Hugh Montgomery, Agent for the Cherokees, and the latter's brother have already been staying in and around Sumak for a couple of weeks to value the improvements of those who want to move west. As we heard, this week and next week 102 persons are moving to the Arkansaw. But these are not, as people say, full blooded Cherokees but are all those who have more or less Cherokee blood, and a large group of Negroes and Negro children. Generally, there are still few or no <u>real</u> Indians who have moved to Arkansaw in the last 2 or 3 years, but only so-called half-breeds and white people who have married Indian women. The above company are making the journey by water, as the boats lie ready for them in the Highwassee River at the Cherokee Agency. People also hear that another company of half Indians, etc., from Goosawaytee and that area will also begin the journey to Arkansaw in a couple of months. Their number should also amount to over one hundred.

Dec. 26. Sr. Delila McNair, who has stayed with us since day before yesterday, set out for home today.

Dec. 30. Br. Clement Vann visited us. He told us that just between here, Rossville, and McNair's, 150 persons — including the above-mentioned 102 persons — have been enrolled for Arkansaw.

[M 415-1b-58: Translated by Julie Tomberlin Weber. Addressed to: Rev. Theod. Schulz, Salem, Stokes County, North Carolina. Postmark: Springplace, C.N., Jan. 1, via Athens, Ga., Greenville, S.C, Morganton, N.C. Free. Gottl. Byhan, P.M. Received Jan. 14.]

Springplace, Dec. 31, 1831

Dearly beloved Br. Schulz,

At the conclusion of this year 1831, which has been remarkable for us here and one we will never forget, I want to send you my sincere greetings in a couple of lines. Full of gratitude toward our dear Lord for His wonderful assistance, which we have enjoyed so plentifully from Him in the year now past, we want to enter into the new year 1832 tomorrow with prayer and pleading that He would also be our Comforter, Helper, and Protector, also that this His work here might not lie undone but might be increasingly supported.

I am sending some more of the Spring Place Diary again, and when circumstances allow, I will continue with this from time to time. Otherwise, we are currently living here in quiet and peace, which is certainly a matter worthy of gratitude. Yesterday we heard that the ever memorable Georgia Guard has been discharged by Gov. Lumpkin. Also that the Georgia Legislature has made a law, or had made one: that the Cherokee Land should immediately be measured out in lots or farms of so-and-so many acres — but this was not approved or sanctioned by Gov. Lumpkin. Time will tell if this will be confirmed. The enrolling business is going very well otherwise; more than 100 persons will be shipped to Arkansaw next week on the Highwassee. We are very eager to hear if and when the wagons arrived back in Salem. Please let us know soon.

5 o'clock in the evening. The Georgia mail has just brought me your kind letter of the 17th, for which we sincerely thank you. Praise God! that the two wagons arrived in Salem so safely and so much faster than we had epected! I also received the *Missionary Intel.* It is a shame that it is not from the fourth quarter of this year, because I already had 2 of the third quarter before, so I now have 3 of the 3rd quarter. I have not received any English Daily Texts either. If you get any, be so good and send us some. If you would send us a German almanac, we would be very happy about it. As soon as I can I will answer your kind letter.

Everyone sends best greetings. And especially receive greetings from your friend and Br.,

Gottl. Byhan

[M 407-2: Springplace Diary.]

Dec. 31. We concluded this year, which was in many respects remarkable for the mission here. We brought our dear Lord emotional thanks for His wonderful and often immediate assistance. Though in the course of this past year it often seemed that the mission here was near its end, the Lord has arranged things so it has remained until this hour, for which we owe Him our deepest gratitude. With thanks we also recognize at the close of this year that our dear Lord has protected us during this year from serious illnesses, so that we all have generally been able to rejoice in pretty good health. Concerning the walk of our Indian Brethren and Sisters, even with all the shortcomings and offenses, we must testify to the honor of our dear Lord that most of them, if not all of them, are concerned only to live for the Savior in this world, which we have clearly seen in confidential conversations with them. During Holy Communion and in the services on holy days we were often able to feel the Savior's presence and His walk in our midst in a comforting and refreshing way, so that eyes and hearts overflow with praise and thanksgiving.

In the year 1831, 1 adult Indian woman and 4 children were baptized. Two persons attained Holy Communion. At the conclusion of this year the Gemeinlein in Spring Place consists of 32 communicants and one non-communicant, 34 baptized and unbaptized children, for a total of 66 persons. In addition to this are the missionaries, 3 persons, one servant Sr., and the single Naeman Rominger from Friedland, 2 persons. In all 71 persons, 8 (4*) more than at the conclusion of last year.

[Br. Theodor Schulz(?) in Salem has penciled in:]

* NB. At the end of 1830 the sum was listed as:

32 baptized adults
31 baptized and unbaptized children
63
5 in missionary family
68

Accordingly I have made my correction in this respect:

Dec. 31, 1831, Br. Byhan notes:

32 communicants
1 noncommunicant
34 baptized and unbaptized children
67
5 in missionary family
total: 72 — 4 more than Dec. 31, 1830

[*Records: N.C.*, 8:3959-60: Salem Memorabilia of 1831. Translated by Douglas L. Rights.]

Among the special happenings in the past year we remember with sadness the calamities which befell our mission among the Cherokee Indians and the present status of the mission which has ever been a first concern of this congregation. Already at the beginning of the year the work of the mission was affected adversely through misgivings and anxieties on account of the passing of political measures. The outcome was that our Br. Gottlieb Henry Clauder was ordered out of the Cherokee territory by the Georgia State military and had to leave his post, "Poyugillogy." He arrived here safely with his wife and little son and the widowed Sr. Anna Maria Gambold on Sept. 2. Br. and Sr. Clauder are waiting only for the "when" and "how" of an opportunity to renew their work among their dear Cherokees.

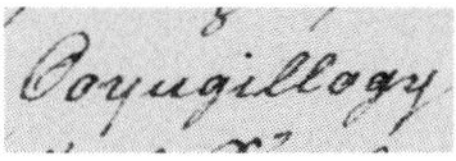

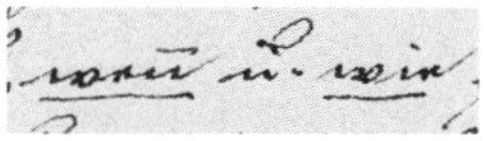

Br. Gottlieb Byhan, as Postmaster of the United States, was permitted to remain in Springplace unmolested; consequently his family was safe and the work of the mission could be carried on.

May the Lord Who hitherto has worked such wonders by His Word and Spirit among this Indian tribe in the thirty years' service of the Brethren, guide all circumstances for the ultimate best of His cause here, even as in all the world He permits His goodness and justice to blossom forth even out of man's failure and misdeeds.

1832, part 1

[M 407-2: Springplace Diary. Translated by Julie Tomberlin Weber. Handwriting is Gottlieb Byhan's.]

Sun., Jan. 1. Because of cold weather and bad roads, only a few people came for the services. Another reason so few Brn. and Srs. came here was that the Agents of the Genl. Government have been staying close by for a while already. They are trying to persuade the Indians to move west, and this worries the Brn. and Srs. more than a little. Even Br. and Sr. Clement Vann, who had already come for the services, were called back home, because these Agents had them told they would like to see them and talk with them in Sumak. However, when Br. and Sr. Clement Vann learned that they only wanted to convince them to move west, they did not go to Sumak, since, as Br. Clement Vann said, they would never move west. At 12 o'clock we were finally able to hold our first service in this year. We asked the Savior to continue to be our help, protection, comfort, and councilor in this new year, as up till now, and to support us in the current oppressed and difficult times, and that many people might come here this year as well who are concerned about their salvation and who want to be saved.

Jan. 6. Epiphany. Most of our Brethren and Sisters came by invitation for the Festival of the Heathen today. In the first service we had a lovefeast with the whole congregation, in which we explained to them the purpose and the reason for today's festival day and read the story of the Wise Men from the East in English and in the Cherokee language. Then they were told various things about our heathen missions. We also read some from the *Missionary Intel.* about our heathen congregations, and this was interpreted into Indian, which was very pleasing to our Brn. and Srs. Afterward we gathered for the enjoyment of Holy Communion, during which the Indian Sr. Lidia Elisabeth, wife of our Indian Br. Boas, participated for the first time after first receiving the confirmation blessing. The Indian Sr. Sophia Carolina watched during this as a confirmand. We felt very happy today among our Brethren and Sisters, and we were powerfully aware of the Savior's walk in our midst. Toward evening Mr. Oppelt from Bethania, N.C., stopped in at our place on his way to the state of Alabama.

Sun., Jan. 8. Since the streams had risen to an unusual level, none of our Brn. and Srs. came for the services today. We prayed the Church Litany with our house family and had a Singstunde.

Jan. 9. Col. Hugh Montgomery, Agent for the Cherokees, and his brother Col. Montgomery from Georgia stopped in at our place with the interpreter Moses Paris. They had been in Sumacktown for a long time already in the enrolling business and now were getting ready to go to Coosawaytee Town to enroll those Indians there as well who are willing to move west or to Arkansaw. In a conversation which Br. Byhan had with the Agent, the Agent assured him, or at least said he believed, that if Br. Byhan remains there or if Br. Clauder should return from Salem, the Georgians would certainly not disturb them in their mission calling, because people say they have never heard of the Moravian missionaries getting mixed up in political matters. Therefore, he, the Agent, believes that we would be able to carry out our calling here without being disturbed.

Jan. 13. Mr. Elsworth and Mr. Thomson stopped in on their way from Brainerd to Hightower and spent the night here. The latter, Mr. Thomson, former missionary in Hightower, had heard that a certain Pettit, to whom he, Mr. Thomson, when he had to flee last year, had temporarily surrendered the mission house, had told the enrolling Agent that the mission buildings were his own and that Mr. Thomson had given them to him. Now since this Pettit had enrolled for Arkansaw, these houses and the improvements belonging to the missionaries were valued and he was paid for this. And so the missionaries are in danger of losing all of their property there. Now things will depend on whether they get their houses and improvements back again from the Agent and enrolling Officers or not.

[M 415-2-2: Translated by Julie Tomberlin Weber. Addressed to: Revd. Theod. Schulz, Salem, Stokes County, North Carolina. Postmark: Springplace, C.N., Jan. 15. Free. G. Byhan, P.M. Received Feb. 4.]

Springplace, Jan. 13, 1832

Dear Br. Schulz,

Your kind letter of Dec. 17th last year, along with *Wöchentliche Nachr.* and a *Missy. Intel.*, arrived here on Dec. 31. Your next letter of Dec. 28, via Knoxville, had already arrived at McNair's on Jan. 7th; however, because of the very high streams I did not receive it until the 11th of this month. From this you will see that the letters via Tennessee reach Spring Place faster than via Georgia. We are sincerely happy and grateful for everything contained in the letters and the rest of the news.

Praise God, we here are living in peace and quiet. The emigration of the Cherokees is going pretty well, but unfortunately it is only those who — because of their character — are not particularly respected or those who have been in debt over and over again, who then, upon selling their improvements, have been put in a position to pay some of their debts. Last Monday Col. Montgomery, Agent for the Cherokees, and his brother Col. Montgomery from Georgia, who along with Mr. Curry is busy enrolling the Indians for Arkansas, stopped in here with the interpreter, Moses Paris, on his way to Coosawaytee. In a conversation with the Agent, he believed he was able to assure me that we, the Moravians, would always be able to remain here undisturbed and to pursue our mission calling, because it was believed that the Moravian missionaries have never gotten mixed up in politics. He also advised us not to sell our houses and improvements to anyone, because the Genl. Govt. would without a doubt pay us for it.

Now concerning our presence here and our progress, I have nothing to say at this time. Our spirits have been very weakened by so much talking and thinking about this matter, and we want to commend this matter to the One who commands everything. And so we do not want to take drastic measures, as you mention, per force. It is just a shame that this was not observed last summer. Humans plan and God acts!

Now I do not believe I can request a blank commission from the Genl. P.M. in order to make a successor in any case, because the Genl. P.M. would naturally want to know immediately who my successor is. If I could name him, then I would have no hesitation.

I would also just like to ask what I should do about our farming. Should I hire a man to help Rominger, since I must have two hands or two people if the farming and all the rest of the work on the place is going to be taken care of. Or should we not plant anything, since we do not know — and no one knows — whether the mission here can be continued or not? Since the time for planting is approaching, I would like to know the thoughts of the Conf. about this matter as quickly as possible. Otherwise, we rely on God to release us soon from this extremely difficult uncertainty, which we have lived in for one year now!

We celebrated Jan. 6th here with our Indian Brn. and Srs. as we did last year. We had a lovefeast and Holy Communion. In the latter, the Indian Sr. Lidia Elisabeth was confirmed for her first celebration of this. We felt very happy among our Brethren and Sisters, and it would be regrettable if we had to leave them, although there is no immediate necessity for this yet.

We have not yet received any English Daily Texts. We are deeply moved by the painful circumstances of our dear children. Words cannot express the emotions we felt when we first saw the news in Br. Schaaf's letter to me. May the Savior comfort the parents.

Time and circumstances do not allow me to send a Diary this time. Perhaps next week. Everyone sends greetings. Especially your familiar Br.,

Gottl. Byhan

[M 407-2: Springplace Diary.]

Sun., Jan. 15. Once again only a few of our Brn. and Srs. were here for the Sunday services. Because we had no interpreter, some of the *Idea Fidei Fratrum* was read.

Jan. 19. Mother Vann visited us and told us that the Georgia Guard was close to us again and set up quarters in Sumak at Mr. Wacasser's yesterday evening. We thought it advisable and necessary for Br. Byhan to go to Sumak Town today and talk with the commanding officer there about our presence here, and especially about Br. Nathl. Byhan's presence and also our workman, Naeman Rominger, and to find out if the latter could also stay here in the future without being disturbed. The commanding officer, Col. Henderson, told Br. Byhan that the laws about white people which had been made in the Georgia Legislature in Dec. 1830 were still valid and had not yet been recalled. Accordingly it was against the laws for Nathl. Byhan and Naeman Rominger to live in the country, and they were in danger of being arrested. When we were asked if the Georgia Guard had not stopped in at our place last year and if we had not been disturbed by them, he was given the appropriate information. Br. Byhan also thoroughly explained what happened to Br. Clauder last summer in Ochgeloogy, and how he had finally received the assurance from Col. Nelson, at that time commanding officer of the Georgia Guard, that he could stay at his post in Och_____y as a missionary without being disturbed, but that this news had arrived here too late, since Br. Clauder had already set out on the journey to Salem. Then he asked if we had come directly into this country here from Salem. We told him yes. After a long pause, and it seemed that he had been reflecting on the matter, he said it was regrettable that we missionaries could not decide to take the oath so that we could live here in the country undisturbed. In the meantime, he said we should just continue on as before. He would write to the Governor of Georgia, and he would let us know as soon as he had received an answer from him. In recent days we also began plowing our land for oats. It is still uncertain whether we will be able to sow and harvest them.

Jan. 20. The Georgia Guard came through our lane without stopping in at our place. They went to New Echota, where they were overnight, as we later heard.

[M 415-2-3: Translated by Julie Tomberlin Weber. Addressed to: Rev. Theod. Schulz, Salem, Stokes County, North Carolina. Postmark: Springplace, C.N., Jan. 22. Free. G. Byhan, P.M. Received Feb. 5.]

Springplace, Jan. 20, 1832

Dear Br. Schulz,

Since my last letter to you dated the 13th of this month, which I sent via Tennessee, something else has happened which I want to report to you immediately.

Yesterday morning old Mother Vann came to our place and told us that the evening before, the 18th of this month, a party of soldiers had passed here and were quartered in Sumak Town at Mr. Wacasser's. She could not tell us what their purpose was, but a certain young white man, Benj. Murry, who was hired by Jos. Vann about 3 or 4 miles from here to sell corn for him, had fled, so we concluded that it was once again the intention of the Georgia Guard to arrest the white people in the country.

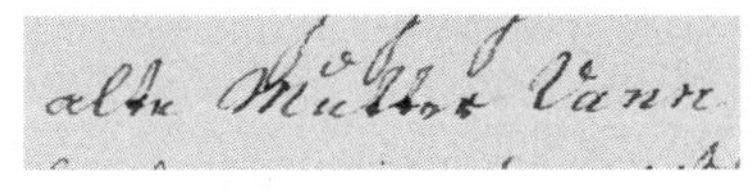
alte Mutter Vann

We thought it advisable for me to go to Sumak right away to see the commanding officier and acquaint him with our situation and circumstances, and especially to talk with him about Nathl. and Rominger and whether they were safe here or if they were in danger of being arrested? Then yesterday afternoon I went there again and had an opportunity right away to explain our situation to the officier both how our things are currently and also what it was like the entire last year. Among other things, he asked if we, that is, here in Spring Place, had not been disturbed and if the Georgia Guard had not stopped in at Spring Place, and he was given the appropriate information about this. He said that Nathl. and our worker, Rominger, certainly did not have permission to live in this country according to the Georgia laws, and they were liable to be arrested, especially the latter, because I explained to him that our son Nathl. had to assist in the Post Office, since this office was a kind of distributing office. After a long pause, he said we should just continue as before. He would write to the Governor on our account. As soon as he had an answer from him he would inform us of this. Then he dismissed me.

This is how things stand now, and it seems as if we will have to spend another year in uncomfortable uncertainty, not knowing if we should continue with the fieldwork or if we should let everything stand and lie. Br. Clauder knows what our situation was like in this respect throughout the entire last year.

My view is that it is pointless for us to wait any longer for the decisions of Congress and the Supreme Court and to count on it turning out favorably for the Cherokee and for the mission. I think, rather, we must now deal with the Governor of Georgia. If he is satisfied, then the Genl. Govt. will not make objections.

Still I do not understand. Our fervent wish and request to God is just that He might soon release us from this confusion!

Today Nae. Rominger got a good start plowing for oats. We might have no benefit from the work being done, and yet something must be done. Otherwise, I know nothing else to report for now.

I learned from Br. Clauder's letter that my letter to you dated the 16th and 17th of Dec. had been opened. I presume it was the same letter that contained 3 key questions for the Conf. I think the Georgians will have received little satisfaction [from it]. I will therefore send my future letters via Tennessee. I think they also go more quickly. At least your letters always arrive here much more quickly.

We have not yet received any English Daily Texts from Bethlehem. Everyone joins me in sending best greetings. Your familiar friend and Br.,

Gottl. Byhan

[B 61-3: Provinzial Helfer Conferenz, meeting in Salem. Translated by C. Daniel Crews.]

Jan. 21. Br. Gottlb. Byhan finally received an answer from the Genl. Postmaster in Washington in regard to his resignation with the charge to suggest someone else as his successor as postmaster in Springplace, but he did not know of any suitable subject to name, and moreover winter was advancing. He therefore, with our permission, reported this to the Genl. Postmaster and that he would be willing to continue in the postmaster's office until the spring.

By this our dear believers of the Cherokee Nation were assured by Br. and Sr. Byhan, and the latter were in a position to accept the formers' loyalty according to the present circumstances. For this we were very thankful, the more so since Br. and Sr. Byhan had indicated, in the face of Sr. Byhan's feebleness, that they were inclined to hold out until then. We confidently hope that our dear Lord will send us more light and clarity in this time about how it will go with the poor Cherokee Nation, and what outcome its — and our Mission's — precarious and ever more complicated situation will take.

Since Br. Byhan has several times in his letters expressed the wish that Br. and Sr. Clauder, if at all possible, return in the spring and take his place, either through our intercession with the Governor in Georgia or with the Genl. Postmaster in Washington, and since he was convinced through the assurance of the Genl. Government Agent Mr. Montgomery and others that Georgia would not disturb our missionaries in their calling, the letter from Br. Byhan received today again contained the request to the P.H.C. that from here the Postmaster Genl. in Washington be asked for a commission for Br. Clauder as postmaster in

Springplace, so that Br. and Sr. Byhan, in accord with their request, could be relieved there in the spring.

We considered this carefully because Br. and Sr. Clauder are most willing to return to their dear Cherokees as soon as the road is passable. They were told by the Georgia Guards that on account of the political circumstances then prevailing (which do not allow an exception to be made for our missionaries) the former favor with which they were regarded cannot last much longer. It is also to be presumed that in case the P.M. General gives his consent for Br. Clauder to serve as postmaster there, he will do this with the consent of the Georgians, and Br. Clauder could remain there unchallenged by the Georgia Governor. In this way the purpose of maintaining our little Cherokee Gemeinlein with the necessary care of the missionaries can be made attainable.

We therefore believed that we could give Br. Byhan the following advice, namely: That he explain to the Postmaster Genl. how he was unable to find anyone in that region to suggest as his successor in the Post Office position, but that the health circumstances of his wife make necessary their return to Salem. With good conscience, however, he could recommend for this place Mr. G. Clauder, who, as a missionary at one of our settlements in the Cherokee Nation, through his character and behavior has sufficiently legitimized himself with the State of Georgia and has gained respect on the part of the Georgia Guard, until finally this indulgence — on account of the particular circumstances of other missionaries — had to stop in the late summer of last year, and he was required to move with his family to Salem. Before his appointment as missionary, Mr. Clauder spent several years as assistant in the Post Office of Gb. Shober in Salem and completed a full apprenticeship in the Post Office and its related business, and if he were installed as his successor, this would also accomplish the purpose that if the Cherokee Nation moves to the Arkansas he would accompany them as missionary.

If this suggestion receives the agreement of the P.M. Genl., then Br. Byhan would request the latter to send the commission to Salem either directly to the Postmaster, Gb. Shober, or to the

Board of Directors. Br. Schulz by today's post will notify Br. Byhan of this in the name of the P.H.C.

[M 407-2: Springplace Diary.]

Sun., Jan. 22. We had no interpreter today and there were also few here who understand English, so after a hymn was sung Br. Samuel gave a talk in the Cherokee language to those Brethren and Sisters who were present.

Sun., Jan. 29. A 5- to 6-inch deep snow fell last night, and it continued snowing today, so no one came to the services. We prayed the Church Litany with the house family and sang some verses.

[M 415-2-4: Translated by Julie Tomberlin Weber. Addressed to: Revd. Theod. Schulz, Salem, Stokes County, North Carolina. Postmark: Springplace, C.N., Feb. 5. Paid 18¾; ½ credit; free. Gottlieb Byhan, P.M. Received Feb. 18.]

Springplace, Feb. 2, 1832

Dearly beloved Br. Schulz,

Your kind letter of Jan. 11 arrived here in Spring Place on Jan. 28. We thank you very much for everything contained in this. This time I am sending the Diary until Dec. 31 of last year, as pitiful as it is. Please be good enough to let me know in due time if you received the things I have sent you from time to time, especially since I saw from Br. Clauder's letters to me that a letter I sent to you with the Diary had been broken open, although nothing was removed from it. It was good that there was nothing to take out.

([Footnote:] I can almost guess where my letter to you was broken open. Recently a large packet directed to Georgia State was opened between here and Athens, Ga. What else could happen when 4-5 people — not including the postmaster — are busy going through the mail when it arrives, that is, by those who have no right to do this.)

Since my last letter to you, dated Jan. 20th, nothing special has happened except that we have had extreme cold. This has bothered us more than a little in our houses, since we have no stoves. On Jan. 26th the therm. stood at 6½ degrees below 0 in the morning, and on the 27th at 8 degrees below zero. We have never experienced anything like this here.

Now I have nothing to say this time regarding the matter of our release, Br. and Sr. Clauder's return, concerning the postal service, and the Indians' move west, etc. However, one thing really makes us uneasy, and that is the uncertainty about our farming in which we find ourselves. The question is this: If we hire workers again and pay them so that the farming will be continued, then it is necessary for oats, corn, etc., to be planted, and yet we always fear having preparations made for fieldwork, since we do not know if the mission will continue here, because if it is not continued here then all the costs would be lost. And if the mission is continued and we have made no preparations for planting, it would indeed be bad for the Br. and Sr. who lived here, since they would have to purchase everything.

I am not writing to you because I believe you could advise me what would be the best and most advisable thing to do in this matter, because we and you all cannot know what the end of the mission here will be. I only add this to show you that this matter and the uncertainty that we do not know what to do about this concerns us more than a little. Otherwise, concerning the uncertainty in which we live, regarding our presence here and the entire Cherokee matter in general, it does not cause us as much unease and worry. This will gradually be cleared up and we commend it to God.

Much about our stay will depend on the answer the Governor of Georgia gives the commanding officier of the Georgia Guard regarding us, about which I wrote you in my last letter. I am inclined to believe that this answer, if another one comes, will have a great influence on our work here and that we might then will be clear about the existence of the mission here. <u>My</u> idea is that we should turn to the Governor of Georgia in matters of the mission among the Cherokee, instead of the Genl. Govt., because it seems the Genl. Govt. has put the Cherokees entirely into the hands of the Georgians, so that the former does not want to have anything more to do with them.

Everyone here sends best greetings. And you are most especially greeted by your loving friend and Br.,

Gottl. Byhan

Feb. 4th. Yesterday Mr. Dav. St. Dazizi came to our place. Through him we learned that things generally look very bad in the Nation, and that if the Georgians do not treat them — the Cherokees — better, they might not be able to endure it here longer than 1 or 2 years. The Nation on the Alabama side is also in the same dilemma that they are in on the Georgia side, because the Alabamans are moving into Cherokee country in throngs, since a law made in Alabama allows them to do this. In the course of this year, much more concerning this Nation will happen.

Now the One who commands everything does not allow anything to happen by chance.

G. B.

[M 407-2: Springplace Diary.]

Sun., Feb. 5. The Sunday services were held as usual. In the first was the sermon and in the second a Bible reading. The latter was repeated in the Cherokee language by the Indian Br. Niclaus Ignatius. In conclusion some hymns were sung in the Cherokee language. We had informed our Brn. and Srs. a couple of months ago that since it looked as if we would stay here through the winter, we would now begin the school again at least for the children of our Indian Brn. and Srs. And so two boys [Jesse Henry and John Shepherd Vann] came to it today, and we began school with them.

Feb. 6. Br. Nathl. Byhan and Sr. Nancy Becker today went to Mr. McNair's, since the former had business there, and returned from there on the 7th.

Sun., Feb. 12. In our service today there was first a brief address to the Brn. and Srs. and then something was read from the *Idea Fidei Fratrum.* Afterward the Indian Br. Samuel held another pretty long talk for the Brn. and Srs. in the Cherokee language. In closing, another hymn in the latter language was sung.

An Indian woman from Sumaktown, whom we had already noticed in our services several times, today expressed to us at her own initiative her heartfelt wish to belong to our Gemeine. She was asked why she wanted to belong to our Gemeine. To this she answered with tears that she had already often heard that humans are bad and sinful, and that she could not get to any good place in this condition and be saved, because she knows that she is also a great sinner, etc. She had also heard that there were ways and means through which one could become good and saved. All of this had brought her to reflect often on herself, and she was convinced in her heart that she could not be blessed in her current condition, because she knows and feels that she is very bad, and more such expressions. Our hearts were warmed upon hearing this declaration, and we directed her to the Friend of poor sinners, that the Savior does not turn away anyone who feels so bad and sinful, and that He came into this world for the good of poor sinners and had shed His blood for poor sinners, etc. She seemed to be very comforted at these words, and we could clearly see in her that she is seriously concerned and worried about her salvation.

This person also told us that she had already been baptized a long time ago by the Paptists. They had just taken her in front of many to the water and dunked her under, and said that this was good for her. But they had not told her what was the reason and the purpose of baptism. The one who had baptized her had not spoken with her before or after the baptism, and so she did not know why she had been baptized. We asked her to attend our services often, which she also promised to do. She lives about 9 or 10 miles from here in Sumaktown.

Feb. 18. A white man from Georgia, although he said he came from South Carolina, stopped in at our place. He told us that he had heard from Mr. Wacasser in Sumaktown that we now wanted to sell our improvements and that he had come to buy them. We told him that for the time being we did not yet want to part with our improvements, since Br. Byhan had the Post Office here and thus could not leave the place. He told us further that on the 27th or 28th of this month this place as well as various other places would be rented to whoever offered the most, and if we did not sell our improvements first, before the place is rented, afterward we would not receive any compensation for it. This Goodman, as he called himself, also strongly advised Br. Byhan to be present when the places, and primarily our place, would be rented. This will take place here in the Nation at Mr. Scudder's, about 65 miles from here.

[M 415-2-5: Translated by Julie Tomberlin Weber. Addressed to: Rev. Theod. Schulz, Salem, Stokes County, North Carolina. Postmark: Springplace, C.N., Feb. 19, via Knoxville, Jonesboro, Ten., Wilkesboro, N.C. Free. G. Byhan, P.M. Received Mar. 5.]

Springplace, Feb. 18, 1832

My dear Br. Schulz,

Although I do not have a lot to write you this time, the little I have to report will perhaps interest you.

About 3 hours ago a white man from Georgia stopped here and asked to speak privately with me. He then told me that he had just come from Mr. Wacasser in Sumak, and he had told him that we would be selling our improvements now, so he had come express to buy these from us. I told him that for now we would not yet let our improvements out of our hands, since I had the Post Office here and so could not leave the place. This man told me that on the 27th and 28th of this month this place — as well as various other places — would be rented to the highest bidder, and that if we had not sold the improvements previously, before the place is rented, we would receive no compensation for them afterward. This man, who said his name is

Goodman, strongly advised me to be present when they rent out the places — including this one — which will be done here in the Nation at Scudders about 65 miles from here. I do not yet consider it necessary to go.

But God! what else will happen, and how will things turn out for us here?? But God will continue to assist us! Perhaps things are not really the way this man says, but it bothers us and keeps us uneasy. We do not know what to do anymore anyway, since the entire work here is so shattered and confused that we will soon not know up from down. — (My writing was interrupted here, because the Georgia mail came and brought me nothing from Salem once again except a German newspaper and 1 English newspaper which Br. Clauder sent.) — Presumably we will now be punished; perhaps we have also earned it.

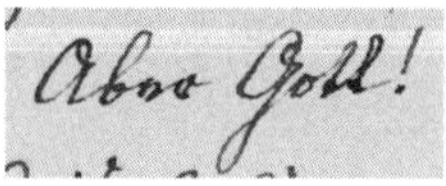

Br. Seidel has not yet sent us an English Daily Text. Please tell Brn. Shober and Clauder that for God's sake they should not send any more *American Tract* magazines here, but I would like to have the Salem newspaper. Perhaps you can subscribe for Spring Place on the mission account?

About 2 weeks ago, we found that our horse Ball, which we brought out with us in the fall of 1830, has the hooks, as people call it, and indeed extremely badly. We had them cut, and then he got lockjaw and 3 days later died.

In addition to our other worries and cares, the following circumstance makes us more than a little worried. Our Nathl. has had a kind of boil or growth for 3 months already — we do not actually know what it is — on the right side of his throat, and it seems to be getting worse. We really wish, and he himself does, that he could get medical advice and assistance. But that isn't available here, and we must be patient until we see what will happen concerning the Cherokee matter in the Supreme Court and in Congress.

Time is short and I must close. Everyone sends best greetings. So does your familiar friend and lowly Br.,

G. Byhan

[M 407-2: Springplace Diary.]

Sun., Feb. 19. Since no one was here today who could serve as interpreter in our services, the Indian Br. Samuel gave another talk for the Brn. and Srs. in the Cherokee language in the closing service, which was also the case on *Sun., Feb. 26.*

[M 415-2-6: Translated by Julie Tomberlin Weber. Addressed to: Rev. Theod. Schulz, Salem, Stokes County, North Carolina. Postmark: Springplace, C.N., Feb. 26, via Knoxville, Ten., Wythe C.H., Va. Free. G. Byhan, P.M. Received Mar. 8.]

Springplace, Feb. 25, 1832

My dear Br. Schulz,

I received your dear letter of Jan. 21, along with *Wöch* and *Monatliche Nachrichten*, on the 4th of this month, as I think I have already reported to you. Last mail day, the 19th, your letter of the 4th of this month and *Wöch* and *Monatliche Nachrichten* also arrived here.

Following the advice of the Helf. Conf., I already wrote with the last mail on the 9th and suggested Br. Clauder as my successor as postmaster here. Time will tell how long I now have to wait for an answer from the Genl. P.M. I have left it up to him to decide to whom he wants to send the commission, either to you or the Directors and Board of Missions or to Br. G. Shober or to Br. Clauder himself or to me. We will see now. I personally wish that he might send it to one or the other in Salem, because it would expedite the matter.

Concerning Nathl.'s sore throat, about which I wrote you in my last letter, we are somewhat comforted again for now, since the ulcer, as it seems to be, was cut off yesterday by Doct. Bean, and it now appears that it will go away, although it still does not look the best.

Nothing new has happened since my last letter to you, although we often hear that the Georgia Guard is visiting this area in disguise. We have seen and heard nothing of them. Next Tuesday and Wednesday the places of emigrants will be rented out, perhaps I can report something about this to you in my next letter.

Br. Seidel in Bethlehem is not sending us an English Daily Texts this year it seems. I would really like to have 4 or 5, because there are requests for them. Please be good enough and pay Sr. A. M. Gambold $1 for her large Bottle, which she sold to Mr. McNair, since I received payment from him for it and will debit the Spring Place mission for it.

The 26th. The Georgia mail yesterday evening did not bring us the slightest thing from Salem. But we hope the Knoxville mail will bring something if it can come today despite the high streams. We still feel as if we have been abandoned when we must survive a mail day without receiving anything from Salem.

A week ago from last Sunday we were happy when an Indian woman came to see us and expressed her desire and intention to become Jesus' property and to belong to our Gemeine. We had often seen this person in our services before, and now she talked contritely and remorsefully about her previous way of life. She was directed to the Best Friend of sinners, who does not turn away anyone, not even the greatest sinner. She promised to visit us often. She lives in Sumak Town about 10 miles from here.

Everyone here greets you in the best way, especially your friend and lowly Br.,

Gottl. Byhan

[M 407-2: Springplace Diary.]

Mar. 1. When Sr. Byhan went into our smokehouse early today, she was aware that there was a large opening way up high in the roof. On further investigation we found that thieves had broken into it the night before and had stolen some smoked ham from it. In general we have noted recently that some Indians in our neighborhood have begun their old way of living again, since no laws are enforced anymore, and they know that no one can punish them for such things anymore.

Sun., Mar. 4. In the first service was a sermon on the words [John 1:29]: Behold the Lamb of God, which taketh away the sin of the world. Afterward was the baptism of the baby daughter born to our Br. Samuel and his wife Sr. Rachel, with the name Elisabeth. In the second service we had a blessed enjoyment of the body and blood of Jesus in Holy Communion. The Indian Sr. Sophia Carolina was a participant for the first time after she had first received the confirmation blessing. Mr. Dav. Steiner Dazizi and his father, who is a member of the Gemeine in Brainerd, were present as guests at this Holy Communion. The former served us today as interpreter in our services. In the evening we had unusually strong storms with heavy downpours of rain and hail.

[M 415-2-7: Translated by Julie Tomberlin Weber. Addressed to: Rev. Theod. Schulz, Salem, Stokes County, North Carolina. Postmark: Springplace, C.N., Mar. 11. Free. G. Byhan, P.M. Received Mar. 26.]

Springplace, March 10, 1832

Dear Br. Schulz,

Your kind letter of the 15th of last month and 2 packets of *Wöch* and *Monatliche Nachrichten* arrived here in Springplace on the 4th of this month. Many thanks for everything. We are always happy when we receive *Wöch* or *Monatliche Nachrichten*, because then we see how things are going in the Unity and in the Gemeine. Gradually 3 *Missionary Intel*s from the 4th quarter of 1831 have arrived here. We will probably not receive any more printed *Nachrichten* for now. I do not know why the *New York Observer* is not being sent here anymore. I did not cancel my subscription. But someone must have written that it should not be sent here anymore, because otherwise he would not have been directed to stop. It always came addressed to John R. Smith, P.M. at Spring Place. We found it strange and it was apparent to us that this newspaper was denied us. In the meantime, it does not matter so much if we know how things are going in the rest of the topsy-turvy world.

From your letters I learned that it was considered unnecessary that when the Georgia Guard was in Sumak last Jan. that I had a conversation with the commanding officier about Nathl. and Rominger. None of us, including myself, agree that it was unnecessary for us to make the effort to explain our situation and circumstances to this person. But since then we have noticed and experienced that this conversation with him was not at all disadvantageous to us, and it was a great comfort to us. We are living in outward peace and quiet. No Georgians, so to speak, come close to us. They know that they cannot do anything to us, and we can and must consider this an example of God's guidance so that His work here does not lie untended. But if only He sends workers more fit than we into the vineyard here. Thus according to all indications the Savior will receive a rich reward from this Nation.

It is extremely remarkable that we have not received the $250 which the government issued for the mission here. One might ask who put this money in his pocket?? We could use some of this again soon.

In one of my previous letters I wrote to you that a white man from S.C. who now lives in Hall County in Georgia or is staying there now, stopped in at our place and positively told me Spring Place would be rented out to the highest bidder on the 26th and 27th of Feb., as well as other places in the Nation from which the residents have emigrated. These last places have now been rented, but naturally not Springplace, which we were worried about. Still our friend McNair told us yesterday morning that they had called out or named Spring Place, but not a single person made an offer for it. They know well where things stand with us and with the place Springplace. I have not yet heard if they wanted to rent out our mission place in Och_____y.

Last Sunday, the 4th of this month, we had a blessed celebration of the body and blood in Holy Communion with most of our communicant members. The Indian Sr. Sophia Carolina was a communicant for the first time after first receiving the confirmation blessing. In the evening on the same day we had a horrible storm with strong downpours of rain and some hail, but the worst weather seemed to move between us and the mountains, because we recently heard that at Mr. George Harlen's 12 miles from here a hurricane-like storm raged which knocked down everything in its path. During the extreme cold in Jan. almost all of the peach blossoms here froze, and it seems that the apple blossoms also suffered. The pears and cherries, however, still seem to be good.

Currently we have 3 boys in the school, but the Brn. and Srs. promise to bring more. The Brn. and Srs. have often asked us if Br. Clauder — if he is supposed to come — will take boys and girls in the school? We really cannot answer this for them.

Everyone here sends greetings, and you dear Br., accept another most sincere greeting from your friend,

Gottl. Byhan

Please give the enclosed letter to our Rachel.

[M 407-2: Springplace Diary.]

Sun., Mar. 11. The services were held in the usual order, although few came for them.

Mar. 16. Br. Byhan, Sr., went to Ochgeloogy to hold serves there for the few Brn. and Srs. next Sunday, and to serve the communicants there with Holy Communion.

Mar. 17. In the morning we had a heavy snowstorm, completely unexpectedly. After this weather had lasted for a couple of hours, it cleared up and got so cold again that all the rest of the fruit, the pears, apples and cherries, which had survived the previous night frosts, were completely frozen.

Sun., Mar. 18. Br. Nathl. Byhan led the Sunday services here in Spring Place. A good number of Brn. and Srs. had come for these.

Mar. 19. Today Br. Byhan, Sr., returned to Spring Place from his visit in Ochgeloogy. He brought along the happy news that the Supreme Court of the U. States has decided that the laws which the state of Georgia made that all white people should leave Cherokee country are invalid and that the Supreme Court has sent a mandate to the Georgians that the missionaries

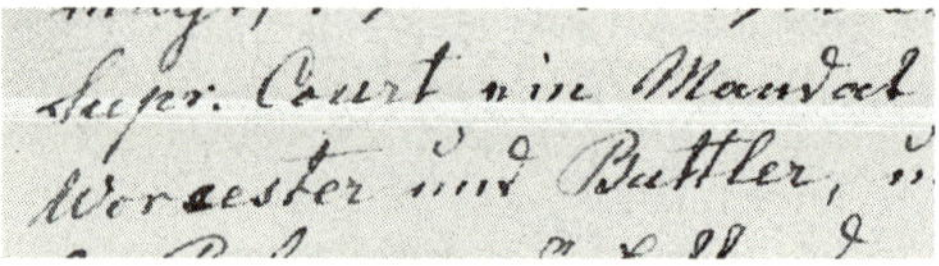
Supr. Court ein Mandat
Worcester und Buttler,

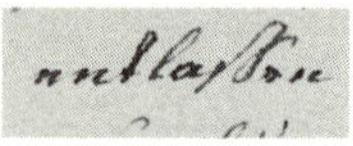
entlassen

Worcester and Buttler should be set free from the penitentiary immediately. Br. Byhan, Sr., led the Sunday services for the Brethren and Sisters in Ochgeloogy and Holy Communion for the few communicants, as only 6 had come. They were very happy and grateful for this. Usually the Brn. and Srs. in Ochgeloogy gather every Sunday and educate themselves together by reading in the Holy Scriptures, and one of the 2 Brn., George Hicks and Christian David — Watty — offers a prayer each time. In conversations with the few Brethren and Sisters there it is clearly noted that they wish more and more to grow in the grace and knowledge of Jesus Christ and to increase, and one can sense from them that they want to become and remain Jesus' property.

Mar. 21. We heard that Doct. Bean's house, kitchen, and storehouse in Sumacktown were burned down. Two travelers were there overnight, so most of the things could be saved although Doct. Bean himself was not home. For a long time already he has seldom stayed at home for many days, since the Georgia Guard tries constantly to find him and arrest him. Today Mr. Dav. Steiner Dazizi also arrived here with his father and three horses and spent the night. In the evening in the 12th hour 2 Indians with 2 horses arrived here. They were lodged in the house where our scholars sleep.

The Sunday services were regularly attended by our Brethren and Sisters during this time, as much as the weather and the distance of their homes allowed. They expressed their joy each time when they heard that it seems more and more as if Br. and Sr. Clauder would return as their future teachers.

[M 415-2-8: Translated by Julie Tomberlin Weber. Addressed to: Rev. Theod. Schulz, Salem, Stokes County, North Carolina. Postmark: Springplace, C.N., Mar. 25. Free. G. Byhan, P.M. Received Apr. 6.]

Springplace, March 24, 1832

Dear Br. Schulz,

I already reported to you on the 10th of this month that I received your last letter to me dated Feb. 15th; it arrived here on March 4. Since then we have remained completely empty-handed and have not seen a single line from Salem. Perhaps the letters are lying somewhere on the way, since the mails currently are going very irregularly, as we see in the newspapers. Everywhere one looks there is confusion, and nothing different should be expected from the postal service. God knows when I will finally receive an answer from the Genl. P.M. to my suggestion that Br. Clauder become P.M. here.

You will probably have heard, perhaps before we did, that the Supreme Court has decided in favor of Mr. Worcester and Buttler. People say this news caused quite a stir among a certain party of people in Georgia. God alone knows what will happen now! And we must patiently await this.

Otherwise, everything here is quiet. We are having cold and dry weather, and the air is so full of smoke that one almost chokes. The reason for this is that there are fires all around in the bush. This week Doct. Bean's house, kitchen, supply house, and smoke house burned to the ground in Sumak. The loss is quite great. He himself, Doct. Bean, a white man whose wife is the eldest daughter of our friend McNair, was not at home, because he has been on the run for a long time now trying to avoid falling into the hands of the Georgia Guard.

On March 16th I visited our Brn. and Srs. in Ochgeloogy, and then on Sunday the 18th I held services for them, and 6 communicants who had gathered celebrated Holy Communion. They were all very pleased with my visit with them. They usually meet every Sunday and strengthen each other in the word of God. Brn. George Hicks and Christian David Watee lead their services. It is their absolute intention and desire through His grace to live only for the Savior in this world and to remain faithful to the grace received. By the way, I felt very happy among these dear people. Old Br. Willm. Abr. Hicks and two of his daughters are currently living in the mission house there, and they are keeping everything in good order.

5 o'clock in the afternoon. The Georgia mail just brought me your kind letter of the 7th of this month after a drought of 3 weeks, for which we were very happy.

I have time to reply to only 2 points. First, concerning the sore on Nathl.'s throat I think I informed you in one of my previous letters that Doct. Bean had cut off this sore after it had grown to a considerable size. Now it is almost completely gone, for which we are very thankful.

Second, you write me that Br. Warner said I had planned and had said that I wanted to buy the Schulz house. I cannot remember ever having said anything like this. If I said such a thing then I have forgotten it. In the meantime, when we are finally in Salem, we can discuss this matter more and talk about it. Meanwhile, I will consider it until we are finally there in person where more things like this can be said. If Br. Warner also buys the Schröther house, then hardly anyone would be found to move into his house. But I do not want to get involved in any negotiations like this as long as we are here. There will be enough time when we are finally there. And I do not want to be in Br. Warner's way if he has a chance either to rent it to someone else or to sell it. We must be there first before we can do anything more in this matter.

You have doubtless also heard the decision of the Supreme Court concerning Worcester & Butler, Georgia and Cherokees. What will the consequences be?? Time will tell. May God be with us!

On Feb. 19 I sent the letter to the Genl. P.M. in which I recommended Br. Clauder as my successor as P.M. here. I have not yet received an answer to it; however, I hope the next mail on the 31st of this month will bring me the answer. I am happy and very glad that Br. Shober also wrote to the Genl. P.M. about

Br. Clauder, so that he can send the commission directly to Br. Clauder in Salem, which would really expedite the matter.

Everyone here sends best greetings. Nancy Becker is very poorly, as the English say, and is never really healthy. She fervently wishes to be back in Salem. Your faithful friend,

Gottl. Byhan

P.S. Please greet our children for us. Today we also received the first Salem Newspaper. Please greet Br. Christian Blum for us and tell him that our health is just so so.

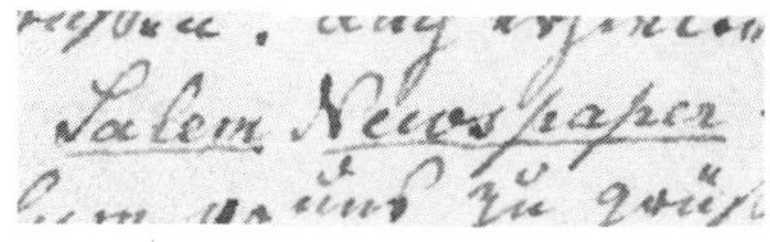

[B 61-3: Provinzial Helfer Conferenz, meeting in Salem.]

Mar. 20. After Br. Gb. Byhan, upon our advice, suggested to the Postmaster Genl. in Washington Br. G. H. Clauder as his successor as postmaster in Springplace, in recent days the official appointment of Br. G. H. Clauder to this office was made by letter from the Postmaster Genl., and thus Br. and Sr. Clauder are in a position to go back to their beloved Cherokees. They are planning to set out in about 14 days with their 2 children. This is the more possible since the Supreme Court of the United States on the 3rd handed down a verdict that the Georgia laws concerning the extension of their jurisdiction over the Cherokees are altogether against the Constitution of the United States and concern the treaties existing with the Cherokees, and for this reason are unconstitutional and null and void. The Supreme Court also orders that the imprisoned missionaries are to be set free.

We now discussed the departure arrangements of Br. and Sr. Clauder, which will require a two-horse wagon for their things in addition to Br. Clauder's small wagon. As soon as Br. and Sr. Clauder arrive in Springplace, Br. and Sr. Byhan and their son Nathaniel return here by the same wagon.

Before Br. Clauder's departure, a visitation of the Brethren and Sisters in Oochgelogy will also be particularly recommended, as well as the best ways for re-establishing the school, which in recent time, despite the special situation of the Cherokees, could receive attention. For this purpose his sister-in-law, the single Sr. Dorothea Rüde, who has been a faithful teacher in the Girls School here and has felt moved to accompany them and render further service there, can render real service in the school.

Because the annual subsidy from the Genl. Government for the school among the Cherokees has not been forthcoming for 3 years, we were thankful to receive in these days, through the efforts of our friend, Mr. Lewis Williams, Representative in Congress, an allocation of $850 from the Treasury of the Government of the United States. This will prove very useful in these present times.

Thurs., Mar. 22. The Confz. agreed that the Negro woman of our married Br. John Henry Shulz, who will be very suitable for the housekeeping of our Br. and Sr. in Springplace and in many other respects, should be bought by Br. Theodor Schulz for the low price offered of $200.

Sat., Mar. 31. Since our Br. and Sr. Clauder are planning to journey to Springplace on Tuesday, April 3, accompanied by the single Sr. Dor. Rüde, the Confz. spoke with the former about their important service among the Cherokees, and urgently recommended to them the faithful conducting of the school with the Cherokee youth, with which Sr. Dorothea Ruede can render real service. We also urged them to diligent visitation with their Brn. and Srs., and at least monthly in Oochgelogy as well. We also urged them to have daily house devotions, and in the school to see that the youth and children be instructed in house and garden and fieldwork.

At the same time Br. Clauder was asked not to enter in the slightest into the internal political situation of the Cherokee Nation, but to have his eyes fixed on his main calling, to lead souls to Jesus and to help to increase His divine Kingdom, and to devote everything possible to this. For this we wished him new blessing, the powerful support and help of God and His dear Spirit.

[*Records: N.C.*, 8:4016: Salem Diary. Translated by Douglas L. Rights.]

Apr. 2. At the close of the monthly prayer meeting led by Br. Schulz, Br. & Sr. Clauder and their 2 children and the single Sister Sophia Dorothea Ruede who leave tomorrow on their journey to Springplace, Cherokee county, were commended to the Lord in earnest prayer.

[*Records: N.C.*, 8:4030: Aufseher Collegium, meeting in Salem. Translated by Douglas L. Rights.]

Apr. 2. The resolution with regard to Br. J. Hy. Schulz of March 19[1] has been voided in that, after he had offered to sell the Negro woman to several neighbors for $200.00, he sold her on his own initiative to Br. Theo. Schulz for service in the Spring Place, Ga., mission (Cherokee).

[M 407-2: Springplace Diary.]

Sun., Apr. 1. The Brn. and Srs. gathered in quite large numbers for the services. We received a letter today from our dear Br. Schulz in Salem with the announcement that it is now decided and certain that Br. and Sr. Clauder will arrive here in Spring Place this month in Br. and Sr. Byhan's place. The Indian Brn. and Srs. once again expressed their joy that they will not be left. Today we also heard that Mr. Wacasser in Sumaktown had the place where blessed Charles Renatus Hicks lived and where his widow, our Sr. Felicitas Hicks, lived until now, taken by white people because he has rented there. Wacasser had our Sr. Hicks get her things and household goods out of the house, and told

---

[1] [(*Records: Cherokees* ed.:) Auf. Col. had resolved to exclude Br. Henry Schulz from Salem because of the "bad behavior" of Betsy. See *Records: N.C.*, 8:3989, 4029.

the white people to move in. And so our Sr. Hicks is without house and home, and now must move in with one of her sons.

[M 415-2-9: Translated by Julie Tomberlin Weber. Addressed to: Rev. Theodor Schulz, Salem, Stokes County, North Carolina. Postmark: Springplace, C.N., Apr. 8. Free. G. Byhan, P.M. Received Apr. 20.]

Springplace, Apr. 7, 1832

Dear Br. Schulz,

We received your kind letter of March 17th on the 1st of this month, and we thank you sincerely for this. In this letter you report that you informed us in a letter dated March 10th about the decision of the Supreme Court in favor of the missionaries and the Cherokees. We have not yet received that letter, that is, the one dated the 10th. I wonder where it might be wandering around, or if it might even just be lying somewhere still? We hear that the Gov. of Georgia is not going to follow the decision of the Supreme Court regarding Worcester & Butler. We must wait to see what the consequences will be.

I also saw from your kind letter that Br. Clauder was accepted as my successor in the postal service here by the Genl. P.M. and that Br. and Sr. Clauder will now set out on the journey here as quickly as possible. The Genl. P.M. has not given me any notice of this. Perhaps I will receive a letter from him today.

I announced this change to our dear Indian Brn. and Srs. last Sunday. They seemed to be very happy about it, and we have reason to believe they are happy that they will not be left by us and that Br. and Sr. Clauder will come in our place.

We will certainly keep Rominger on in the field and garden work. We have, so to speak, everything going well, and we are generally further along with our work in the fields and garden. According to the time of year, we are 2 or 3 weeks earlier than we were last year when the Georgians were on all backs all the time, so that we could not get on with the work.

It is a matter worthy of much praise that our annuity from the government, through the efforts of Mr. Lewis Williams, will be paid, which will be a great benefit to the mission finances.

I have already informed you of my thoughts about Warner's house in my previous letter. I can do nothing in this matter until we are finally there. I do not know what Br. Warner is asking for it either. I must first see it before I can buy it. Br. Warner might have improved it so much that it will cost more than I can afford. In brief, I cannot do anything about it for now, and I must wait until we finally get there. Perhaps Br. Benzien, the congregation business manager, still has a little place where he could lodge us in the meantime — out of old friendship — until we can look around a little. Dear God has always provided for us. He will continue to do so!

Otherwise, we are living in peace and quiet here. We hear and see little or nothing of the Georgians. Perhaps the decision of the Supreme Court has caused them to reflect a little. Those white people who live here in the country and have sworn allegiance to the laws of Georgia are not at all fond of the statements of the highest authority, and they do not really trust the peace, since they do not know if it will now be their turn to have to leave the Indians' country. Still they threaten everyone with beating, etc., if they say anything favorable about the Indians. Particularly our Wacasser in Sumak is very indignant about the decision of the Supreme Court. It is good that we do not need to fear him. It is actually more laughable the way they behave.

Apr. 8. I wrote this far yesterday. But yesterday evening in the eighth hour the Western mail brought me your kind letter of March 10th as well as Br. Clauder's letter of the same date. These letters completely missed the road to Spring Place. The fault probably lies with the Knoxville P.O. Now we are happy that they have finally arrived here, and we thank you sincerely for these. Unfortunately, however, all the messages in your letter, and primarily in Br. Clauder's letter, arrived too late, because

Br. Clauder is without a doubt already on his journey here. The Daily Texts you sent here, 7 in all, all arrived correctly. I have taken care of those for Worcester and Butler. I will send the other 3 I still have on hand to the missionaries in Brainerd who have asked me for them. I think it would be impossible to refuse something like this?

The wish in your dear letter of March 10th, that I might be the first here in this country to know of the decision of the Supreme Court, could not be fulfilled. I was the first, however, who brought it from Ochgeloogy and New Echota to the area of Spring Place. It was announced in Och_____y on the evening of the 16th, and I brought the news to Spring Place on March 19th. At first the people were so overjoyed they could hardly believe it. Now we will see how the Lord will assist further! It is known that the Georgians have not accepted the decision.

I must close. My time is short. Excuse my scrawl. Everyone here greets you in the best way. Today I am expecting another letter from you and further news about Br. and Sr. Clauder's journey here. You are especially greeted by your familiar friend and Br.,

Gottl. Byhan

[M 407-2: Springplace Diary. Handwriting is Gottlieb Byhan's.]

Sun., Apr. 8. Because of the constant rain yesterday and the flooded streams only a few of our Indian Brn. and Srs. were here. Through a letter we received today from Br. Theod. Schulz in Salem we learned that Br. and Sr. Clauder are planning to begin their journey from Salem to Spring Place on the 2nd of this month, so that we can expect this Br. and Sr. here during Passion Week. Today we also heard that the Methodists in Chatuga want to hold a large common service, or Camp Meeting, next Easter Sunday in Chatuga, about 12 or 15 miles from here. Our Brn. and Srs. were told that we would have Holy Communion on Easter Sunday. They promised to come for this.

[Handwriting is now Henry G. Clauder's.]

Apr. 15. Palm Sunday. The Sunday services were held in the following manner. In the first service we prayed the Litany of the Life, Sufferings, and Death of our Lord Jesus Christ. In the sermon which followed, the Brethren and Sisters were reminded that we are once again entering into Passion Week, during which we are especially to consider the sufferings and death of our Lord Jesus Christ, and we asked our dear Lord to let the consideration of this be blessed for our hearts once again. After this the Brn. and Srs. were invited to the enjoyment of Holy Communion next Easter Sunday.

Apr. 19. We had the joy of welcoming dear Br. and Sr. Clauder and the single Sr. Sophia Dorothea Ruede, along with the driver Fredrick Clayton, to our place. The former will replace Br. and Sr. Byhan in service to the mission here in accordance with their call. Br. Clauder will also take over the Post Office here, which Br. Byhan has taken care of almost 5 years now.

Apr. 20. Most of our baptized people came for the services on Good Friday. On this occasion they sincerely welcomed Br. and Sr. Clauder. We had no interpreter during the services, but the Passion story of our Savior according to Matt. 27 was read in the Cherokee language by the Indian Br. Solomon, and finally an appropriate hymn was sung from the new Cherokee hymnal. The tears of those present testified to the fact that the presence of Jesus could be powerfully felt during the services today. A wild, unconverted Indian considers it shameful to shed tears, but when he has come to the knowledge of the truth and hears the story of the suffering and death of his Savior and that of the entire world, then an otherwise very hard heart melts, and the the Wellspring of tears brings forth tears like melting ice freely flowing.

Sun., Apr. 22. On Easter Day we first prayed the Easter Litany. Then a brief talk was held with an interpreter and the resurrection story was read. In the third service we refreshed our needy souls through the enjoyment of the body and blood of our redeemer in Holy Communion, during which, with the addition of several guests from other confessions, about 35 Cherokees participated. We left this blessed meal with strengthened courage and faith and refreshed souls. Br. and Sr. Byhan bade a sincere and emotional farewell to the communicants on this occasion and commended their successors to their love and confidence. An Indian woman who had already expressed her desire to belong to our Gemeinlein, declared her intention anew today. We were happy about this and advised her to examine herself further and give her heart completely to the Savior.

Apr. 23. In the morning after a sincere farewell, Br. and Sr. Byhan began their journey to Salem accompanied by our best wishes for happiness and blessings.

1832, part 2

[M 415-2-10: Translated by Julie Tomberlin Weber. Addressed to:

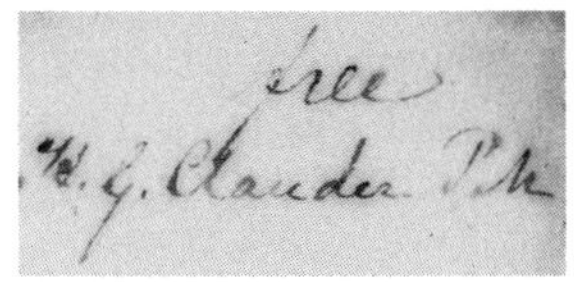

Revd. Theodore Schulz, Salem, North Carolina. Postmark: Springplace, C.N., Apr. 24. Free. H. G. Clauder, P.M. Received May 9.]

Spring Place, Apr. 23, 1832

Dear Br. Schulz,

Last Thursday the 19th we arrived here safely in the afternoon. In recent days we had rain and bad roads, and we also saw snow on the mountains on this side of Maryville, T. On Friday we had the joy of being able to see most of our Indian Brn. and Srs. and being welcomed by them. In the services on that day as well as yesterday they were very emotional, especially during Holy Communion. On this occasion, Br. and Sr. Byhan said farewell to the Indian Gemeine and commended us to their further love and confidence.

This morning at half past 8 Br. and Sr. Byhan began their journey to Salem accompanied with our best wishes. Br. Byhan took one of the horses that was here, and I have kept three here since I will probably have use for them. This week we will first settle in and become familiar with the various things here and next week we will begin the school.

My expenses for the trip here including the toll for Clayton's wagon at the ferry and bridges amounted to $39.25, which I am adding here as you asked.

Greet my dear parents sincerely for us. Our children and we are all well except for a little cold among the latter.

More soon from your faithful friend and Brother,

H. G. Clauder

[M 407-2: Springplace Diary. Translated by Julie Tomberlin Weber. Handwriting is Heinrich Gottlieb Clauder's.]

Apr. 27. We had a soaking rain. Toward evening some surveyors came close to us. They are now busy measuring off this whole country into lots of 160 acres, to distribute it through a Lottery in the future according to the custom of the Georgians.

Sun., Apr. 29. We had rain the entire day. At 11 o'clock we gathered with many brown and black people to pray the Litany. Then the words of Matt. 7:13,14 were discussed, during which those who understand English listened attentively. In the second service Luke 15 was read in English and Cherokee and in conclusion some hymns were sung. It was also announced that the school will now be started again, so that those who had children here could send them here again. Our Indian Br. Nicolaus Ignatius came here today to help take care of our fieldwork throughout the summer. The following day we began with the school, which will be taken care of primarily by Sr. Ruede. In the evening our friends Mr. and Mrs. McNair came here on their trip home from their children in the southern part of the Nation. They spent the night here and continued on the following morning.

May 2. Br. Clauder went to Oochgelogy on a visit, where he was taken in cordially by the Brethren and Sisters and friends. Wm. Abraham Hicks lives with part of his family in the mission house there where services are held every Sunday by both the Indian Brethren George Hicks and Christian David Watee, for the instruction of the rest of those who have been baptized.

When Br. Clauder visited the latter Brother in his home on the 3rd, he could not adequately express his pleasure at this and said repeatedly that he thanks the Lord from his heart that we have returned to this country, even if we cannot be in the same spot where we were once before. We had to submit patiently to the ways of the Lord who arranges everything for the best. Accompanied by him, Br. Clauder went to an Indian house close to there where one of his former scholars lived. As soon as she saw that her former teacher was there, she came running toward him with her hand outstretched and let her childlike joy at this be seen, and she did not leave his side. Several weeks later this young girl [Delila Emilia?] came to the school in Spring Place.

May 5. Mrs. Bean brought three of her children [Tolbert Gains, Emelia] to the school here. In the evening three more of Br. Samuel's girls [Gateya, Gatege, Charlotte] came.

Sun., May 6. In the sermon we considered the words of Jesus in Luke 9:62, during which David Tatsizi interpreted. In the second service Matt. 22 was read in both languages and in the same way a number of hymns were sung. Today some children came to the school again, which now consists of 12 scholars. In our evening devotion we asked together that the Savior would turn to us in grace and support us in our work and bless our weak efforts.

May 7. We had unusually strong winds, which brought a heavy storm in the afternoon. This continued throughout the entire night and soaked the earth so that for several days no work could be done in the fields.

May 9. An Indian came here who had had a fight while drunk and was pretty badly injured. He asked for brandy wine, and since he did not receive this he asked for vinegar. We gave him ½ a pint of this, which he then drank. He also wanted us to treat his hand, which was bitten badly in the fight. When he saw that we did not take note of such requests, he soon left us.

[M 415-2-11: Translated by Julie Tomberlin Weber. Addressed to: Revd. Theodore Schulz, Salem, North Carolina. Postmark: Spring Place, C.N., May 13. Free. H. G. Clauder, P.M. Received May 26.]

Spring Place, May 12, 1832

Dear Br. Schulz,

You have probably received my last letter of Apr. 24th [23rd]. Since then we have been busy enough in the garden and fields, and nothing unusual has happened since that I needed to report to you, so I let the writing go until now.

Last week I visited in Ochgelogy and found everyone there well except Christian David's wife, Sister Sussana Charity, who has been suffering from consumption the entire winter. Christian David was very happy about my visit and immediately shared with me the news that his brother, Major Ridge, recently converted and was baptized by the Presbyterians at Turnip Mountain (Doct. Butler's station). I joined him in sincerely rejoicing.

The Brethren and Sisters in Ochg. are supporting each other diligently every Sunday, led by Watee and George Hicks, at the mission place and are very happy about the former, who is the elder, and he is faithfully supported by his assistant George. I was sorry that George was not at home when I went, and so I have not yet seen him. Our faithful old William Hicks still lives in peace at our dear old Ochgelogy, with his daughters Margaret Mary and Ruth. The latter has still not been baptized, although she is the elder. I found everything in quite good order there and just as we had left it last July. I set Holy Communion for the 31st of this month there and I am planning to visit there every 4 weeks and hold services.

Br. and Sr. Byhan will probably have arrived at your place this week. You can learn more details about our post from them personally. I cannot write much, I just wanted to remind you of one matter that Br. Byhan had promised to discuss with you. For some time now, an Indian woman has been coming here for services and asks to be counted as a member of our community. She was already dunked in water 8 years ago by a Baptist who was traveling through. This was called a baptism, but at that time she herself did not know what was meant by it and was afterward as godless as before. But now she has a better understanding of the meaning of this proceeding. Now what should we do in this case? Is it necessary to have her baptized again after special instruction? Or should she just be accepted into the Gemeine through the handshake and considered already baptized? I would like to hear the advice of the P.H.C. about this soon.

Since our arrival here, we have had to turn away 10-12 children who were offered for us to educate and lodge, because we have our hands full with the 16 boarders (6 are yet to come). The Negro woman Betsy has been diligent thus far and very orderly. If she continues like this we will have much cause to be happy and grateful.

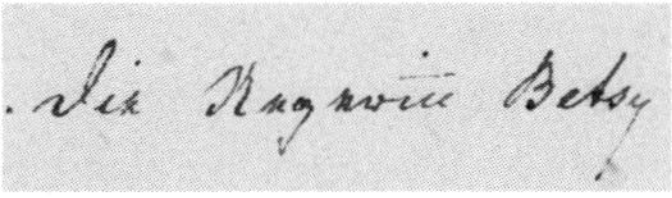

We have seen little of the surveyors who are in the country measuring it into lots. Generally it seems that everything around here is much quieter than I had expected. Some say that the chiefs negotiated with them this summer to make a treaty, but I do not know at whose authority this news came out. We here hear little about political matters of the country, and we are happy about this.

I had forgotten to include my travel costs in my last letter, and I will do this now as your notice for the account. The expenses for our 16-day travel thus added up to $39.25.

In the hope that I will receive something from you with the Georgia mail this afternoon, I will not yet close these few lines.

4 o'clock in the afternoon. We did not receive anything from Salem with the Georgia mail, so I have nothing else to add. I commend myself and mine to your loving remembrance. I remain your obliged friend and Brother,

Clauder

[M 407-2: Springplace Diary.]

May 13. Two more children came here to the school. Although we had not wanted to take any more, we could not deny the request of these children's parents, who belong to our Gemeinlein. The sermon at 11 o'clock in the morning was on Luke 16:19-31. Then in the second service the Litany was prayed by Nicolaus Ignatius. We hope to be able to use this young man as an interpreter in the services pretty soon. He was completely raised here and understands the English language pretty well.

This evening Mr. Henry arrived here with his wagon from Augusta and brought us coffee and sugar at a very low price. This week we were busy making hay, for which our heavenly Father gave us beautiful weather.

May 20. First was the sermon and then Br. Solomon read Matt. 17, sang some hymns, and closed with a prayer during which the rest of the Brn. and Srs. showed much emotion. There was a sweet feeling among us today, as there also was among the Brethren and Sisters, and the expressions of many of them brought us much joy, since they illuminated for us their walk with their unseen but close Savior. In the evening after our usual evening hour the children were encouraged again, especially to diligence both inside and outside school and to obedience, and some rules which we find necessary for order were announced.

Since we found that our supply of meat and corn was out and such groceries are not only very expensive but almost not available for purchase in this area, I went to Tennessee with our wagon this week and bought everything necessary there for a very low price. During my absence the Georgia surveyors were busy close to us and also passed through our fields.

[M 415-2-12: Translated by Julie Tomberlin Weber. Addressed to: Revd. Theodore Schulz, Salem, North Carolina. Postmark: Spring Place, Cher. Nation, May 27. Free. H. G. Clauder, P.M. Received June 4.]

Spring Place, C.N., May 26, 1832

Dear Br. Schulz,

We were delighted to receive your kind letter along with written *Nachrichten* on May 19th — after the packet had been on its journey here since the 20th of last month. I cannot write much at this time since the status quo has pretty much continued since my last letter to you of the 12th.

Since our bacon supply was almost gone, I made a journey to Columbus on the Hiwassee this week with our wagon and 2 horses, and there I bought 250 pounds of bacon at 8 cents a pound, along with 18 bushels of corn at 33 and a third cents per bushel, through which we had approximately $10-12 less in expenses than if I had bought these articles here. Along with the 50 bushels of corn which I had gotten for a supply from J. Vann at 50 cents a bushel, now I hope to have enough to last until October. During my 2½-day absence, the Georgia surveyors passed through our farm. One corner post stands in our yard several steps behind the drying house, which you can tell Br. Byhan. He will probably know which area it is in. Since then [page torn] they made their camp at the large spring near Vann's.

This week we had lots of rain and occasionally strong storms which damaged some of our garden plants pretty badly. The school which Sr. Rüde has gladly taken care of thus far is now being attended by 14 scholars, many of whom have made good progress in spelling and reading. Because reading is the most essential thing, we follow the plan of the other teachers in this country and limit ourselves to this until a child can read well. Through this they also learn to speak English faster, and only then are they instructed in writing and arithmetic.

Next week I am planning to go to Och_____y to hold services there and to serve the communicants Holy Communion. I will pray for our Lord's gracious assistance for this proceeding.

We are otherwise healthy, as are our children, and we are grateful to our dear Lord, who is always better inclined toward us than we know or earn, for allowing us, His unworthy tools, to be active again in His beautiful work here among the Cherokees. May we help increase His calling and provide a powerful witness to Him through word and deed. Greet your dear family as well as my dear parents, from your poor fellow servant of the Lord,

H. G. Clauder

[M 407-2: Springplace Diary.]

Sun., May 27. The services were as usual. The Indian woman Si.nas.te, who wants to join here, expressed herself today especially open-heartedly and complained to Sr. Clauder of her distress and the persecution and insults she has to endure from her husband and her natural sister, because she seeks our community and has renounced further service to sin. We tried to comfort her as well as we could, and taught her our Savior's rule to repay evil with good, and to seek help from the Savior in her distress. He does not fail to reward any disgrace suffered for His name's sake. Upon leaving after this conversation she said thank you for all that we had told her, and added that now she already felt much relieved.

May 30. Br. Clauder went to Ochgelogy where he preached on the following day and then celebrated Holy Communion with the few communicants who were there. Old Christian David could not come, because he had a bad knee injury from a kick by a horse.

Sun., June 3. Completely unexpectedly, our friend Boudinot came to the service at our place today. Since last winter he had been in the northern States on business for the Nation, and today he arrived here from Washington with his comrade John Ridge. Dazizi also came and served as interpreter during the sermon. Br. Samuel admonished the Brethren and Sisters in the second service to remain faithful to the Savior until the end and not allow anything to separate them from Him and His Gemeine.

June 10. On Pentecost most of our baptized people came. Many of them had already come the previous evening and had spent the night here. At 10 o'clock the Indian Solomon held the first service, consisting of singing some hymns and a prayer. At 11 o'clock was the sermon for which there was, however, no interpreter. During the enjoyment of Holy Communion, with which we concluded this important holy day, a very heavenly feeling prevailed. We began singing appropriate hymns from the Cherokee Hymn Book, through which the communicants, most of whom are real Indians and neither understand nor speak English, received instruction for their edification and were certainly encouraged and strengthened to remain in the saving faith in the Savior.

[M 415-2-13: Translated by Julie Tomberlin Weber. Addressed to: Revd. Theodore Schulz, Salem, North Carolina. Postmark: Spring Place, C.N., June 12. Free. H. G. Claude, Post Master. Received June 27.]

Spring Place, C.N., June 12, 1832

Dear Br. Schulz,

We received your kind letter of May 11th with the Knoxville mail last Tuesday, the 5th of this month. We thank you sincerely for this.

By now both of my letters from the 12th and 26th of May will probably be in your hands. The first included a question about how we should act regarding the Indian woman whom we have already mentioned frequently, Sinas-te from Sumake. She was baptized by the Baptists 8 years ago without personally understanding what happened to her, and now she really wants to be baptized by us and to join our fellowship. We would really like to have information soon on this point from the P.H.C. The said Indian visits us regularly every Sunday, and she is waiting eagerly for her official acceptance into the church and the fellowship of believers. She was previously one of the godless people. Her completely changed mind and behavior now cause more than a little amazement and attention from her neighbors and acquaintances, and she has to tolerate more than a little scorn and mocking from them.

I visited in Oochgelogy during the last days of the previous month, and I preached before a very small number of people there and then celebrated Holy Communion with 4 of the Brn. and Srs. who were present. Old Christ. Dav. Watee was not present, since he had been injured by a strong kick from his horse on his way home from a service in Ooch_____y. Because of this he was not able to go home, and it took a lot of effort for him to be taken to Billy Hicks's, where I visited him. His wife, Sr. Sussanah Charity, has been ill with consumption the entire winter. Old William Abraham continues to live in his sad, dark way, and he is still excluded from Holy Communion. I often feel powerless about him, since my efforts seem to bear so little fruit. The Good Shepherd alone can find him again and bring him back to the flock. However, despite all this, he is not apathetic or spiritually dead — at least his statements seem to indicate the opposite.

Concerning our life here in Spring Place, I must confess with much gratitude and great joy that we have been able to pursue our calling in peace and quiet both outwardly and inwardly so far. The Lord has given us the appropriate health and the strength and courage necessary for this, and we want to thank Him sincerely for this and try to use all of these essential gifts for His glory.

The school is currently attended by 16 children, of whom 14 (6 boys and 8 girls) live here. The girls live in a room in our house, where they can be supervised all the time. The boys live in the old mission house and have the yard behind it and the schoolhouse for their use except during school time. In this manner we believe we can keep good discipline and prevent disorder. Sr. Rüde takes care of the school alone in the morning from 8 until 11, and we cannot be happy and grateful enough for her assistance and willingness to help. In the afternoons, I instruct the boys while she holds sewing school in her room for the girls. This is also 3 hours, from 2 until 5. In this way, we have school for the children 6 hours each day, and in the time in between they are given various handwork, and so far they have shown a pleasing willingness to do this. We expect 4 more children of Brn. and Srs. George and William Hicks from Ochgel.

Aggy Sanders, who assisted us for several weeks but did not please us, went home last Sunday. We were completely disappointed in her. We are happy that we can manage without her and have capable help in the Negro woman. We also have Peggy Samuel, whom we taught in Oochgel. We took her in to help us with her father's permission. In exchange for this we provide her with appropriate clothing.

Last Sunday was Holy Pentecost, and we had a very pleasant holy day with most of our Brn. and Srs. During Holy Communion, I had appropriate hymns sung from the Cherokee hymn book for the pleasure of the Indian Brn. and Srs., and they showed encouraging emotions during this. It seems to me completely appropriate to have them sing hymns in their own language at all services — or to sing with them — especially during Holy Communion, since it is mostly singing, and not a single Cherokee voice is to be heard during the English hymns. How do your views on this compare to mine?

One more question about Cherokee services. Is it in accordance with church order that an exhorter like Br. Samuel, for example, or someone else who is not ordained, says the apostolic benediction at the conclusion of the service? The Methodist exhorters do this, which is probably an example for Br. Samuel. The Presbyterians, on the other hand, do not allow any of their so-called catechists. David Steiner Dazizi brought this point to my attention. If it is the same with us as with the latter confession, I will instruct Br. Samuel appropriately about this. He is, by the way, making good and pleasing progress.

Please greet Br. and Sr. Byhan for us as well as my dear parents and all the Brn. and Srs. who take loving interest in this mission. I hope Henry Schulz does not forget his promise to write to me first. A special sincere greeting to him in the meantime.

I am especially happy this morning about both swarms of young bees I safely caught yesterday, the first this summer —

actually the first in my life. Our hired workers had left early yesterday for Ochgelogy to fetch a couple of cows from there, so I had to make the attempt with my wife, and it worked quite well, you see, although my love was stung by 10 bees and had to leave the place very quickly.

Yesterday the Georgia surveyors drew another line through the Spring Place improvements. Another important question just occurred to me. A certain Georgia officer is giving public "Notice 'for the last time' that he will attend at ______ on 31st July for the purpose of receiving the list of taxables not yet given in, etc." Should I go and report, or wait until a constable comes to collect and then pay him for it? Your answer to these various questions is requested as soon as possible.

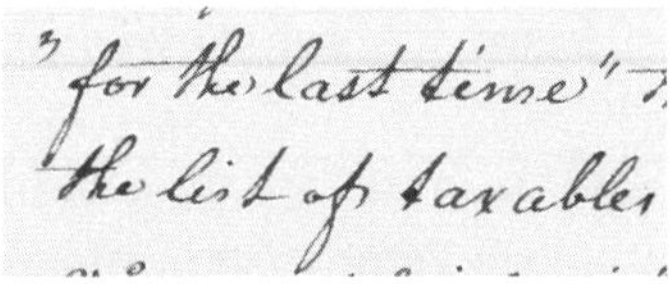

From your faithfully obliged, poor fellow Brother,

Clauder

[M 407-2: Springplace Diary.]

Sun., June 17. For the first time we had the joy of having our Nicolaus Ignatius assist as interpreter in our services. He received good marks as a beginner from those who can judge better than we ourselves can. We will try to use him for this purpose in the future. Today only a few listeners were present at the services, since there was preaching at other places in the neighborhood.

June 23. In the evening our Br. and Sr. George Hicks arrived here from Ochgelogy with their two children for our school. Annie Hicks came with them for the same purpose. She was formerly at our school in Ochgel.

Sun., June 24. Once again we had a pleasant and blessed day of services. Most of those baptized were here. First Br. Solomon prayed the Cherokee Church Litany. Then was the sermon on the words of Col. 3:11: Christ is all and in all. (See the English translation.) During this Br. Hicks interpreted, and the listeners delighted us with their attentiveness. In the third service Br. Samuel admonished those present to pay attention to the words of their teachers, who had left their home and friends to tell them in their poverty and blindness that Jesus Christ had come to rescue them from their misery. Finally he spoke especially with the children and said that the purpose of their presence here was to be instructed in useful things and that they must use their time here well and not make their teachers sad through laziness and disobedience. It was pleasant for us to see that during this talk, the contents of which we did not learn until later, many of the children as well as some of the parents were moved to tears. This gives us hope that the children will try with new diligence and courage to make progress in useful knowledge.

June 27. We went to Ochgelogy, where we arrived late in the evening pretty soaked. We had stayed with our friends in New Echota for several hours, and since it began raining heavily soon after our departure from there, we had to stop in at a house until the storm was past. The following day there was supposed to be a service there; however, Br. Clauder became so unwell that nothing came of this. The missionary Jones from the Vally Towns gave a brief but quite appropriate and edifying talk to the few who were present.

Toward evening we went to our Watees, both of whom have been lying ill for some time. Both of them were extremely happy about our visit. On a chair beside Christian David's bed lay many books in Cherokee. Among these was the Gospel of Matthew. When I remarked that he had his advisors and comforters, these books, very close to him, he said: Yes, I spend most of my time with them and receive much comfort from them. Before we went to bed he handed us an English Bible, called his family together, and then he and his wife propped themselves up on their bed and sat there so respectfully and with visible emotion while Br. Clauder read a chapter and offered a prayer. The next morning they repeatedly expressed their gratitude for our visit, and then we began our return journey to Spring Place.

On the way home we visited our friend Elias Boudinot in New Echota. There was an ambassador there who was the bearer of suggestions from the government of the United States to the Cherokee Nation concerning a treaty which the President of the United States wants to conclude with this Nation. It is expected that the Cherokees who now agree more and more that they must expect much oppression here will finally leave their land and move to Arkansas. The suggestions are very advantageous, and if everything promised to them is carried out properly, the Cherokees will hardly find reason to regret their move.

1832, part 3

[M 415-2-14: Translated by Julie Tomberlin Weber and C. Daniel Crews. Addressed to: Revd. Theodore Schulz, Salem, North Carolina. Postmark: Spring Place, C.N., July 1. Free. H. G. Clauder, Post Master. Received July 11. Br. Schulz has written in the address: Proposals fr. the Gl. Government & Br. Clauder's report for the Secy. of War.]

Spring Place, C.N., June 30, 1832

Dear Brother Schulz,

Last Tuesday I wrote you a letter to send to you with the Knoxville mail. However, since it did not come and a number of very important things have become known, I will replace my letter to you of the 26th with this one today and not send that one.

First, however, I must inform you that I received your kind letter of May 26th and June 2nd which arrived in good time, and I thank you for this. Yesterday we returned from Ochgelogy where I attempted to hold services on the 28th, but I could not carry out my plan because I did not feel well and had a bad sore eye. I almost fell unconscious and had to lie down as quickly as I could. I am now pretty well recovered again except for my left eye, which is very inflamed and is usually very painful in the evening. May the Lord grant me strength and grace to be able to lead the services here tomorrow, since the Indian Sinas.te is supposed to be accepted into the Gemeinlein.

The above-mentioned important things that have become known concern the political circumstances of this country, and since things will without a doubt soon lead to a treaty with the Cherokees, I want to report to you the proposition which the Cherokee I saw and spoke with yesterday in Echota brought here from Washington, as much as I can still remember.

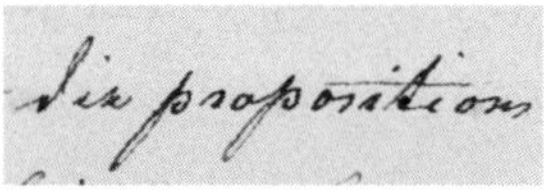

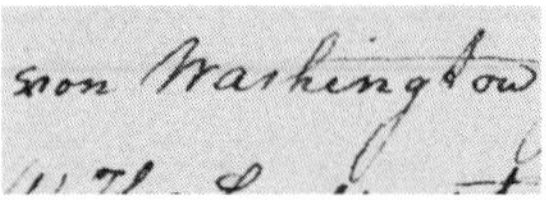

[Br. Clauder writes the following in English:]

(1) The Land west of the Mississippi shall be secured to the Cherokees, and shall be sufficiently extensive & suited for agricultural purposes. (2) The U.S. promises to protect them from invasion of other tribes. (3) The U.S. Will provide them with teachers — build churches, Council houses & houses for a few of the chiefs. (4) The Cherokee shall have an agent residing at Washington City at the expense of the Genl. government. (5) The Cherokee shall have the right to make their own laws & have their own government. (6) No white people shall be permitted to enter their Country, excepting those having a permit from the U.S. Agent. (7) The U.S. provides Mills, Blacksmiths, Iron, steel, hoes, ploughs, &c., for them. (8) Each adult in the Nation shall have a gun, & each family shall be provided with a sufficiency of Blankets. (9) Provision is made for all orphan Cherokee children. (10) They shall be removed at the expense of the U.S. & subsisted 1 year after their arrival in their new home. (11) The U.S. pays them for their improvements & stock of every kind left here, &c.

[Br. Clauder returns to writing in German:]

In all there are 17 articles — which exceed all treaties in liberality — which are known to me. Next Tuesday there will be a gathering of the Chiefs at John Ross's, to take these propositions into consideration.

During our absence from here Mr. Currie spoke. He has returned from Arkansas and left a letter from the War Department addressed: "To the Superintendent of the schools of the United Brethren in the Cherokee Nation." I share with you its contents:

[Br. Clauder copies the War Department letter in English:]

Sir,

To enable the Department to submit a Report of the Disposition & use of the Civilisation Fund at the next session of Congress, you are requested to transmit by the 1st of Novem. a statement of the Concerns of the institutions under your charge, as they may be on the 30th of Sep. next. Your statement will be confined, as far as practicable, to the schools, unconnected with those of the Missions, & will shew the following particulars:

1. The date of the establishment of the School.
2. The sums annually applied by your Society to each Society ([margin note:] school, I think he means), distinguishing its own funds from those granted by the government.
3. The number of school houses, the scite & cost of each.
4. The value of the School lots, & of the fixtures & appurtenances.
5. The sums received & expended for education.
6. The amount of debts & incumbrances, if any, incurred for the support of schools.
7. The number of teachers, & of other persons employed in connexion with the school, their names, duties, & pay.
8. The number & names of the pupils, distinguishing males & females, & showing how many entered & how many left since the preceeding report. To this tabular statement, remarks will be appended, specifiying the branches of knowledge cultivated, the proficiency of each pupil, & his or her capacity to be useful & in what way.

You will also report the intentions of your Society as to future operations should the tribe remove.

Very respectively, your obed. Servt.,

Elbert Herring

[Br. Clauder continues his letter to Br. Schulz in German:]

In order for me to be able to make this requested and very detailed report, I would like to ask your counsel, especially in regard to nos. 4 and 5 of the above which seem to me to be ambiguous, and which I do not understand as appropriate. In No. 3 is the Ocgelogy schoolhouse to be taken into consideration although at present there is no school there? How is the worth of the lots (No. 4) to be found I do not know. The worth of the "fixtures & appurtenances" can probably be valued. (I do not know how No. 5 is to be taken; this obligation is already included in No. 2.)

The Georgia Guard has recently been around here to capture our neighbor Vann because he along with Capt. McNair and several others arrested a Georgia surveyor and took him to Tennessee and charged him "for violating the intercourse law." The judge, however, who questioned him, let the poor fellow go. Although this is now only a scouting party for Capt. McNair, it may seem a more serious matter to the Georgians, and it could have unpleasant consequences, for I hear that Capt. McNair is of a mind to resist the Guard if they come over the border.

Yesterday evening after sundown we heard three musket shots over at Vann's set off by the Guard, but Vann was nowhere to be found, and they had to leave with their purpose unaccomplished. However, we saw nothing of them and hopefully will have nothing to fear from them.

We now have all the children here whom we promised to take. The total number of scholars is 19. All of them will have to stay here except for 2: James and John Vann. Peggy Samuel, whom we took in the place of Aggy Sanders, is getting on well and seems to receive our admonitions well.

I am expecting, however, that if a treaty comes into effect I have little doubt that such complications will not arise that it will bring an end to our and all other schools in this Land. Should anything else of importance arise, I will report it to you next week. For now, though, I have nothing more to bring up, other than a heartfelt greeting to our dear parents and your dear family from your true friend and fellow Brother,

Clauder

[M 407-2: Springplace Diary. Translated by Julie Tomberlin Weber. Handwriting is Heinrich Gottlieb Clauder's.]

Sun., July 1. The Indian woman Si-nas-te, who was baptized a number of years ago by a traveling Baptist preacher, was present in the sermon on the Doctrinal Text [Luke 15:6] for today. She seems to be thoroughly converted and sincerely longs to be taken into our Gemeine.

Sun., July 8. The services were held as usual. Only a few of our Brn. and Srs. came for them. However, a good number of Vann's Negroes were here, so that our Saal was still completely full. If souls come only for the service, then it is always encouragement enough for us to proclaim the sweet Gospel to them, no matter what color and Nation they are from. Everyone has an immortal soul for which the Savior suffered and died and won life and salvation.

July 9. We sent both of our day workers to Tennessee with the wagon to get groceries, primarily cornmeal, from there, since all the mills around here are in disrepair and you cannot get anything milled.

July *11.* They returned.

July 14. Br. Clauder received a pleasant letter from the missionary Worcester. It is known that since last September he has been held as a prisoner in the state prison of Georgia because he refused to recognize the legitimacy of the laws of Georgia extended over this country.

July 19. According to an announcement by the head Chief of the Nation, all Christian confessions in this country observed a day of repentance and prayer in consideration of the oppressed situation of the Cherokee Nation. We asked the only wise Regent of the circle of the earth to grant the leaders of this people wisdom to recognize what will be best for them, to prevent all bloodshed, and if it is His will that the Cherokees should move to the west, to go with them in grace and power and protect them from all further dispersal. Most of our Brn. and Srs. were present at the service, and the Indian Brn. Samuel and Solomon sang and prayed in the Cherokee language at the close of this.

July 20. We visited some of the Brn. and Srs. on the Connesauga River, where we found the married Sr. Esther lying sick on a straw mattress in a hut. Since she was very weak we had some refreshments sent to her, through which she completely recovered in a number of days. This evening we were delighted by a visit from our friend Butrick.

[M 415-2-15: Translated by Julie Tomberlin Weber. Addressed to: Revd. Theodore Schulz, Salem, North Carolina. Postmark: Spring Place, C.N., July 22. Free. H. G. Clauder, Post Master. Received July 30. Br. Schulz writes: Butrick's books.]

Spring Place, July 20, 1832

Dear Br. Schulz,

Herewith I am starting to send you a copy of the Diary from here, and next week I will continue with this. I will also send you my account current in the same manner. I still have some money in my account, and if I should be lucky enough to collect the notes of the Ochgelogy concerns, I will be able to manage for a long time. Our large school adds a lot to this, and it is fortunate that there is plenty of food to be bought for a good price in nearby Tennessee. I was there once already in the month of May and bought cornmeal and beans. However, I did not have nearly enough, and last week I sent our small wagon there once again and had 250 pounds of beans and 18 bushels of cornmeal sent. This should keep us on into fall, we hope.

Last Saturday the 14th we were delighted to receive both of your kind letters of June 19th and 28, the former containing *Wöchentliche Nachrichten* of the U.A.C. I think I informed you a long time ago that I received the *Missionary Intel.* and some written *Nachrichten* in the month of May. If I am mistaken, then it has now been done.

Yesterday we held a day of prayer with most of our Brn. and Srs. following the announcement of Chief John Ross, which you will have seen from the *Phönix.* Next Monday the large and important Council begins. This could decide whether they (the Cherokees) will make a treaty and accept the proposals (which I wrote to you) or not. It is said that John Ridge is heading a party which has a plan to make a treaty with the United States and then to emigrate to the other side of the Rocky Mountains, where he, as chief, will form a Colony of Cherokees. John Ross is not satisfied with the Delegates, who are all for the treaty, as is E. Boudinott. He still wants to wait things out here and hope, even though there is nothing to hope for. His father was a Scot, and they are known to be a stiffnecked people. Now may the Lord arrange everything for the best and grant the chiefs wisdom in their deliberations.

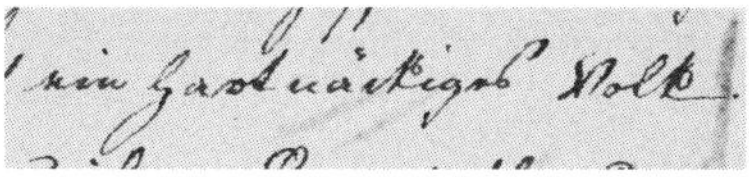

This morning my wife and I are planning a joint visit at Josua and Israel's and in the area on the River there.

I am enclosing a $2.00 Newbern note, which is not accepted here according to the Georgia laws and thus is useless. I will write again next week, and in the meantime I remain your friend and Brother,

H. G. Clauder

The 21st. Our friend Butrick ordered the following English books from me, which he would like to get at the first opportunity. Heckewelder's *Narrative of the Mission among the North American Indians*, Loskiel's ditto, ditto. Heckewelder's *History of the North American Indians*. Holmes's *History of the U.Br. Church*. Holmes's *Historical Sketches of the Missions of the U.Br. Church*. 1 copy of each work.

H. G. Clauder

[M 407-2: Springplace Diary.]

July 23. The Council of this Nation gathered to consider whether it is to the advantage of the people to emigrate west or not. The latter was once again the decision reached by the Chiefs. Most of our Brethren and Sisters went there, and so our services were not so well attended.

July 26. We received a visit from some Methodist missionaries. In the evening one of them led our usual evening devotion in an edifying manner.

[M 415-2-16: Translated by Julie Tomberlin Weber. Addressed to: Revd. T. Schulz, Salem, North Carolina. Postmark: Spring Place, C.N., July 29. Free. H. G. Clauder, P.M.]

Spring Place, C.N., July 26, 1832

Dear Br. Schulz,

Herewith you will receive the Diary from Spring Place through the end of June. I sent the beginning of this last week via Petersburg, Ga. Please let me know how many days it takes the letters to get there.

Last night we had Col. Montgomery spend the night with us. He is a brother of the Agent and is riding around in the country to enroll the Indians to emigrate to the west. From him I learned that William Hicks wants to acquire our place in Ochgelogy as his own property and told him he would take a reservation there himself. I have harbored suspicions for a long time that Will. Hicks might have the place valued and keep the money for it and then emigrate. And so I acquainted Mr. Montgomery with the entire matter, that Hicks is just our tenant, and no one but you (or I in your name) has the right to sell the place. Montgomery will tell the rest of the Agents, and he told me it was good that I had given him this notice to prevent deceit from happening.

A similar situation happened at the mission in Hightower, which put it into the hands of the Georgians, when the Indian tenant whom Thompson put into his house had the place valued and emigrated to Arkansas with the money.

Without a doubt there will soon be a split among the Cherokees. They are already divided. One party is for selling the land, but by far the largest part of the nation, led by John Ross, is against it. I have not yet heard anything from the Council, which began last Monday. People say it will last 4 weeks. Even if no treaty is made, many will emigrate next fall.

Be so good and inform me of your opinion about the place at Ochgelogy. Should we try to sell it to Willm. Hicks or someone else? Or should I announce that we are the legal owners of the place so that he cannot secretly sell something he has no right to?

We are longing for rain. It has been 3 weeks since we had rain. We are all well, as are our 20 scholars, and we pursue in our calling in peace and quiet, externally and internally. We are quite satisfied that Sunday services are well attended. Please send me the note from Wm. Abr. Hicks for $105, which I cannot find among notes you gave me, in your next letter. Just a few days ago I found out that it is not in the papers where the others are, and since I have not seen it since my arrival here, it is apparent that this note was left behind — this note is due now, and I will try to collect the money.

I remain your loving friend and Br.,

H. G. Clauder

I received the July 12 letter with *Nachrichten* on the 28th.

[M 407-2: Springplace Diary.]

Sun., July 29. The sermon was on Rom. 8:32, and the listeners were also encouraged to put their trust in God in all external shortcomings and needs. Since He did not spare His only begotten Son but gave Him up for the sins of the world, He will not withhold smaller gifts, but will give us everything in the right measure which can serve our best interests. In the second service we read some mission news, the contents of which were interpreted into the Cherokee language.

Aug. 10. We received a visit from General Newnan, who is a member of the Congress of the United States. He asked about the current state of the Nation and what the opinion of the Indians is about moving away.

1832, part 4

[M 415-2-17: Translated by Julie Tomberlin Weber. No address; no postmark. Received Aug. 26.]

Spring Place, C.N, Aug. 10, 1832

Dear Br. Schulz,

Last Tuesday the 7th the Council broke up, and since I have heard about the negotiations there I want to share this with you by the first post.

Mr. William Rodgers and his wife are spending the night here on their way home, and I learned from him that the Cherokees absolutely do not want to hear anything about new treaties. The party which considers it best to accept the offers of the Government and to which Rodgers, John Ridge, Boudinott, Coody, Martin, and others belong, was hardly able to explain its thoughts. As soon as they said anything about emigrating or indicated this, the other party became angry and made the bitterest accusations that they were not the friends of the Nation. They were traitors and had been bribed by their enemies with money, etc. Boudinott resigned his editorship of the *Phönix* and explained his reasons, and it is said this newspaper will no longer be published. Rodgers seemed more than a little uneasy and also said he would not stay here to watch the degradation of his people. He had suffered long enough and hoped for better things, but in vain.

The Nation is obviously divided, and John Ross is the cause of this. If he had harmonized better in this Council in a more reasonable manner, then they could have reached an agreement.

The U.S. Commissioner, Mr. Chester (the same one who traveled through Salem last March) was treated with open disdain, in that they they did not want to reply through him to the suggestions he delivered, but rather would have the Nation's answer delivered to the Government in another manner. Chester was dismissed with few words and even fewer signs of friendship. He is supposed to have left the Council enraged.

I also learned from Mr. Rodgers about the plan those who now want to emigrate are now harboring. Their intention is to start a colony west of the Rocky Mountains. The land offered in Arkansas is in all respects objectionable. Many of the emigrants who went there last winter returned recently and assured that all the talk about lack of water and wood there was not made up, that the land on the river was of excellent quality but that the sickness there was so great that no one could live there. And if a treaty is made with this Nation sooner or later, it will certainly not move to the Arkansas area. Everyone is unanimously against this. All those who are in favour of a removal talked only about the area to the west of the Rocky Mountains.

The argument John Ross is making is foolish in my opinion. He still believes that the decision of the Supreme Court will finally be be carried out, although Justice McLean clearly explained to him that it will only be carried out in as far as it refers to the missionaries Worcester & Butler. Ross's plan ended with a treaty & removal, but he set the time in 12 months. Ridge and his party are for taking this step now and escaping the oppression, irritation, and suffering which is going to be showered upon this Nation in the coming 12 months.

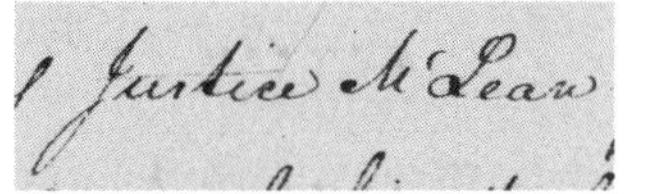

I heard sad news from Ochgelogy. William Hicks has handed our old place over to one of the enrolling agents named Hardin. His family moved into this country some weeks ago. We were aware that Hardin had brought his family into this country to spend the hot summer months here, and it is possible that their stay in our buildings in Ochgelogy is just temporary. I canceled my visit in July, because the Council had just gathered and everyone had gone there. As long as his family is living there it is pointless to try to hold a service there, since no Cherokees would come. On my previous visits there, there were never more than 4 of our Brn. and Srs. present. Soon I will visit our Brn. and Srs. there in their homes and try to learn more about the circumstances which allowed Wm. Hicks to take a Georgia family into our houses.

The services here are not as well attended as they were some time ago either. There seem to be other causes responsible for this than pure indifference, such as distance and work in the fields during the week which tires the Brn. and Srs. and their horses, so they spend the Sabbath rest at home. Otherwise the Gemeinlein continues as usual, as far as I know.

Everything here and in our own circle also continues as usual. However, the black woman Betsy hurt her back some time ago when she was careless in lifting an iron in the kitchen. This week she is completely unable to work and cannot even help with the work. If only my dear wife had more strength, then everything would work better. But as it is she is often completely exhausted and lethargic. Twenty-two children are attending the school and keeping Sr. Rüde and me busy enough. Most of them are delighting us with their progress in learning.

This summer we have had few visitors, for which we are happy and grateful. Last summer Mrs. Vann was not at home, and all the travelers came here. As long as she remains here at home we need not fear being overburdened by travelers.

If you have any Georgia money on hand or that you can get, please be good enough to send me some of it. My cash box still has over $40, but I expect a draft soon for $30 from the Genl. P.M., so I must keep some for this. The expenditures in the past month were great, because the school grew a lot and almost all the corn and bacon and also coffee and sugar had to be purchased. For your notice I must inform you that the notes of the Macon Bank are no longer accepted. The Bank is broken, as people say. I got this news some days ago in a note from Macon. Unfortunately I had $7 of those notes in my cash box when I received the news. In my last letter to you, postmarked July 29th,

I asked you to send me the note of hand of Wm. Hicks, since it is not to be found among the notes you gave me.

The postal work is set up again now so that one mail arrives here on Sunday at 11 o'clock. However, I always try to hold a service before the mail arrives.

3 o'clock P.M. Several hours ago Genl. Newnan was here on his way home to Georgia from Washington City. He regrets very much that the Cherokees absolutely do not want to make a treaty. From here he wants to go to Ridge's ferry to visit John Ross and try to persuade him that all of his hopes for Clay's election and then anticipated help for the Cherokees are unfounded. He will not be able to get anywhere with Ross. He told me the Legislature of Tennessee would gather next month, and the laws of that state would certainly be extended to the Cherokees within the borders once again. The Lottery in Georgia will be over in a few weeks now, and then hundreds and hundreds of emigrants will move into this country. Then the destruction and ruin of the Cherokees will be complete.

If only they had not let things get this far. I fear the internal and external destruction will be so great that all hopes for improvement among the Indians will have to be completely extinguished. The condition of the Nation is already pitiful now. What else will happen. One hears comments everywhere: "Now is the trouble begun."

Now it turns out that John Ross was the author of the arrest of the surveyor. McNair, Vann, and others were actually hired by him to do this, and the Georgia Guard, which allowed the Council to pass peacefully, will catch Ross and his helpers soon now. Our poor Br. James is also very mixed up in this affair. The Guards were already at his house a number of weeks ago to arrest him, but they could not find him, and I would not wish them better luck, because he was just being used by McNair as a spy and did not lay a hand on the surveyor. Since then however, he has not come back to the services here.

It does not seem necessary to list the special expenses for each year since 1800 in the required report for the Secretary of War. I suppose he just wants to know what the average annual expenses are, and 2nd, how much has been spent since the beginning of the mission. I can make more use of the copy you sent to me in your last letter in preparing the report than the various and partly confused accounts that are here, and I thank you many times for your efforts. In a few weeks I will enclose the required report for you, and you can then send it on to Washington.

Sunday the 11th. With today's mail I received the *Missionary Intel.* from you. 2 weeks ago I received 2 copies of the same issue directly from New York, not including the one for Mr. Butrick.

Greet the dear Brn. of the P.H.C. as well as your family and my parents. I remain your obliged, poor Brother,

H. G. Clauder

[M 407-2: Springplace Diary. Translated by Julie Tomberlin Weber. Handwriting is Heinrich Gottlieb Clauder's.]

Sun., Aug. 12. Most of the Brethren and Sisters were here for the services. Br. Samuel brought a request from one of the Indian women, in which she expressed her desire to become a member of this Gemeine. We sent her sincere greetings and word that it would be necessary for us to speak with her ourselves first before we could think about giving her hopes that her acceptance could take place. Samuel said she is planning to come herself next Sunday.

Sun., Aug. 19. Among the visitors on this day was also the above-mentioned person. She is the only daughter of our Sr. Sophia Carolina. She was raised in Brainerd and speaks English well. In Oct. 1829 she was married by Br. Byhan to the Indian James Sanders. She said it had already been some time since the desire arose in her to become the Savior's property. She wishes to receive the waters of holy baptism and join the community of believers. We encouraged her to surrender herself completely to the guidance of God's Spirit, who certainly will complete the work of grace which has begun in her heart. It gave us great joy to accept this person as a candidate for holy baptism. In the sermon on Ps. 126:3 we remembered with grateful joy the charity and mercy which was made ours through Jesus Christ the Redeemer, that all who believe in Him are saved, and that this happy news of peace has also been preached for 100 years through the witness of the people of the Brethren in many areas of the earth and to many people with blessings for their hearts. On this day, since we were celebrating the anniversary of the 21st early, we celebrated Holy Communion with most of our communicants.

N.B. The wish of the U.A.C. that this anniversary day should not be celebrated until next Sunday was not known by us until after this date.

Aug. 22. Br. Clauder visited Sr. Sussannah Charity, who is ill, in Ochgelogy. She is near her end, judging by all appearances, and she is happy she will soon be freed from all suffering. Her expressions about the state of her heart were pleasing.

[M 415-2-18: Translated by Julie Tomberlin Weber. Addressed to: Revd. Theodore Schulz, Salem, North Carolina. Postmark: Spring Place, C.N., Aug. 26. Free. H. G. Clauder, Post Master. Received Sept. 5.]

Spring Place, Cher. Nat., Aug. 25, 1832

Dearly beloved Br. Schulz,

I received your kind letter of the 2nd of this month, along with *Monatliche Nachrichten*, 8 days ago today on the 18th. We are currently all in good health, for which we want to be sincerely grateful to our dear Lord whose help and support delight us.

We are also encouraged to continue faithfully in our calling despite the prevailing difficulties, since we still see signs of the Holy Spirit's work in the hearts of some Cherokees. This is especially the case with 2 young women who have requested the bath of holy baptism since my last letter to you. One of these individuals is the daughter of our Sr. Sophia Carolina, who was educated in Brainerd and was married to the Indian James

Sanders in 1829 or '30 by Br. Byhan. She seems to be seriously concerned about her eternal well-being. The other is our Peggy, Br. Samuel's daughter, who was educated completely by us and at that time was distinguished from the other children by her quiet, serious nature. The admonitions which she often received from us, as well as from her father, did not remain without fruit in her heart, and some days ago she told Sr. Clauder that she also wanted to join the people of God through holy baptism and to belong to the Savior.

This week I visited in Ochgelogy. It turned out that the news about the mission place being rented out by Wm. Hicks to a Georgian was completely unfounded. Wm. Hicks did not know anything about this and assured me that he was not intending to do anything like this. During our conversation I also discussed with him the on-going circumstances. Wm. Hicks wants to purchase the place from us. In my opinion, it is the safest thing to let him have it, since it can be expected that it will be taken next winter by the individual who gets it in the coming Lottery if we have not previously given up our claim to it.

I do not know for sure yet what will happen with our place at Spring Place. I am often worried about this. The Lottery will be held in October, and it is said Gov. Lumpkin will distribute the grants to those who win the lots without distinction or special consideration.

By the way, it is completely impossible to make a single prediction about what the Cherokees will do in the latest case, because there has been indescribable confusion and chaos since the Council. The treaty party is trying in many ways to raise itself up and get the majority of the people to join it.

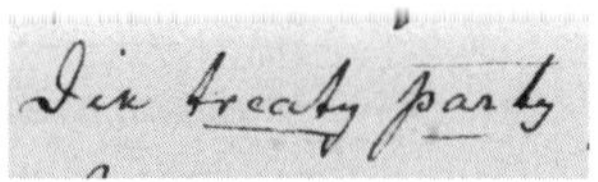

Sr. Sussannah Watee is near her end. She might perhaps suffer for 3 or at most 4 more weeks now. My visit there (in company with Geo. Hicks) was a very pleasant one. Her peace and quiet is a good model to observe. Her comments show the blessed state of her heart and with what joy she looks toward the goal of her faith. We sang a few verses and prayed at her bed. Dear old Christian David is able to get around again with the help of crutches. His leg is still very weak and not completely healed yet.

Some weeks ago I received a long letter from Mr. Hallock the Secretary of the American Tract Society in New York, with the news that that the society has given Br. Schweinitz the sum of $200 to support the circulation of tracts to the Brethren's mission stations. Mr. H. promises me he will assist the people among whom I have the grace to work by contributing money, or through tracts when it is requested, to spread the word of the Cross. After thorough consideration and discussion with Elias Boudinot, I believe I can do some good in this manner, that is, through the circulation of tracts in the Cherokee language. And so I want to ask you to write to Br. Schweinitz about this and ask if a sum of about $30 from the contribution of the American Tr. Soc. can be obtained to have an order of about 2,000 copies of an evangelistic Tract printed, that is, translated into Cherokee.

The desire of Cherokees for texts in their language is very great. The speed at which they learn characters and can then immediately read is amazing. There are known cases in which Cherokees learned their letters in the brief span of 3 hours and could then also read their language. The great desire for texts is not limited to the Cherokees here. Mr. Boudinot told me that several days ago he received an order from Arkansas for 600 copies of the Gospel of Matthew. Mr. Boudinott is no longer editor of the *Phönix* now, and he wants to spend his time translating. He told me that he would translate an instructive text into Cherokee without payment as soon as someone asks him to do so. It is known that the few Cherokee writings which we have thus far have been very beneficial, and I absolutely agree with Mr. Boudinot's comment that "a Cherokee tract has done more good in a short time than 4 missionaries can accomplish in a long period of time."

On the 12th of this month I sent a long letter along with my cash account by way of Knoxville, and I hope you have received this by now. Since then, I have received approximately $80 in cash, first from Mr. Ellsworth in Brainard $50 for the small mare which Clayton brought here 6 years ago and for which we had little work and even less feed. And Mr. Boudinott paid me $32 in full for his note. Since I expect a letter from you with the mail today, I will not close this until after the arrival of the mail.

4 P.M. I just received your letter of the 11th of this month with both notes enclosed. In my opinion the fact that the Indian Solomon held the first service on Pentecost is no reason to accuse him of self-righteousness or arrogance, since he, as little as any other Indian, will not believe he was especially honored. I know that I have the prerogative to hold the first service on holy days or usual Sundays, but I did not believe I was giving away anything special when I found it appropriate, due to circumstances, to ask an Indian Brother who possessed the appropriate grace and gift to do this. From my diary of June 10th you will see that there was no interpreter here on that day, and so I could not hold a special holy day talk as usual, since I had few English listeners. If the Indian Brn. and Srs. can improve themselves through singing and praying in their language, I do not want to hinder them, and it is more appropriate to occupy them in this manner than to have them spend the time sitting on the porches of our house and talking and laughing until the usual hour for services (11) strikes.

On this occasion I must repeat the old request: "come and see." It has been 6 years now since a Brother from the P.H.C. visited here. Since then, there have been many and great changes here which cannot be very accurately described with a quill any more than the special circumstances which often take place. More in the future.

Greet the dear Brn. of the P.H.C., as well as my dear parents. My handwriting has gotten bad in my haste, so I must ask for patience. Finally I commend myself and mine and the work here to your further prayer, and I remain your poor fellow Laborer,

H. G. Clauder

I presume you do not have any Georgia newspapers available, so I am sending you mine from time to time.

[*Records: N.C.*, 8:4050: Bethabara Diary. Translated by Douglas L. Rights.]

Aug. 26. After Br. and Sr. Byhan had received their call to the pastorate of the Bethabara congregation, Br. Byhan preached the introductory sermon here to a large congregation. Toward evening he went back to Salem.

[*Records: N.C.*, 8:4048: Aeltesten Conferenz, meeting in Salem. Translated by Douglas L. Rights.]

Aug. 29. The single Sr. Nancy Becker, formerly of Friedland, who for some years assisted Br. and Sr. Byhan faithfully and diligently in the Cherokee Mission, asks for permission to join the congregation here and to be received into the Choir House of the Single Srs., where she would be busy with all kinds of handwork. Since she was born in Salem, Conference has no objection.

[B 61-3: Provinzial Helfer Conferenz, meeting in Salem. Translated by C. Daniel Crews.]

Tues., Sept. 6. From a letter from our Br. G. H. Clauder dated the 25th of last month and received yesterday we learn, as the report is there, of the speedy move of the Lottery winners over the surveyed land of the Cherokee Nation, and that the Governor himself is going to issue grants to all the single plots bought through this on the built-on land and the portions cultivated by the Cherokees. This disturbs Br. Clauder very much in regard to our two mission places. This raises the question: "Would it not be better to sell our houses and improvements to Indians?" Br. William Abr. Hicks would be willing to buy the ones in Ochgelogy.

However, because we began this mission with the permission and support of the General Government, as well as with the agreement of the Cherokee Nation, and it is hardly to be doubted that in case of the moving away of the Indians to the West the

Genl. Government will reimburse us for our improvements and the Cherokees as well, we may negotiate only with the Genl. Government and the Cherokee Nation. Thus our opinion in all our negotiations is to keep this steadfastly in mind: Not to get mixed up in dealing with individual Indians concerning our houses, etc. Such dealing is contrary both to the existing Cherokee laws and to their treaties with our Government. Through these, individual Cherokees are supposed to have reason to make their dwelling places more secure against the wishes of the United States Government, or if they do depart through full compensation for those improvements, for which the Government itself is to provide a part, they are not to be taken unjust advantage of. Br. Schulz is to give Br. Clauder clear information about this and seek to reassure him.

[M 407-2: Springplace Diary.]

Sun., Aug. 26. It rained heavily the entire day, so that no one could come to our services.

Aug. 28. There visited us a young preacher named Adams, who had previously worked among the Chickasaw Indians but now is employed by the American Sunday School Union in the southwestern states establishing Sunday schools. On the following day he visited our school and held a very impressive talk for the scholars, who listened to him very attentively.

Sun., Sept. 2. In the last service was the wedding of a young Indian couple who are connected with the Methodists.

Sun., Sept. 9. There was a heathen ballplay near us. In the evening a number of Indians passed by here, some of them drunk and with noise and yelling. However, we were not further disturbed by them, although they camped close to our spring. Drinking and heathen games have been taking place near us almost every Sunday for some time already ([added by another writer:] since the laws of the Cherokee Nation have been invalidated by Georgia).

Sept. 12. I (Br. Clauder) visited our famous friend Butrick at

Candys Creek about 40 miles from here. The following day was the beginning of services which were supposed to continue there 4 days in a row. The people who attend these services had constructed numerous small houses and huts close to the meeting house, in which they lived for these days. On this day there was a prayer hour first. In the afternoon Mr. Adams preached through an interpreter, and in the evening by light Br. Clauder preached on the words of Jesus from Mark 8:2: I have compassion on the multitude.

[M 415-2-19: Translated by Julie Tomberlin Weber. Addressed to: Revd. Theodore Schulz, Salem, North Carolina. Postmark: Spring Place, C.N., Sept. 18. H. G. Clauder, Post Master. Received Oct. 6.]

Spring Place, Sept. 17, 1832

Dear Br. Schulz,

With the last mail I received your kind letter of Aug. 28th along with the enclosure of 2 odes dated the 21st and $160 cash, and I thank you sincerely for this. We are all enjoying our usual health and until now we have been able to continue with the school and mission work in external and internal peace and quiet.

On the 21st my wife and I are planning to visit the Brn. and Srs. in the Chatoogeta area and, the Lord willing, preach there. It is an Indian settlement, and the straw fire that was lit there some years ago by the Methodists has long been extinguished. Br. Samuel lives in that same neighborhood and is trying to be effective among his countrymen. Next week I am planning to return to Och____y and preach there and serve Holy Communion to the few dear communicants there. Poor Sr. Watee is still here below, according to the most recent news, and is suffering terribly.

On the 30th of this month the baptism of the adult Peggy, daughter of Br. Samuel, will take place here. She was formerly a scholar in Ochgelogy, and immediately after our arrival here she came back along with her 2 sisters Anny and Charlotte and is helping with the work.

Last week, at our Brother Butrick's repeated invitation, I visited at Candy's Creek, about 20 miles northwest of McNair's. A so-called 4-day meeting was taking place there, which was favorably distinguished from a Methodist Camp Meeting in that there was no confusion and deafening noise. I could spend only one day there, because the Saturday postal work here requires my presence. In the evening before my departure from there I had an opportunity to give witness to the Savior of sinners' mercy, during which I was assisted by an excellent interpreter.

There have been some changes in the postal work here, because of which the business is no longer as complicated as it used to be. The Georgia mail now comes on Saturdays at 10 A.M. instead of 3 P.M. and leaves again immediately for Head of Coosa, from where it returns Monday evenings and then departs for Georgia Tuesday morning. And so I have a chance to answer letters with Tuesday's mail. This arrangement will last only until the new year, however. Then stages from Georgia and East Tennessee are supposed to meet here 2 times a week. It is said the road between Coosawaytee and the Chatahoochie River on the Georgia post road is supposed to be improved soon and made suitable for a stage, and then will have occasional passengers, and so will put this burden on our backs. God alone knows what things will look like by then in this country, because if Georgia really draws for the land and divides it among her citizens, the one who receives this Lott will certainly do his best to take it if there is still a prospect of it being a profitable stage establishment. However, I have hope that Georgia will not draw for the land and the lottery will be postponed for some time until after the presidential Election.

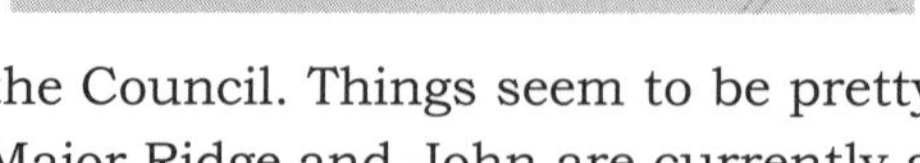

In 3 weeks there will be another gathering of the Council. Things seem to be pretty quiet among the Indians. Major Ridge and John are currently at the Creek Council.

I already informed you in my last letter that Wm. Hicks still occupies our place in Oochgelogy alone and wished to purchase it. I would really like to get your views and instructions. My opinion is that the best thing would be to sell the place to Wm. Hicks.

Greet my dear parents as well as Henry A. Schulz. His letter of Aug. 27th arrived with the last post. Remember all of us in your prayers and especially your poor, faithfully obliged Brother,

H. G. Clauder

[M 407-2: Springplace Diary.]

Sept. 21. Br. and Sr. Clauder visited our Brethren and Sisters and friends in Chatoogeta. Through Br. Samuel, Br. Clauder had announced a service there. So that we would not get lost on the way to his home, Samuel had sent his son here yesterday evening to serve us as guide. This morning it rained a little, but we confidently began our visiting journey in the hope that the rain would soon be over. Unfortunately, it turned out otherwise, and we were completely soaked a long time before we arrived at Samuel's. However, we found a dry little house there and a good fire by which we could dry our clothes. After an hour we went to the meeting house built by Indians, about a mile farther, and found about 10 Indians there despite the heavy and continuing rain. I gave a talk for them about the bliss which God's children enjoy here already. Samuel's son, Flea, a former scholar in the school here, served as interpreter during this. In the evening we returned home alone with the sincere desire that the Lord might let our visit with these Cherokees be a blessing to them.

[M 415-2-20: Translated by Julie Tomberlin Weber. Addressed to: Revd. T. Schulz, Salem, North Carolina. Postmark: Spr. Place, C.N., Sept. 23. Free. H. G. Clauder, Post Master. Received Oct. 3.]

Spring Place, Ch.N., Sept. 22
10 o'clock A.M.

Dear Br. Schulz,

With the mail this morning I received your kind letter of the 6th of this month, and I am hurrying to send you a few lines with tomorrow's Knoxville mail reporting that I received your kind letter of July 31st as an enclosure to some *Missionary Intel.* and also one dated Aug. 4th along with *Monatliche Nachrichten* and a counterfeit $10 N.C. I just exchanged this $10 note with Mr. John Martin through the post rider, who brought me another note for it this morning. In my letter of the 18th [17th] which I had sent via Washington, Ga. (a new distributing P.O.), I informed you of the receipt of the said letter as well as the one of Aug. 28th with $160, which arrived here 8 days earlier.

I was very happy and grateful to learn the thorough and good views of the P.H.C. regarding the Ochgelogy place, with today's mail, since I have to visit there next week and thus can give Ab. Hicks clear information about his request. I will follow your thoughts precisely, although my views were originally different from these and I believed that the sale of those improvements would protect the mission from loss. I do believe the views of the P.H.C. are better and will avoid all suspicion by the Cherokees and also will not interfere with our further usefulness among them. Wm. Hicks is very much under the influence of his son Eli, who does not mind small or large fraud when he has the opportunity, and if he or his father cannot buy that place I fear they will attempt to make it theirs.

Perhaps next week I will send you the report which the Secretary of War requested. The old accounts that are here are so confused that I cannot compare them with the copies, and so I must rely on the latter alone, which are a great help to me.

I am very sorry that in my haste I led you to assume that your comments about my Diary of June 10th were not accepted in the spirit of Brotherly love, and I trust that your love for me will bring you to excuse this mistake which I cannot excuse and which I sincerely regret. In the future I will try to be clearer in my Diary in order to avoid misunderstandings.

Yesterday it rained heavily the entire day while my wife and I were visiting Samuel in Chatoogeta. The path was so overgrown with hedges and bushes that we could not use an umbrella. I had my overcoat, and my wife had a coat and wool hat. We were completely soaked long before we arrived there, but we found a good fire there where we were able to dry out. Samuel is better off than we had assumed. We found a good dry log cabin lined with clapboard inside, beds on proper bedsteads, good chairs and a walnut wood table, iron fire dogs and shovels, all made by Cherokee craftsmen, even a spacious horse stall where our horses were taken to dry, which is unusual among the Cherokees.

After we had enjoyed a good lunch we went to the meeting house one mile from Samuel's home, which was built by the neighbors without assistance or support and is open for missionaries of all confessions. It is a spacious house of studded logs, built to last, and it even has a high pulpit which one needs long legs to ascend. Instead of benches there are cut logs on which the listeners sat while I delivered a sermon through Flea (Samuel's son). In the evening we returned home in all the rain and were soon happily by a good fire remembering our wet visit in Chattoogeta.

We lost a significant part of our feed corn because of the rain. It was lying on the field when it began to rain. I really doubt if we will get enough corn to make it through one year. Our crop is not very good.

Along with a sincere greeting for the Brethren of the P.H.C., I commend myself to your prayer, and I remain your loving, poor fellow Brother,

H. G. Clauder

[M 407-2: Springplace Diary.]

Sun., Sept. 23. Once again we had conversations with Aggy Sanders (a single person) who had helped us in our household work a number of months ago. She had already ignored a number of warnings she received, and although she was often moved on such occasions to tears, the impression seemed to have no lasting impact. Therefore, it gave us special pleasure when we learned already last Sunday that she wanted to speak with us, as she was now seriously worried about her condition. And so today we also found cause to believe that she is an object of the work of grace of the Holy Spirit, since she now gave a contrite confession with many tears and asked for the waters of holy baptism. We were happy to accept her among the baptismal candidates.

Sept. 26. I went to Ochgelogy for the purpose of preaching the following morning and celebrating Holy Communion with the communicants there. Because of the heavy rains, however, which had begun the previous night, no one could come to the services. The following day, the 28th of this month, I returned home.

Sun., Sept. 30. We had the joy of baptizing one of our adult scholars, Br. Samuel's daughter, into Jesus' death with the name Eliza Louisa. Our Saal was completely filled with listeners on this occasion. At this event as well as at the enjoyment of Holy Communion with our communicants which followed, a sweet feeling of the presence of Jesus prevailed. During this many hearts melted in tears. May the Lord make us, his weak tools, worthy to spend more days here like today, to His honor.

[M 415-2-21: Translated by Julie Tomberlin Weber. No address; no postmark.]

Spring Place, C.N., Oct. 1, 1832

Dear Br. Schulz,

Yesterday we experienced the sweet feeling of Jesus' love and presence as we rejoiced over the baptism of our adult scholar Peggy Samuel into Jesus' death, with the name Eliza Louisa. The Saal was completely filled on this occasion with attentive listeners, some of whom were emotional, including our neighbor Vann's wife Jinny. This person has already shown us much friendship since we have been here and attends the services every Sunday and seems to have good impressions. She often stands at the point of renouncing the world and its vanities and becoming Jesus' property, but unfortunately something holds her back from such a step. Jesus and His salvation are not yet more important to her than everything else. However, we hope that in the end God's Spirit will succeed in winning her heart completely for the Savior.

A healing spiritual change also seems to have been brought through God's Spirit in Aggy Sanders, who caused us more than a little worry and aggravation last summer. She has attended services diligently since we dismissed her last June. 14 days ago her mother acquainted us with her situation, and at the first opportunity we had a thorough and frank talk with her. She really regretted having used her time so poorly and with many tears declared her remorse over her sinful state. Then with warm hearts we directed her to Jesus and His salvation and merits. She is now one of the candidates for baptism.

My visit in Ochgelogy last week was rendered pointless by the heavy rains, because of which no one could come to the service. I also visited Sr. Watee, who is still here below but is hurrying rapidly toward her end. On my return journey I spent the night with Mrs. Worcester in Echota, who had returned from visiting her husband in Milledgeville Ga., the previous day. It is expected that as soon as the land lottery is over, the 2 poor imprisoned missionaries will be released unconditionally. Worcester and Butler were both well and received many signs of

Mitleiden von dem Gefängnißwärtern,

sympathy from the prison guards, who allow them as much freedom as possible in their circumstances.

We are having a cold and gloomy fall day today, so that one really needs a fire in the sitting room. Next week there will be another meeting of the Council. I am planning to attend it. It is said Gen. Corrol from Tennessee will come for it as Jackson's designated Treaty commissioner.

Today I still have to finish the quarterly post account. This and the other usual business require me to make this report hastily and briefly, since the post leaves here tomorrow.

I am enclosing the report required by Sec. Cass, which you will send on, since he wants to have it by the first of November.

I commend myself to your further prayer as your unworthy,

H. G. Clauder

Excuse my bad handwriting this time.

[*Records: N.C.*, 8:4050: Bethabara Diary.]

Oct. 14. At the morning service the diary of Ochgeloogy for the year 1831 was read.

[M 407-2: Springplace Diary.]

Oct. 9. I (Br. Clauder) went to McNair's to receive a gift of 5 bushels of wheat, which Mr. McNair had given us. The following day, however, it rained very heavily, so that I could not go home, and so I had to wait there until

Oct. 11 before I could begin my journey home. The streams were still very flooded, and while crossing a creek 5 miles from Spring Place the wagon was almost thrown over by the torrential current, and some time passed before I was finally able to get safely across. In the meantime it turned night and new difficulties arose. Once I completely missed the road and got lost in the bush, and already thought I would have to spend the inclement night there without fire or food. But then it pleased the One who gives clouds, air and wind, makes roads and paths, to let the light of the moon break forth. After this I soon found my way and reached Spring Place at half past 8 in the evening.

Oct. 12. It rained very hard again the whole day. In the evening the missionaries Butrick and Proctor came and spent the night with us.

Oct. 16 and 17. I visited the Council on business and had the opportunity of seeing and speaking with many of our Brethren and Sisters there who live far away. The proceedings of the Council were of no particular importance, although 2 commissioners from the U.S. government were there and tried to move the Cherokees to a treaty to emigrate to Arkansas.

1832, part 5

[M 415-2-22: Translated by Julie Tomberlin Weber. Addressed to: Revd. Theodore Schulz, Salem, No. Car. Postmark: Spr. Place, C.N., Oct. 21. Free. H. G. Clauder, P.M. Received Oct. 31.]

Spring Place, C.N., Oct. 20, 1832

Dear Brother Schulz,

On the 7th of this month your last two letters dated the 18th and 24th arrived here, the first as an enclosure to the most recent *Wöchentliche Nachrichten*. I would have reported receiving your kind letters earlier, but I did not find the appropriate time and also because I wanted to let the Council reach its end so I could give you news from it. This meeting has not yet concluded, but it is not expected that anything of importance will take place. Mr. Chester and Col. Montgomery are there and pushing for a reconsideration of the earlier propositions for a treaty, which are known to you, but in vain. The head chief and a few of the others are still showing the most stubborn steadfastness, to the obvious harm and ruin of the lower class of the people. In the meantime, the time is approaching when the lottery for the distribution of the land will begin, after which the settlement of the white people will begin without recourse.

Major Hardin, one of the former enrolling agents, stopped in here yesterday for an hour. I asked him the question about what would happen with our improvements here at Spring Place, since 2 or 3 lots on which our fields partially extend are connected with the improvements of our neighbor Vann. Under these circumstances he thinks the future owner of these lots would have no claim to them as long as Vann owns the fields bordering ours. However, Vann has a large piece of land, and it is probable that soon a Law will be passed which will reduce all Cherokees to a mere competency of land, and thus many of them will lose their fields. The Georgia law protects only Indian improvements, all the rest will be given to the owner designated by the lottery without consideration. Otherwise, the Cherokees agree more and more that their stay here will soon come to an end, and if Jno. Ross would think of the well-being of the people (instead of his own interests), he would take the advice of the last Cherokee delegation and others and save his Nation from unavoidable ruin.

The Ochgelogy improvements will be taken by white people very soon, without a doubt.

This week I paid a brief visit at the Council but found little there to interest me, nor could I learn what the negotiations were.

With the exception of our little Ann Eliza, our usual health continues. Her sickliness seems to come from slow teething.

We are now busy harvesting the corn. I doubt if we will get more than 300 bushels. If we should have as large a family to feed again next year as we had this summer, I will have to buy corn again, and that seems to be very costly.

For this reason I want to raise the question whether we should not try to reduce the number of scholars, or if we will continue regardless of the costs, as previously? We sometimes feel almost hopeless when we consider what misery and unavoidable ruin the Cherokees are quickly approaching, and that our efforts to educate their growing youth and to civilize them promise to be as fruitless as a battle against the wind and storms. The good seed which is scattered here cannot flourish here under the current circumstances, and the plants which are greening so nicely here and there will wilt again like shucks, I fear, and die an eternal death.

Our Br. Boudinott recently expressed his thoughts in the following sad words to me: "If the Cherokees remain here, their

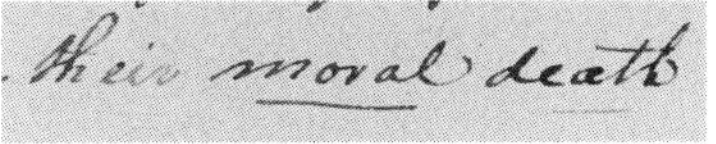

moral death will be as certain as a natural death is to you & me."

On the occasion of my visit at the Council, I extended your greetings to Major Ridge, who still remembers you very well, as well as Henry, who visited here in 1828. He also asked about Br. Steiner and asked me to extend his greetings to you and Henry and Father Steiner. His inner spiritual change can be seen in a sweet manner, and he does not appear to be far from his brother, Christian David Oatee, in humility.

Next week Mr. Boudinott and I will select the little tract that will appear in print. He thinks "something of the narrative kind would be easiest translated & increase the desire of reading among the Cherokees."[1] Since the American Tract Society has helped us with the means, it seems appropriate to make a selection from their publications, which are all evangelical and not sectarian. Mr. Boudinott, who knows the taste of the Cherokees better than I, suggested the well-known tract, *Sarah, the Poor Indian Woman*, for translation. This selection seems completely appropriate to me. The Easter Litany is actually incomparable, but it would not be as easy to understand and interesting to the common people as that moving story. Besides the translation would be much more difficult.

However, this is just preliminary.

Thank you for all of the news items you shared. Greet the dear Brn. of the P.H.C. from all of us. Sr. D. Ruede went along to the Council and found much of interest there. Last week I visited at McNair's. He gave us a gift of 5 bushels of wheat. Some weeks ago a panther (feminine gender) that was quite large was killed in the area there. In the *Southern Recorder* of Oct. 11, you will see 2 articles of importance, Maj. Curry's account of his expedition to the Arkansaw Cherokee Country & something about the Land lottery.

Along with sincere greetings, I remain your loving, poor fellow Brother,

H. G. Clauder

---

1 The quote is in English in the original German manuscript.

[M 407-2: Springplace Diary. Translated by Julie Tomberlin Weber. Handwriting is Heinrich Gottlieb Clauder's.]

Sun., Oct. 21. First was the sermon on Phil. 2:5, which Dazizi interpreted and was attended by a significant number of reverent listeners. Afterward was the baptism of the child of our Br. and Sr. James and Rossanna, with the name George. This evening Br. Clauder was informed through a couple of lines from Elias Boudinott of the blessed homegoing of his mother, our Sr. Sussannah Charity Watee in Ochgelogy, with the request that he take care of her burial on the following day.

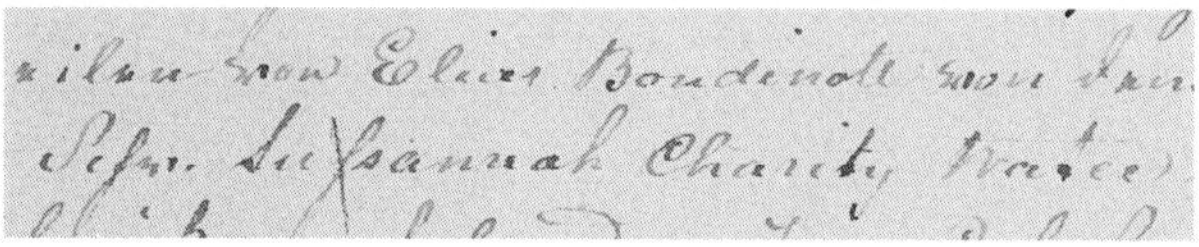

Oct. 22. Br. Clauder left for there very early during heavy rains which continued 3 to 4 hours, and arrived at sundown at the home of the now departed one. It was the family's wish that the body not be taken to the grave until the following day, but signs of rapid decay made it necessary to hold the burial right away. The grave was about a mile from the house, on a hill where the bones of many of the family rest. And so it got completely dark by the time the wagon arrived there with the body and the rest of the company all on horse. First a fire was made and torches were lit. Then everything was gotten into appropriate order. After some verses were sung and a prayer, Br. Clauder spoke on Heb. 4:9, "There remaineth therefore a rest to the people of God," which Elias Boudinot (son of the deceased) repeated sentence for sentence in Cherokee. Then the body of our now deceased, resting Sister was laid in her earthen bed during the praying of the Burial Litany. The whole train of people stayed at the place until the grave was filled with earth. Then everyone returned quietly and orderly, as far as such is possible on horse by night. It was a remarkable sight to see such a gathering of people at such an hour of the night in the wild bush. The cause and purpose of this, as well as all the circumstances associated with this, were especially suited to bring about healing reflections and impressions.

Oct. 23. I visited many of our Brn. and Srs. and friends in the Ochgelogy area. Some of them still gather on Sundays at the mission place and edify themselves with reading, singing, and prayer. Their numbers are often not more than two or three. Sr. Hicks said on such an occasion when only three were together the feeling of the presence of Jesus which prevailed during this was still impressive, and when Watee sang some verses alone, it was no different than if many tongues had joined in.

Oct. 24. A few came to the service there, where they were encouraged to continue looking to the Lord, to remain as faithful to Him as their redeemer and payment for sins, and to love Him above everything. William Abr. Hicks seems to be completely sunk in earthly chaos and separates himself completely from his family. All the warnings given until now remain without fruit, and instead of leaving his dark ways of error, he seems to get deeper into them. May God's Spirit touch him again powerfully. After the service I began my return journey to Spring Place in the company of both Indians Dikuyiski and U-kill-a-nieka. The latter is taking his young daughter Lissy home from our school for several weeks to visit. It is noticeable that he also gives us hope that he is an object of the work of grace of the Holy Spirit.

Oct. 25. General Newnan from Georgia passed by here on his way to Washington. He stayed here for an hour and took some refreshments. He assured us that we would not be disturbed in the possession of this post by the division of Cherokee land among the citizens of Georgia. However, it later turned out to be the opposite. See Diary of 1st Jan. 1833.

[M 415-2-23: Transcribed by Grace S. Robinson. Addressed to Theodore Shulze, Esq., Salem, N.C. Post stamp illegible. Postmark: War Department, Lew Cass; Office of Indian Affairs, Elbert Herring. Free.]

Department of War
Office Indian Affairs
Oct. 27, 1832

Sir,

I have the honor to acknowledge the receipt of your letter of the 20th inst to the Secretary of War, enclosing the School Report of Revd. H. G. Clauder of Spring Place, Georgia.

I am instructed to say that the report is altogether satisfactory; that the Secretary of War cherishes for the institution the kindest feelings, believing it to be under judicious management and therefore very useful; and that the former allowance of $250 toward supporting the establishment will be continued. With high respect, Your hubl. svt.,

Elbert Herring

To Theodore Shulze, Esq., Salem, N.C.

[M 415-2-24: Translated by Julie Tomberlin Weber. Addressed to: Revd. Theodore Schulz, Salem, North Carolina. Postmark: Spr. Place, C.N., Oct. 30. Free. H. G. Clauder, P.M. Received Nov. 10.]

Spring Place, C.N., Oct. 29, 1832

Dear Brother Schulz,

With these few lines, written in great haste, I wanted to inform you that I received your kind letter of the 13th of this month, along with the 3rd booklet of printed *Gemein Nachrichten* and to thank you for these.

It pleased our dear Lord to complete in blessing our Sr. Sussannah Watee, after a long illness, on the 21st of this month. I was informed of this on the evening of that same day through a couple of lines from her son E. Boudinott, with the request to take care of her burial. And so I set out on the road very early on the 22nd in a heavy rain, which I never got out of, to Watee's home 35 miles from here. My overcoat served excellently during this, but I missed having a good Umbrella! At sunset I arrived there at the last minute, so to speak, to attend the burial, since the corpse was quickly deteriorating, and it had to be buried that evening. You will see the rest in the Diary, which I will soon copy to send you.

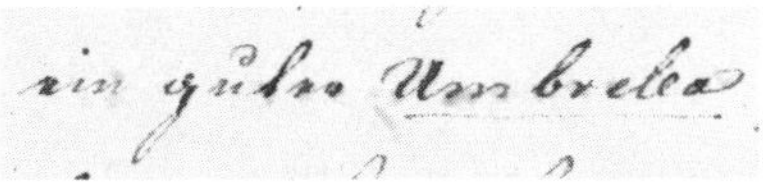

We are now busy bringing in our corn and are very overwhelmed with work. I am planning to go to Ochgellogy with a wagon tomorrow to pick up most of the things we had left there. Wm. A. Hicks is seldom there. Both his daughters who kept house there are gone, and he stays with his son Eli most of the time, where he gets his food. But he always spends the night at our place. Things keep getting worse for him. He has completely separated from his wife. I fear he will come to a bad end, but I will continue to hope the best and not tire of admonishing him lovingly as well as I can.

Genl. Newnan was here last week on his way to Washington. He accepted some refreshment and was very friendly. He gave us good hope that we will not be disturbed in our possession of this post after the division of the land. He said he had personally spoken with Gov. Lumpkin about us and that he is very well inclined toward us as Moravians. We leave this entire matter up to the one wise and just Lord and put little hope in humans. The Lord will protect His work and guide it as He wants to.

It is a great joy and encouragement to us that our dear Lord has once again given approval to serve two persons with holy baptism at our next Holy Communion on the 25th of Nov., the married Dorcas Sanders, previously Fields, and Aggy Sanders, who seems to be thoroughly changed and we hope converted. We are also expecting two new baptismal candidates, a man and wife from the Ochgelogy area who seem to have been thoroughly awakened through the efforts of Watee.

We have much cause to thank the Lord for the health we all continue to enjoy. Along with sincere greetings to my parents and your dear family, I remain your sincerely loving, obliged Brother,

H. G. Clauder

[*Records: N.C.*, 8:4056: Bethania Diary. Translated by Douglas L. Rights.]

Nov. 8. This was election day for electors. Rainy weather kept many voters away. Of the few votes the majority was for Jackson.

Nov. 11. In addition to the preaching there was the reading of a report from Oochgelogehy on the "Oppression by Georgia," which threatens to end our mission among the Cherokees.

[M 407-2: Springplace Diary.]

Oct. 30. I went to Ochgelogy with our wagon to collect various things we had left there last year.

Oct. 31. I returned safely home.

Sun., Nov. 4. Only a few Brethren and Sisters arrived here, since a number of them have recently gone to the gold mines by the Vally Towns.

Nov. 10. One of our young scholars experienced a special protection of his life when a heavy but overloaded wagon went over his body without seriously harming him. The Lord blessed the household remedy we used so that the child was completely recovered in a few weeks.

Nov. 16. I went to Chatoogata again and preached on John 3:16,17 before a small number of Cherokees who were very attentive. I also passed out a number of Cherokee Litany booklets and found willing takers.

Nov. 24. In the evening many of our Brn. and Srs. came for tomorrow's services at our place, so that we had our hands full. During the night some blankets in the girls' room caught on fire while some children were sleeping under them. Luckily some of the Indian Sisters who were sleeping in the upper part of the house were awakened because of the smoke, through which the threatening misfortune was prevented.

Sun., Nov. 25. Two persons joined Christ's Gemeine through the waters of holy baptism. As usual on such occasions our Saal was filled with listeners. Those being baptized joyfully answered the usual questions in the English language. During the enjoyment of Holy Communion in the second service, a sweet feeling could be sensed and our dear Brn. and Srs. seemed to be very deeply happy in this pasture for souls.

Currently there are many white people from Georgia here in Cherokee country who are looking for their lots, which have been awarded them in the current land lottery. They are very rude and often offensive, especially toward the poor Indians, who tolerate everything with exemplary composure.

[M 415-2-25: Translated by Julie Tomberlin Weber. Addressed to: Revd. Theodore Schulz, Salem, North Carolina. Postmark: Spr. Place, Ga., Nov. 27. Free. H. G. Clauder, P.M. Received Dec. 15.]

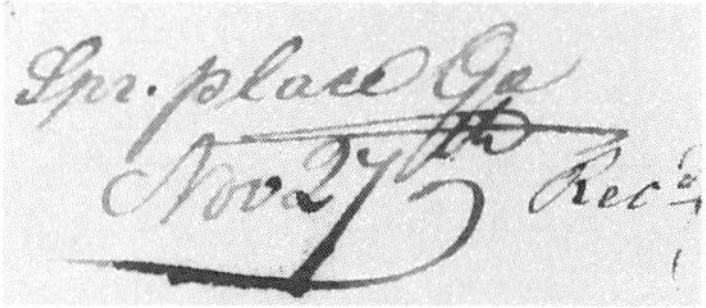

Spring Place, C.N., Nov. 26, 1832

Dearly beloved Brother Schulz,

Yesterday we were delighted to receive your kind letter of the 13th with the Knoxville mail as an enclosure to the *Missionary Intelligencer,* and we have heeded it since then in the services. The holy baptism service which I mentioned in an earlier letter and for which you had extended your best wishes for blessings had just taken place when the post brought us your dear letter. We can and must acknowledge with grateful joy that this opportunity served to touch hearts and to encourage our brown flock, which was here in pretty good numbers, including Sr. McNair, who seemed to be very well for the first time since we have been here.

You can register the names of the individuals who were baptized in your Catalogue as: 1st, Agatha Sanders, daughter of our Br. and Sr. Richard Daniel and Salome Elizabeth Sanders, and 2nd, Dorcas Sanders, previously Fields, wife of James Sanders, and daughter of our Sr. Sophia Carolina. This last person, Sophia Car., could not be present for the baptism of her daughter Dorcas because of illness. On such occasions we usually have the familiar and faithful Tazizi as interpreter. He visits us quite regularly, usually on Sundays, and always expresses joy at helping me as interpreter. No new baptismal candidates have talked with me since these 2 individuals who were baptized yesterday.

Otherwise, the progress of this congregation is overall pleasing. Until now we have not had disturbances of any kind. The Indian Sr. Agatha, who was accepted last July and against whom all sorts of accusations were made, such as adultery and drunkenness, attends services regularly, and all my inquiries to reach the truth of the matter have remained fruitless. I am more inclined to believe that she is innocent, which she always asserts with tears. Nor can I ever find the actual witness. Everything is just hearsay evidence. However, the matter did not cause any other disturbances among the rest of the Brn. and Srs.

Day after tomorrow I am planning to go to Ochgelogy and make another attempt to hold services there. I am almost ready to lose heart about visiting there during the week as previously. No one comes to services, and it seems pointless to me to make the long and extremely unpleasant trip there this time of year so frequently for nothing. Also I have plenty to keep me busy at home.

Last Saturday during the night we experienced the merciful protection of the Lord when some blankets in the girls' room in our new house caught on fire where the children were sleeping under them. Some of the Indian Sisters who were sleeping upstairs in the house smelled it, looked for and found the cause of it, and extinguished it without disturbing us in our sleep, and we did not learn about it until yesterday morning.

This matter seemed to us to be a finger pointing to our plan to let the children go home on the 2nd Sunday in Dec. during the coldest part of winter for a few weeks. We decided this yesterday, and the parents of the children were informed of this and gave their complete approval. At the other mission schools here in this country it is usual to have a vacation in August and September, but that time seemed like the most pleasant to us, and we kept the school going then with few interruptions and the children together, with the purpose of giving them an opportunity to go during the cold winter months and also to save us much work and to avoid all danger of fire here. Toward spring we will start holding school again — the Lord willing — because until then a lot concerning the circumstances of this people can change.

I did not expect my report to be well received by Sec. Cass, and I am joyfully grateful that it was, because I had little joy in preparing it, and I often secretly thought about the matter with fear. We had a visit last week from the Georgia land speculators, and we can probably expect more. This week I received no *Recorder*, and so I cannot know what is happening in the Legislature. We still have no white neighbors, although many lots in our neighborhood have been drawn. Unfortunately, it seems Jackson was elected again, so we would prefer to go to the other side of the Rocky Mountains with the Cherokees, so that we do not have to witness the demise of the Union!! The Constitution will probably be changed soon, so that Jackson can be president for life.

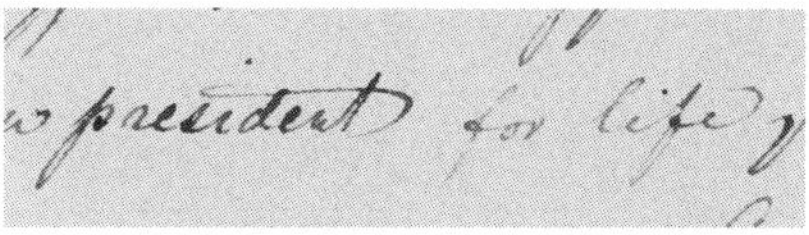

Greet my dear parents and all my friends, your faithfully obliged Brother,

H. G. Clauder

[M 407-2: Springplace Diary.]

Nov. 27. In the evening our Sr. Mrs. McNair returned here from Echota. She had visited her son-in-law there, David Vann, who is ill.

Nov. 28. I went to Ochgelogy and the following day held a service in our former house there. Afterward I began my return journey and arrived safely in Spring Place at 9 o'clock in the evening. During my absence the Flea, a former scholar here and son of our Br. Samuel, came here to spend the night. He engaged in such talk among the scholars, however, scolded and cursed us all, so that the children themselves came to Sr. Clauder and told her. So she told him that the sooner he left the better, which he did immediately to the joy of all those present. This young man was persuaded by a Methodist preacher to go with him to West Tennessee a couple of years after he had been dismissed from the school here because of bad behavior, to get further school instruction there. But during the last summer he ran away from there and came home without having learned anything good, but rather the godless ways of the whites.

Dec. 4. During the night an axe which was lying outside of our shop was stolen and the springhouse was broken into with this and some small articles of little worth taken from there. We suspect some white people who were camping close to our spring were the perpetrators. This country is being visited more and more by wandering white riffraff who amuse themselves with thievery and various kinds of dishonesty and oppress the poor Indians. We know of many cases where such white people have taken or killed the Indian's cattle before their eyes, and the latter did not dare claim their property.

The frequent rainy weather and resulting high streams in the last half of December made it impossible for our Brn. and Srs. to make it to the services on Sundays. On first Advent as on the two following Sundays, we held services with our scholars in our house.

Sun., Dec. 9. Most of our scholars went home for a while, because for various reasons we decided not to hold school during the most severe wintertime.

1832, part 6

[M 415-2-26: Translated by Julie Tomberlin Weber. Addressed to: Revd. T. Schulz, Salem, North Carolina. Postmark: Spr. Place, Ga., Dec. 18. Free. H. G. Clauder, P.M. Received Dec. 27.]

Spring Place, Dec. 15, 1832

Dearly beloved Br. Schulz,

With the post this morning I received a letter from Genl. Hardin dated Milledgeville, Nov. 30, and I will share its contents with you.

[Br. Clauder copies Gen. Hardin's letter in English:]

"Sir, I have taken the liberty of addressing you through the medium of this letter, though I have but a limited acquaintance with you. The cause arises from an inquiry you made of me when I called on you as I returned from the late council. It was in relation to the right of occupancy of those lots which had Indian improvements. That law remains yet unaltered. But from the surveyors' return the lot you reside on does not fall in the class of Indian improvements. The return only says & reports a Mission station. It is drawn by James Nix of Henry County. It is the only lot drawn as yet in that neighbourhood of any value," etc., etc.

[Br. Clauder continues his letter to Br. Schulz in German:]

I have not yet seen or heard anything from the current owner of this place, and therefore I am more than a little uncertain about what to do. The report of the surveyors is obviously very incomplete, because most of these lots are cultivated by our neighbor Vann as his property. Otherwise, you will also see from the *Recorder* that a deceiver was discovered among the Lottery commissioners and that he has been impeached, that the Land Lottery has been interrupted for this reason, and it is to be expected that the entire matter will have to be started again.

I ask you now to let me know your thoughts on this as soon as possible, whether I should begin correspondence with James Nix and inform him of the circumstances of our presence and that our lots were originally owned by James Vann, deceased, etc., and they are now completely connected with the fields of Jo. Vann according to the lines. Personally I am not inclined to undertake this negotiation. If the proprietor ever appears there will be time enough to give him the necessary explanations and learn from him what he plans to do. He will not be able to order me away before the Post Office is occupied anew. Mr. Vann told me that this man was here a long time ago and secretly looked over the place, but I cannot believe this since we cannot remember having seen anyone unfamiliar here.

We also are sorrowfully touched by the early homegoing of the dear and honorable Br. L. Benzien, about which we learned from a note from Br. Schaaf, also with today's mail. The ways of our good Lord are unfathomable. What else can we poor ones do but humbly surrender to them. The Gemeine has suffered a significant loss and is certainly generally convinced of this.

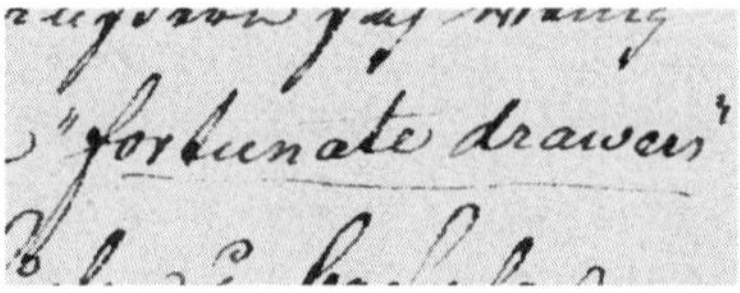

With the exception of insignificant colds, we are well. Last Sunday most of our scholars went home, and so we have had a chance to take care of some other necessary work. The translation of the little tract *Poor Sarah* will be started soon by Mr. Boudinott, and I am planning to go to Athens, T., day after tomorrow to pick up the paper needed for printing it. The Cherokees have said little since Jackson was re-elected. The so-called "fortunate drawers" of the land can be seen frequently; they are finding their lots and looking them over. In the meantime, there is a heavy emigration from Tennessee to the Creek country. Around here there are no new settlers.

With this I must close for now. Unfortunately my writing is barely legible since I cannot write as I would like to due to a lack of time and quiet. Greet the dear Brn. of the P.H.C. as well as your dear family and my dear parents. Your faithfully obliged Br.,

H. G. Clauder

P.S. I would like to ask you to have the amount of $2.50 sent to the publisher of the *New York Weekly Messenger*. This should have been sent long ago, but I neglected to do so. Mr. Vann will leave for Washington next week. In the meantime he is allowing me the use of his *Nat. Intelligencer*. I have not yet received Daily Texts for 1833, and I would like to ask for them, especially some English ones. I pray that the Lord might reveal Himself to you in the coming Christmas holy days, your friend and poor fellow Br.,

Clauder

[Br. Schulz writes:] Answered Dec. 30 & wrote to A. H. Shepperd, S. G. Mony.

[M 407-2: Springplace Diary. Translated by Julie Tomberlin Weber. Handwriting is Heinrich Gottlieb Clauder's.]

Dec. 16. Br. Clauder went from here to Tennessee to pick up some printing paper from there. This is supposed to be used for the publication of a small tract in the Cherokee language. Our friend Elias Boudinot is planning to begin the translation of this from English as soon as possible. Our scholar James Vann accompanied Br. Clauder on this journey and had an opportunity to see a number of things that were interesting to him.

Dec. 21. Br. Clauder returned home safely. In recent days we learned that in Pinelog settlement last week a white family consisting of a husband, wife, and her mother, and some children were killed by a fire in their home. Nothing of this horrible event was discovered until a number of days later when some people accidentally found the charred ashes and bones of the victims. There is strong suspicion toward some Indians, that they were the perpetrators, since they were not supposed to be in the best relationship with this white man, who by the way is supposed to have been a worthless person. Still until now nothing has been discovered. The Indians say that the whole family was drunk, the house caught on fire itself, and they had suffered misfortune in this way, which is also not unlikely.

Dec. 22. We had the first snow this winter. However, it did not stay long and on the following day

Sun., Dec. 23, it melted away completely. On this day we first edified ourselves in our family circle by singing some hymns from the German hymnal. At 12 o'clock many of our Indians had gathered. With them we prayed the Litany in English and Cherokee in our Saal. In the second service the Doctrinal Text for today, John 1:1, was discussed and then a young child of our neighbors and friends Joseph and Jane Vann was baptized into Jesus' death. The mother of the child, who does not belong to any church confession but almost always attends services here, said in a conversation we had with her about baptism that it is her earnest desire for her children to become the Savior's property. She knew well that if she brings her children for baptism she obligates herself to raise them as Christians through word and example, as far as it is within her power.

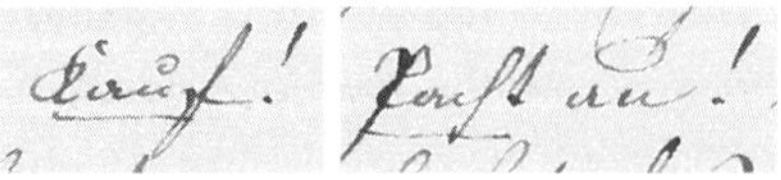

Dec. 24. This morning a man from Georgia came here and showed Br. Clauder a power of attorney which he claimed to have gotten from the person who received the Lott in the lottery on which Spring Place stands. With the most sinful curses and oaths he declared that he was now the owner of our place and offered to sell it to us! Or to lease it! And when he was given a negative answer, he demanded formal possession of it, which was also denied him on the basis that the laws protect all the private property of the Indians, and the largest part of this lot belongs to our neighbor Vann and is cultivated by him. This man saw that he could not do anything, and Br. Clauder told him we would not give up our property under any circumstances until we were forced to do so. And so he promised to send us a court official as soon as possible and

tried through all sorts of threats to achieve his wrongful plan. Finally he had to go away without accomplishing his purpose, but said that he will lease this place to whoever offers the most, and we would then be in an unpleasant situation, etc.

This whole matter worried us more than a little.

In the evening three more white men from Georgia came here and wanted night lodgings. We tried to send them to Vann's, since we had many of our Brethren and Sisters to take care of, who had come for tomorrow's Christmas Day celebration. However, they said they wished to speak with Br. Clauder about the person who had been here this morning. Then we let them dismount and provided them hospitality for payment, as well as we could. They told us that although the previously mentioned man belongs to the Baptists, he has a very bad character and is little respected in his homeland, and that we had done very well not to get involved with him at all.

We felt somewhat comforted by these people's words, but we could not get rid of the worrisome thoughts in order to rejoice as we would have wished with our dear ones in the Gemeine of the meritorious incarnation of our Savior. Before we went to bed and long after everyone else had gone to bed, however, we sat around our fire and threw a glance in spirit to the manger and the newly born Savior, and asked for ourselves a part in the blessing which His servants and followers in other places are enjoying on this evening.

[M 415-2-27: Translated by Julie Tomberlin Weber. Addressed to: Revd. Theodore Schulz, Salem, North Carolina. Postmark: Springplace, Ga., Dec. 25. Free. H. G. Clauder, P.M. Received Jan. 12, 1833.]

Spring Place, C.N., Dec. 24, 1832

Dear Br. Schulz,

At this time I have a matter of great importance to report, and I am more than a little concerned. My last letter to you contained the news that this place was drawn by a man, James Nix in Henry County. This morning his Agent came with appropriate power to look over the place, to rent it out or take possession of it. He assured me that the Governor of Georgia published his Grant, and that therefore the claims which our neighbor Vann has to this Lott at the same time no longer protect our possession of this improvement. I asked the man to wait a couple of weeks until I could get news from my Directors and that we might rent this place from the current owner, explained our entire situation to him and also that a Post Office is maintained here and that I could not leave this place under any circumstances until I have a successor in the Post Office. But he asked me punctiliously if I would give him possession of this place, and when I refused just as punctiliously (everything in the presence of 2 witnesses), he then said the law would have to give him possession of it, and I should prepare myself for the officers to dispossess me and to undergo an interrogation by a Court within a short time, etc.

Now I am prepared for the worst, and I expect no favors or protection. Certainly I would like it if all disputes before the Law could be avoided. But our neighbor Vann, who left for Washington last week, asked me to claim the place as long as possible and not to let anyone into it. If I did the exact opposite now we would turn him into our enemy.

Otherwise, the man requested $300 annual rent for this place, a sum which is too much for it.

I request an appropriate response now as soon as possible about how I should act. Perhaps the horrible Georgia law will determine the designated direction. In the meantime, our Ochgelogy improvements were also drawn by white people. Everywhere you go, you find the consequences of the Georgia laws, and the poor Indians will find their horrible situation soon enough.

Last week I picked up the paper needed to print the little tract from Athens, Ten., and I hope to see it in circulation soon. Tomorrow is the holy Christmas festival and we expect most of our Brn. and Srs. for services. We also comfort ourselves in our oppressed circumstances with the saving birth of our incarnate

Savior. Thus we will experience things similar to what we did in 1831. The Lord, who so comfortingly helped us at that time, will continue to do so, and we are sincerely committed to His holy will.

If we are driven from here, we hope to find a place of refuge at Mr. McNair's. (In haste.) I remain your faithfully obliged friend and Brother,

H. G. Clauder

[M 407-2: Springplace Diary.]

Dec. 25. For the celebration of Christmas Day most of our baptized ones and many Indian friends came to our place, and we had very blessed services with them. Our well-known friend Dazizi, who helped us in the services as interpreter, spent the night at our place. When we sang verses from the English hymnal in the evening, he asked us to sing the verses, "Jesus makes my heart rejoice," and "I, I and my transgressions," etc., which he had previously learned in the school here from the blessed Sr. Gambold. He joined in during the singing of these.

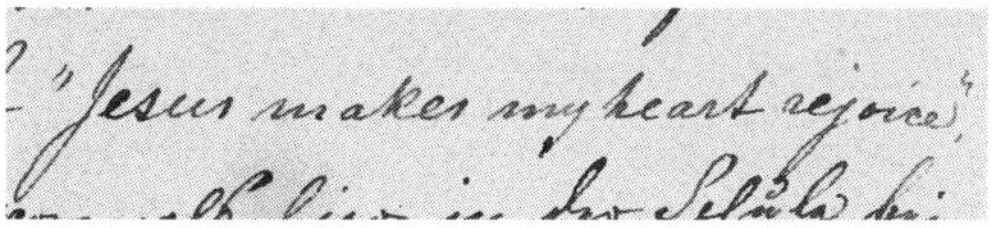

Dec. 26. Br. Clauder and Sr. Dor. Ruede went to Oochgelogy. The well-known Holly Creek was very swollen by the recent rain, so that we ourselves crossed on a log but the horses were driven through and had to swim. After we had lodged in New Echota with our friend Mrs. Worcester, we went to our Br. George Hicks on the 27th, where the service was held this time. Encouragingly, there was a nice number of Brethren and Sisters and friends to see there to whom the saving incarnation of the Word in John 1:14 was proclaimed. Finally the baby daughter born a week ago to our Br. and Sr. George Hicks was baptized into Jesus' death. After the service we rode to the house of our Sr. Sarah Bethia Hicks and spent the night there. During the night we were all

disturbed by a number of drunken Indians who stayed near our house for an hour with wild yelling, noise, and rollicking. However, they did not attempt to enter.

Dec. 28. Br. Clauder went home alone. Sr. Ruede stayed for a number of days with our friends in Ochgelogy and New Echota, when she returned to Spring Place on Dec. 31.

[M 415-2-28: Translated by Julie Tomberlin Weber. Addressed to: Revd. Theodore Schulz, Salem, North Carolina. Postmark: Springplace, Ga., Dec. 30. Free. H. G. Clauder, P.M. Received Jan. 10, 1833.]

Spring Place, C.N., Dec. 29, 1832

Dear Br. Schulz,

My last letter dated the 24th of this month included various pieces of unsettling news. Since then it appears more and more apparent that the man who demanded ownership of this place is very bad and worthless. Through lies and threats he tried to move me to give him possession of this post peacefully. On the evening of the same day that supposed Agent had come here, 3 other Georgians came here and asked about him, and they said I did very well to claim this property, because no human has the right to make a claim to it according to the current Laws of Georgia, any more than any other Lott which contains Indian improvements, that Gov. Lumpkin has not yet given any Grants, and he would not do so either, at least not in cases like this one.

The Laws of Georgia specify that no Lots that contain even one part of an Indian improvement could be taken by white people. However, if the occupant of such a part peacefully surrenders his possession, then no objection can be made. And since two-thirds of our Lotts are owned by Jo. Vann, this bad person tried in a deceitful way to force his way in here. From Mr. Hardin's last letter to me, you will see that this Lott is absolutely named a Mission Station in the Surveyors' Reports and makes no mention of the Indian claim made on it. Gov. Lumpkin could therefore be moved to give a Grant under the presumption that he would not come into contact with Indian improvements by doing so. And so with the last mail I took the liberty of politely presenting the circumstances regarding this to him, and I also informed him of the deceitful attempt to tear us and our neighbor Vann away from this Lott and asked him to inform me if he had ever actually given a Grant for it. Perhaps it would be appropriate if you also wrote to Gov. Lumpkin in the name of the P.H.C. and commended us to his protection.

During my visit in Oochgeloogy this week another man came here, the infamous Wacasser, and he tried to bother my wife with all sorts of lies. But she told him that we would not leave here under any circumstances until the Law forced us to do so. This person, who by the way also tried to take a bull that belongs here, is now trying to get the Post Office moved from here to his house, and I hear someone is supposed to have written to the Genl. Postmaster about this. Since it actually appears that a stage route from Tennessee to Georgia might be accomplished, I will not be sorry if the P.O. is removed from here, but I really doubt if the Genl. Postmaster will do anything in this matter if we remain quiet. I am indifferent about this. It is no longer necessary to have such commissions from the U.S. Government in order to remain here peacefully. The law concerning the Oath of Allegiance, which has caused so much confusion and loss, has been repealed as far as we know.

Yesterday I returned from Ochgelogy where I had held a service at Br. George Hicks's house the previous day. Sr. D. Ruede went there with me for a visit, and I left her in the area there. She will return next week when she has an opportunity. Our friend Isaac Proctor recently asked for an English Daily Text, and I gave him hope that he could get one, and so I herewith request this for him.

I expected a letter from you with today's mail but did not find one. Instead of that, I received a little note from Br. Schaaf along with some odes which were used at the wedding anniversary of my old master and uncle Shober. Since the Vorsteher work is also being carried out by you now, I cannot expect letters from you as often as before. In our current situation, however, I must ask you to let me know your thoughts about our current circumstances as soon as possible. I will send this letter with tomorrow's Knoxville mail. I also wanted to ask you to send all letters and packets by way of Tennessee, since I find the Knoxville route as fast as via Georgia, and I consider it safer.

Since Br. Byhan's times, a certain mail contractor who lives in Kentucky named Dobbins has kept his quarters here. His rider comes here every Saturday evening, spends the night, and gets supper & breakfast, etc. He now owes approximately $40. I have written him numerous times already and insisted he pay, but in vain. 2 weeks ago I gave him definite notice that I expect the outstanding payment by the end of this year, and if he does not act accordingly I could not possibly lodge his young man any longer. I was expecting an answer and money with today's mail, but neither came. Now the question is, should one force him through the Law to pay his debt here, or give him more time and lodge him as previously. We would be sincerely happy if he would find lodging elsewhere.

This year will end soon, and by the time you have received these lines another one will have begun. May the Lord comfort us and strengthen us in all the continuing trials and keep us with Him. Greet the dear Brn. of the P.H.C. and all who participate in this work. Your faithfully obliged friend and Brother,

H. G. Clauder

[M 407-2: Springplace Diary.]

Sun., Dec. 30. Not many Indians came for the service here. In the afternoon we were very delighted by the receipt of some *Gemein Nachrichten* and letters from Salem, and spent the evening with these.

Dec. 31. When evening came a 6 span wagon arrived here loaded with part of the possessions of some families who have leased this place from the man who was here on the 24th, without our knowledge but completely according to our expectation, and who now are planning to live here. The people are not expected here until tomorrow. In the meantime the driver went with the things to Vann's and spent the night there. On this unpleasant and rainy night we sent our faithful Nicolaus Ignatius to our friend McNair to get some advice in our critical situation, with the request that he come to help and advise us.

Now at the conclusion of this year when need and hardship were the order of the day and it absolutely appeared that we would be torn from our dear Springplace by force and it would fall into other hands, we asked the Lord very sincerely to take us into His further protection, to arrange everything so that it pleases Him, and give us patience and faith in the current trouble. We also thanked Him for the unending blessings and charitable deeds we have so richly enjoyed in the year now past. We also had to confess, however, our lagging behind in so many duties, our many mistakes and sins before Him who knows hearts, and plead for His forgiveness and further patience and forbearance.

At the conclusion of the year 1832 the Gemeinlein in Spring Place consisted of 33 communicants, 4 non-communicants, and 27 baptized children. Altogether 64 persons. The Gemeinlein in Ochgelogy is numbered at 10 communicants, 2 non-communicants, 19 baptized children of the Brethren and Sisters, altogether 31 persons. In addition there are approximately 18 children in the school. In our care are thus a total of 113 souls. We commend them along with ourselves to the prayer of all of our dear persons in the Gemeine,

Heinrich Gottlieb & Charlotte Elis. Clauder

[*Records: N.C.*, 8:4012-13: Salem Memorabilia of 1832. Translated by Douglas L. Rights.]

Our mission among the Cherokee Nation, in which this congregation takes a more active part than in other mission fields of the Unity, has not experienced any extraordinary difficulties and disturbances this year; however, unsettled political conditions have kept the Cherokees restless all year as to how these conditions might work out. Naturally, the same circumstances occupy the hearts and minds of our dear missionaries there. Consequently this work also was an object for intercession before the Throne of Grace in public and private prayer.

After Br. Heinrich Gottlieb Clauder had been appointed postmaster at Springplace and thus his unmolested residence in the Cherokee country was safeguarded, the wish of Br. and Sr. Byhan to be relieved of mission service and to return to Salem could be granted. Rejoicing at the turn of events, Br. & Sr. Clauder with their two children set out on the journey to Springplace on Apr. 3. With them went our Single Sister Sophia Dorothea Ruede, hitherto a teacher in our Academy, who had volunteered to go to help them with their family work wherever possible and particularly to follow an inner urge to be of service to the Saviour in this mission in the teaching of children. On Wednesday of Holy Week this company arrived safely in Springplace and right after Easter Br. & Sr. Byhan with their son, Nathanael, and the Single Sister Nancy Becker and the Single Br. Naeman Rominger, started on their journey to Salem, arriving here on May 11.

Br. Byhan accepted the call to serve the Bethabara congregation and Br. Nathanael Byhan fitted up his trade as saddler.

1833, part 1

[M 407-3: Diary of the Mission to the Cherokee Indians. Translated by Julie Tomberlin Weber. Handwriting is Heinrich Gottlieb Clauder's.]

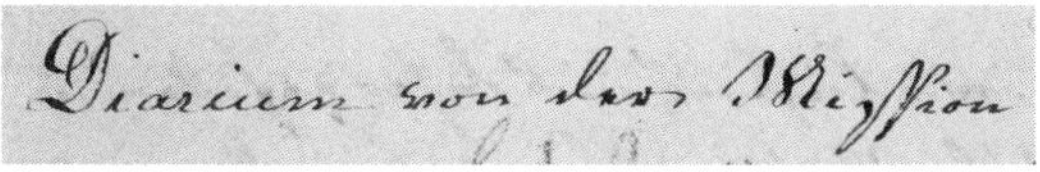

Jan. 1. Before daybreak we had the joy of seeing our friend David McNair here with us. We had asked him to come here today to give us his advice, since we can expect our peaceful possession of Springplace to be disrupted today. Since our houses are situated on Vann's property, which is protected by the laws of Georgia, we still hope to be able to remain secure and presume that our current concern is just the work of an enemy who is trying to act against law and justice. So we anxiously awaited the arrival of the white people who want to displace us and take away our property in Spring Place. Many of our friends and neighbors had come here during the day to see how things turned out. Finally at 3 o'clock in the afternoon 5 wagons and some carts and 15 to 20 people arrived here and demanded possession of all of our houses. Br. Clauder refused to concede anything to them and referred to the laws as far as he was familiar with them, as well as to the assurances of the Surveyors who had measured this district that we did not need to fear any disturbance. In this way evening came on. The drivers began to get impatient and angry. They wanted to get rid of their load, and the people themselves got increasingly insistent in their claims, so that we were

afraid of being personally mistreated. They finally used force, and forceful entry took place. The people promised that if their behavior was unlawful they would move out again. Now things were unloaded and they demanded the key to the church, but this time we succeeded in protecting this house dedicated to the Lord from such quartering. Among the things which were put into the workshop were some barrels of rum, wine, and whisky, and it was soon also apparent that these people really misuse these items. The drivers also stayed here in our yard overnight, all of which upset us more than a little, and we hardly knew where we could still find a peaceful little spot. Our Br. Richard Sanders, who was also here, came late in the evening and with tears expressed his compassion for our unpleasant situation. He said if we could no longer stand it here, he would help us set up a little place outside of the boundaries of Georgia with the assistance of the other Indian Brethren.

Jan. 2. Since we realized that we could no longer get along with such people and also did not know how soon the authorities would require us to leave this place completely, we sent some cases of our things with some Tennessee drivers to McNair's, in the area where Mr. McNair once again had assured us of a place of refuge. The people who are here demanded our smokehouse so they could hang up their meat, which is almost rotten, in it. We were not immediately willing, since we ourselves had lots of meat in it, so they became angry and cursed us more than a little. And so we agreed, and took our meat out and took it elsewhere for security. We slaughtered pigs with the help of some Negroes and Indians, which made the day very busy.

Jan. 3. A man named Banks, a stage contractor, came here and tried to make preparations to set up a post carriage from Augusta to here and on to Tennessee. On his advice, Br. Clauder wrote a letter to the commanding Officer of the Georgia Guards with news of our desperate situation and the request to free us from this if possible. However, we received no answer to this.

Jan. 4. Many people came to see our new housemates, and there was more than a little noise during this, which somewhat tested our patience, our courage, and faith. Still we felt submissiveness to the will of Him who knows our difficult situation and will come to help us at the right time.

Jan. 5. We had the unexpected pleasure of welcoming Brn. Adam Butner and Henry Fockel from Salem at our place on their journey home from the southern states. Br. Butner expressed his willingness to stay with us until it is clear if the new residents of Spring Place will move away or not, which we hardly expected. From day to day it looks increasingly clear that we cannot possibly stay in this situation longer. It is clear that we must seek shelter somewhere else if the authorities do not free us from these burdensome residents.

Sun., Jan. 6. Many of our Indian Brethren and Sisters arrived at our place and expressed their compassion for our bad situation. Our Brn. and Srs. and we were disappointed in our expectation of celebrating the festival of the heathen in a solemn manner with our dear Indians, since the arrival of some Georgians right before the service brought us new troubles. Among these was a man named Bishop, who expended great effort trying to persuade us of the impossibility of our staying here longer, since the laws of Georgia could not provide us any protection. Because our place was built by whites (missionaries) and the laws protect only Indian improvements, the Governor of Georgia had issued the Grant for this Lott, and now we have no more right to this property. Therefore, the sooner we go the better. We were greatly tested in our hope of receiving some news soon from Governor Lumpkin, to whom Br. Clauder had already written on Dec. 24th, or from his Agent the Officer of the Guards, since no answer arrived from these authorities. In this great distress we sighed unceasingly to our faithful and all wise Lord for help and counsel. Since time did not allow us to wait for advice and the instructions of the P.H.C. in Salem, we found ourselves stripped of all Brotherly advice. And so this evening and in the following days we took a careful look at the situation of this post, which now according to the laws of Georgia had been given to other owners, and we as missionaries can expect no protection at all under them. After thorough consideration we decided to use the current opportunity and make arrangements to move away, since a longer stay in

Spring Place not only seemed pointless, but also exposes us to involvement in unpleasant legalities. A not insignificant reason for worry was also the current extensive establishment of the post business. This would be especially difficult for us since we have to provide the food and lodging for postillion and passengers under the current arrangements, and under such circumstances we would be largely, if not completely, prevented from carrying out our actual calling. Our friend McNair, who may well have realized during his visit here that we could not stand it here much longer, had offered us a place of refuge on his farm on the border of Tennessee where we could easily arrange to continue the school and without great expenses. We now decided to accept this friendly offer since we see ourselves forced by circumstances.

Jan. 7-13. And so we spent this week taking our things, along with cattle and pigs, to our new living place. Many Indians helped us with this. Since the buildings on the place shown to us needed some improvement first, we were welcome guests at Mr. McNair's, where we stayed more than a week.

[M 415-3b-1a: Translated by Julie Tomberlin Weber. Addressed to: Revd. Theodor Schulz, Salem, N.C. Postmark: Spr. Place, Ga., Jan. 10. Free. H. G. Clauder, P.M. Received Jan. 21.]

Springplace, C.N., Jan. 9, 1832 [1833]

Dear Br. Schulz,

Since my last letter to you, you probably have been anxiously awaiting another one, and I would have written you a long time ago if I had had time for this and could have shared something with you with any certainty. Now I am hurrying to share with you in these few lines the sad news that we are absolutely being forced to leave this place.

On the 1st of this month the place was taken by Georgia rent people, that is, 3 families, altogether 18 persons. We ourselves have been limited to one-half of the mission house and by next week must clear out of this as well. Right now, there is not enough time for me to write you in detail about everything, since we are in a tumult of packing and moving. We are happy and grateful that our dear Brn. Adam Butner and H. Fockel arrived here on the 5th of this month and have been helping with their wagon to get our belongings to safety, and they are not planning to begin their journey from McNair's until next Monday. Day after tomorrow we will go there, where Mr. McNair has given us a spacious house for now.

Since Dec. 31st we have enjoyed little peace, and there are already 2 parties in law concerning this place, and those who are here now will not easily yield. If Br. Butner comes home before I have the opportunity to write you in more detail, please ask him to tell you personally what he saw here, etc.

So far I have sold few articles, nor will I. Tomorrow I will drive our cattle and pigs to McNair's. I am now relatively free of the Post Office, because a certain Bishop will move in here next week, and he will take care of the mail until a new postmaster can be appointed. I would like to ask you to send all letters and newspapers to the Connesauga Post Office via Knoxville.

We have both been unwell for a number of days with a cold. In our current difficult situation we ask for the merciful help of our dear Lord and the loving compassion of all of our dear Brn. and Srs. and friends. Give our greetings to our dear parents and all who are interested. Your faithfully obliged friend and Brother,

H. G. Clauder

[M 415-3b-1b: Translated by Julie Tomberlin Weber. Addressed to: Revd. Theodore Schulz, Salem, N.C. Postmark: by Br. Ad. Butner.]

Connesauga, Cher. Nat., Jan. 13, 1833

Dear Br. Schulz,

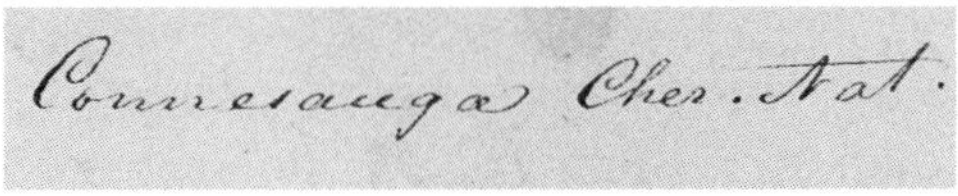

Since Br. Adam Butner is planning to begin his return journey home tomorrow, I want to write a few lines this evening to send with him.

Our dear, honored Spring Place is now almost in the hands of the Georgians, as we had long feared. The ones who had leased the place and who moved in there somewhat stormily on Jan. 1st provided me with frequent opportunities to rent it back from them, and they asked $150 for this. Since then I have found myself entangled in a lawsuit, because Genl. Hardin purchased the place after it had already been taken by previous renters. 3 families who moved in there will soon move out again, since they relinquished their claims to Wm. N. Bishop, who bought their rights for $260 for just 1 year. If we had simply remained there, our activity in our real calling would have received a great [page torn: hindrence?] because the stages from Tennessee and Georgia would have had their gathering place [page torn], we also would have had to take care of the passengers, and there were not enough stalls either or space for horses and people. However, I will remain silent about this here until the thorough future letter I have promised. For now, we are all here at our dear McNair's until the house designated for us has received some repairs.

Yesterday my family moved here. I had all the cattle and pigs, 70 of them, driven safely here and I had 7 Indians help with this. Most of our things are here, and what was left behind will be brought here soon. Our dear Br. Butner was a great help to us, since his wagon made the trip here from Spring Place twice, loaded with our things. I also received $150 from Br. Butner on the mission account, since I am almost out of money. Our Indian Brethren are prepared to assist with repairs to the house. They also want to build a schoolhouse, if you approve of this, in which the neighbors' children can be taught. Otherwise, we want to continue the mission work as previously, as far as the Lord provides the opportunity. I also came here after my family today, since I had remained behind in Spring Place yesterday to get everything in order.

I will probably never be able to describe the confusion prevailing there, which is still continuing, no matter how often I attempt to do so. In haste.

I greet you with love and remain your poor Brother,

H. G. Clauder

P.S. The money I received from Br. Butner consisted of U.S. notes and silver, except for $37 in Georgia notes.

[M 415-3b-2: Translated by Julie Tomberlin Weber. Addressed to: Revd. Theodore Schulz, Salem, North Carolina. Postmark: Springplace, Ga., Jan. 28, 18¾. Received Feb. 25.]

Connesauga, Ten., Jan. 17, 1833

Dearly beloved Br. Schulz,

Both of my last letters to you included the brief announcement that our dear Spring Place is now in the hands of the Georgians. In those letters I also promised to send you a thorough report about our move and all the circumstances surrounding this as soon as possible. I will do this now in the evening hours as well as I can. However, I would prefer it if you were here yourself so that everything could be discussed in person.

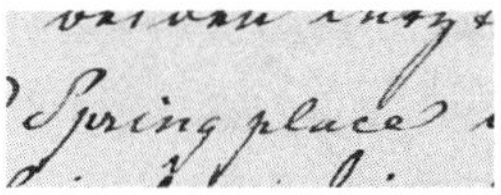

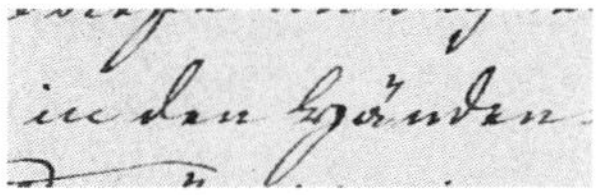

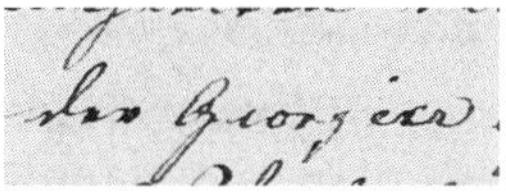

But where and how should I begin, since an indescribable confusion surrounds the entire matter, and I do not feel I am in a position to offer a coherent explanation. Still I will share what has happened as well as I can.

After the visit I received from Mr. Townsent on Dec. 24th, I heard nothing else from him or about the lease of Spring Place until the evening of Dec. 31, when a man from Tennessee arrived at our place and brought the crushing news that an entire large caravan of people and cattle was coming and planned to occupy Spring Place. I immediately had our faithful Nicolas Ignatius ride to McNair's and ask Mr. McNair to come down immediately to advise me what the best thing to do as soon as possible in this trouble. As unpleasant as this unforgettable night was, we still had the joy of seeing Mr. McNair at our place the next morning, Jan. 1st.

Now we were all heavy-hearted and expected the arrival of the people from whom we could expect little mercy. Finally at 3 o'clock in the afternoon 3 large wagons, 2 small wagons, and some ox carts appeared in our lane. Some of the men who had leased the place came onto the porch and showed me their written right to take possession there now according to law. Several hours were spent disputing the illegality of their actions. I referred to the law of Georgia which positively forbids a lot on which there is an Indian improvement from being occupied by the fortunate drawer or his agents, and I assured the entire company that they could not take possession here by any means other than force, and that I would first have to be evicted by force. Then one of these lawful robbers grabbed me and pushed me outside in a forceful manner. Then I saw that half of our new house, both old houses, etc., had been occupied. Many barrels of rum, whisky, and wine and cases full of dry goods were unloaded and some taken into the shop and some into the house. The evening and night passed in this manner with indescribable confusion and noise.

They also wanted to occupy the church but I absolutely refused to give them the key, and so I saved it for now.

On January 3rd Mr. Banks, stage contractor, arrived at our place and tried to make arrangements to lodge his driver and horses at our place. This was a new problem in which we did not know what to do. However, since he saw our predicament he was satisfied with the most basic hospitality we could provide him. Mr. Banks was planning to take a letter from me to the commanding officer of the Guard, in which I asked him to send me help if possible and to order these intruders away from here. But if his authority did not extend this far and the people had the protection of the Georgia law, I asked him to give me written notice of this.

Until this day I have not received any answer from him, any more than from Gov. Lumpkin to whom I had previously written to learn if he had issued a Grant for this lot.

On January 4 a certain Wm. N. Bishop arrived at Spring Place and looked over all the buildings very carefully, but he did not have anything to do with me and stayed completely away from me. This led me to presume that he was not at all kindly inclined toward us. Sunday, the 6th, Bishop returned here to our place accompanied by the infamous Wacasser, one of the greatest deceivers in this country. As we presumed, it turned out that Bishop had indeed bought one part of the possession of Spring Place and was planning to move into his place soon. Several days later he bought the other two parts for $260 in all, so that the 3 families who first took possession of Spring Place now had to leave again, and Bishop is the sole owner.

Some days after Bishop became the lessor of Spring Place in the above-named manner, I received another letter from Genl. Wm. Hardin in Milledgeville, in which he writes among other things: "The Lot whereon you reside is drawn & the Grant for it is issued. Mr. James H. Bryan is the purchaser from Nix, the drawer, & I have this day purchased the place from Mr. Bryan. I ask the kindness of you to take the usual good care of the houses, fences, orchards, gates, etc., & to consider yourself at home upon these conditions etc." He also writes, among other things: "I wish to board my wife & three children with you during the spring & summer etc."[1]

If I had received this letter before the other party had taken possession of the place, who also received his right from James Nix, we might have been able to spend several months there as Hardin's tenants under great adversity and distress. However, since it was completely otherwise, and the parties, Bishop and Hardin, are entangled in a lawsuit, I saw no possibility of enduring the pressure, since in addition to all of this not a single point in the entire law of Georgia assured me ownership of the place as missionary or as postmaster. The only way we would be protected would be under the law recently passed for the protection of Indian possessions, and then the lawyers would be of different opinions, since they would not recognize our place as an Indian possession.

And so we moved here last week to a little place at Capt. McNair's, where his son-in-law Neely used to live. We were lucky

---

[1] The quotes are in English in the original German manuscript.

enough to bring all the cattle belonging to the mission here. The church in Spring Place is filled with our things, which we are planning to gradually get. Mr. Bishop is deputy postmaster in Spring Place for now. With today's mail I wrote a thorough letter to the Genl. Postmaster as well as Genl. Nunan in Washington announcing my resignation, and made the suggestion that the Post Office be moved from Spring Place to the main road from Georgia to Tennessee.

Regarding the mission work, the following should be noted. For now I am planning to visit Brethren and Sisters in the different neighborhoods and hold services in their homes. Here we have the Indian families of Richard Sanders, James, Jeremias, William Henry, Boas, John Jacob, closer than we had them before at Spring Place. The Brethren and neighbors around here are willing to build a meeting house at their expense, which is desirable in my opinion. Also they are going to turn an existing house on this place into a schoolhouse soon, which can be done without much expense and effort. For now I do not see anything we can do on the mission account except repair our house, which will cost perhaps $15-20. Our friend McNair is giving us possession of the place at no cost, as long as there is no other use for it.

The buildings at the place consist of a spacious log house, a kitchen, smokehouse, stalls, shop, 2 corn houses and a spacious smith shop, which will be turned into a schoolhouse by the Indians. Most of the scholars will come from the neighborhood, but I should think that we could also board 6 to 8 children using the $250 which the Secretary of War has promised us, as we did with 17 in Spring Place. I would like to ask you to share your thoughts about this point with me and to send them, since I told the Indian Brethren and Sisters that we could not take any children into our household until we have learned the thoughts of the P.H.C.

The 22nd, evening. Since the Knoxville mail has not come twice now, I could not send this letter as I had wanted to, but in a few days I can send these lines to Calhoun, T., with the post, and so I will fill this page.

And before I go further, I have been asked to make the following request for Sr. McNair: an English Daily Texts for 1833. Also for Mr. Wm. Rowles, a Methodist preacher who is staying with his wife at McNair's and who previously lived in Harper's Ferry and is well known in the Pennsylvania Gemeinen, a copy of Heckewelder's *History of the North American Indian* and 1 copy of Loskiel's *History of the U. Br. Mission among the N. Amer. Ind.* Hopefully an opportunity to send these books will present itself, as well as the one we already ordered for Mr. Butrick last summer.

Last Saturday the 19th many of our Brn. were here busily repairing the houses, and today 9 Indians including 4 members of the Methodists were here to turn the old Blacksmith shop into a schoolhouse. Tomorrow they want to continue with the work, and they are planning to be finished with this in 2 days. If we begin a school, it will just be a so-called neighborhood school for now.

I am completely convinced of the necessity in the current times of trouble and sorrow of staying with the Cherokees, as great as the temptation is among them to drink and game, especially on the Georgia side. Still the grace of God can be powerfully felt among our dear Brn. and Srs., and thus far God has mercifully protected them from all evil. However, I fear that if their teachers left them they would soon, like the Ochgelogy flock, fall into ruin and destruction, and a heavy blame would fall somewhere. There is also hope that the delegates who are now in Washington will begin some action to save their poor, oppressed people when they return. If it finally comes to a move, which we sincerely hope, we are still prepared to go with them in God's name, and because of that we wish even now to remain with them as long as possible.

Otherwise, I sincerely ask that a Brother appointed by the P.H.C. might come out here to investigate all the circumstances in detail and to give me instructions now. The Georgians did not allow me any time to write and ask what I should do, but in the indescribable confusion and haste, I just had to act according to my best understanding. During this I had no one to help me but our dear Brother Ad. Butner, and our old friend McNair. If it is possible for a Brother to pay a visit here for the above-stated purpose, then I sincerely request this, because never has such a visit been as desirable and necessary as right now in these times.

Next Sunday I will hold a service in Ochgelogy and on the following Sunday in this area.

Herewith I commend myself to the special prayer of all friends of God's work among the heathen, and I remain your loving, poor Brother,

H. G. Clauder

[B 61-3: Provinzial Helfer Conferenz, meeting in Salem. Translated by C. Daniel Crews.]

Tues., Jan. 22. A letter dated the 9th of this month received from Br. Clauder in Springplace brought us the not entirely unexpected sorrowful report that on the 1st of this month three families of Georgians consisting of 18 persons came there asserting that they had won Springplace with the land belonging to it in the drawing of the Georgia Lottery. They claimed they had the right to take possession of the houses and half the Mission House, and that more were coming in a couple of days for this, so that Br. and Sr. Clauder with their family and things were required to leave Springplace and to accept the offer of our friend Captn. McNair, 18 miles from Springplace on the Connassauga in Tennessee, where a house has been temporarily emptied for them. To their comfort and aid they had on the 5th a visit from our Brn. Adam Butner and Fockel, who were there on their return journey from Florida. These afforded them real service in packing and removing their things to McNair's.

On the 11th they planned to leave Springplace entirely for a time, and Br. Clauder had made arrangements to hand the Post Office over to a certain Mr. Bishop. Br. Clauder does not say in the letter whether he has any prospect of being able to get rid of these people through the help of the Georgia Guard or the Agent of the Genl. Government. Of course this could hardly be managed since it has been confirmed that the Springplace lot was actually drawn in the Lottery at Milledgeville.

Time will show whether or for how long Br. and Sr. Clauder will be able to stay at Mr. McNair's for the profitable exercise of their chief calling, since the larger part of their baptized members live nearer to Mr. McNair's than they do to Springplace, or whether their situation there will be suitable for his making visits to the Cherokee Land under Georgia jurisdiction, or vice versa. They cannot return at this time of year, and for now must be patient in their place of refuge and wait and see how the Lord will preserve them in their dismal situation.

Since Br. Clauder in his dismay has perhaps forgotten to report the necessary things concerning the Post Office to the P.M. Genl. in Washington we considered it necessary for Br. Schulz to report these events to him by the next post to Washington.

As for what concerns our reimbursement for our now abandoned houses and improvements in Springplace and Oochgelogy, Br. Schulz at the end of Dec., as soon as we received the news from Br. Clauder that the lots there had been drawn in the Georgia Lottery, appealed to one of our Congressmen in Washington about this to find out through him the opinion of the Secretary of War. We are still waiting for his answer. Presumably we will have to send a written petition about this to the next Congress, since the present one ends at the beginning of March.

[M 407-3: Diary of the Mission to the Cherokee Indians.]

Jan. 21. We were far enough along with the repairs of a little house that today we could move into it and were sincerely grateful to our dear Lord that we once again have our own place in peace from the outside, and could continue in our calling. In recent days the Indian Brethren Richard Sanders, John Jacob, William Henry, Boas, Jeremias, and James, as well as 4 Indians who belong to the Methodists, came to our place and helped us 3 days with the improvement of the out buildings on this place. These dear Indians also went to work with courage and diligence and prepared a little house for the school we are planning to hold here in the future. It served as more than a little encouragement to us to experience these unexpected proofs of love and compassion from our Indians. They also expressed their willingness to build a meeting house here as soon as we give them instructions for this.

Jan. 25. I began my visitation journey to Ochgelogy, which is now a distance of 45 miles from our home. I spent the first night with our friend and former neighbor Vann near Spring Place. The following morning,

Jan. 26, I went on to New Echota where I arrived at noon. Since our well-known friend Worcester recently was set free from his imprisonment in Milledgeville, I took the opportunity to visit him and found it impossible to turn down his cordial invitation to stay with him until morning. His imprisonment had lasted 16 months, during which time he had to do hard labor as a carpenter. He and his companion in this humiliating imprisonment, Doct. Butler, found it pointless to take their case further in the higher courts of the United Sates, since their decision in their favor had remained unfulfilled, and they had no reason to harbor the hope that this would ever be carried out. As a result Gov. Lumpkin, who was happy enough to have a good reason to let these missionaries go, pardoned them without being forced to do so by a higher authority, and let them return home to their families. This part of Indian country will now be divided through the Lottery game to the residents of Georgia, and they also have legal power to take their winnings. For this reason Mr. Worcester will also have to leave his post sooner or later, following the example of what recently happened to us.

Sun., Jan. 27. Early in the morning I left my friendly lodgings and set out for our Br. and Sr. George Hicks, where the service was supposed to be held. The Brethren and Sisters, however, had not received my announcement, and so no one was there. A Baptist preacher was also preaching a mile from Hicks's, where everyone was running. And so I spent the day with Br. G. Hicks in conversations about those things closest to the heart of a believer. In the evening before we lay down to rest we commended ourselves in prayer to the further guidance and merciful care of our dear Lord, which Br. Hicks repeated on the following morning,

Jan. 28, in a very childlike way. After I had visited some more friends and Brethren and Sisters in this neighborhood, I began my return journey.

Jan. 29. I arrived safely and gratefully at my dear ones, happy to find protection from the rain which had lasted the entire day today. In the mission buildings at Oochgelogy, which we had to leave in July 1831 and which had been occupied by Wm. Ab. Hicks since then, there are now two white families from Georgia who have forced their way in there. The houses and enclosures there, which we built with effort and expense, are very dilapidated, and the otherwise pleasant place is almost unrecognizable.

Sun., Feb. 3. Since we had arranged for the service on this day at our Brother John Jacob's, we drove there with our children in our small wagon. We were more than a little happy when we found not only all of our Brethren and Sisters who live in this area but also many unknown Indians gathered there upon our arrival. Brethren Josua and Israel from the Spring Place area had also come. The joy of seeing so many Indians together was great, and a very sweet feeling prevailed in the sermon. The Indian Brother Nicolaus Ignatius served as interpreter. He has made very good progress in this work. The large house was completely filled, and all those present could not fit in, so some had to stay outside in front of the door. This test of holding future services in the homes of our Brethren and Sisters turned out to be a great encouragement to us, and since they do not live so far as from Spring Place, they can easily come to the service from home on the same day and also return there. The great effort and cost of feeding and lodging the visitors, which was unavoidably the case in Spring Place, is thus now no longer necessary.

[M 415-3b-3: Translated by Julie Tomberlin Weber. Addressed to: Revd. Theodore Schulz, Salem, Stokes Co., North Carolina. Postmark: Connesauga, C.N., Feb. 4. Free. H. G. Clauder, P.M., Springplace, Ga. Received Mar. 2.]

Connesauga, C.N., Feb. 2, 1833

Dearly beloved Br. Schulz,

After a long wait, we were very happy on Jan. 31 to receive another kind letter from you, dated January 10, along with 2 English Daily Texts, one of which Sr. McNair has already received and the other of which is designated for Mr. Proctor.

You will already have received my thorough letter from January [blank; 17th] and seen from this that your expectation and mine, that Grants would not be issued before the end of the Lottery, was not correct. Gov. Lumpkin has already issued many Grants, as can be seen from his letter to me, which I finally received last week. I am now sending you a copy of this. I had already followed his advice that I should turn to Col. Williamson, the officer of the Guard, a long time ago and indeed in vain, since I never once received a letter from him, not to mention that he would have assisted us.

On my recent visit to the area of Ochgelogy, I found Genl. Hardin in possession of the mission buildings, although Wm. Hicks still considers this his property. Hardin is planning to move to Spring Place in a few days, and I see very clearly that he was secretly happy that we were driven away from there, although his last letter to me said otherwise. His assurance that Secretary Cass was authorized to pay us for the Ochgelogy and Spring Place improvements was just intended to prevent criticism from our side. In the meantime, Mr. A. H. Shepperd, whom you had written, will report this if it is true.

I also had the opportunity to visit Mr. Worcester in Echota, and I found him expecting to experience the same fate we did any day and to be evicted.

Here in our new home, we are enjoying extraordinarily good

health and my health is able to tolerate the many tasks which occupy me daily, some of which are quite difficult. Even before my last letter was sent to you, we had moved into our little house which is actually intended to be a kitchen, and although we are somewhat crowded, it is a little refuge of peace under the Lord's assistance and protection, and we are quite content in it. The Indian Brethren continue to come and help us with their work and are prepared and willing to continue helping. Sr. D. Ruede is still living with the McNairs for now, until the home here is renovated and we can move into it.

In my last letter I asked for the P.H.C.'s instructions and advice concerning a school and boarding a small number of scholars. There are many conveniences in carrying out such a plan here, and the expenses associated with it will not be as great as those in Spring Place in any case. Since the Genl. Govt. is willing to contribute a significant sum and the Indians themselves are building a little house for it here in the hope of getting a school for their children in this way, our friends and Brethren and Sisters are eagerly anticipating receiving an answer of approval from the dear Brn. of the P.H.C.

I cannot report much yet regarding the mission work. For now I am planning to hold services in the homes of our Brethren and Sisters in the different areas. The plan is incomparably difficult for me since I am away from home every Sunday, but easier for us in other regards and also for the Indian Brn. and Srs. Through this [plan], unfamiliar Indians who would not come to our place come to the services as well. If only we enjoy the Lord's approval and can rejoice in His merciful glance, then we will not lack for anything.

In the poor Cherokees' current difficult situation, which must certainly come to an end soon, they need much comfort and encouragement, and the faithful hearts among them cannot be abandoned by their teachers as long as they seek to remain faithful to their Savior and Redeemer. In the meantime, it is my expectation that the Nation's issues in this country will reach one end or the other this summer. Many are just waiting on the return of the Delegation, and as E. Boudinott explicitly said to me: "If Mr. Ross returns with his usual flattering hopes, the people will not endure longer. His return is the utmost bound of their endurance." The treaty-making party, to which Ridge's family and many others belong, will then become stronger, and without fail they will take measures to emigrate.

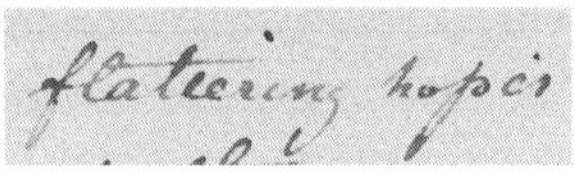

On the other side, you will find Gov. Lumpkin's letter.

[Br. Clauder copies Gov. Lumpkin's letter in English:]

Executive Department
Milledgeville, Ga., Jan. 3, 1833

H. G. Clauder, Springplace, Ga.,

Sir: In answer to yours of the 24th ult., received this morning, I find on examination of the records that on the 8th of last month, December, Lot No. 244 in the 9th district 3 Section of Cherokee was granted to James Nix of Henry County.

Upon enquiry at the Surveyor General's Office, I find the Surveyor General did not from the return of the Surveyor of said District feel himself authorized to refuse a grant for said lot, as it had not been recognized as a lot having an Indian improvement thereon. I find also that lot No 245 is returned without any note or mark of Indian improvements. I can assure you, Sir, that the Surveyor General as well as myself are anxiously disposed to do justice to the unfortunate Indians to the full extent that the laws of the state will authorize, and that we are extremely careful not to grant any lots, which are returned as being occupied by the Natives. But several cases have already occurred, which justifies the belief that the Surveyors have not been as careful as they ought to have been in making their returns of Indian improvements, which we fear will produce litigation and injury to the natives. So far, however, as may depend on my vigilance & disposition to do justice to the Natives, you may rest assured that nothing shall be omitted.

Col. Williamson, under the provisions of a late act of the Legislature, has recently been appointed and instructed, as the agent of the State to superintend the rights & interests of the Indians within the limits of Georgia & see that justice is administered to them according to the existing laws of the State. I therefore would recommend to you, and all others, who may have similar cases of difficulty to apply to Col. Williamson as a Gentleman in whose capacity, honor, & integrity you may safely confide.

I am, dear Sir, your obdt. servt.,

Wilson Lumpkin

[Br. Clauder concludes his letter to Br. Schulz in German:]

Already on Jan. 3 I wrote urgently and pleaded with Col. Williamson, whose honor and integrity were so highly recommended, but he has left me in confusion about the housing and destruction. So much for Georgia protection!

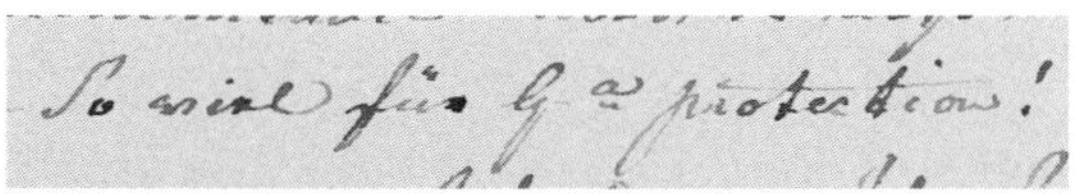

Your friend and faithful fellow Brother,

H. G. Clauder

[*Records: N.C.*, 8:4060: Salem Diary. Translated by Douglas L. Rights.]

Feb. 2. This evening the Brn. Adam Butner and Heinrich Fockel returned after a twelve weeks' journey in the interest of the business of the former. They went all the way to Florida and back. On their return they were from the 5th to the 14th of January with Br. and Sr. Clauder at Springplace, to their great encouragement and help in their distressing situation, since according to the laws of Georgia they can no longer remain on Cherokee land, and they will be driven out by those who are awarded the land by the lottery of the state. The aforesaid Brethren helped Br. and Sr. Clauder with their wagon to move to our friend McNair in the state of Tennessee, 18 miles from Springplace, where they had a friendly reception and found the necessary dwelling.

[B 61-3: Provinzial Helfer Conferenz, meeting in Salem.]

Mon., Feb. 4. Our Br. and Sr. Clauder and the single Sr. Dorothea Rüde are now in a separate little house at our friend McNair's (Tenesse district) where Br. Clauder hopes his chief calling can still continue. Br. Schulz has already the close of last [month] written to the Postmaster Genl. in Washington. We have also received favorable reports from our Congressman and the Secretary of War concerning our reimbursement for our vacated mission places. In these we are advised to have these appraised and to send this appraisal to the next Congress with a petition to the Secretary of War in Washington.

[M 407-3: Diary of the Mission to the Cherokee Indians.]

Feb. 4 and 5. Nine of our Brn. and Srs. came here again and worked diligently on the schoolhouse. Our neighbor Childress, who owns a sawmill, gave us the boards required for this as a gift. The following day the Indians finished the little house, which gave us more room.

Sun., Feb. 10. The service was held at Br. Josua's house, and those present were told how much better it is to gather riches in heaven than to seek such in this world and to attach our hearts to these. More than 40 Indians were attentive listeners. Br. Clauder spent the night with our friend Vann and had the opportunity of seeing with sorrow how our dear Spring Place, now occupied by Georgians, has been changed into a place of drinking for the Indians. A number of Indians had gotten whisky there and rollicked throughout the entire night and disturbed us at Vann's, where they came. One of them had even given the clothes off his back for whisky. Such cases are now frequent in this part of the Nation.

1833, part 2

[M 415-3b-5: Transcribed by Grace S. Robinson. Addressed to: Revd. Theodore Schulz, Salem, North Carolina. Postmark: Connesauga, Cher. Nat., Feb. 12, 18¾. Received Mar. 7.]

Connesauga, C.N., Feb. 11, 1833

Dear Brother Schulz,

Your esteemed favours of Jan. 15th & 17th, the former containing the Report of the Male Missy. Soc. & the latter containing several little German publications, came to hand last week to our great joy & satisfaction.

The perusal of the German Accounts alluded to in your favour of the 17th would afford us great pleasure & profit, & we sincerely hope an opportunity for sending them to us may present itself before long.

I have just returned this evening from a visit to our Brethren in the neighbourhood of Spring Place. Yesterday I preached at Br. Joshua's to about 40 Cherokees, many of them perfect strangers who never visited us at Springplace. The same was the case on the Sunday before, Feb. 3, when our meeting at John Jacob's 9 miles from here was attended not only by everyone of the members of our Church in this settlement, but also by a considerable number of heathen whom we never had the pleasure of seeing at Springplace. We are therefore greatly encouraged in our labours, while we see that our dear Cherokees are attentive to the means of Grace in spite of the confusion & persecution thrown into their way. We entertain strong hopes that under the Devine blessing our present plan of operation will prove successful, both in edifying & strengthening the hearts of our people as well as in gaining from among the heathen an additional reward for the travail of our Redeemer.

The situation of the poor Cherokees is deplorable, & my feelings are still bleeding when I reflect on the scenes I witnessed yesterday. While we were returning from Joshua's to Mrs. Vann's we met about 8 or 10 Indians in a state of beastly intoxication. Some even unable to walk lay aside the road in death-like silence. And where did they get the liquor? At Springplace, a place which for 30 years sent forth its rays of light to guide the erring heathens into the way of salvation. Now since it has fallen into the hands of the Georgians it has become the abode of drunkards, gamblers, & swindlers. Oh! That the Lord had consumed the place by fire from above six months ago. But while I mourn over this state of things I must praise the Lord for the Grace He has thus far imparted to our Brethren & Sisters, who thus far have walked worthily of the name they bare, & while their evil countrymen endeavour to ensnare them & to get them to become associates in drunkenness, they remain firm & immovable in their refusal to touch or to taste or to handle.

The schoolhouse mentioned in my last was completed last week by our Indian Brethren, & it is quite a comfortable & suitable cottage. Our labourer, Br. Nicolas, who by the by becomes more and more useful as an interpreter, occupies the house at present & will continue to do so for the present. We, viz., my own family & black Betsy, still live in the kitchen without suffering any material inconvenience, but we hope to move into the commodious dwelling house in the course of two or three weeks when the repairs will be completed. Our good friend Capt. McNair permitted us to cultivate a small tract of land, but it will not be sufficient to raise our supply of corn, which is moreover unnecessary, as I have made arrangements to get as much corn as we shall need this summer from Mr. McNair, & next year I shall get 125 bushels from Mr. Jo. Vann, who purchased our corn at Springplace to spare us the trouble of transferring it hither.

The longer we are here, the better are we pleased with our new situation, & the good Lord gives us good health, so that with moderate exertions we shall soon be conveniently fixed to continue that important branch of missionary labour, a school.

It is more than probable that our Indian Brethren will move over to the Tennessee side where we shall have them nearer to us than ever. Br. Samuel is now building over on this side of the line to avoid trouble & oppression, & many others are now following the same plan. Thus while the State of Tennessee does not extend jurisdiction, this part of the Nation will afford a refuge from personal oppression.

I have in my last letter endeavoured to point out the necessity of a visit from one or the other of the Brethren of the Conference. I would therefore conclude these few hasty lines with a renewal of the petition that some Brother may be sent to view the state of things here, & to advise & direct me how to proceed.

I have commenced transcribing the Diary & shall perhaps get a sheet ready next week, as I have no other time but evening to devote to writing. It is slow & bad at that.

With much love, I remain your unworthy Brother,

H. G. Clauder

[M 407-3: Diary of the Mission to the Cherokee Indians. Translated by Julie Tomberlin Weber. Handwriting is Heinrich Gottlieb Clauder's.]

Sun., Feb. 17. It rained in the morning. However, contrary to our expectations, the service at John Jacob's was still attended by about 30 Cherokees and their children. At the beginning of this they were especially advised to love God their Savior, who did and still does so much for them, and that they should show this love to their parents through obedience according to the Savior's example, or toward their teachers. The sermon was on Ps. 107:20. Finally, some news from the mission in Jamaica was shared from the *Missionary Intel.*, and this brought special attentiveness and interest.

[M 415-3b-4: Translated by Julie Tomberlin Weber. Addressed to: Revd. Theodore Schulz, Salem, Stokes Co., North Carolina. Postmark: Connassauga, C.N., Feb. 19, 37½. Received Mar. 9.]

Connesauga, C.N., Feb. 18, 1833
Monday Morning

Dear Br. Schulz,

Yesterday evening upon my return from John Jacob's, I was overjoyed to receive your kind letter of the 3rd[?] of this month, along with a *Missionary Intel.*, and to learn that you finally received the sad facts personally through Br. Butner, as well as through my letter, regarding our removal from Spring Place.

We are all enjoying our usual health, and with God's help and blessing we think we will be able to continue with school soon. We are just waiting for the approval of the P.H.C. and have no doubt it will grant us this joyfully. The Indian Brethren have finished the little house needed for this without any cost, and since last week I have engaged a carpenter at our future home to make a few windows (I brought the glass for this from Och-geelogy) and some stairs and other improvements.

We like the plan to hold Sunday services in the homes of the Indian Brn. and Srs., and this pleases the Indian Brn. and Srs. themselves more and more. Through this we will not have to house and feed them and their horses on Saturday evenings, as we did at Spring Place. This was always very difficult and expensive for the mission, and yet it could not be changed if, for example, the most distant of them wanted to attend services on Sundays. Now, in contrast, the Indians do not need to leave home before Sunday morning, since they do not have to travel as far as to Spring Place. Also because of this there are always stranger Indians at the service who never came to Spring Place. Furthermore, they are moving increasingly to this side of the southern line of Tennessee. We hear nothing from them anymore about the Treaty of Removal.

A certain mail contractor near Murfreesboro, T., whose rider we boarded and housed in Spring Place for an entire year, owes the mission the sum of $41.75, and all my requests to send me the money remain fruitless. What should we do now? I do not know if the man is solvent or not, and I really do not know what to do to collect the money. And so I wanted to ask for your advice.

I hope to get the cash soon from Wm. Hicks for his notes. Because of this, I hope to get enough money to meet the now low expenses of this mission for now. I sold the herd of pigs, which I brought here from Spring Place but did not have enough corn to keep, to Capt. McNair for $100, and I will probably use most of this amount for corn for us.

In Spring Place we had almost 125 bushels of corn, which I sold to Mr. Vann to avoid the expense and effort of transporting it here. And so Mr. Vann owes us $62.50, which he will pay upon his return from Washington.

Yesterday it rained heavily that I was not enthusiastic about going the 9 miles to Jacob's, since I did not expect anyone. However, I went and rediscovered what I had experienced many times previously, that the Indians do not allow heavy rains to prevent them from coming to the services. I found about 30 Cherokees — Moravians, Methodists, and heathens — there, and we had a quite richly blessed time there during which we felt Jesus' presence quite powerfully. My dear Nicolas was also quite fluent while interpreting, and he himself was quite emotional. The entire last night we had rainstorms, which caused the Connesauga River to overflow its banks and into low grounds, and it swept thousands of Capt. McNair's fence rails away with it. But they will hardly reach Mobile!

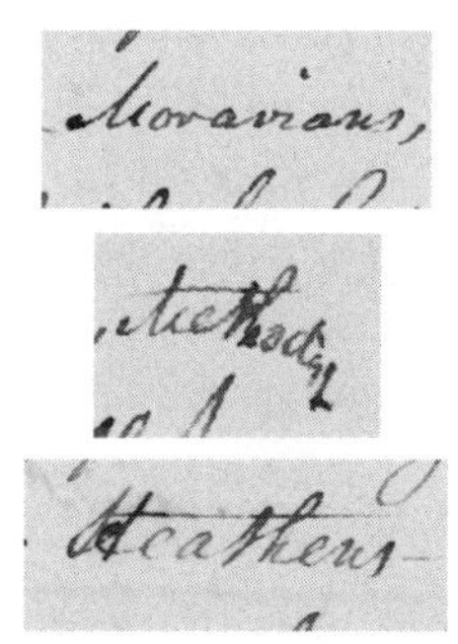

Herewith I am finally sending you a page with the continuation of the Spring Place Diary, which I will finish next week. During the day I have no time at all to write, since there is so much work in the garden and otherwise. And so I must use the evening hours for this. Please greet my dear parents. Tell J. C. Blum he should send my *Reporter* via Knoxville to Connesauga, Cher. Nat. Herewith I must close after signing as your faithfully obliged and unworthy fellow Brother,

Clauder

[*Periodical Accounts*, London, 12 (1832-34), Quarterly Extracts, Feb. 1833, 387-88.]

The following information respecting the Mission among the Cherokees, is contained in a letter from Br. Bechler, of Salem, in N. Carolina, dated Feb. 26.—

"The State of Georgia has divided that part of the Cherokee territory lying within its frontiers, among the remaining inhabitants, by lottery; and those to whom the property has by this means been appropriated, are now endeavouring to eject the former possessors. In consequence of this, the Missionary settlement at Oochgelogy was occupied by strangers. Br. Clauder hoped, however, that Spring-place, being a post-station indispensable to the United States, would not be included in this violent measure; but, on New-Year's Day, he was obliged, by a company of three families, comprising eighteen persons, to give up one half of the Mission-house. A few days after, there appeared a so-called agent of the government of Georgia, who drove away the above-mentioned company, but proceeded to compel our Missionaries to quit the premises altogether. In these difficulties they were greatly relieved by a company of brethren and sisters [*Records: Cherokees* ed.: Brn. Adam Butner and Johann Heinrich Fockel] from Salem, who that day arrived at Spring-place, on a journey of business. The latter assisted our Missionaries in removing all their goods and cattle to the residence of Captain Macnair, (whose wife is a communicant of the congregation at Spring-place), in the state of Tenessee, a distance of eighteen English miles. Here they not only met with a welcome reception and a temporary residence, but they continue to enjoy an opportunity of labouring among the Cherokees, as some of the members of their congregation reside near this place. They hoped also to commence a school in a short time.[”]

[M 407-3: Diary of the Mission to the Cherokee Indians.]

Sun., Feb. 24. The services were held at our Br. James’s, about 5 miles from our home. The house was extremely full of Cherokees, so that some of them had to stay just outside the door. The closeness of the Lord could be felt during this service and blessed it to comfort and edify many souls. Some who are still heathen but who have already often heard the Word of God without concerning themselves any further about it, were attentive and some of them emotional listeners. In conclusion our Br. Samuel stepped up and in a loving and urgent manner advised all present to remain faithful to the Savior, who loves them so deeply, and to turn to Him in prayer when external difficulties and sorrow come to them, since He is a helper of the poor and oppressed, etc. During this talk general emotion prevailed among those present. Everyone, however, was quiet and orderly. It was an encouraging sight and certainly is and remains the desire and intention of our Indian Brn. and Srs. to live for Jesus and to be his property eternally.

Mar. 1. Br. Clauder planned to go to Ochgelogy where Holy Communion had been set for next Sunday the 3rd. But the streams were so high from heavy rains which continued the entire day today that they could not be crossed. And so the visit in Ochgelogy had to be canceled this time.

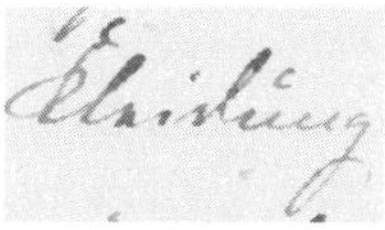

Sun., Mar. 10. The service was at the Indian Br. James’s. The sermon was on the parable of the sower [Matt. 13:3-9]. The number of listeners was unusually large. Many had to take a place outside the door and behind the house. Especially remarkable to us among the latter were 4 Indians who lay in their original clothes in quiet contemplation on the ground and listened to the words of the interpreter. During this we sincerely wished that the good seed of the word of God might not fall in vain on their ears and hearts. In conclusion a Cherokee who was present, a brother of the well-known Young Wolf, spoke to the gathering with sincere warmth.

On this day Br. Clauder had the opportunity of speaking with the very old grandmother of our Sr. Betsy Sanders. She said she also wishes to walk on the good road on which are most of her descendants, and also to be there where they are one day. She also often prays to God that He might accept her. She was told that Jesus Christ died for sinners and if she, as a sinner who has nothing but bad, calls to Him for comfort and help and would put her hope in His merit alone, she would one day be united with all of her descendants who have become believers in endless peace with Jesus.

Mar. 11. Since we had business at the Agency we (Br. and Sr. Clauder) went there today on horse. We passed by the mission post at Candys Creek and found loving acceptance and lodging there with our friends Mr. Holland and Mr. Butrick. The next morning after we had been commended to the faithful protection of the Lord in the house service, we continued our journey farther to the Agency, where we arrived in a couple of hours and were cordially taken in by Mr. Lewis Ross. Afterward we went toward home, but were overtaken by night and turned in at our friends Mr. and Mrs. Proctor, who received us extremely lovingly and gave us lodging. On the following day,

Mar. 13, we arrived safely home.

Sun., Mar. 17. We once again had an inclement, rainy day. I (Br. Clauder) nonetheless went to the place where the service was announced for today, presuming that only a few would have come there. But I was pleasantly surprised when approximately 50 Cherokees, among others also more heathen from Sumak, gathered and listened to the sermon on Paul's words from 1 Cor. 1:18 with the usual attentiveness. The example of the Indians who do not allow themselves to be stopped by unpleasant weather from attending the services humbled and encouraged me more than a little. Generally a new spirit seems to rule among them since the services have been held in their homes. Each time some who never or only extremely rarely visited at Spring Place come.

Sun., Mar. 24. Br. Clauder visited at Br. Josua's in the area of Springplace, with the intention of holding a service there. However, only a few could come because of the frequent rains and resulting high streams. Also no interpreter was present. First, some Cherokee hymns were sung with those present. Then Br. Clauder read aloud part of a Cherokee tract and then in a prayer commended the mission work in this Nation to the further protection of the faithful Shepherd of souls. The Indian Br. Israel closed the service with singing some hymns and a prayer. Shortly after the service a covered boat with a load of flour came down the River and stayed a while at Br. Josua's house.

The services on Palm Sunday as well as on Good Friday were attended with attentiveness by most of our Indian Brethren and Sisters, and we hope that a good impression of the memory of the suffering and death of our Savior remained with them.

Sun., Apr. 7. On the holy festival of Easter, we held services for the first time at this place on the Connesauga River, since our house has been thoroughly repaired and is sufficiently spacious. First was the sermon on Ps. 16:8-11, for which about 50 attentive listeners were present. In the 2nd service we celebrated the memorial meal of our Redeemer and Savior with our communicants. Most of them were present for this and received a rich blessing. A baptized Indian watched during this as a candidate for the first time.

[M 415-3b-6: Translated by Julie Tomberlin Weber. Addressed to: Revd. Theodore Schulz, Salem, North Carolina. Postmark: Connesauga, C.N., Apr. 9, 18¾. Received Apr. 24.]

Connesauga, C.N., Apr. 8, 1833

Dear Brother Schulz,

We were delighted and encouraged to receive your kind letter of March 23, which last week arrived as an enclosure to the

Missionary Intelligencer, as the 4 English Daily Texts safely arrived at our place some weeks earlier. Some have already reached their designated recipients.

We continue to enjoy good health, for which we are sincerely grateful to the Lord who gives all good things. We have been busy laying out and working a small garden, which we have partially hoed and planted, as well as sowing oats and grass seed in several acres of the field received from Mr. McNair. We are planning to move into our recently repaired house and leave the small and dark kitchen which we have occupied since Jan. 23 and just to use it as a kitchen. On the 22nd of this month we are planning to begin our school. We will not know until then how many students we will have.

Concerning the spiritual progress of the Indian Gemeinlein, we note with joy and gratitude that although sins and temptations are gaining more power, our Brn. and Srs. continue as usual in their quiet and truly Christian walk, often encouraging each other in their houses with singing and prayer and trying to learn the portion of God's word which they have in their own language. Yesterday on the holy celebration of Easter we once again celebrated Holy Communion for the first time in a long time, and 22 Cherokees were present for this. On this occasion our Brn. and Srs. showed the usual and frequently mentioned emotion. Oh, may the tears have been those of true contrition. During this Holy Communion Agatha Sanders, who was baptized on Nov. 25 in Spring Place, watched as a candidate for the first time.

After the conclusion of the service we discussed various things with our Indians concerning the school, and the conclusion of this was that for now 6 of their children would be boarded, and they will go home (if this is not too far) to get their clothing washed at home. This will relieve our Sisters from a great burden.

Now I must also extend the greetings which some of our Brethren send to the Brethren of the P.H.C. in the name of all the rest. Richard Danl. Sanders said: "We have been thus far preserved in peace & unity, & I trust our Saviour will help us to continue in peace to our end."[1] The otherwise very quiet and shy Br. Boas said (through Sr. McNair as interpreter): "We are thankful to God that He has still permitted our teachers & the teachers of our children to remain near to us & that we can hear their words. This is the Lord's doing for which we are glad & thankful." Many others wanted to express their feelings and to greet all of the Brethren and Sisters in Salem. It was a day of true joy for us, as we have not experienced in a very long time. One Indian named Turnover, who visited us regularly in Spring Place, belongs to the Methodists, and has often enjoyed Holy Communion with us as a guest, informed me that he was planning to end his relationship with the Methodists, because he did not receive any more instruction from them, and he always felt very happy to be with us. I did not try to persuade him or dissuade him but told him that the external name was not important; everything depended on one's heart loving the Savior and standing united with Him, etc.

I must postpone the valuation of Spring Place until we see what Jo. Vann gains through the Law, since he is planning to begin a suit in the Georgia courts to get Spring Place back.

In a few weeks the Council will gather, and then the delegates will give their report. It is said Ross turned down $3,000,000 as payment for the Cherokee Land. May the Lord rule everything according to His will and also be an eternal blesssing for this oppressed people.

Please be content with these few lines for now. More soon from your faithfully obliged Brother,

Clauder

[1] The quotes are in English in the original German manuscript.

[M 407-3: Diary of the Mission to the Cherokee Indians.]

Apr. 12. We finally moved into the home designated for us here at our place of refuge, after it had been thoroughly improved, which means fitted with windows and floors and doors, and the large openings between the blocks closed with stones and lime. Now we will finally be in a position to begin the school, for which the Indian Brethren long ago constructed the little house required for this.

Apr. 15. Br. Clauder went to Spring Place on business regarding the Post Office. The man who was temporarily assigned by Br. Clauder to take care of the postal business upon our departure has now officially been assigned this office by the General Postmaster. And so today after balancing the accounts Br. Clauder was free of obligations regarding the Post Office in Spring Place.

Apr. 18. A company of U.S. Regulars marched through this neighborhood to drive out the white people who have been called intruders here in this country. However, they limit themselves only to that part of the Nation over which the laws of individual states have not yet been extended. In Georgia and Alabama, where the oppression by the white people is the worst, nothing takes place in favor of the Indians.

Sun., Apr. 21. Br. Clauder preached at our Indian Br. John Jacob's. Among the visitors were many white people from the neighborhood. The child of our Br. and Sr. John Jacob was also baptized into Jesus' death.

Apr. 22. We began the school with 12 scholars.

[M 415-3b-7: Translated by Julie Tomberlin Weber. No address; no postmark. Received May 8.]

Connesauga, Cherokee Nation, Apr. 24, 1833

Dear Br. Schulz,

Herewith I am finally sending you the end of the Springplace Diary from last year, 1832. Because of all the work we had to do to set up this place, which we have now finished with God's help,

I had to postpone copying the Diary. Since I have more time now, I will send the one for this year until the beginning of Apr. as soon as I can.

I am happy and grateful that I am finally able to report the beginning of the school here with 13 scholars (6 of them are boarders here). We started it day before yesterday on the 22nd. Among the scholars are Polly and Amos Bell, 2 white children who live near here and whose father, a trader, pays us $4.00 per quarter for their children's instruction. More white students will probably come, and we are planning to accept them in exchange for payment. We are not having any problems with our 6 boarders since we now have enough space to house them. At our request, the parents of those who do not live too far away also agreed to take care of the laundry for their children. We never had the advantage of being able to do this at Springplace.

The following things should be noted about the establishment of the place here. The house here built by McNair's son-in-law Neely had not been finished and was completely unusable for our purposes. Since Mr. McNair had a lot of boards here and provided us with even more from his sawmill, I thought it would not cost more than $50-60 to have this house finished. To that end I spoke with Mr. McNair, who gave us the place and all the buildings to occupy "as long as we wanted to stay here." And so Mr. McNair had a carpenter come. He made 2 good floors, 5 windows and window frames, 5 doors, a staircase, and 2 partitions, upstairs and downstairs in the house. His bill came to $59. I also had a mason fill the spaces between the blocks with stones and plaster and then painted with lime, the fireplace re-bricked and plastered, and he also built an oven next to that. The mason's bill came to $12. These are all the expenses we considered necessary to establish this place. The glass required for the windows, the frames for a window, and door hinges were left over from the construction at Spring Place and were useful here. We made a small garden ourselves and put a fence around it and the yard with the help of our Nicolaus.

We now have plenty of room and are happy and grateful that we can continue in our calling without having anything to do with the miserable laws of Georgia or having to fear them. If we were still in Spring Place now, we would have the entire burden of the Post Office including 3 stage drivers and 2 horses along with passengers, on our back. The stages are now running and it is astonishing that there are already travelers in them. The Genl. P.M. has installed Mr. Bishop as my successor in Spring Place, against my recommendation, and last week I closed the P.O. accounts to the beginning of April. Now I have nothing more to do with the Genl. P.M. except to pay some small drafts that add up to about $20.

I hardly think that Mr. Vann will start a suit to get Springplace back although he might succeed, since many Cherokees have already gotten their places back by law. Last week I saw a company of U.S. Regulars under Capt. Gardiner at McNair's marching to Camp Armstead in the Valley Towns to chase out the so-called Intruders. This company had marched to Augusta some months ago to be near the nullifiers in S.C. When this absurd Demonstration passed by without any bloodshed, these troops returned to their assigned place, Camp Armstead.

I also had the opportunity recently of becoming acquainted with one of the Arkansas Delegates, Mr. Drew. I found his tales of earlier forays against the Osages and his description of the Buffaloe chaces on the endless prairies in Arkansas very interesting.

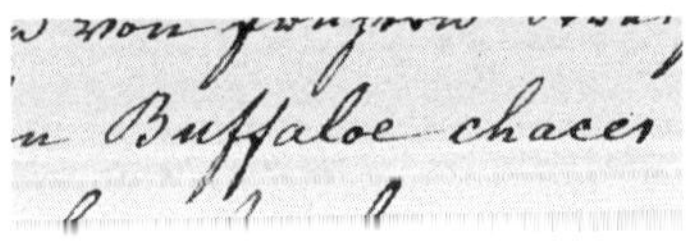
Buffaloe chaces

We would really like to receive the *Gemein Nachrichten*, books, and other texts. May the Lord soon provide an opportunity for this. I am pleased to hear that you have received Krummacher's Sermons Br. Benzien ordered for me, and I would like to ask you to have Clewell bind them nicely for me. My dear father will take care of payment for this as well as for the book itself.

Along with a sincere greeting to dear Brethren Bechler and Schaaf, I remain your poor fellow Brother,

Heinrich Gottl. Clauder

N.B. Do you by any chance have any Georgia money on hand? If you do, please send me some, since I still cannot reach a settlement with Wm. Hicks, who owes me more than $100. He has no money.

[M 407-3: Diary of the Mission to the Cherokee Indians.]

Sun., Apr. 28. Br. Clauder preached at the home of the Indian Br. Boas in Sumak.

Apr. 30 and the following days we were busy in our garden and fields.

[M 415-3b-8: Translated by Julie Tomberlin Weber. Addressed to: Revd. Theodore Schulz, Salem, North Carolina. Postmark: Connesauga, C.N., Apr. 30, 18¾. Received May 25.]

Connesauga, C.N., Apr. 30, 1833

Dear Br. Schulz,

Last week I received your kind letter of the 12th of this month, along with our blessed Br. Benzien's memoir and $100 cash enclosed. We were delighted to receive this and I thank you sincerely for it. In the $100 is $30 on the Merchants & Planters Bank of Augusta, which unfortunately has a bad reputation now and payment refused. The Directors, however, supposedly said they would do their best to restore the bank's credit. In the meantime, however, circulation of their notes has been suspended. I am bringing this to your notice so that neither you nor anyone else in Salem accepts any more notes like this for now.

I also want to share my views with you about another issue — the arbitratorship and valuation of Spring Place, which are not feasible now for the following reasons. Mr. Vann, on whose lots our Spring Place improvements stand and to whom everything within the bounds of his lots is secured by the Georgia laws, recently appealed to the new Indian agent for Murray County to remove the Georgians from Spring Place. They then received strict orders from that agent, Williams (not the former one), to clear the place within 10 days. This time will run out in a few days, and although Bishop is not yet making any preparations to remove and refuses to do so, it is the duty of the agent to evict him by force and put Vann in possession. Bishop further appealed to the Court where Vann must defend his rights. Mr. Vann is planning to [page torn: do his best?] to get us poor pilgrims back to Spring Place, which indeed eventually could well happen when the suit is finally decided and everything is quiet again.

On the other hand, if we receive damages for Spring Place from the U.S. Government (which according to this is more likely) then the place would fall into the category of the so-called enrolled emigrated places, and then we would counteract Mr. Vann, who was always a patron of the mission, in his suit. Therefore, I must wait, along with Mr. McNair, with whom I have discussed the valuation.

Mr. Vann is doing this only for us — as well as to get rid of a bad neighbor — and we should certainly be the last ones to oppose the Cherokee complainant through hasty steps. By moving here we have escaped these difficulties, since as a missionary I could not have been a party in law, nor would I have wanted to be one. If Springplace should be regained, we can have the Post Office moved somewhere else and return next year. However, if the Georgian, Bishop, asserts his right, then we could easily and soon have the value of the improvements determined. I will be able to say various other things about Ochgelogy in my next letter since I am planning to go there day after tomorrow, the Lord willing. People say Wm. Hicks has asserted his right as occupant of our houses there after he personally talked with Gov. Lumpkin in Milledgeville.

We continue to enjoy our usual state of health, as do our children. This week 14 children are coming to school. Things are set up now so that we do not need as many hired workers as we did in Spring Place, and I am planning to let our Nic. Ignatius go for a while and manage the outside work alone.

I am very happy to hear that there was an opportunity to send news and books here. If Clewell can just send the box to Knoxville or Maryville right away, there is always a chance to send things on from there with traders — from Maryville I can pick up the box myself in 4 days if there is no other way.

Along with sincere greetings to your dear family from Sr. Clauder and me, I remain your faithful friend and Brother,

H. G. Clauder

[M 407-3: Diary of the Mission to the Cherokee Indians.]

May 3. Early in the morning, I (Br. Clauder) began my journey to visit in Ooyugilogy. At noon I arrived at our friend Vann's near Spring Place and found everyone in deep mourning over the death of their 5-month-old baby daughter, who had died the day before as a result of so-called blue cough. In the evening I arrived at our well-known friends Mr. and Mrs. Worcester in New Echota and spent the night there. After I had visited some more friends there on the following morning, I went on and arrived at noon at our Br. George Hicks's at Ooyugillogy. The following day,

Sun., May 5, most of our Brethren and Sisters and friends gathered there. Then there was first a sermon on Luke 14:16-18, and then the child of our Sr. Sarah Bethia Hicks and Wm. Hicks was baptized. After the visiting friends had left, the few communicants in this area, a remnant of the former Gemeinlein at Ochgelogy, enjoyed Holy Communion for their strengthening and encouragement. During this a tender feeling of the gracious presence of the Savior prevailed. Afterward some of them gave a very pleasing testimony.

May 6. I decided to visit our Sisters Ridge and Fields, who live far away on the Coosa River, since we had not seen them for almost 2 years. On my way there I stopped in at a school being held by a certain Mrs. Stone from Connecticut. Ten of her scholars were reading in an English Testament, some others were spelling. Among them was a small 4-year-old girl who distinguished herself by spelling 4-syllable words. At the teacher's request, I gave a small talk for her scholars and encouraged them to diligence, honesty, peacefulness, and love toward God their Savior, and commended them and their teacher to the faithful guidance and support of the Savior in a prayer on our knees and that He might give the scholars new hearts and might give and maintain for the teacher those gifts which are necessary for her calling. Then I took leave from them and went on. A long time before evening I arrived at our friend Major Ridge's and found his brother, our dear old Christian David (Watee) there as well. Because of the presence of his daughter Sally, as well as later the arrival of his son John Ridge, I had good interpreters, so that the evening passed by unnoticed with conversation, praying, and singing, and not until midnight did we go to bed.

The following morning I paid a brief visit at Sr. Fields's and was happy to see that she has a relationship with her Redeemer. After I had taken sincere leave from these dear friends and received repeated invitations to come again soon, I began my return journey and arrived back to my dear family the evening of the following day, after an absence of 6 days and a journey of 130 miles.

May 10. This evening we received a visit from Mr. Worcester and Stephen Foreman, who spent the night and left for Candys Creek early the next morning. Mr. Foreman is a converted Cherokee and recently returned from Princeton in N. Jersey, where he studied a number of years.

Sun., May 12. We have had heavy downpours of rain since yesterday evening, which also continued the whole day today. Despite this some visitors still came to the service here.

[*Records: N.C.*, 8:4112: Friedberg Diary. Translated by Douglas L. Rights.]

May 14. I [*Records: Cherokees* ed.: Henry A. Schulz] spoke with the single Br. Miles Vogler about his often expressed wish to become a messenger of the Lord to the heathen.* I advised him to become well acquainted with the Holy Bible, hymns of the church, and the history of the Brethren's Church, and that if time and circumstances permitted, I would be glad to instruct him in geography, history, English, and other branches of learning, with good, if not erudite instruction.

* Miles Vogler later served as a missionary to the Cherokee Indians.

[M 407-3: Diary of the Mission to the Cherokee Indians.]

May 15. Br. Clauder went to the Council in Red Hill on business. The Delegates who had attended the last Congress gave a report on their negotiations with the Secretary of War and the President concerning the situation of this Nation.

May 16. Br. Clauder returned home.

Sun., May 19. Some of our Brn. and Srs. gathered at John Jacob's, where the usual services were held.

During this week with the help of some of our neighbors we built ourselves a springhouse for the storage of milk and butter. A shelter for our wagons was also built. After finishing this work we let our hired workers go, since we hope to manage alone with the necessary work at this time.

[M 415-3b-10: Translated by Julie Tomberlin Weber. Addressed to: Revd. Theodore Schulz, Salem, North Carolina. Postmark: Connassauga, C.N., May 21, 18¾. Received June 4.]

Connesauga, May 20, 1833

Dear Brother Schulz,

Yesterday evening we were delighted to receive your kind letter dated May 5 along with the Salem Diary and Memorabilia, which occupied us in a pleasant and instructive manner until late in the night. I was already planning to write you last week but my visit to the Council prevented me from doing so. And so

I will now prepare a letter to send with tomorrow's Tennessee mail.

Since my last letter to you several things have happened which might be of interest to you and with which I will begin my simple tale. First, I will report on my journey to visit in Oochgelogy and from there on to Major Ridge's home. You will later learn about this in more detail from the Diary for here. On the first Sunday in this month the small gathering, the remainder of our former dear Ochgelogy flock, was served Communion. This was a blessing and refreshment for them, and it took place at our Br. George Hicks's home. Our Brn. and Srs. George & Lucy Hicks, Lydia Chisholm and her mother, old Hannah (Qualiuku), Sr. Sarah Hicks, and Nancy Hicks (Charles Renatus's widow) were present.

The interesting old Christian D. Watee was visiting his married daughter in Wills Valley, but the following day I found him on his journey home at his brother, Major Ridge's. My visit here was very interesting for me. Sr. Ridge, Sally, and Major R. were very friendly. The latter asked about you and Br. Abraham Steiner, Sr. He is about as good at speaking English as I am at Cherokee. Then among other things, I want to provide a brief description of our conversation. We sat in the shade by his house. Watee was also there. I said Br. Abraham Steiner had been "utlonka" (sick), meaning he was very weak and frail because of old age, etc. Major Ridge later learned this opinion, and he quickly replied with his usual laughter, "Stiner no sick here (pointing to his legs), bone sick, no walk." Now he had sufficient reason to laugh at my Cherokee, as I had about his English.

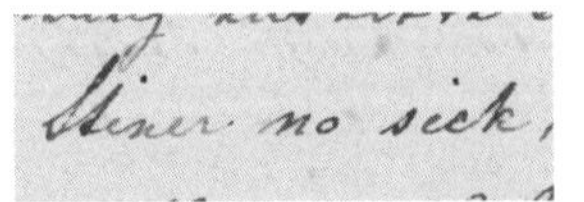

His son John also came and spent the night there. His head was full of great plans for taking the Cherokees across the Rocky Mountains and establishing a large kingdom there, gathering all the Indian Nations there and establishing a border between them and the white population.

He demonstrated a certain eloquence in his arguments which revealed a special talent. Among other things he said, "We want

"We want the Missionaries to go with us,

the missionaries to go with us, & the United Brethren who have established their Missions on the inhospitable shores of Greenland, they will, I trust, feel willing to go with us." I told him that I had no doubt that our missionaries would accompany them with the approval of the U.S. Government.

However, it is impossible that the Cherokees will cross the Rocky Mountains. There are many among them who would probably move there if the journey did not have to go through the great desert. And how should a Nation trudge through this with all their elderly and weak, women and children?

Gov. Lumpkin has confirmed Wm. Hicks's possession of our Oochgelogy houses, and the white people who had forced their way in there had to yield. However, Hicks had had a white family from Tennessee come, and they are living there now and working the fields. He also had a large new field cleared there. From all of this it is clear to see that he has taken possession of the place. He is also supposed to have said he will never again give up his rights. If he is planning to enrich himself through dishonesty, the sooner we can try to get the valuation of the place the better. In 2 weeks I am going back there, and I will see what can be done. I also hope to get the requested valuation of Spring Place by September, since by July or Aug. it will be known whether Vann will get the place or not, which seems very improbable to us.

Regarding the Ochgelogy improvements, I believe it is Wm. Hicks's intention to compensate us for them, and since the law of Georgia gives him complete rights and protection, it is my view that we should accept or request compensation from him to avoid all cause for bitterness. Last week I had a thorough conversation with Major Currie, the special agent of the U.S., whom I met at the Council. He would be willing to undertake the valuation of both abandoned mission places, and since he is personally known by the Secretary of War and Jackson, he and Col. Montgomery would be the most appropriate individuals to get this matter in order. Curry traveled to Arkansas last year with a number of Emigrants. He gives a good description of the land and the improved situation of those Cherokees who are already there.

The Council is still working, and I hear that both parties are supposed to have united again, which leads me to think that Ross now understands how essential it is to send an exploring party to the west. Last week Ridge was planning to submit a memorial to the Council to reach this end, and a reconciliation would hardly have been accomplished if the Council had decided against it. Already by last week when I visited the Council I believed that I could note from Ross's public talk that it would come to the point of sending an exploring party. Oh, if the Indians would just understand for once that they cannot remain here and not console themselves any longer with unfounded hopes.

The U.S. troops who recently moved through here actually drove all the intruders out of the Tennessee part of the Nation, but in Alabama and Georgia everything remains status quo, because the laws extend over both of these states. This is just a policy of Jackson to get Tennessee to extend its laws over the Cherokees as well, so that there would be no more interference from the U.S. government.

Concerning us here, we should note with gratitude toward our dear Lord that although we are not enjoying such good health as we did previously, we can still be on our feet and take care of our business. Sr. Clauder has been suffering for several weeks from a painful tooth and from headaches caused by an earlier cold. Several days ago our young Ann Eliza was also sick with fever from a tooth. However, the raging hooping cough did not reach our little one. Mrs. Vann at Springplace lost her little 6 month-old baby daughter to this. Our dear and good McNairs are also more than a little concerned about their eldest daughter Mrs. Been, who left her 6 children 6 weeks ago and secretly ran away with a white man named Ware. So far there has been no news from her. Everyone presumes they have gone to Missouri.

The children are all with their grandparents and 3 of them come to the school here. Her former husband, Been, with whom she did not have a happy marriage, had left her more than a year ago.

I have not yet heard anything about the box from Mr. Clewel. Was my payment for my *N.Y. Weekly Messenger* made through Henry Sch.? I have been receiving the *N.Y. Observer* for a number of months, although I did not order it. This makes me think that the payment was made to the *Observer* instead of the *Messenger*, which is a much more interesting paper for me and avoids all sectarianism.

Wm. Hicks finally paid $95 on his notes and is still in debt approximately $50 including interest. Unfortunately, however, I had to take $40 Darien notes, which are not in the best credit, like all Georgia notes in these times.

It should also be noted especially for Br. Byhan that recently the excellent horse he received from Sam. Henry died very suddenly from the so-called Botts. Greet Br. and Sr. Byhan for us. We have not received anything from them since last September, although I sent them some letters which presumably never arrived, just as a letter to you between Feb. 18 and Apr. 8 was lost on the way.

Along with sincere greetings to your dear family, I remain with love, your faithfully obliged Brother,

H. G. Clauder

[M 407-3: Diary of the Mission to the Cherokee Indians.]

Sun., May 26. Pentecost. Many of our Brn. and Srs. gathered at Br. James's, where Br. Clauder held the festival sermon. This was translated as usual through an interpreter, which was now all the more necessary because only Indians were there. Finally Br. Samuel gave an admonition and prayer, which made an impression on the listeners. Br. Clauder then returned by foot accompanied by the Indian Br. Israel, who had come to visit. He spent the night with us.

June 1. Br. Clauder went to Ochgelogy, where on the 2nd he first preached at George Hicks's and in the evening at Sr. Sarah Hicks's. Christian David (Watee) was also at the first-mentioned place and read the 2nd chapter of Acts, which was recently translated. Finally he gave some admonitions to those present and concluded with a prayer. Afterward Br. Clauder had another conversation with this interesting old man, during which, among other things, he explained the cause of his peaceful and cheerful nature: "When I think about my former ways, it is nothing other than a miracle of my Savior's grace that I do not walk in this anymore, and that He has taken away all my great and frequent sins and accepted me as a follower. This is what I always gratefully rejoice over." Since his wife has gone to her rest, he has given his own farm to his stepson John Candy and lives in peace with his son Elias Boudinot in Echota. Here he spends most of his time reading the few available Cherokee books.

Since Br. Clauder was busy preparing a tract translated into the Cherokee language in New Echota entitled *Poor Sarah*, he did not return home until the 5th. An edition of 3,000 copies was printed of this text. Some of them are supposed to be distributed here in this country, and some of them among the Cherokees in Arkansas.

[*Records: N.C.*, 8:4061: Salem Diary. Translated by Douglas L. Rights.]

May 22. In the evening in the 6th hour the widowed Br. Abraham Gottlieb Steiner fell asleep in his 76th year.

Memoir of Br. Abraham Steiner

Autobiography of the widowed Br. Abraham Steiner, gone home at Salem in North Carolina 22 May 1833

I was born Apr. 27, 1758, at Bethlehem in Pennsylvania and baptized by Br. Peter Boehler. After I was a little over a year old I was, according to the custom of the time, placed by my parents in the institution for small children at Old Nazareth. . . .

After a number of years I was placed in company of thirteen children of the same age in the Boys School at Nazareth Hall in which I spent my remaining years of childhood and several years beyond. . . . Limited as my training was, had I not received it there I would have received none or else a much more imperfect one. Further, it was here that the foundation of my dependence upon the Brüdergemeine and its ordinances was laid; and finally it was here that love for the Lord's work in general, but especially among the heathen, and the desire to serve Him was aroused in me. . . .

At that time many Indians still came to Nazareth Hall, from Friedenshütten as well as from the upper Susquehannah region and from other communities, and I acquired an attraction to these people which always remained. At the departure of the Brn. Zeisberger, Senseman, Heckewelder, and others into Indian country, likewise at the equipping of Brethren for the West Indies Islands, Br. Tiersch always presented the work of missions among the heathen in such a light that it necessarily made a deep impression upon our young hearts. At that time I mostly saw the missionaries set forth on foot with their bundles on their backs, and I always imagined a missionary as a servant of Jesus who did not hold his life dear, goes his own way in poverty, often sees no prosperity for himself, depends entirely upon His grace, and I could think of nothing more honorable upon earth. . . .

From the bottom of my heart I said to the Saviour: Today I give myself anew to Thee. At another time my grandmother Boerstler, from Oley, visited me and said in parting: “Hab’s Lammlein lieb!”[1] Those few words pierced my heart and had a greater impression on me than the longest and most learned sermon.

So my childhood years sped by, by no means without impressions upon me of my Redeemer’s love but without having made many especially spiritual experiences. . . .

Once a report of an Indian congregation was read during which I was so moved that on that and the following day my eyes seldom were dry, particularly when I considered how much I lacked in comparison with these Indians, in love and grace and loyalty. This was noticed, and I was asked what was the matter. But I told no one. At that time, and long afterward, I could have offered up everything, body and life, to be a Moravian missionary to the heathen, preferably among the Indians, and I really often wished my conversion an accomplished fact and real soon to be able to consecrate my life to such a service. . . .

Since from earliest times I had a special love for the Indians and would have liked to spend my days in service among them, I approached Br. Heckewelder, who was on his way to make a journey into the Indian country, and asked to be permitted to accompany him; that desire was granted. We departed in Apr. 1789. The purpose of this journey was to gather information whether the tract of land granted in trust to the Brethren along the Muskingum could be surveyed, and how soon this work could be begun. . . . During this journey I learned how one subsists in the bush, which was of great advantage to me in later times. . . .

This was the beginning of war between the Indians and the U.S. which came to an end only after many years after the

---

1 “Love the little Lamb.” Br. John Gambold also recollected Sr. Boerstler’s words. See *Records: Cherokees*, 5:2586.

complete victory of Gen. Wayne over the united Indians. During the entire journey not the least danger threatened us, though the Indians who accompanied us declared they saw evidence of warriors near several places we passed. . . .

In Aug. I received an offer to take over the store at Bethabara in Wachovia. . . . On Oct. 16, 1789, I reached Salem. The simplicity of the prevailing customs here pleased me very much. This, in addition to the meeting of many former friends, soon helped me to feel at home, and when on Nov. 1, the entire congregation joined in the hymn I was overwhelmed by the words: “Salem that is above” with an indescribable experience. . . .

I was in Salem on Oct. 17 [1799] at the meeting of the Society for the Propagation of the Gospel among the Heathen, in which I felt strongly moved to say much about the fact that we have been so long in North Carolina without having done anything in the cause of the Lord among the nearby heathen, and named the Indians in particular who were nearer to us than the northern Indians in Pennsylvania, that it was high time that we here made effort to carry the Gospel among the heathen. Many objections were presented, and I had to fight opposition, but several Brethren strongly supported me. The occasion for this was an article by the preacher Joseph Bullen. . . . [Here Br. Steiner recounts his journeys to the Cherokee Nation and the beginning of the Springplace mission, as documented in *Records: Cherokees*, volumes 1-5.]

I was charged with the oversight of the Girls Boarding School in Salem in 1806 and took residence there in Oct. . . . With the supervision of the Girls Boarding School I entered upon an entirely new field of endeavor. This institution was still new, had rapidly increased in patronage, but now it was definitely on the decline again, and it seemed as if all had lost confidence in it. This was gradually regained. I won the good will of scholars and teachers, and soon the confidence of parents, and patronage was restored so that many applicants had to be refused for lack of room. My duties increased, for I also taught, so that my strength was taxed. I became weak; a severe recurrent headache afflicted me, and finally no week passed that I did not have to spend at least one day in bed, unable to do any work. Naturally the duties of the work piled up. So I found it necessary to hand in my resignation, which was accepted in 1816.

Now I began a journey to Pennsylvania, which I had left 27 years ago. This journey was not only beneficial, but also served to completely restore my health. . . .

In the summer of 1819 I accompanied Br. Samuel Gottl. Kramsch to Raleigh, where he submitted to an eye operation. . . . After my return I received an assignment from the Prov. H. Conf. to visit in Springplace. On Sept. 17 I set out upon this journey in company with Br. Samuel Thomas Pfohl, and arrived there early in Oct., to the heartfelt joy of Br. and Sr. Gambold. Twenty years had passed since I first entered Cherokee Land. What changes had taken place meanwhile! At that time the wares had to be transported on pack horses following narrow trails. Now there were wide roads built for the comfort of the travelers, upon which wares and provisions were hauled by wagon by natives of the land. Then only small huts were to be seen; cultivation of the soil was just beginning; the Indians mostly lived in villages and supported themselves primarily by the chase. Now there were no more hunting reservations; many individual farms were established with well cultivated fields with good, yes, even some beautiful, houses; and most of the inhabitants supported themselves by farming and raising cattle. Then there were no schools and no religious services in the land, and the whites and half-breeds desiring to have their children instructed were compelled to send them away to white people. Now schools and mission stations were established; the Word of God was proclaimed in the land to the profit of many. Then darkness held sway; now many of my former acquaintances had become redeemed children of God. This change rejoiced me greatly. I had a number of consultations with Br. and Sr. Gambold concerning our plan in Cherokee land, and especially in regard to Springplace. A small congregation had been established. They lived scattered but came to Springplace to church, and consisted of solid, dependable people who had laid a good foundation. I rejoiced to find many of my former acquaintances among the members and had the privilege to baptize, before partaking of their first Communion, my old friends Clement and Mary Vann. Twice I partook of the Holy Communion with the little group of believers at which the presence of the Friend of sinners, full of salvation and grace, was sensibly felt in our midst and the spirit of real Brotherly love was effectually working. It was a means of grace when First-Love and real simplicity dominated. Also many heathen came, tearfully complaining because of their unblest circumstances and desiring counsel, whereby I learned to hold in high regard the constant concern of the missionaries for the salvation of souls. Sr. Gambold especially was untiring in her efforts to lead souls to Christ and encourage them. The number of scholars at Springplace was small, but under Sr. Gambold's instruction they were taught basic things.

We visited many Indian Brethren on their farms, among others also my former acquaintance, Br. Charles Renatus Hicks, in whose house I conducted an evening meeting. On that occasion we also visited Brainerd, where the missionaries received us most cordially. The school had a board floor; male scholars predominated. Before leaving I addressed the student body, and upon being asked to read a chapter from the Bible, I read Isaiah 60, with application to the Cherokees. In departure the scholars sang two hymns, one in the English, the other in the Cherokee language, as well as a hymn from the Brethren's hymnal which Sr. Gambold from Springplace had taught them.

Since a new seat of the Cherokee Government had been laid out about 20 miles from Springplace, named Newtown, and a new Council House built, in which the first Assembly for Council was to be held, I was requested to hold a service there before its opening. Upon our arrival many Cherokee Chiefs were already present, among them Br. Charles Renatus Hicks, and many other people. A Baptist preacher was also present with the intent to secure permission from the Council to establish a mission in the valley towns in the mountains, which was granted with the consideration not to interfere with other missions. On several evenings before the opening of the Council meetings he read a few chapters from the Law of Moses, whereupon I followed each time with several chapters from the Gospel. The inaugural festivities of the

Council House were held on a Sunday, during which many Indian and white people gathered at the Council House. After the Chiefs occupied their seats the Speaker of the Nation, Major Ridge, first addressed the chiefs and the National Committee, reminding them of their duties, to which several chiefs replied. The Speaker then addressed the people in a short address, which was followed by a shout of approval. Shortly thereafter the tobacco pipes were handed out and announcement made that the service was about to begin and that today no more business would be transacted. I then took my place in one of the open buildings, where I could be seen and heard by the Assembly, and the Baptist minister stood beside me.

First of all I declared the purpose of that gathering in a short address; then we sang a hymn. After a prayer, particularly on behalf of the Cherokee Nation, I preached a sermon on John 3:16, “For God so loved the world, etc.,” dealing with God’s counsel for our salvation, the content of which was repeated by Br. Charles Renatus Hicks in the Cherokee language. Then the Baptist preacher gave an admonition in which he urgently besought the listeners to give admonition to the truth just proclaimed and live accordingly, that the one who first preached the Gospel among them was standing before them, perhaps for the last time because of his advanced age, and that he had proclaimed the Gospel of Peace and they might well heed it. This address was also interpreted by Br. Hicks. Then the Baptist minister started a hymn out of our English hymnal and offered the closing prayer, in which he interceded that God’s blessing might particularly rest on their present and future Council meetings. During the services, at which many of the listeners had to stand for lack of seats, silence reigned supreme in a reverent manner. One saw many standing quietly, devoutly, with folded hands and bowed heads, and the half-Indians considered this gathering as the dedication of their Council House.[1]

We set out from here for Oochgeelogy to view an area where

---

[1] See Br. Steiner’s 1819 account of the dedication of the Council House, *Records: Cherokees*, 5:2469-71.

an awakening had been in progress for some time. This had its origin through Bible reading, and the inhabitants had expressed their desire to have a missionary couple in their midst. Especially at William Hicks's and Major Ridge's we received a loving welcome. Upon our return to Springplace, we discussed plans how the serving of this place, a day's journey away, could possibly be accomplished, and we had the joy that our Lord had inclined two of them to desire baptism.

The building of the church in Springplace was so far advanced that it could be consecrated, and Nov. 14 was set for this. . . . On that occasion two adults from Oochgeelogy were baptized by Br. Gambold and me.

After a short morning farewell from our dear Indian congregation we began our return trip on Nov. 17th and arrived safely in Salem the first week in Dec. . . .

Beginning of the year 1822 I was asked to take charge of work among the Negroes in Salem and vicinity. I did not accept this call willingly but from a sense of duty. I began to hold special meetings for them on 24 March 1822. At first I held meetings every four weeks, but soon, upon the request of the Negroes, every 2 weeks on the various farms, and each time a goodly number of listeners gathered. O, how often I prayed that the Savior would give me the message I was to proclaim to these people and to apply the words to their hearts, or rather to speak through His Spirit to their hearts; for daily I realized my insufficiency, and I never spoke to them publicly or in private without first praying for grace, anointing, and wisdom. In 1823 a house of God for these people was erected at Salem and dedicated the same year on Dec. 28th, and the first adult Negro woman was baptized on this occasion. . . .

Salem, North Carolina
Jan. 25, 1827
Abraham Steiner

Supplement on 24 Sept. 1832

Since composing the above memoir I have suffered more from the sicknesses and weaknesses of old age than formerly. The Lord also bereft me of my helpmeet on Aug. 17, 1829. The future I submit to Him and I do not worry. My only concern is my slackness in running the race set before me. . . . My evening walks in the moonlight have since then been discontinued, but the secret conversations with my dearest Friend are carried on nonetheless. What more can I say? My insufficiency is great, the Savior's supply sufficient. This has been my life's experience. When I consider how long the Lord has cared for me and still receives so little honor and glory for His diligence, I wish most heartily that I might please Him more. I shall never be able to thank Him sufficiently for His mercies toward me. The thanks and praise which He deserves I will render unto Him when I see Him face to face. Meanwhile, I will kiss His bloody hands here already as best I can, in which He bears me up with all my misery.

So far he himself. Added after his demise:

During a very active course of life, old age had gradually caught up with our departed Br., and the more he realized his strength was waning the more urgently was he concerned about his inner condition, the soul's struggle of his youth was accentuated by age as his autobiography amply shows. . . .

On the evening of 22 May 1833 it was evident that the end was near. The blessing of the Lord and the congregation was bestowed upon him in the presence of his children and a number of other Brethren and Sisters, and at 2 o'clock he departed, ending his pilgrimage of 75 years, 3 weeks, and 4 days. . . .

Gravestone of Br. Abraham Steiner, pioneer missionary to the Cherokee Nation, in the Salem God's Acre.

1833, part 3

[M 415-3b-9: Translated by Julie Tomberlin Weber. Addressed to: Revd. Theodore Schulz, Salem, North Carolina. Postmark: Connassauga, C.N., June 7, 18¾. Received June 19.]

Connesauga, Ch. Nat., June 6, 1833

Dear Br. Schulz,

Today I received your kind letter of May 26th along with *Monatliche* and *Wöchentliche Nachrichten*, and this was a great encouragement to us. Yesterday evening I returned from Ochgelogy and New Echota. I had spent 1½ days at the latter place to finish the tract *Poor Sarah*, which has now been printed with the assistance of Mr. Worcester. The appropriation of $40, which you and Br. Schweinitz made for this purpose, was sufficient to have an edition of 3,000 copies printed. Mr. Worcester asked for 1,000 copies to send to Arkansas, and I gave them to him. Although you will not be able to make further use of it, I am sending you a copy. I had the woodcut you will see on the outside sent from N. York last winter by mail.

Since my last letter to you, I have learned more about the union that has taken place between Ross and Ridge and about the decisions reached by the Council. The reason for their agreement is that they want to watch until the next Congress. If they are not given any assistance, they want to proceed seriously and seek another place to live. The head people of both parties have committed themselves to this agreement by signing their names. This was actually the point Ridge was working toward, that John

Ross should reveal the ultimate aim of his stay and the reasons for his continuing "good hopes." Since he lacked this, he preferred to get assurance of the other party's patience and trust until the end of the next Congress. However, since one can predict with relative certainty that nothing will happen in Congress according to the Cherokees' wishes, one can certainly expect a treaty and the resulting move of the Cherokees. In the meantime, the matter has broken, and the Indians speak more about their situation than previously, and at least Ridge's party, which is in favor of removal, will no longer be seen as unfaithful — as traitors.

For this and other reasons I also finally see an opening to take steps to estimate the value of both of our mission places, and I will be able to send the required papers in July. Genl. Hardin, who was assigned this task by the U.S. Government last year and therefore is known by Sect. Cass, was immediately willing to take care of this matter for me. It is now clear that Wm. Hicks is definitely planning to sell our Ochgelogy place at the first opportunity or to sell it to the U.S. as his property if the enrollment of emigrants should begin again. Wouldn't it be advisable to inform Col. Montgomery or Sec. Cass of that post's situation to prevent this planned deception?

Our health continues to be good, and the school, which has about 7 regular scholars, is also in a routine under Sr. Rüde, accompanied with our dear Lord's blessing. We believe we can see the miraculous hand of God ever more clearly in our being driven out of Spring Place. Oh, how faithful and good He is toward us, His children, who are so often unfaithful. When we left Spring Place we were bitter about the Georgians, in the way of human sinners. However, we see that whatever the Lord does or allows to happen works out well in the end. Our prayer is that He might continue to be with us in love and goodness, and that He will strengthen and bless us and all His servants in their callings and offices. Your loving, obliged Br.

H. G. Clauder

N.B. I have sued the mail contractor in West Tennessee who owes us $40 for food, etc, through Mr. David Wendell of Murfreesboro, and proved my account before an Esquire from McMinn

County and sent it with the County seal and Clerk and presiding chairman's signature, and I hope to get what belongs to us.

[M 407-3: Diary of the Mission to the Cherokee Indians. Translated by Julie Tomberlin Weber. Handwriting is Heinrich Gottlieb Clauder's.]

Sun., June 9. The service was held at our Br. Josua's. All of our Brn. and Srs. from this area, as well as our friend Tazizi, had come for this. From conversations with many of those baptized, their wish to be the Savior's property and to remain faithful to him until the end could be seen.

Sun., June 16. A large number of Indians gathered at our Br. James's. Unfortunately, however, our interpreter Nicolaus Ignatius was sick and could not be present. After singing some hymns, part of the Cherokee tract *Poor Sarah* was read. Then at Br. Clauder's request a Cherokee who was present, an exhorter among the Methodists, gave a talk. Our Brn. and Srs. were invited for the enjoyment of Holy Communion at our house in 14 days.

June 18-20. We had 2 to 3 strong storms with rain and wind each day, which was very harmful to the oats and corn. During these days a traveler named Week from Macon in Georgia visited us. He said he used to be a member of the Brethren's Society in New York and was in the service there of a Brother named Tenbrock. In 1817 he had gone to Georgia and run a business in Savannah and Macon until a number of years ago he had lost almost everything in a fire in the latter place and a serious illness which followed. He visited our school here and showed compassion for our situation.

Sun., June 30. We had many visitors here since the services were held here. In the sermon on John 3:3 the listeners were reminded that the new birth of the heart does not merely consist in baptism or in an external moral and legal nature, but is rather effected through the power of the Holy Spirit in the heart and indeed in all who notice His tugs and follow them. After confirmation, the single Sr. Agatha Sanders participated today in Holy

Communion for the first time. On this occasion we felt the merciful presence of our Lord in a manner rich in blessings to our comfort.

[M 415-3b-11: Translated by Julie Tomberlin Weber; transcribed by Grace S. Robinson. Addressed to: Revd. Theodore Schulz, Salem, North Carolina. Postmark: Connassauga, C.N., July 5, [paid] 75¢. Received July 15.]

Connesauga, July 2, 1833

Dear Brother Schulz,

[Br. Clauder begins his letter in English:]

Herewith you will receive our Diary for the past half year from which you will learn some further particulars concerning this Mission. That my imperfect sketches of the past may still be interesting to you is my sincere wish. Our Lord & Saviour has thus far supported us under various trials & perplexities, & permitted us to labour in this part of His extensive vineyard for which I trust we feel truly thankful, & that He will carry on this work among these poor Cherokees in spite of existing obstacles, is the subject of our daily prayers & supplications.

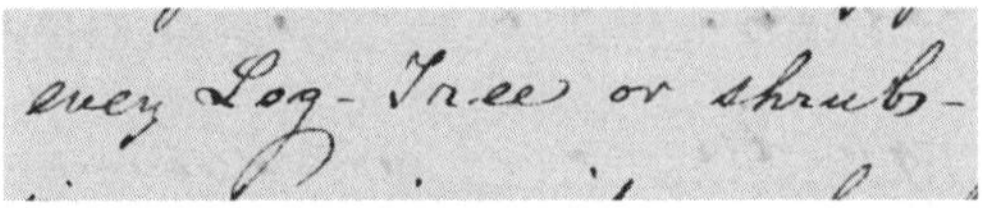

Your esteemed favour of the 20th ult. together with a copy of the last No. of the *Miss. Intellg.* came to hand last Sunday the 30th & gave us great satisfaction. With regard to the fraud to be apprehended from Mr. Hicks I am happy in saying that on my last visit in Ochgelogy about the beginning of June I took measures to get our abandoned improvements valued, which valuation I have in my possession & would forward it on at this time were it not for a small amendment which is necessary & concerning which I have written to Genl. Hardin. From the same gentlemen I also expect by every mail the valuation of the Spring Place improvements, which he promised to make out for me. The valuation of the Ochgelogy improvements amounts at present to $1,284.50. Genl. Hardin was very particular in making out this amount, specifying every Log, Tree, or shrub, etc., on the place, but in his efforts to take notice of minor items he forgot the Brick chimney of the Mission house, the valuation of which I have yet to receive.

[Br. Clauder continues his letter in German:]

Since I copied the above hastily this morning in English, I received the valuation of Springplace, and I will send both papers to you as soon as I receive the complete one from Ochgelogy. I will write soon to Mr. Montgomery and Maj. Currie, the special enrolling agent, so that they become acquainted with Hicks's plans. It is really almost unbelievable that he should have such thoughts, but it is commonly said in his neighborhood, based on his own talk, that he is planning such and such. Hicks himself was in Milledgeville at Gov. Lumpkin's, who gave him a certificate so that the drawer by lottery should not disturb him in his possession. Genl. Hardin, however, thinks that according to their law Hicks could not possibly claim the place and Lumpkin's certificate is not worth anything. Otherwise, in my opinion, this does not concern us, since we have the valuation and need to turn with it directly to the Genl. Government.

In our actual calling here everything is continuing as usual. Last Sunday the 30th a great many people came here for the sermon. Many could not get into the house, because there was not enough room. The Indian Turnover (Josua's cousin) came back with his request to become a member of our Gemeine, and he had already asked his former teacher for a certificate about his association with the Methodists, since the Methodist missionaries who previously made so much noise and trouble have completely abandoned their work and are no longer roaming around the country to win proselytes. Many of their church children are now essentially abandoned and are trying to join elsewhere. I thought it would be my duty to give this Indian some hope that his wish might possibly be granted in time. Doct. Rowles, who seems to be a reasonable man and last worked on this Circuit, found it pointless to continue in their previous manner, and for a number of months he has been living in another area where he, like us, holds a school and on Sundays preaches there.

Also of further interest, I would like to report that the single Indian woman Agatha Sanders participated for the first time in Holy Communion last Sunday after her confirmation had been completed. Until now no new baptismal candidates had come. Things are not going well with the Indian Agathe (her Indian name is Si-na-sta), who was accepted into the congregation last summer in Spring Place. We often hear bad news about her, but cannot find any positive proof or accusers. She rarely visits us and is very reserved. She is not yet one of the communicants.

We heard the news a long time ago from my relative Mrs. Clewell that the box had been sent to Col. Williams in Knoxville, but I have not heard anything from him, although I wrote him long ago asking him to send said box to Athens (by mail stage), where I could easily get it.

Corn cannot be purchased here at all. Many Indians have nothing to eat but blackberries and blueberries. Many hungry people come here looking for something better to eat or to trade their berries. Last week I got some corn from our friend Cobb in McMinn County, where I got it for 40 cents per bushel. Mr. McNair was seriously ill for a number of weeks, but now he is up again. Greet my dear friend Henry in Friedberg for me. I would really like to receive something from his own hand. Give my sincere greetings to the dear Brethren of the P.H.C.

I remain your loving, obliged Brother,

H. G. Clauder

[M 407-3: Diary of the Mission to the Cherokee Indians.]

Since our usual interpreter Nicolaus Ignatius became ill at the beginning of July and a number of weeks passed before he completely recovered, the usual Sunday services were canceled several times. The Brn. and Srs. still gathered often and edified themselves by singing, reading, and praying in their language. Some of the so-called Class leaders of the Methodists also held exhortation talks a number of times at our Brethren and Sisters' services.

July 18. We received the news that the United States Government has opened anew the voluntary enrollment of Cherokee emigrants to Arkansaw territory, through Major Currie. Along with others also, William Hicks, who formerly belonged to the Gemeine in Ooyugillogy, has had his name listed.

[M 415-3b-12: Translated by Julie Tomberlin Weber. Addressed to: Revd. Theodore Schulz, Salem, Stokes Cty., North Carolina. Postmark: Connassauga, C.N., Ju~~ne~~ly 23, [paid] 56¼¢. Received Aug. 17.]

Connesauga, C.N., July 22, 1833

Beloved Brother Schulz,

I hope that by now my last letter to you dated the 2nd of this month, along with the enclosure of the Diary to the first of this month, will have reached you safely. Since it was sent, we have continued with our usual routine, but each of us has had to tolerate a small illness or another. You will have learned from the newspapers that the greatly feared cholera is killing people in this state of Tennessee, especially in the western and middle sections. May the Lord in His great mercy and goodness protect us from this.

On the 11th of this month Mr. McNair and I were called to Vann's to serve as witnesses in the matter of Vann vs. Bishop. The latter, however, avoided a trial for now by a writ of injunction he received for this purpose, and which postponed the matter until the next Supreme Court in September. Then we must appear there as witnesses. Mr. Vann believes he can prove that the missionaries received the Spring Place place from his father James Vann for no payment in 1801 on the condition that if they ever had to leave it he (Vann) would pay for the improvements and the place would fall back into his possession. From

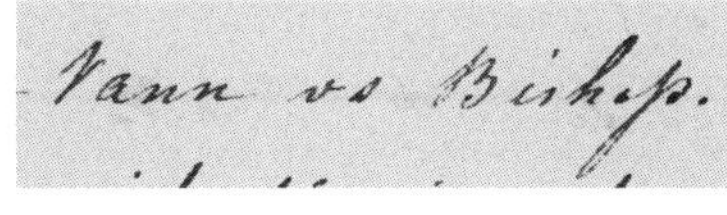

the Diary[1] here, it can be seen that Vann bought this place from Mr. Brown and gave it to the Brethren. However, I cannot find anything about a price the Brn. are supposed to have paid for it, and therefore I believe that Vann always tolerated them as tenants on Spring Place.

Mr. Vann really wants you to wait with the petition concerning the Spring Place improvements until the Court's decision. However, this will be in the fall anyway, since the decision of the Court will doubtless take place in September, and then there will be enough time until the beginning of Congress. Even if Vann should win his suit, he will hardly be able to remain peacefully in possession of Spring Place, since the law of Georgia that entitles him to it now can easily be changed, and indeed many expect this to happen.

Last week I had the opportunity of talking with Wm. Hicks at McNair's in McNair's presence as you advised, and I explained to him the insignificance of his claim to the Ochgelogy improvements. He said little or nothing, but he admitted that he was planning to enroll our improvements there, etc. I protested against this and explained to him that I would do my best to prevent him from doing this, since not he, but we were still owed a lot of money for these, and we were entitled and also hoped to receive this.

Yesterday I heard from Mr. McNair that Wm. Hicks has enrolled for Arkansas, along with many others, but I still do not know if he has actually listed our place or not. Last week I informed Col. Montgomery about the saga of our place and asked him not to pay attention to Wm. Hicks's claims. It would also be advisable to write to Gov. Lumpkin about this, since he has certainly not heard the truth from Hicks, but through false representations of the one who wrote that letter, on which he (Hicks) bases his claims.

The emigration business is starting again. I doubt whether the goal will be reached in this way, because many of the previous

---

[1] See Springplace Diary, April 30, 1801, etc., *Records: Cherokees*, 1:258, etc.

Emigrants are here again now since the road back here cannot be blocked!

The situation of the Cherokees is regrettable. Many of them are suffering starvation. There is no corn to be had for any price here. Wheat is not planted much, and the little of it there is is very bad.

Regarding the mission work here, I should mention the following. The outlook is very gloomy. The temptation to drink and all the other vices are seen frequently, and those who are not associated with one Christian confession or another show a great apathy toward the word of God and services. Among this large group, there is a prevalent belief that all missionaries are trying to persuade them to emigrate. Although we really cannot discuss this with the Indians, it is still desirable for it to come to this soon, because if the Cherokees hold out here with their previous infatuation, it is obvious that they will be spiritually and physically ruined and all efforts against this will remain fruitless. And so we really hope that this Nation might accept the liberal offer of the Government and leave this unfortunate country, and the sooner the better.

This month the usual Sunday services had to be canceled, since an illness prevented my interpreter Nic. Ignatius from coming to help me with these. The school here is continuing in a blessed routine under Sr. Ruede and is attended daily by 15 to 20 scholars who are all making very good progress in learning. It would be very regrettable if Sr. R., who seems to be very content here and is certainly occupied in a useful manner, returned to Salem for the sake of her friends, which is sometimes mentioned.

The heat is very extreme every day. Yesterday afternoon at 3 o'clock it was 100 degrees Fahrenheit. There is also a great drought, which is harmful to the crops and garden. Unfortunately I have not yet received the box of books, and today I must once again write to Knoxville about this. We are longing for the *Gem. Nachr.* contained in it. Mr. McNair has completely recovered from his recent salivation. He and his son James, who is our closest neighbor, constantly show us much love.

Our friend and closest colleagues, Mr. and Mrs. Proctor in Ahmohee, who have served in this country for approximately 15 years, are getting ready to return to Boston. The number of missionaries here decreases from year to year.

I am enclosing the paper with Genl. Hardin's valuation of our abandoned improvements. I have not yet received the Supplement for Ochgelogy. I will send it in the future, as soon as I receive it. Sincere greetings from all of us. I remain your obliged friend and Brother,

H. G. Clauder

[M 407-3: Diary of the Mission to the Cherokee Indians.]

Sun., July 28. The service was held at Sanders's. During this our friend Young Wolf interpreted, and then himself preached in Cherokee.

Sun., Aug. 4. I preached at our Br. George Hicks's in Ooyugillogy, where I had the joy of seeing together all the Brethren and Sisters who belong to the Gemeinlein there. Many white people from the area were also present. An Indian named Du-na-ne-la, who regularly attends services, expressed his desire to join our community through holy baptism and to become a follower of the Lord Jesus. Brn. George Hicks and Christian David, who had already spoken with him often, gave a good testimony of him, because of which I felt joy at accepting the said Indian for further instruction in the truths of salvation.

Aug. 8. I went to Tennessee to fetch a small wagonload of wheat from there. This kind of grain turned out badly this year, and is rare and expensive. Still I was lucky enough to get a sufficient supply and a good price from an old, familiar friend, Cobb.

Aug. 9. I returned home. On the way home I paid a farewell visit to our familiar friend and colleague, Isaac Procter in Ahmohee, who is getting ready to move to Indiana with his family.

Aug. 10. We were delighted about receiving a refreshing rain, which gave the thirsty ground and plants long desired refreshment.

Aug. 11. Early in the morning I set out on the road to Josua's, where the service was supposed to be held. It was about 12 o'clock noon when I arrived there and found a large number of Indians gathered there. Unfortunately, however, there was no one among them who would have been able to serve as interpreter, and so a chapter from the translation of the Gospel of Matthew was read, and some hymns were sung. Then I closed with a sincere prayer, and with a heart sorrowful over the shortcomings of our poor and imperfect service began the rest of the journey home.

Aug. 12. This evening we received a delightful visit from our friends, Mr. and Mrs. Butrick, who are on their return trip to Carmel, a post which they were required by the Georgia Guard to leave in 1831. Mr. Butrick gave us the gift of some books which can be used at our school.

[M 415-3b-13: Translated by Julie Tomberlin Weber. Addressed to: Revd. Theodore Schulz, Salem, Stokes County, North Carolina. Postmark: Connesauga, C.N., Aug. 13, 18¾. Received Sept. 2.]

Connesauga, C.N., Aug. 12, 1833

Dear Br. Schulz,

My letter containing the Diary to July 1st left here on July 5, followed by another one containing the valuation of both abandoned mission posts. I would love to hear that these letters have reached you safely. In your last kind letter, dated the 14th of last month, nothing was mentioned about mine dated [posted] the 5th. I hope that it and the other one have been in your hands for a long time now.

Our health remains the same, and our work is about the same as usual. My visit in Ochgelogy on the first Sunday in this month was especially encouraging to me, since I had the pleasure of seeing all of our Brethren and Sisters there gathered together, including Sussanah Fields. I had heard incorrectly that she had decided to become a Methodist, but she seems to be far from taking this step. A man named Du-na-ne-la was also there. At his request and based on the good testimony of Brn. Christian David and George Hicks, I accepted him into the class of new people so that in time he can reach the further grace of the Gemeine. He always attends the services of the Brn. and Srs. at George Hicks's and seems to be thoroughly awakened. He is an unmarried man and works at Chisholm's.

On the occasion of my visit in that area, I ran into Maj. Currie with whom I had a private conversation in which I explained to him the situation at the Ochgelogy Mission place. Since Wm. Hicks is currently his interpreter, I suspect that Currie considers our improvements there to be Hicks's property and will accept this from him. I wrote to Col. Montgomery about this a long time ago. Currie had indeed seen this letter, but he would not assure me that Wm. Hicks has no claims to these improvements. Still he admitted our right to be paid for this and said: "The U.S. government will compensate Mr. Hicks for his trouble in taking care of the Station, & will also fully satisfy your board for the same."[1]

The Emigration of the Cherokees is not proceeding as intensely as was expected, and at this date only a few have agreed to do it.

I would like to learn the P.H.C.'s opinion on two questions.

1. The Indian Turnover and his wife have asked repeatedly to be accepted, and they have received a good testimony from their preacher (Young Wolf). After they have been accepted through the Lot in the usual manner, can they then join our other communicants in Communion immediately without consulting the Lot again about Holy Communion? Both have already frequently attended with our Gemeine as guests, and it would probably seem strange to them if they had to undergo a waiting period as actual members of our Gemeine.

2. Regarding the acceptance of new people, that is, those who want to be baptized and therefore need our special consideration

---

[1] The quote is in English in the original German manuscript.

and instruction, it seems appropriate to me to accept such people publicly and in ceremonial manner, since this makes a good impression on the hearts of all those present, and in this way the "newlings" themselves declare their decision to seek the One Thing Needful. I experienced a delightful example of this during the acceptance of the Indian Dananela in Ochgelogy. However, before I continue in this trial, which seems appropriate for this people and not at all outside of the "Brotherly Way," I want to ask for the view and sanction of the elder servants of the Lord, "for the spirits of the prophets are subject to the prophets" [1 Cor. 14:32.]

After my return from Ochgelogy last week, I went to Tennessee with our small wagon and picked up wheat that I had bought there for 62½ cents per bushel. This grain is quite bad throughout the country this year and also not very plentiful. Flour is now already $7 per barrel, and if the corn crops really turn out as badly as people everywhere presume, it will become even more expensive. There is an overabundance of fruit everywhere.

Yesterday (Sunday) I left here early in the morning in the rain to go to Josua's where a large congregation of Indians had gathered. In that service 2 children were baptized. Today I am feeling my ride yesterday of 42 miles.

Our school is limping along, since the scholars come extremely sporadically. For this reason, as well as the fact that no school can be held in the winter, our dear Sr. Ruede feels moved to return to Salem at the first opportunity, especially since she cannot forget her dear Springplace and does not feel at home here, and we will probably never occupy that place again. Our situation here does not allow us to expect that much good can be accomplished through a school here, so we cannot oppose our Sr. R. If an opportunity should present itself this fall, she wants to return.

Perhaps Br. Timothy Vogler will visit us this fall. If his load allows it, we would like to get some articles and items of clothing for winter: 2 pairs of pantaloons for everyday & 2 vests for myself & cassinett or cheap woolen cloth for a suit for little Charles.[1]

---

[1] The list items are in English in the original German manuscript.

Unfortunately the box sent with Clewell has not yet arrived; however, I hope to receive it soon through a driver from Columbus who recently went to Knoxville.

My dear Elisabeth is pretty strong again, praise God, and currently busy drying peaches and cuttings. The dear young ones are all well. Please greet my dear parents and your dear family and especially Henry in Friedberg, whom I often think of lovingly. Herewith I commend myself to you as your faithfully obliged Brother,

H. G. Clauder

[M 407-3: Diary of the Mission to the Cherokee Indians.]

Sun., Aug. 18. Our Brethren and Sisters gathered at Sanders's, where I preached on Matt. 26:41, with the help of the previously mentioned Young Wolf. After this the Indian Br. Boas gave a sincere and very appropriate talk and advised those present to watchfulness and to prayer in these evil times of temptation and decay.

In the last half of the month (August) I went to Tennessee once again to pick up the part of the wheat and flour supply we had bought and left there. During my 3-day stay there, I had the opportunity one evening of bearing witness in a Methodist service to the Savior's love for all men.

Aug. 25. A Baptist preacher preached in our neighborhood. We also went there and found many white people gathered there. Most of the few Cherokees who were there belonged to our Gemeine. After the singing and prayer, the preacher stood up and said, "I have learned that Br. Clauder is present, and I wanted to ask him to take a seat by me here in the house." At this public invitation I went up, after which he asked me to preach at the close of his talk on Rev. 1:7. I did so with the merciful help of the Lord. Afterward the preacher continued, through an interpreter, to talk to the Cherokee Brn. and Srs. and then in English again in such a loud and ranting manner that some of those present left, some of them cried in great disorder and waved their hands around. We were happy to leave this outrageous scene of disorder as quickly as possible and go home convinced that we do not get to know Christ in this way. Following this incident I took the opportunity to make some explanations for our Brn. and Srs. about the mind and spirit which prevails in such services and that such a thing is not from God's Spirit but surely from the evil spirit or from some human spirit. I advised them in love in the future to keep their distance from such occasions, which just lead them astray. They also considered this to be the best thing and promised to do so.

Sun., Sept. 1. The small number of our Oochgillogy Brethren and Sisters gathered at Br. George Hicks's where the sermon was on John 19:4,5, in preparation for the enjoyment of Holy Communion. We then celebrated this to our strengthening and refreshment, aware of the Savior's presence.

The young man Du-na-nela, who upon my last visit had expressed his desire to join the congregation through holy baptism, expressed himself in such a way that the Holy Spirit's work of grace in his heart could be seen. He testified that he feels great pain at the poverty and wretchedness of his heart and that he pleads in silence daily for a merciful glance. With warm hearts we spoke words of comfort to him, and assured him that a heart which feels its poverty would be a sacrifice the Lord would not scorn, but would accept with special favor, and that he could therefore continue confidently on the beautiful path he has begun and which leads to eternal life. Br. Hicks says that this Indian attended the services every Sunday and that he is a good singer and really helps a lot to liven up their singing.

Sept. 3. Our former neighbor Vann has begun a legal case through the Indian Agent against the current resident of Spring Place (Col. Bishop) to get back the property which has been secured for him until now by the law, and so I had to appear as a witness at Vann's side at the court in Murray County. The matter was not completely closed. From the Judge's (Hooper) statements, however, the conclusion could clearly be drawn that Mr. Vann will win his case and that Bishop, whom we met last Jan. and who came into possession of Spring Place in an illegal manner, will now have to give in. This later turned out to be the case. But through the obstreperous manner of this evil person and the yielding of those legal servants who were supposed to carry out the above decision, out of fear of Bishop or secret enmity toward Vann, this man claimed further possession until finally the legislation of Georgia made such changes in the previous laws that he as well as all Cherokees were very limited in their possessions. Then Vann forever gave up any future claims to Springplace, and thus also our chances of perhaps returning to Spring Place disappeared forever.

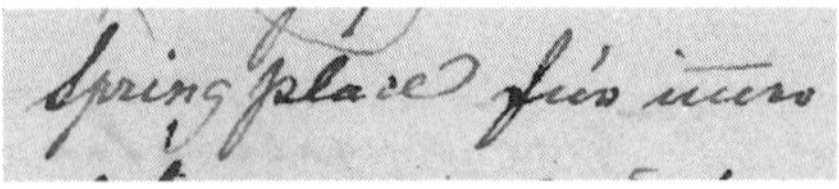

[M 415-3b-14: Translated by Julie Tomberlin Weber. Addressed to: Revd. Theodore Schulz, Salem, North Carolina. Postmark: Connesauga, C.N., Sept. 6, 37½. Received Sept. 30.]

Connesauga, C.N., Sept. 5, 1833

Dear Br. Schulz,

I was overjoyed to receive your kind letter of Aug. 22 just now and to learn that both of my earlier letters had been safely received. I also finally received the outstanding supplement about the Ochgelogy improvements, and I am enclosing it.

Yesterday I returned home again after an absence of 7 days while I was visiting in Ochgelogy and in attendance as a witness in Vann's suit vs. Bishop at the Supreme Court of Murray County, Georgia. The Court lasted only 2 days, because the Judge had other business, so the suit will be brought up again on the 30th of this month, and McNair and I must be present there again. The Grand Jury found a true bill against Bishop for trespass on Vann's lots, and without a doubt it will be given to him. This can also be concluded from the Judge's explanation of the law.

It would therefore be very advisable if the petition for the payment for Spring Place improvements were still deferred;

otherwise, Bishop might enter a plea because of this to claim his possession and thus cause us an unpleasant enmity with Vann. Bishop explains he would lease the place in spite of the law, which does not concern us anymore, but before we follow our intended course further, we should let the Indian Agent attempt to remove Bishop. This will probably happen very soon. If he manages this, then it is doubtful whether he (Bishop) would not claim his place through an appeal to the higher courts in the end. And so it would perhaps be the safest thing for us if the petition concerning Spring Place were deferred this year and remain until a future Congress. Still this is just my opinion. It can hardly be expected that we or other missionaries will live in Spring Place again.

In the meantime, a treaty might finally be arranged, although the prospects of this now are very gloomy and one or more years could easily pass before that happens. I reported earlier that the Emigration of individual people and families is underway again, and I know a number who are going, and they then influence others to do this. But our people are all quiet and are not being challenged by the Georgians.

My visit in Ochgelogy was especially encouraging, since the still and quiet routine of the little gathering there shows the Holy Spirit's internal work of grace. The statements of the young Indian Du-na-nela were especially pleasing to me. He explained quite humbly that he senses the poverty and depravity of his heart quite keenly, and yet he would so gladly live to honor the Savior. Such statements always provide reason to extol the Savior's great love for sinners to such uneasy souls. A sweet feeling prevailed during Holy Communion as well. We are planning to enjoy this high good here with our little flock next Sunday, and we sincerely pray for the Savior's merciful presence during this.

Concerning the question in my last letter regarding Turnover, whether he and his wife, both of whom belong to the Methodists, can be admitted to Holy Communion without the use of the Lot after they have been accepted: I found a similar case in the books from Ochgelogy, and this provides me with an example, and at the same time it also offers the practical answer to the above question. Our Sr. Lucy Hicks was a full member with the Methodists and was immediately admitted to Holy Communion after her acceptance in our Gemeine.[1] Turnover (who is supposed to have another name by the way) had previously made a number of statements to me concerning his intention and received my opinion about Holy Communion, and he will also receive further instruction.

The little tract *Poor Sarah* is frequently read by the Cherokees and hopefully with blessings. Mr. Worcester is pretty much finished with the translation of the Acts of the Apostles, and he wants to have a thousand copies of Matthew and Acts properly bound with an appendix of the Hymn Book, so I wrote Br. D. Clewell about his desire.

We are having exceptionally dry and hot weather. No significant rain since June.

If you have any Georgia money on hand, I ask you to please send me some, since I am unfortunately out again. I have had approximately $40 of Macon and Planters & Mechanics banks on hand for a long time now and not spent it. In addition there is the fact that in Georgia no paper money of any kind at all under $5 is payable and under penalty of $100 fine & 6 months imprisonment, and yet little silver money is circulating in the country. I would also like to ask you to pay a debt of $13 at the Mission Diacony and to debit it to me or deduct the money from the interest of my capital. This debt just arose today, when I had my artificial teeth, which I lost 6 weeks ago, replaced by a skilled dentist from Savannah. These are very useful to me when talking. Please be good enough to pay this debt from my money.

I recently received a letter from Br. Tim. Vogler and in addition to my request to bring us some necessary items and articles of clothing, etc., I sent him an answer on this point, a memorandum to you, since I was not able to send you any specific communication at that time, asking him to send that list. The box with *Nachrichten*, which Clewell sent to Knoxville, I received week before

---

1 See *Records: Cherokees*, 8:3922-23, 3962.

last in Columbus, T., and we are strengthening our hearts with its contents.

Praise God, we are all healthy and well. We are finally almost finished drying peaches and have gathered more than 2 bushels of them. This will serve us well in the winter, since unfortunately we could not plant any cabbage in our garden due to the heat and drought.

Please give my sincere greetings to the Brethren of the P.H.C. and your dear family from all of us. We thank you for your loving interest, and we greet the Brethren of the U.A.C., and commend ourselves to their further compassion and intercession.

I remain your faithfully obliged friend and Brother,

H. G. Clauder

[M 407-3: Diary of the Mission to the Cherokee Indians.]

Sept. 8. The services were held here at our home. After the sermon in English, the Indian Br. Samuel gave a brief talk to those Cherokees present. During the blessed enjoyment of Holy Communion which followed, the older girl Eliza Louisa watched as a candidate for the first time. Her sister Gategy, or Anny, as we now usually call her, who was formerly a scholar of ours in Oochgelogy and Spring Place, sent us a request through her father (Br. Samuel) for the waters of holy baptism. She repeated this request insistently herself, because of which we accepted her at that time as candidate for holy baptism.

This week we were busy making hay, for which we found and used a natural pasture, or savannah about 3 miles from here. We also had a new wooden chimney covered with plaster built onto our kitchen, since the old one was very bad and recently caught on fire, but which was discovered in time and further damage was prevented. After an unusually hot spell and drought of 6 weeks, when the grass for the cattle in the bush completely dried up, on

Sept. 14 we received a lasting rain.

[M 415-3b-15: Translated by Julie Tomberlin Weber. Addressed to: Revd. Theodore Schulz, Salem, North Carolina. Postmark: Connesauga, C.N., Sept. 20, 37½. Received Oct. 8.]

Connesauga, C.N., Sept. 19, 1833

Dearly beloved Brother Schulz,

Last Sunday the 15th I received your kind letter of the 3rd of this month. It brought us joy and encouragement.

I thank you especially for the answer it included concerning the Indian Turnover and his wife, and concerning the public acceptance of baptismal candidates or new people. I really am sorry that my first question was stated so unclearly that you had to guess my opinion, although you did so correctly. Both were communicants with the Methodists and as such enjoyed Communion with our Brn. and Srs. in Holy Communion. In my last letter to you, I wrote that I found a similar case described in an old report from Ochgelogy which provided me with an example, and which was also in complete agreement with the answer included in your dear letter. By the way, the Savior approved of the acceptance of both, and our Communion day Sunday before last was designated for this. But since they live very far from here and no announcement could be taken to them, they did not come. And so Sept. 29, when Br. Josua will lead the services, has been designated for this.

Concerning the acceptance of baptismal candidates, it was my assumption that our Brethren in the various missions have observed no particular method or rule in this regard, so that the various nations follow different rules which seem to be the most appropriate to make a healthy impression and touch the hearts. And so it seemed best to me to suggest this method, since this is more comparable to the way our colleagues work in this country and is popular among the Indians now. In a similar manner, the Presbyterians and Methodists gather numerous members; by far not all have earned the name of mere proselytes, but through word and deed show the truth of their conversion.

Fortunately, the Indians generally are completely unfamiliar with the controversies surrounding theological points. The teaching of the fall of man, the redemption of the Savior, and faith in Him, etc., are commonly preached by the missionaries of various confessions and believed by the Indians. And so all the missionaries explain the same thing, so why is it that if an Indian is awakened in our sermon, he leaves our fellowship and joins somewhere else? The answer is clear to me from observing individual cases: because there was not an invitation through which he could immediately show his desire to move closer to the Gemeine. He finds this opportunity elsewhere and does not hesitate to use this. Of course it does not matter who sows and who harvests, but the friends of the mission are always happy when the number of their faithful followers increases. In the meantime, I remain willing and happy to follow your advice in every respect, with the hope that the spirit of God might lead many more souls to us.

Herewith I am finally sending you the conclusion of my cash account, which goes back to Aug. 1 of last year. I should note here that the expense for the repairs to make the houses at this place habitable has raised the total by about $100 more than it would have been otherwise. Also the costs for paper and printing loan for the tract appear as extra expenses. I must admit, the sight of the total shocked me more than a little, since we all try to be as thrifty in our affairs as circumstances allow, and still we have spent almost $700 in the last 13 months. In our current small household I have tried to manage without the help of a hired worker, but since I often have to visit people who live far away, I found it necessary to take in a boy here whose mother is a widow and lives in the neighborhood. I pay her $3.50 per month for her son's work, and he can take care of our work and small field under my supervision.

This week many of our Indian Brn. and Srs. are setting out on a journey to the gold mines in the North Carolina part of the Nation, where they can carry out their work undisturbed by whites.

Today I am more than a little disturbed about the illness of our only horse (the large Hicks) which has a hard lump beneath his breastbone and is so stiff in all his legs that I doubt he will recover, although we have already tried various means.

Otherwise, our children, Sr. Ruede, and we are healthy. I am also happy to report that our Sr. Ruede has resolved anew to stay with us for at least one more year and lead the school as before. This week we have 6 Indian boys with us for instruction and to feed. However, they go home every Friday and return here Sunday evenings.

I have been receiving the *N.Y. Observer* for a long time now, although I do not want and did not subscribe to it. Please be good enough to tell the agent for this newspaper, Br. Shober, Sr., that he should cancel it. We have so many interesting *Gem. Nachr.* to read now, we have no time to read the newspapers.

All of us send sincere greetings to the Brethren of the P.H.C., and I remain your loving friend and Brother,

H. G. Clauder

[M 407-3: Diary of the Mission to the Cherokee Indians.]

Sun., Sept. 20 [*Sept. 22*]. We went to our Br. and Sr. Sanders's, where the service was supposed to be held. But it turned out that almost all of our Brethren and Sisters and friends had gone to the gold mines some days ago. Among them was also Nic. Ignatius, the interpreter, so that we had no opportunity to give a talk for those who were present there. And so our Br. Boas gave a brief talk about the Savior's suffering and death. I was very happy to see that our few Brn. and Srs. currently at home are seeking their edification in this manner. At their small services of the type just mentioned, great attentiveness to what is being talked about prevails each time, along with childlike simplicity. These can be taken as a proof of the earnestness with which they seek the salvation of their souls.

Sept. 28. We (Br. and Sr. Clauder) went with our children on a visit to the Spring Place area, where we were cordially received by our well-known Vanns. The following day,

Sun., Sept. 29, we went with some other friends to Br. and Sr. Josua's, where we found the Indian Brn. and Srs. and friends gathered. Fortunately Dazizi was also there and served as interpreter during the preaching, during which the Lord revealed Himself in grace. Since we spent the night at Vann's again, I (Br. Clauder) had the opportunity of holding a service for the Negroes at this farm in the evening. Unfortunately, however, only a few came for this, since most of them do not seem to be concerned about their salvation. Those who attended the service belong to the Baptist confession but never receive visits from their teacher. And so they expressed their joy over mine and wished that I would often hold a sermon for them.

Sun., Oct. 6. Most of our Brethren and Sisters came to our place. In the preaching was the reception of the Indian Turnover, along with his wife, who earlier had belonged to the Methodists and had been baptized by them and attained Holy Communion. Upon their acceptance into our Gemeine an almost universal emotion prevailed among those present, and the richly blessed presence of Jesus could be powerfully felt.

[M 415-3b-16: Translated by Julie Tomberlin Weber. Addressed to: Revd. Theodore Schulz, Salem, North Carolina. Postmark: Connassauga, C.N., Oct. 8, 18¾. Received Oct. 28.]

Connesauga, C.N., Oct. 7, 1833

Dearly beloved Brother Schulz,

Sincere thanks for the box & keg sent with Brn. Reich and Vogler.

I also want to send you a few lines to share with you the news that our Sr. D. Ruede is planning to use this opportunity to return to Salem. She hopes to visit just until next spring. She could not ignore the request of her sister Reich, who is still ill, in the same way we hope she will not be able to forget the friendly thoughts expressed by the Indian Brn. and Srs. yesterday that she will return here before the opening of school next spring. Her brother-in-law Reich promises to be helpful in this regard. Her services at the school will remain as blessed memories of the scholars' parents as well as ours, and she herself can remain assured of the love of the Indian Brn. and Srs.

The guns and shoes of Brn. Reich and Vogler [page torn: will serve us] quite well, because I can get corn and pork from the purchasers in exchange for these. Otherwise, I would have had to purchase them with cash. And so I gave these Brn. a draft for you, and I hope you will be good enough to pay it for them. They are planning to begin their return journey day after tomorrow, on the 9th, via Abingdon and Wythe Courthouse. Yesterday the Indian Turnover and his wife were accepted into our Gemeinlein here, and there was an emotional awareness of the merciful presence of our Lord and Savior during this. We hope this occasion also left a blessed impression on our visiting Brn.

We hear that the Indian Agent forced Intruder Bishop in Spring Place to move out. I will probably learn soon if this is really true. But now he can appeal and still get the matter in the Court. In the meantime, we will go [to see] what the Indians did in the Council which was convened over 8 days ago, or what new laws concerning the Cherokees are being enacted in the Georgia Legislature.

That's all in haste. I send sincere greetings and remain your faithfully obliged friend and Brother,

H. G. Clauder

1833, part 4

[M 407-3: Diary of the Mission to the Cherokee Indians. Translated by Julie Tomberlin Weber. Handwriting is Heinrich Gottlieb Clauder's.]

Oct. 9. Brn. Emanuel Reich and Timothy Vogler, who arrived here on the 2nd on a private business visit from Salem, left us and began their return journey. Our Sr. Sophia Dor. Ruede, who has taken care of the school here and in Spring Place with faithfulness and blessing since Apr. of last year, returned to Salem with them. Many of our Indian Brn. and Srs. had come here and gave an emotional farewell to this traveling company. Since I (Br. Clauder) had business in Athens, Ten., I accompanied them about 20 miles and took leave from them on the following day.

Oct. 12. A large ballplay took place near us. And when we drove to the service at Br. and Sr. Sanders's on the following day, *Sun., Oct. 13*, we met crowds of Indians who were drunken and painted, but they did not try to cause us the slightest problem. During the sermon a drunken one came up to the door and tried to cause a disturbance, but since he was not heeded he soon left again. We were happy and grateful to our dear Lord that all of our Brethren and Sisters have been prevented through grace from participating in this game, where there usually is no lack of temptation to sin, or from wanting to attend it as observers.

Sun., Oct. 27. The Baptists had a large service near us here, which was primarily attended by white people and Negroes. Our Indian Brethren and Sisters all gathered at James's, where a sermon was held. After this the Brn. and Srs. sang some hymns, and Br. Samuel gave a talk in which he admonished those present to follow the example of the Savior in love, humility, gentleness, and patience, and to show that they are His true disciples.

For years the number of traveling traders in this country has increased greatly, and the Indians are very inclined to buy on credit without exerting the appropriate effort afterward to pay their debts, through which they expose themselves to much trouble if their creditors seek to collect what is theirs through the law. And so we talked seriously with our Brn. about not getting in debt with the white people, but to pay right away for everything they find it necessary to buy if possible, or preferably to completely forego the purchase if they can manage. Time will tell whether this admonition will have the desired effect. They made no comments afterward.

The last days of Oct. were distinguished by unusually harsh weather.

[M 415-3b-17: Translated by Julie Tomberlin Weber. Addressed to: Revd. Theodore Schulz, Salem, North Carolina. Postmark: Connesauga, C.N., Nov. 1, 18¾. Received Nov. 11.]

Connesauga, C.N., Oct. 29, 1833

Dearly beloved Brother Schulz,

I was ready to answer your kind letter of the 10th of this month, but I wanted to wait for the Council of the Nation, so I could inform you of the final decisions of the head chiefs. This meeting ended recently without considering the question: "What should we do for the good of our people in our oppressed circumstances?" So now I am hurrying to express my sincerest gratitude for everything in your dear letter.

No one can really explain to me what the actual purpose of the Council's gathering was, because nothing else was done there that was of any significance. We hear that a relatively strong delegation is being sent to Washington to stay there during the session of Congress. If only the poor people would finally realize that such attempts to claim their land are in vain.

You probably already know that the Tennessee laws have also been extended over this part of the Nation. We do not really know yet what kind of laws these are. Hopefully, however, we do not need to worry that test oaths will be required of us, or that the scenes of 1830-31, which I will never be able to forget, could be renewed here as in the Georgia part of this Nation.

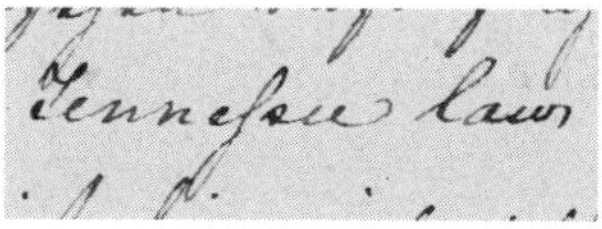

For a number of weeks we have not heard anything else about the progress of the so-called enrolling. I have already reported to you that our familiar friend Young Wolf, along with many others in his neighborhood, will go to Arkansas this winter. Young Wolf was one of the most popular native preachers here, and it almost seems as if the entire mission work of the Methodists here in this country depended on him. Since he agreed to be registered for Arkansas his work here is over, and his fellow believers who do not want to follow him there are trying to join our Gemeinlein. Last Sunday a young Indian who was a "class leader" for the Methodists, along with some others, informed me of their desire to be allowed to join our fellowship, and I advised them to await the decision of the Methodist Conference first and to see if a teacher would be sent for them, although this is doubtful.

I will continue to follow the instructions of the P.H.C. regarding official services in the Spring Place Gemeine, such as baptisms, communion, etc., as far as I am able. However, the Ochgelogy Gemeinlein is too far from here for us to expect the members (mostly Sisters) to be here for Holy Communion. Br. G. Hicks owns a very spacious house, and our communicants there have enjoyed Holy Communion there several times completely undisturbed. If it should become clear by next spring that our stay here should last longer, then I am inclined to join our Indian Brethren in building a simple and inexpensive meeting house, because our house is too small for the preachings which are held here from time to time, in addition to all the inconvenience which is associated with this otherwise.

Concerning the spiritual life of our Gemeinlein, we note with gratitude toward the faithful Shepherd of souls that His work continues calmly and quietly externally, but internally with power and truth in the hearts of our dear Indians, and that everything clearly indicates that they mean it seriously when they say, "follow Him through scorn and mocking." During the services on Sundays they are usually all here, listen with quiet reverence, often with tears, to the words of their poor unworthy teacher, and sometimes also express with words what they are feeling internally.

Among those whom the members strengthen through a talk, one of the most pleasant for a long time has been the dumb and quiet old Br. Boas. And those who understand him, for example Sr. McNair, Young Wolf, Nicolas Ign., give him a good testimony. Still I should say that of those who sometimes lead a prayer at the conclusion of a service, or if no interpreter is present, Brn. Israel, James, and Solomon besides Boas, only Samuel can be viewed as a speaker. Solomon and Nic. Ignat. are only singers, and the latter is also interpreter. Often there is no interpreter at my planned services, and so I have one or the other of the above Brn. offer a prayer, and they are always glad to do so, and with humility and trembling.

You will also be wanting to hear something from Vann's suit vs. Bishop, since I was called to go to the Court as a witness on Sept. 30, along with others. But nothing was accomplished at this court. Since then, however, I have learned that the Indian Agent, following the earlier decision of the Court, tried several times to evict Bishop. But since the latter stubbornly refused, nothing further has been done about it and probably will not be until the next Court in April '34. In the meantime, others will likely come, so that Spring Place will probably never fall back into our hands or Vann's.

Tomorrow I am planning to go to Ochgelogy on a visit. In the meantime the school, which I have continued as well as I could, will be canceled. Since the children are beginning to come very irregularly and in small numbers, and I am often short on time, I almost think it is necessary at this time to stop the school for now. Hopefully our Sr. Ruede will return here next spring and continue to care for her dear Cherokee children.

Because Brn. Vogler and Reich left their guns and shoes here, all of which have been sold now, I had no difficulty trading for a sufficient supply of corn and pork. I get the latter from Capt. McNair. I also took in about $70 in specie. As soon as I can close the accounts of these two Brn., I will have their respective credits sent to you with the request for you to pay this to them.

Once again we thank you sincerely for the box of clothing articles, etc., sent with the last wagon. May our dear Lord bless all the friends and supporters of this mission one thousand fold and grant them the joy of seeing many of these poor Indians leave the darkness and shadow of death and enter the saving light of the Gospel. That is our daily prayer and that is the goal of our poor efforts. It is often tempting to lose faith when we see so little fruit from all of our work while the work of the evil enemy can be seen on all sides. So many surrender enthusiastically to the works of darkness. Yet the Savior, who knows and watches everything, grants us new courage and a desire for His work, which He will also certainly complete in a blessed manner. May He continue to grant us faithfulness and love for this. You will surely help us to pray for this.

Along with our dear children, we are all well and we lovingly commend ourselves to you. Your faithfully obliged Brother,

H. G. Clauder

[M 407-3: Diary of the Mission to the Cherokee Indians.]

Sun., Nov. 3. I visited in Ochgelogy and held a service there, which was attended by the few Brn. and Srs. there. Most of the people in the Ochgelogy area do not seem to be concerned about their eternal salvation and attend the services little or not at all. It is a painful thing to note when one compares the worldly spirit which rules there now with the former better actions and deeds of the people. Still with praise and thanks to the faithful Shepherd of souls, I note that with few exceptions the members of our small company there have remained faithful to the Savior and the Gemeine, and in these evil times of temptation hold to Him as children.

Sun., Nov. 10. After the usual service was the marriage of a young Indian couple. The man, named Su way kee, has been an exhorter with the Methodists until now, but some time ago asked for acceptance into our community, since, as he says, his teachers are not concerned about their church children here. His wife was formerly a scholar in Spring Place and was mostly raised by our Sr. McNair.

The Baptists for some time have been preaching in the neighborhood here once each month, and their preacher, named Buckner, was very indignant, because the last time he visited I held a service with our Brethren and Sisters on the same day 5 miles from his church. He said this prevented them from attending his. And so I took the opportunity of discussing this with our Brethren and explaining to them that they should not let themselves be led astray by other voices. Their comments were very encouraging to me and were as follows: We are building a congregation for ourselves. You are our teacher and sent to us for this purpose, and so we want to seek no other teachers, but attend our own services. This explanation showed a solid walk in faith, the fruits of which are noted generally in their other actions.

Sun., Nov. 17. I went to Josua's with our Nicolaus Ignatius, where the service was held. In the sermon on Matt. 13:24-30 the Brn. and Srs. were admonished to watchfulness over themselves, so that they would not follow the temptations of the enemy and with sins fall into danger and in the end be overcome by it.

When we returned to Vann's, where we spent this night, we learned that a tragic accident had just taken place there. A company of so-called horse racers from Kentucky had been there for a number of days already. On this holy day they wanted to set up practice for betting races on Vann's riding ring. Their plan was thwarted when one of their horses shied and threw the rider, so that he broke his arm. Despite this warning incident the evening was still spent pretty loudly. During this brandy wine was also drunk in excess.

Nov. 26. Our hired worker had an immediate protection of his life. He was busy driving in a load of rosin torches, which is very common here and can be used instead of lights, when his horse shied and could not be controlled until the wagon and harness were torn up and the horse had finally run away. The young boy got a serious wound on his right leg, because of which he had to use crutches for months.

Nov. 30. I rode to Oochgellogy where the service took place the following day. The Daily Text [1 Tim. 3:16] provided a good opportunity to proclaim to those heathen who were present the message of peace that God appeared in the flesh for their eternal salvation.

Dec. 2. I visited the school in that area, which Mrs. Stone holds there. At the teacher's request I gave a talk for the children. A young boy was asked if he could remember something which had been said during my visit the past year and he answered, "You told us to pray, 'Oh Lord Jesus give me a good heart!'"[1] When he was asked if he asks daily for a good heart in this way, he said yes, because he would also like to go to heaven one day.

This evening I stopped in at New Echota where I attended the monthly prayer service at our honorable friend Worcester and gave a brief talk about the spread of God's Kingdom among the heathen.

---

[1] The quote is in English in the original German manuscript.

Sun., Dec. 8. First the Litany was prayed, during which the Indian Brethren and Sisters repeated those lines which are to be prayed by the congregation. Then there was a sermon as usual. The Indians are currently very upset about the new oppressive laws, which are threatening to be carried out in the Georgia district. According to these, the Indian families are supposed to be very limited in their individual land holdings, because of which many of them will lose considerable parts of their farms. They will also be very oppressed in other respects, which will finally leave them no alternative but to bring themselves to move to Arkansaw.

[M 415-3b-18: Translated by Julie Tomberlin Weber. Addressed to: Revd. T. Schulz, Salem, Stokes County, North Carolina. Postmark: Connesauga, C.N., Dec. 7, 18¾. Received Dec. 26.]

Connesauga, C.N., Dec. 5, 1833

Dear Brother Schulz,

Many weeks have passed since we received your kind letter dated Oct. 31, along with 2 English almanacs for 1834. We thank you sincerely for these.

For a long time I have had numerous important points on my mind, and I would like to learn the views of the P.H.C. about these. Yet I hardly know where and how I should begin with this. It is a shame that we cannot discuss these in person. In the meantime, I will try to clarify these questions for you.

The political circumstances of this nation are getting worse from day to day, without the least signs of willingness from the head chiefs to escape their unavoidable ruin here through a treaty and move away. Perhaps you know that the Tennessee laws now extend over this part of the Nation. These laws are really mild in comparison with those of Georgia, as you can see from the Tennessee newspaper that I will send along with this. However, the laws just passed by Georgia are really too horrible and set everyone in commotion and fear. There is one law which takes away the right of the so-called reserves from 1817 and '19 to own a single foot of land unless they paid a white citizen for it, and among these reserves are John Ross, Lowry, Richard Taylor, John Martin, and many other first men in the country. And so their farms stand unprotected, and the so-called fortunate drawers in the Lottery can now receive the Grant for these lots, evict the Indian occupant, and settle on it himself. This law concerns only the reserves — a small part of the people.

Another law, just as horrible as it is unjust, concerns all Indians in the Georgia part. It takes away the right of the Indian occupant to own more than one lot, the one on which his home stands. He is therefore limited to one square of 160 acres. Through this law many, for example Jos. Vann and others, will lose three-quarters of their farm. Under these circumstances it is impossible to avoid a treaty and move to Arkansas.

Since it seems it has finally come to this, many questions rise. First. Is it not better to gather together in one place those Cherokees who make up our congregations when they settle down, as for example in Fairfield? In my opinion our Brn. and Srs. should come to an agreement now, that they should be acquainted with the plan and explained from the history of the Indian missions the usually prevailing rules and arrangements. If they are generally opposed to such arrangements, the question could perhaps be raised whether we could accompany them to an unspecified place in an unfamiliar land where they would live scattered, especially since missionaries from various confessions are already there, and they could join them. This is not what we hope for; on the contrary we are prepared and sincerely willing to join our Cherokees in seeking a land of peace and quiet.

One more question arises which I would also like to present and to which I request an answer. Since the news concerning the condition of the land in Arkansas is very ambiguous, and one also knows little or nothing about the trade and transport channels (commercial channels), and also about the fields which are available for the use of missionaries there, it seems to me very necessary that we make an exploratory journey there to become acquainted with the character of the land, the circumstances of the people there, and all sorts of things, for example whether a spot can be found where a congregation of Christian Indians could settle, whether such an establishment could be established there at all, what kind of opportunities are there to work among the people, where and how can we get foodstuff, groceries, and other essentials. Such a journey, which would not need to be very expensive, seems appropriate to me and I would be willing to undertake this along with a Brother from Salem, and the sooner the better.

Perhaps I am premature with these questions, but in my humble opinion these points will come up in the course of the next year. Be good enough, dear Brother, to inform me first of the thoughts of the P.H.C. about the preceding.

Some days ago I returned to Oochgeelogy. Our dear old Christian David Watee shared with me his plan to enter into marriage again. He had asked Mr. Worcester to perform the wedding, but a question arose that resulted in postponing the marriage for now. The one Br. Christian David is planning to marry is the widow of his deceased nephew or son of his sister. Mr. Worcester doubted the appropriateness of such a relationship. However, the relationship does not seem as close to me as those in which a man marries the sister of his deceased wife, and there are examples of this in Salem. And so I concluded that Br. Christian David's plan could not be contrary to our rules, and I promised to perform the marriage on my next visit in Feb. If the views of the P.H.C. are in agreement with those of Mr. Worcester, please inform me of this along with the reasons for it, so that I can better instruct our dear Brother. His bride is a member of the congregation in Turnip Mountain and has an upright character.

Our dear friend Worcester is somewhat apprehensive about his expected eviction by the Georgians who own his Lot. Doct. Butler in Turnip Mountain has already received notice to leave by Jan. 1st or to be forced out (like us). The Acts of the Apostles has now appeared in print in Cherokee. Unfortunately, however, Mr. Worcester will soon be finished with his work, since his departure from New Echota is very probable and his Cherokee printers, Wheeler & Candy, are at the point of going to Arkansas. William Coody is also going there. He is a former delegate to Washington. Boudinott and Jno. Ridge could also follow soon.

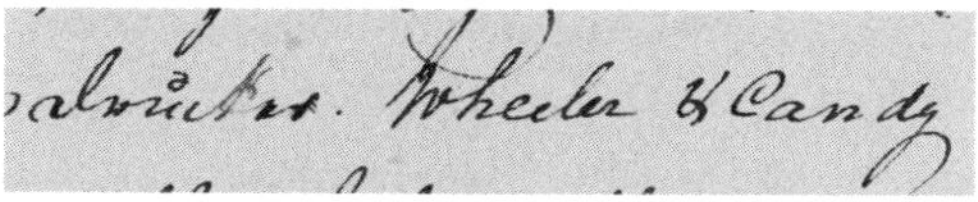

There is great confusion among the people. Drunkenness, thievery, and such vices are very common. It is not difficult to see in advance that if the Indians do not hurry with their departure, they will be ruined here on earth and eternally.

Some months ago I asked you to pay to the mission account a debt of $13 from the capital I have with you. Please be so good and inform me whether this matter has been taken care of so that I can balance my account in the cash book here.

The 6th. Yesterday evening Capt. McNair brought your kind letter of Nov. 11, along with *Monatliche* and *Wöchentliche Nachrichten.* Your comments concerning the poor Cherokees are very fitting; everything is now being fulfilled. Br. Em. Reich has credit on my ledger for $32.50, so you can settle this amount with him. He has some more outstanding with his customers here, and this will gradually come in. Br. Tim Vogler also has credit of $100, which I took partly in cash, partly in corn and pork. Be so good and pay him this amount in the meantime, and when you have done this inform me so that I can debit the accounts of these two Brn.

Greet my dear friend Henry in Friedberg, as well as your dear family. Your faithfully obliged friend and Br.,

H. G. Clauder

Corn is very rare and expensive. However, I was fortunate enough to trade shoes and guns for more than 250 bushels at 50 cents per bushel.

[M 407-3: Diary of the Mission to the Cherokee Indians.]

Dec. 20. I visited the Agent, Col. Montgomery. From him I learned the news that the number of new emigrants to Arkansaw already adds up to 900 souls, who will begin their journey there at the beginning of February. He expressed the wish that we might also move there with our Indian Brethren and Sisters, and indeed the sooner the better, since a longer stay here by the Indians will expose them to various bad things and types of oppression which they can only avoid by moving. Col. Montgomery assured us that the government would be willing to cover all of our travel expenses to Arkansaw if we would emigrate there with our Gemeine. But there is not yet the slightest inclination among them to take this step, and the positive explanation of our Brethren shows that they want to wait until the Chiefs have a different opinion about it than previously.

Dec. 25. Christmas Day. The service here was attended by a large number of Indians, who listened to the message that the Son of Man has come to seek and to save the lost, Luke 19:10. In the following services we celebrated the memorial meal of His suffering and death with the blessed feeling of Jesus' presence.

Sun., Dec. 29. Our Brethren and Sisters gathered at Br. James's where we considered in the service the blessings and good deeds we have received from our dear Lord in the now past year, and brought the proper thanks to Him, the faithful Head and Shepherd of His people. Among those present was an unbaptized Indian who has often attended our services recently. Since he was very moved by the sermon, I took the opportunity afterward to speak with him individually and found a sinner very concerned about his sins. With tears he explained that he also wishes to attain forgiveness for his sins and be saved. He said he was previously associated with the Methodists, but was misled to drinking by his heathen friends, and since then had kept his distance from all worship services. However, now he wants to begin attending them anew and seek forgiveness for his sins with Jesus. Finally he expressed his desire to receive the waters of holy baptism and to enter into our community.

At the end of the year 1833 the Gemein here consisted of 36 communicants, 2 baptized non-communicants, 2 baptismal candidates, 30 baptized children of the Brethren and Sisters under 12 years old. A total of 70 souls. The Gemeinlein in Ochgelogy consists of 10 communicants, 2 non-communicants, 1 baptismal candidate, 18 baptized children of Brethren and Sisters. A total of 31 souls.

Heinrich Gottlb. Clauder

[B 61-3; *Records: N.C.* 8:4094-95: Provinzial Helfer Conferenz, meeting in Salem. Translated by C. Daniel Crews and Douglas L. Rights.]

Fri., Dec. 27. We took the questions laid before us by Br. Clauder in his letter received today into close and thorough consideration, namely:

a. The widowed Br. Christn. David Wattee, a member at Oochgelogy, wished to enter into matrimony again with a widow of his nephew, the son of his sister, and who is a member of the Presbyterian congregation there. They asked Mr. Worcester about the wedding, but he was doubtful about such a union's conformity to Scripture. To Br. Clauder this did not appear to be sufficient, but he wanted to learn the thoughts of the P.H.C. before he performed the marriage. Since this widow is not considered to be blood kin of Wattee, and the Levitical regulation (Lev. 18) mentions nothing against it, the Confz. agreed with the views of Br. Clauder and had nothing against the marriage.

b. According to Br. Clauder's description of the ever increasingly perplexing and hard pressed situation of the Cherokee Nation, there is now added the fact that the State of Tennessee also has extended its jurisdiction by law over that portion of the Cherokee Land which lies within the borders of Tennessee. As the Cherokee Nation will be forced to give in to this, he asks: Would it be advisable to persuade the believing Cherokees who belong to our fellowship — if they move to the Arkansas — to settle there as a fellowship in one place, and to acquaint them with the plan beforehand, so that they can be brought to such an understanding? If they were against such an arrangement, then the question is whether in such uncertainty we could accompany them into an unknown land where they would live scattered from one another? Would they not rather join themselves to the missionaries of other persuasions who are already there?

Because the reports of the quality of the land on the Arkansas are so varied, as well as communication with it and the mission field itself [so uncertain], therefore Br. Clauder asks: Should a reconnaissance journey be undertaken? He himself is willing to do this if a Brother from Salem goes along to accompany him. With this he expresses to our great joy his and his wife's unceasing disposition to move with their dear people wherever they may go.

The precarious situation of this oppressed people and our mission among them has been for several years an important topic of our deliberations, and especially the possibility of their being driven from their Land, which we expected would happen earlier. Partly because of the wish of our Cherokee Brn. and Srs. themselves, and partly because of our high calling to serve the heathen people here with the Gospel, which is joined with the obligation of the legacy which lies so near to our hearts, nothing else could be reached but the decision: Yes! We may have to give up the Cherokee Mission [as it now is], but with full confidence in the Lord we still leave to the believers of this Nation the hope that our missionaries will move with them.

And so it was very comforting to us to learn that Br. and Sr. Clauder have renewed their old promise not to forsake their dear small flock. We wish from our hearts that if it comes to a real departure that the Lord will allow us to find a Brother who will move with them as their assistant. Although at present the Cherokee Nation remains undecided and has not come to a decision regarding their move, but on the contrary has once again sent delegates to the Congress in Washington, in order presumably to make a last attempt for the maintaining of their legitimate property, we can only expect that they will finally have to decide on a complete move. The specific character of this people, however, nevertheless requires from us the greatest caution. The Confz. therefore decided to advise Br. Clauder to do nothing which might give even the slightest appearance that the missionaries favor the move of the Nation until they themselves come to this decision. This may still take some time.

The life of the Cherokees up to now hardly leaves any expectation that they will consent to living all together in one place in the new land. In case they do decide to move, the earlier advice given to our missionaries there is to be followed by Br. Clauder, if the Cherokees give occasion for it: That they are to be given to understand that they shall not be forsaken by us, with the request

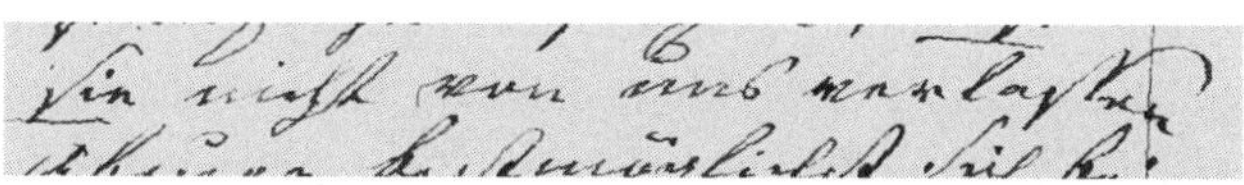

that in the move they keep together as well as they can, and that upon arrival in the land of their future repose that they also build as close as can be beside one another around their teachers.

Since a large part of the Cherokee Nation has already moved to the Arkansas, among whom missionaries have already settled, and Br. Clauder also cannot leave his little congregation, a reconnaissance journey there would have little purpose, and in addition would be very expensive, and we do not know whether the remaining part of the Nation will really proceed to the Arkansas, we therefore decided that in any case, nothing of the sort be undertaken before the Nation has reached an absolute decision. The Conferenz cannot at all advise a reconnaissance journey, but rather thinks that if the Nation comes to the decision to move to the West there will still be time then to speak with Br. Clauder about what is necessary for this, such as whether we can find a reliable Mission Agent in the States of Ohio, Missouri, and Mississippi for our mission affairs, and whether our best suggestions would be that the missionaries go right away with their Indian Brn. and Srs. on the journey to their place of refuge. The General Government no less has in addition attested that it will give its help and support for the construction again of mission buildings where our missionaries without fail will find a suitable place to build in the midst of their Brethren and Sisters.

[M 415-3b-19: Translated by Julie Tomberlin Weber. No address; no postmark. Diary address: Revd. Theodore Schulz, Salem, North Carolina. Diary postmark: Connesauga, C.N., Jan. 1, 1834, 37½. Received Feb. 1, 1834.]

Connesauga, C.N., Dec. 31, 1833

Dear Br. Schulz,

Since I am planning to send you my Diary from the last half of this year with tomorrow's post, I wanted to inform you as well about how we are all doing here.

The Christmas celebration was a period rich in blessings for us and for our Indian Brethren and Sisters who came here in large numbers along with their friends. Our friend Young Wolf and his wife, m.n. Hildebrant, were also here, and the former provided good service as an interpreter. We have another day of blessings ahead of us on Jan. 6, the day our Indian maidservant Jinny, daughter of our Br. and Sr. Boas, is supposed to receive the bath of holy baptism. Some others also have this grace ahead of them. This girl went to the school in Spring Place, as did Br. Samuel's daughter Anny, who is also a candidate for baptism. It is very encouraging to us that so many of our scholars are eventually asking to receive holy baptism and to join our Gemeine.

Members of the Methodist Society continue to come and ask for acceptance since they have been almost completely abandoned by their teachers, and they still want instruction and teaching. What should I do with them? Couldn't we accept them all at one time, or is it better to accept these poor souls individually? Please be good enough to inform me of your views about this matter as soon as possible.

The Emigration of the Cherokees to Arkansas continues slowly. 900 souls are on the list now, and it is probable that the number will surpass 1000 by February when they are planning to leave.

From the Diary you will learn that I recently visited Col. Montgomery at the Agency. Since then Maj. Currie stopped in here. Both hope that our Brn. and Srs. might be willing to move to Arkansas, and they (the Agents) promise us they will cover our journey expenses completely, which we meanwhile want to note.

However, last Sunday our Brn. and Srs. declared positively that, "We wait untill our Chiefs fail." So for now it will be difficult to

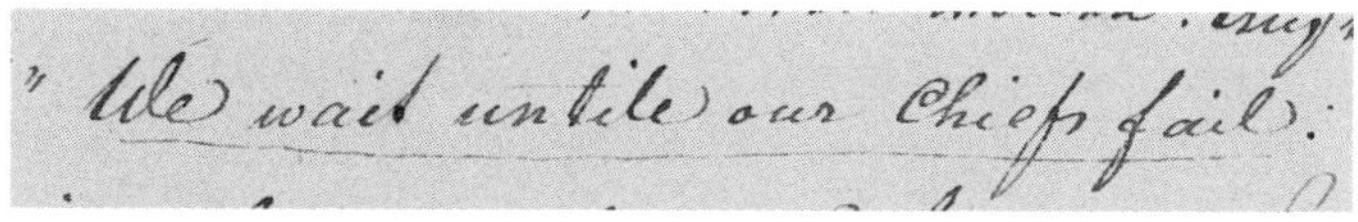
"We wait untile our Chiefs fail.

persuade them to enroll. But that Jno. Ross can avoid a treaty longer is almost impossible to believe. Time will tell everything. In the meantime we must watch patiently.

I asked Col. Montgomery if he had received the usual support for our school from the Secretary of War, to which he replied no. He says: "Your Directors ought to notify the Department thereof, as no Mony has been received at this Agency for the benefit of your School." Eighteen months have passed since we received all that was outstanding 2 years ago, and during this time school here and in Spring Place was continued. Perhaps Mr. Lewis Williams will be good enough to mediate for us again.

Yesterday we saw from the *Reporter* that it has pleased the Lord to call home dear Br. Reichel as well as your granddaughter Eliza Carolina Stiner. The homegoing of the former once again leaves a hole in your row of servants, as was the case with blessed Benzien one year ago.

We now stand at the end of a year we will never forget, and the Lord alone knows what lies ahead of us in the coming year. However, we already owe Him praise and gratitude for countless proofs of His love and assistance, which we experienced in blessing, and we comfort ourselves that:

God will arrange
For everything
To work for salvation.

Along with best wishes for blessings in the New Year, I remain your loving friend and Brother,

H. G. Clauder

Glossary-Index

For the most part, sources for this glossary-index are:

Records of the Moravians among the Cherokees (*Records: Cherokees*), volumes 1-9 (1752-1833) and forthcoming volume 10 (1834-38);
Records: Cherokees, forthcoming volumes 1838-62;
"Catalogue of Scholars at Springplace, Cherokee Country, 1804-1842," unpublished ms., Moravian Archives, Bethlehem, Pa., box 197, folder 5;
Records of the Moravians in North Carolina (*Records: N.C.*), translated and edited by Adelaide L. Fries and Douglas LeTell Rights (Raleigh: State Department of Archives and History, 1954, v. 8 (1823-1837), https://archive.org/search.php?query=moravians%20north%20carolina;
Dienerblätter, multivolume set containing brief biographical sketches of every known servant of the Moravian Church; compiled by the Unity Archives in Herrnhut, Saxony;
Periodical Accounts Relating to the Missions of the Church of the United Brethren (London: Brethren's Society for the Furtherance of the Gospel among the Heathen) v. XI, 1829-1831; XII, 1832-34, https://catalog.hathitrust.org/Record/100432371;
McClinton, Rowena, *The Moravian Springplace Mission to the Cherokees* (Lincoln, Neb., and London: University of Nebraska Press: 2007);
Phillips, Joyce B. and Paul Gary Phillips, *The Brainerd Journal, a Mission to the Cherokees, 1817-1823* (Lincoln, Neb., and London: University of Nebraska Press, 1998);
Moulton, Gary E., ed., *The Papers of Chief John Ross* (Norman, Okla.: University of Oklahoma Press, 1985).

Thanks again go to Jack D. Baker and David Hampton of the Cherokee Nation for their assistance in reviewing the Cherokee relationships in this glossary-index. Any errors are strictly my own.

Richard W. Starbuck
May 21, 2019

— A —

— B —

— C —

— D —

— E —

— F —

— G —

— H —

— N —

— O —

— P —

— Q —

— R —

— S —

— T —

— Y —

— Z —